COMPANION TO
IRISH HISTORY
1603–1921

COMPANION TO
IRISH HISTORY
1603–1921
From the Submission of Tyrone to Partition

Peter R. Newman

Facts On File
Oxford • *New York*

COMPANION TO IRISH HISTORY

Facts On File Limited
Collins Street
Oxford OX4 1XJ
UK

or

Facts On File, Inc.
460 Park Avenue South
New York NY10016
USA

A British CIP catalogue record for this book is available from the British Library.

A United States of America CIP catalogue record for this book is available from the Library of Congress.
ISBN 0–8160–2572–X

Facts On File books are available at special discounts when purchased in bulk quantities for businesses, associations, institutions or sales promotions. Please contact the Special Sales Department of our Oxford office on 0865 728399 or our New York office on 212/683–2244 (dial 800/322–8755 except in NY, AK or HI).

Manufactured by
Derek Doyle & Associates, Mold, Clwyd
Printed and bound in Great Britain by
Biddles Ltd, Guildford and King's Lynn

10 9 8 7 6 5 4 3 2 1

This book is printed on acid-free paper.

To Gareth, for the days that were.
Castlerock 1970–71

CONTENTS

INTRODUCTION

The capitulation of the Earl of Tyrone in 1603 may justifiably be seen as the closing act in the long struggle of the native Irish to co-exist with the steady encroachment of English domination in Ireland. It did not mark the end of resistance, but the nature of that resistance altered in substance and in purpose as the ensuing centuries unfolded. It is arguable that the defeat of the Ulster Irish was already accomplished with the disastrous battle of Kinsale and the subsequent Treaty of Mellifont, but only with the departure of the defeated leadership in 1607 was the way wholly cleared for wholesale English conquest of Ulster. The last of the Irish provinces to resist, Ulster, proved to be the most thoroughly restructured, to such an extent that, with the coming of Partition in 1921, Ulster clung tenaciously to the British link steadily forged in the seventeenth century. This *Companion* covers a 300-year period in the history of Ireland, from 1603 to 1921. It seeks to explain, through its various topics, the complexity of Irish history, whilst at the same time seeking to avoid an Anglocentric viewpoint.

When it is considered, for example, that for the whole of the nineteenth century, Ireland was governed directly from Westminster, it may be thought difficult and even tendentious to try to avoid an Anglocentric approach. A way around that is to consider the impact within Ireland, of legislative measures taken in London: to look at what was intended and what actually ensued from colonial rule. It was the perception of many Irish people leaders and followers who were seeking firstly legislative independence and secondly full separation, that British rule was, essentially, colonial. Even the behaviour of the Protestant Ascendancy in the eighteenth and nineteenth centuries betrays that assertive identity peculiar to colonialists in an annexed territory.

The very fact of the creation of the Free State in 1921 was a consequence of continued, prolonged and bitter struggle between the colonial power and the colonized, and alliances of interest developed that would have been impossible in the centuries before 1603. The 'Irish', in the wake of the collapse of the Earl of Tyrone, and slowly and painfully over the generations, developed a national identity rooted in old regionalisms, perhaps, but transcending them. The evolution of Irish national identity, and hence the creation of an independent Irish state, ran concurrently with English colonization and exploitation. The assertion of English sovereignty, a matter that became pressing for England only in the sixteenth century and had hardly concerned medieval kings, ultimately proved conducive to the development of Irish identity. The many risings and insurrections which this *Companion* deals with, were vitally important moments in the emergence of a free Ireland.

English dominance in medieval Ireland, exercised directly over much of Leinster and Munster and indirectly through subservient Gaelic chieftains elsewhere, began to decline by the end of the thirteenth century. A distinction began to emerge between the English community in Ireland, descended largely from Anglo-Norman adventurers, and the government of Ireland exercised from Dublin on behalf of the English crown. This distinction is reflected in the dichotomy that came to exist between areas of English influence – cultural, social and political – and areas of direct administrative control, which came to be confined to the area known as the Pale, centred upon Dublin and the eastern coast, and extending into Meath and Kildare counties, which were medieval English creations and precursors of subsequent 'shiring' in Ulster after 1603. The English crown had always claimed to possess the overlordship of Ireland, but this claim had never been pressed into full-scale conquest and assertion of its pretensions. Independent Gaelic chieftains existed beyond areas of English influence, for example in Ulster, and co-existed with the colonists whilst pursuing their own objectives and observing their own laws. English governmental priorities were always limited, either to defence of the Pale – particularly as it shrank in face of spasmodic indifference in London and assertiveness by Gaelic chiefs – or to piecemeal campaigns aimed at reducing particularly troublesome chieftains to some form of obedience. This reflected an English polity which saw the divisions within Gaelic Ireland as in some ways necessary for the integrity of the colonized areas. Given the commitments of English kings elsewhere, and particularly in France, Ireland was peripheral, requiring to be contained and controlled in some way, but not to become a drain upon the resources of government whether in money or men. Indeed, revenues accruing to the crown of England from its Irish territories, went to help fund policies elsewhere; this drain of money away from the Dublin government, limited its effectiveness, and during the course of the fourteenth century resurgent Gaelic chieftains encroached steadily upon the settled English lordship.

Neglect from London, and consequent Gaelic revival, brought about the critical situation which Richard II sought to remedy by his massive armed expedition to Ireland in 1394 and again in 1399, on the eve of his own deposition and murder. If the object of Richard's campaigns was to restore the decreasing revenues coming out of Ireland, he was only partially successful. He, no more than any earlier king, and despite the armed gesture, relegated Ireland and its problem to secondary importance when weighed against the European dimension of English policy, or, indeed, against the maintenance of royal authority in Wales.

Considerable power, therefore, devolved upon Anglo-Norman landowners in Ireland as representative of government in far-off London. FitzGeralds and Butlers, and others like them, pursued personal aggrandizement, ritualized rivalries and government policy as it suited them. Their descendants became the Old English, whose position in late Tudor and Stuart Ireland was wholly altered by the religious issue.

Tudor expansion in Ireland, inherent in King Henry VIII's assumption of the 'crown' of Ireland, was a reflection of the centralizing tendencies of Tudor government. In the reign of Queen Elizabeth I, this went hand in hand with zealous propagation of the reformed, Protestant religion, and an articulated mission to civilize the 'wild Irish' and their society. The English nobility and landowners in Ireland, because of their vital role in the maintenance of the English lordship there, were scarcely affected by the religious changes in England which, during the course of the sixteenth century, made Catholicism synonymous with latent or active treason. The native Irish and the English in Ireland were not united by a common religion, indeed, Gaelic Catholicism and that practised by the colonists had little in common. The threat of Protestantism and enforced conformity did not make itself felt in Ireland until the last great Gaelic chieftains had been swept away in the wake of 1603. It can be argued that what eventually gave identity of interest to Old English and Gaelic Catholics was not so much the threat of Protestantism, but the increasing determination of government in England to exercise full political control throughout the whole of Ireland. Then, and perhaps only then, did Gaelic and Old English Catholics find in their religions a common banner under which to unite to resist that encroachment. The Great Rebellion which began in 1641 and dragged on into 1653, was a struggle of the Irish – whether native or settler – against the principle of direct control by the enforced seizure and redistribution of land by Westminster to create a Protestant political nation.

The shiring of Ireland, begun in the Middle Ages, was carried through, and with it went the local government patterns and machinery familiar in England. The expropriation of land, striking first at the Gaelic Irish and then at the Old English whose Catholicism rendered them suspect, and whose tolerance of things Gaelic made them seem effete, gave to later nationalist aspirants the single most effective propaganda weapon they were to possess, the land question. From the moment that Ulster was parcelled up and handed out, the divorce of the Irish from their land fuelled resentment and resistance.

The *Companion* seeks to lay stress upon the land issue, covering many aspects from the expropriations themselves, through the campaigns to restore Irish land to the Irish that eventually bore fruit in the nineteenth century.

The struggle for independence from English, latterly British, rule, which may be said to have culminated in the war for liberation of 1919–21, is a common thread throughout the entire period covered by this book. Indeed, it was an objective shared for a time by the dominant Protestant minority, the Ascendancy, which may serve to show that nationalism or separatism are not synonymous with a specific religious observance. Modern republicanism, for example, which sees the task of liberation as not yet completed, has never been religiously exclusive.

The history of any country, of any period, is complex. This *Companion*, whilst setting out to explain and perhaps to simplify issues and events, should really, in doing so, serve to emphasize complexities and remind us that the modern history of Ireland is compounded of all the elements of its past, not just religious confrontation.

The criterion for selection of biographical data in this *Companion* is that the central figure with which the brief biography is concerned, should in some way or other illuminate or exemplify aspects of Irish history or crucial and central themes of that history. There is every reason to include, of course, figures such as Daniel O'Connell, Isaac Butt, John Mitchell and Henry Grattan; many others necessarily demand inclusion. The agents of British rule, such as Drummond and Trevelyan, whether immediate or remote, are of more importance than an endless citation of British prime ministers and monarchs. Indeed, the often-remote nature of British sovereignty is best illustrated by omissions. The inclusion of Irish figures for sometimes purely illustrative purposes is more readily justified.

The *Companion* adheres to the calendrical change of 1752: throughout, the year is taken to commence on 1 January.

A

Abercromby, Sir Ralph (1734–1801)

Abercromby was Commander-in-Chief of the British army in Ireland, appointed in November 1797. He was an experienced commander, having fought in Flanders and in the West Indies expedition against the French in 1795. On the eve of the rising planned by the UNITED IRISHMEN in 1798, a republican movement seeking separation from Great Britain, Abercromby denounced the indiscipline of the troops at his command. The government, which had been pursuing a policy of repression backed by localized but considerable violence, forced his resignation and replaced him with General LAKE. The Irish administration at the CASTLE in DUBLIN seems to have been instrumental in ridding the army of Abercromby's restraining influence.

Abjuration, Oath of (see also CATHOLIC CLERGY, Proclamations and Legislation against)

The Oath of Abjuration was primarily an anti-Catholic measure intended to force renunciation of papal authority and doctrine and express unreserved loyalty to the reigning monarch. Such an oath was imposed in Ireland following the conquest by CROMWELL in the 1650s, and was imposed again in 1691 in contravention of the terms for the surrender of Limerick. The Treaty of LIMERICK had specifically required Catholics to take an oath of allegiance to King WILLIAM III, but no more than that, following the struggle between the Protestant supporters of William and the Catholic followers of the deposed King JAMES II. On 27 February 1703 an abjuration act passed the English House of Commons requiring recognition of the lawful sovereignty of Queen Anne. In August 1709 an oath of abjuration specifically aimed at Roman Catholic clergy in Ireland required them to renounce publicly the pretensions to the throne of the Stuarts, but it seems that of the approximately 1,000 registered Catholic priests, barely 30 or so took the oath.

Abstentionism

A policy of the republican SINN FÉIN party developed in 1917, by which Sinn Féin candidates standing for election to the Parliament at WESTMINSTER, made it known that if elected they would decline to take up their seats there. Abstentionism reinforced Sinn Féin's claim not to recognize British authority. Count PLUNKETT, who won the Roscommon by-election on 3 February 1917 against a HOME RULE candidate, was the first MP to decline to sit. Joseph McGuinness, who on 9 May 1917 won the Longford South by-election for Sinn Féin, was anyway a prisoner in Lewes gaol in England and so therefore unable to sit. Sinn Féin took the endorsement of its candidates as good ground for setting up an independent assembly in Ireland (see DÁIL ÉIREANN).

Administrative Structure of Ireland

Government and administration in Ireland during the period from 1607, was modelled upon that which had prevailed in England since the early Middle Ages, and which was wholly an English introduction into Ireland. 'Shiring', or the creation of counties, first began during the Anglo-Norman conquests, and was progressively brought to completion over ensuing centuries. The administrative structure reflected the ancient provinces of Ireland, ULSTER, LEINSTER, MUNSTER and CONNACHT, or Connaught, but there had been modifications of ancient boundaries, as for example in the shifting of county of Cavan from Connacht to Ulster. Ulster was the final province to be 'shired', the identified and named counties arrived at in 1585 being made a reality by conquest in 1603. The final county distribution was Ulster: Antrim, Armagh,

Cavan, COLERAINE (later DERRY or Londonderry), Donegal, Down, Fermanagh, Monaghan and Tyrone. In Leinster: Carlow, DUBLIN, Kildare, Kilkenny, Laois or Leix (also known as Queen's County), Longford, Louth, Meath, Offaly (or King's County), Westmeath, Wexford and Wicklow. In Connacht: Clare, Galway, Leitrim, Mayo, Roscommon and Sligo. In Munster: Cork, Kerry, Limerick, Tipperary and Waterford. Within the counties, the next subdivisions were those of the BARONIES, and within the baronies were the towns, townlands and lesser units of population. With the counties came the officialdom of English administration, the sheriffs, Justices of the Peace, high and petty constables, imposing and executing English law in place of and against the rules and procedures of native, Gaelic, social structure and territorial administration. 'Shiring' represented an aspect, and an important one, of a general policy of ANGLICIZATION.

Adventurers, The

The IRISH REBELLION of 1641 broke out initially in ULSTER, but rapidly spread throughout Ireland, requiring immediate and effective military measures by the Parliament at WESTMINSTER, itself already locked in a series of constitutional crises with King Charles I. The Parliament created what amounted to a lottery, to raise money to finance the war against the rebels, by offering land, which was yet to be forfeited, to those prepared to invest in its outright purchase. Those who opted to take land on such terms were called Adventurers. By Act of Parliament of 19 March 1642, subscriptions from £200 upwards were invited for lots of 1,000 acres. (The Irish acre was considerably larger than its English counterpart, consisting of 6,046 square metres). Effectively some 2½ million acres were set aside to satisfy the claims of the Adventurers. As the war in Ireland dragged on and regular forces from Britain became engaged against the rebels, the government also found it necessary to use forfeited lands to reimburse soldiers for arrears of pay and to provide security for official loans. In

consequence, the scramble for land in the 1650s after the suppression of the rebellion was muddled and corrupt, involving wholesale movement of populations to make way for investors and soldier-settlers. It has been estimated that in 1641 some 60 per cent of Irish land was held by Catholics, whether native Irish or OLD ENGLISH. By 1660 this figure had been reduced to 9 per cent, although subsequent land settlements caused it to rise again to nearly 20 per cent of the land area.

Agrarian Outrages/Agrarian Violence

Incidents of rural and agrarian violence are bound up both with the issue of land in Ireland, and also with the nature of peasant society (see FEUDS and FACTION FIGHTING). Almost all outbreaks of concerted aggression directed at landlords and at large farmers during the eighteenth and nineteenth centuries, such as that of the WHITEBOY movement, originated in grievances over landholding and related issues such as TITHES. Precise records relating to outrages began to be compiled by the CONSTABULARY only in 1844, and seem to relate to specific indictable offences such as murder, assault and incendiarism. The records reveal certain areas of the country to have been more prone to violent outbursts than others, for example, Connacht experienced less than did Munster, and within Munster, County Tipperary more than other counties. Nineteenth-century agrarian violence was predominantly the protest of smallholders and small tenant farmers against the spread of pastoral agriculture, with its emphasis upon consolidation of holdings and cut-back in the area devoted to tillage, which required a larger manpower to work. There was also a strong correlation between the increase in EVICTIONS of tenants from their farms, and the number of outrages. In 1880, for example, there were 2,000 officially-executed evictions and 2,500 or so reported cases of agrarian violence. In some instances (see WHITEBOYS, SHANAVESTS) the violence had tendencies towards political action, but for the most part it was parochial, sometimes regional, and largely occurred within the peasant communities themselves. LAND LEGISLATION from the 1870s onwards helped ameliorate some of the pressing problems.

Agricultural Co-operative Movement

Co-operation for producing and selling agricultural produce as a way of alleviating rural distress, developed in the 1890s largely from the initiative of the Irish Agricultural Organization Society. By 1910 there were some 996 local co-operative groups, including more than 390 creameries. This development coincided with the spread of general agricultural societies and clubs, and the creation of small credit banks.

Agricultural Labourers' Union, The Irish

Between the date of the first reliable census (see POPULATION) of 1841, and 1901, the number of rural labourers in Ireland plummeted by more than 70 per cent, to around 295,000 so described in the census of 1901. EMIGRATION, the FAMINE, consolidation of farms and increase of pasture at the expense of tillage, combined to drive labourers away from the land. In consequence, unionization was never very effective. The first Irish branch of the English Agricultural Labourers' Union was founded in Kanturk, County Cork, in August 1873, with ISAAC BUTT as its President, and the English Union leader Joseph Arch present at the foundation meeting. Under the influence of Butt and others, the Irish Union began to devote itself to political issues that Arch considered were unrelated to the problems of the labourers. In particular, emphasis was placed upon emigration as a solution to rural poverty and distress, and which amounted to a Union policy based upon the belief that nothing could be done within Ireland to remedy the problem. In consequence, the Union virtually faded into inactivity, obliging labourers to take localized action for higher wages or better conditions, as in the strike at Kanturk in 1880. A resurgence of formal Union activity by agricultural labourers was noted in the 1890s, when some joined DAVITT's Democratic Trade and Labour Federation. But, in reality, the Irish rural labourer had no 'voice' at all, and manifestations of AGRARIAN OUTRAGE were often his sole vehicle for registering protest.

Agricultural Organization Society, The Irish

The Society was founded on 18 April 1894, almost entirely on the initiative of the farmer and landowner Horace Plunkett. Plunkett had returned from farming in America with a passionate conviction that the Irish land problem was wholly rooted in social and economic matters and not a consequence of political factors. He set up the Agricultural Organization Society to provide direction for the spread of co-operatives, which he saw as a solution to rural poverty. Plunkett himself was a landlord and a Unionist, although he later converted to the cause of HOME RULE. In setting up the Society, he put into practice his belief that the land issue could be remedied within the context of the UNION, a position he abandoned before 1900.

All For Ireland League *see* O'BRIEN, William

America, National League of

The National League of America was a politically moderate body established to provide financial backing for the HOME RULE movement in Ireland in the 1880s. The importance of America to the more radical struggle of the FENIANS and other republican groups in Ireland was immense, and consequent upon the EMIGRATION to America of thousands of Irish during the nineteenth century. The National League was, because of its moderate stance, less in touch with Irish-American opinion than other bodies, and its fund-raising success was limited.

American Association for the Recognition of the Irish Republic

The American Association was primarily a fund-raising body formed in November 1920 during the WAR FOR INDEPENDENCE in

Ireland between the IRISH REPUBLICAN ARMY and the forces of the British government. The Association drew upon strong Irish-American feelings, and within 12 months was reckoned to have 800,000 members. EAMON DE VALERA acted in America as 'official head of the Republic' set up in Ireland by the Irish people, and the formation of the Association gave co-ordination to fund-raising bodies. Some $10 million was remitted to the republic in Ireland between 1919 and 1921.

American War for Independence

The struggle between the American colonists and the British government, which broke out into armed confrontation at Lexington in 1775, and which originated over the question of taxation, had a direct Irish connection. EMIGRATION of thousands of predominantly ULSTER Irishmen to America during the eighteenth century created familial and cultural links, and certainly among Irish PRESBYTERIANS there was considerable sympathy for the American cause. The Irish Catholics, on the other hand, were by and large loyalist in their sympathy. The loss of the colonial markets in America as a result of the war threatened Irish trade, and obliged the British government to purchase the support of the Irish PARLIAMENT by concessions that angered the English House of Commons, particularly during April and May of 1778. There seems to have been genuine fear and concern amongst the PATRIOT group in Ireland that a defeat for the American colonies would encourage the British government to adopt policies of taxation without representation in Ireland, and there is no doubt that the example of the struggle in America inspired the formation of VOLUNTEER forces with a conditional loyalty to the British constitution. The first Volunteers enrolled in BELFAST in March 1778, less than two years after the formal declaration of American independence on 4 July 1776, and in November 1779 a massive Volunteer demonstration in DUBLIN called for the lifting of commercial restrictions imposed upon Ireland from WESTMINSTER.

Amnesty Association

The amnesty movement in Ireland began in 1868 with the primary objective of securing the release from prison of FENIANS gaoled following the abortive uprising of 1867. In August 1868 Cork City Council moved resolutions calling for the release of political prisoners. Mayor of Cork Daniel O'Sullivan, a forthright Fenian supporter, had to resign in May 1869 to preclude measures to disqualify him from office being taken in the House of Commons at WESTMINSTER. On 5 November 1868 John McCorry founded the Irish Liberation Society to channel the efforts of amnesty groups, and in response to reports of ill-treatment of prisoners circulating freely in Ireland. ISAAC BUTT chaired an amnesty meeting in DUBLIN in November 1868, and a massive demonstration on 26 January 1869 in Dublin was followed in February by the release of 49 Fenians, more than 30 of them from exile in Australia (see TRANS-PORTATION). These were nearly all non-military Fenian members. The Amnesty Association proper was founded on 28 June 1869 with Butt as President, and at once embarked upon a series of major public meetings to rally popular support and to pressurize the government, such as the rally at Cabra near Dublin of 100,000 on 10 October 1869. Some politicians, sympathetic to the cause, nevertheless felt that the pressure would be counter-productive and could turn the government away from clemency and amnesty. The campaign kept the issue in the forefront of the public mind. In January 1871 a further 33 were released, including O'DONOVAN ROSSA, JOHN DEVOY and THOMAS LUBY, leading Fenian organizers. The public campaign took on a new lease of life in September 1873 with meetings such as that at CLONTARF attended by an estimated 250,000, and the final rally at Glasnevin near Dublin on 23 November 1873, of some 300,000. Under the influence of Butt, the Amnesty Association began to concern itself also with questions of LAND LEGISLATION, and by doing so alienated the IRISH REPUBLICAN BROTHERHOOD who saw such additional emphases as detracting from the purpose of the Association.

Ancient Order of Hibernians

The Hibernian Order was a significant development in extra-parliamentary politics in the 1880s and 1890s. It was vigorously Catholic, and probably rooted in the RIBBON movement of earlier in the nineteenth century with its sectarianism and confrontational attitude to the ORANGE ORDER. Essentially a secret society, and so in a way linked to the agrarian movements of earlier times (see WHITEBOYS), the Hibernians came under attack from the CATHOLIC CHURCH. One leading churchman castigated them as 'an organized system of blackguardism'. Their primary strength lay initially in ULSTER, where the sectarian confrontation of Catholic and Protestant, orange and green, was most marked, but the movement grew strongest in America, particularly in 1898. The American example inspired a rejuvenation of Hibernianism in Ireland around 1902. It may be compared, in its championing of Catholics and their rights, with the DEFENDER movement of the late eighteenth century which had itself arisen in response to sectarian violence from the Protestants in Ulster, the Ribbon movement marking a transitional stage. Hibernianism was characterized chiefly by militant Catholicism in a sectarian and not in a theological sense, rather than by doctrinaire nationalist or republican beliefs, and because of that it helped to maintain the developing sectarian rift in Ireland. In its name it appeared to link itself to benevolent society traditions, but its secrecy lay firmly in the Whiteboy inheritance.

Anglicization

The English policy for Ireland that produced PLANTATION, that is the introduction onto Irish land of English and Scottish Protestants as a means of controlling Ireland and stabilizing it in English interests, also gave rise to Anglicization. This expressed itself in the wish that the Irish should become 'in tongue and heart and everything else English, so as there will be no difference or distinction', as was remarked in the early seventeenth century. The success of Anglicization was mixed, but its best chance to succeed came after the battle of KINSALE in 1603 and the defeat and surrender of the Gaelic nobility of ULSTER led by the Earl of TYRONE. Its application involved the immediate imposition on the native Irish of the oath of supremacy, which required recognition of the English monarchy and constitution, and the piecemeal implementation of English law (with particular emphasis upon landholding). It is shown in the preferment of Protestants to positions of authority and the necessary exclusion of Catholics during the seventeenth century, and its repressive nature can be seen in the PENAL LAWS enacted against Catholics, particularly after the deposition of King JAMES II in 1688. The idea of Anglicization was still current in 1858, when a nationalist writer in the journal *The Celt* observed 'To be Anglicised is to lose our national and characteristic identity, to merge everything Irish and Celtic in, not a British union, but a British supremacy.' Outwardly, Anglicization as envisaged by the English governments of the early seventeenth century was successful: English law, English administration and English religion did replace the Gaelic order of things. Gaelic chieftains abandoned their ancient powers and titles in favour of English legitimization, although that process of appeasement had marked the Gaelic nobility, even in Ulster, for several centuries prior to 1603. Anglicization failed, however, in that power was never entrusted to Gaelic or OLD ENGLISH who clung tenaciously to their Catholicism, and so was exercised always and virtually exclusively by the Protestant minority of NEW ENGLISH and Scots who were synonymous with the PROTESTANT ASCENDANCY which ruled Ireland through the eighteenth and much of the nineteenth centuries.

Anglo-Irish Treaty

The Anglo-Irish Treaty of 6 December 1921 was the outcome of negotiations between the British government and the DÁIL ÉIREANN, a delegation from which journeyed to London for the talks. It marked the end of the WAR FOR INDEPEN-

DENCE waged by the IRISH REPUBLICAN ARMY and SINN FÉIN against the British government since 1919. A truce had been agreed on 11 July 1921 following preliminary discussions involving DE VALERA and ARTHUR GRIFFITH. De Valera and Lloyd George met on 14 July, and established that Lloyd George would not recognize the Irish Republic, and that Sinn Féin would not accept HOME RULE, which was now wholly discredited. In September the Dáil delegation – Griffith, MICHAEL COLLINS, Michael Duffy, Robert Barton and Eamonn Duggan – went to London for formal talks. De Valera believed that the solution for Ireland was to secure 'external' association with Great Britain, whereby King George V would be head of an association of states but not king of Ireland.

The delegation, however, was offered a take it or leave it dominion status from which, advocates of the Treaty argued, a secessionist Republic would ultimately be able to emerge. The Treaty consisted of 18 articles, and was imposed upon the Irish delegates by Lloyd George, who threatened them with renewed war unless it was signed. The Treaty was finally approved by 64 votes to 57 on 7 January 1922. The delegation had secured independence in domestic and fiscal matters and had achieved dominion status within the Empire. They had accepted the PARTITION of Ireland which created the new 'state' of Northern Ireland from the SIX COUNTIES of ULSTER, but there were promises of a subsequent boundary commission by which, at most, the counties of Tyrone and Fermanagh might be restored to the FREE STATE. British withdrawal from three of Ireland's four provinces (see ADMINISTRATIVE STRUCTURE) had been achieved. The opponents of the Treaty, chief of whom was De Valera, regarded it as a betrayal, primarily because the Republic had not been secured, and secondly because it accepted partition of the 'seamless garment' of Ireland.

The Treaty plunged Ireland into a bitter civil war between the pro and anti-Treaty sections of the IRA and Sinn Féin, with the eventual triumph of the pro-Treaty forces, who were supplied by the British government.

Antrim, Randall MacDonnell 2nd Earl of (1609–83)

MacDonnell was the leading Catholic nobleman in ULSTER when he succeeded his father in the earldom in 1636. The MacDonnells, although not Irish, having originated in Scotland and settled in Ulster from the fifteenth century onwards, had survived the fall of TYRONE and the Gaelic chiefs of Ulster in 1603 and had submitted to the government of King James I, accepting the earldom in 1620, a symbol of their conformity to English practice. The second earl emerged as the leader of the Catholic Irish in Ulster, and was seen by King Charles I as a counter-balance to the strong Scottish PRESBYTERIAN influence in the province. As relations between Charles I and his kingdom of Scotland deteriorated, largely because of the king's religious policies, the Ulster Scots of Protestant persuasion began to be suspect as well, and Antrim began to be used by the king as an implicit threat to keep the Ulster Scots quiet. The king's VICEROY in Ireland, THOMAS WENTWORTH, put no faith in Antrim, but found himself by-passed by royal policy. Historians have debated Antrim's role in the build-up to the IRISH REBELLION of 1641, but there seems little doubt that Charles I considered him the man capable of raising the GAELIC IRISH in support of the crown in the event of a war with Scotland. In 1644, Antrim did invade Scotland whilst the king was locked in the civil war in England, and his departure from Ulster gave the Scots there the opportunity to inflict defeats upon the Irish rebels in the province. Antrim was largely ineffectual, but was seen, certainly by Protestants in Ulster and in England, as a more serious threat than he proved to be.

Apprentice Boys

Following upon the deposition of King JAMES II in 1688 the Catholic Irish rose in arms against the authority of King WILLIAM III, and Ireland entered upon a brief period of savage civil war. On 7 December 1688 Catholic forces in ULSTER under the command of Alexander MacDonnell 3rd Earl of ANTRIM, advanced against the strategic port of DERRY.

Protestant apprentices (one of them was reputedly a Catholic) caused the city gates to be shut against Antrim, an act of defiance that signalled the subsequent siege of DERRY. The actions of the Apprentice Boys came to be commemorated in Apprentice Clubs, formed from 1814 onwards, and vigorously Protestant in their religion. The modern Apprentice Boys parade in Londonderry is a triumphal assertion of the actions of December 1688.

Ardee, battle of

The battle of Ardee, County Louth, was fought on 23 March 1642 between forces of the CATHOLIC CONFEDERACY and government troops under the command of Sir Henry Tichborne. The Confederate army was defeated.

Arklow, battle of

The battle of Arklow, County Wicklow, was fought between insurgent forces commanded by Father MURPHY, and government troops under General Francis Needham, on 9 June 1798. The insurgents, predominantly Catholic peasantry, had risen as part of the rebellion of 1798 led by the UNITED IRISHMEN which aimed at overthrowing British rule in Ireland. The rebels, although numerically superior, were out-fought by trained troops. An uprising in DUBLIN, often postponed, was timed in such a way that its outbreak coincided with this major setback for the rebels.

Armagh, James Ussher Archbishop of (1581–1656)

Armagh city was the episcopal centre of Ireland, equivalent to Canterbury in England, and the archbishops of Armagh enjoyed the Primacy of all Ireland. Ussher had been appointed Professor of Divinity at TRINITY COLLEGE, DUBLIN, in 1607, and was elevated to the archbishopric in 1625. Predominantly an absentee, residing ordinarily in England, he exerted a powerful influence upon the CHURCH OF IRELAND from as early as 1613, when he began work on drafting the articles of faith for that church. He

resisted the imposition of articles in line with those of the Church of England in 1634, and lost ground to the LAUDIAN reforms in the Irish church that were promoted by THOMAS WENTWORTH as LORD DEPUTY. The appointment of John Bramhall to the bishopric of DERRY in 1634 was a direct challenge to Ussher, who chose to stand aloof from future confrontations. In England in 1640/41 he began work drafting a scheme for a modified episcopal structure in the Church of England to avert confrontation between King Charles I and his Parliament, and sought to save Wentworth's life. A bitter critic of the WESTMINSTER ASSEMBLY OF DIVINES in the 1640s, he died in retirement in receipt of a pension from the government.

Arminianism

A religious doctrine reputedly evolved from the works of Jacob Arminius (1560–1609), a Dutch theologian who challenged Calvinist orthodoxy by laying emphasis upon free will as against predestination. Arminianism was espoused by the reform movement within the Church of England associated with the name of Archbishop William Laud (see LAUDIANISM). Laudian reforms were introduced into the CHURCH OF IRELAND through the appointment of Arminians to bishoprics, such as that of DERRY in 1634 and Limerick in the same year, Down and Connor and Waterford and Lismore in 1635, Cork and Ross in 1638 and Elphin in 1639. The shift in doctrinal emphasis was disapproved of by the Irish primate, James Ussher, archbishop of ARMAGH, but was forced through by THOMAS WENTWORTH, whose nominee John Atherton was appointed to Waterford and Lismore. The tiny proportion of the Irish population that the CHURCH OF IRELAND catered for, rendered the reforms in Ireland of less political importance than similar developments in England, but they reflect the close identification of interest between the two churches.

Article Men

The Article Men were those entitled by the terms of the Act of SETTLEMENT of 1662 to have their claims to restoration of their forfeited lands considered on the grounds that they had abided by the negotiated peaces of the IRISH REBELLION in 1646 and 1649. At the restoration of King Charles II, attempts were made to resolve the chronic predicament in which former royalists as well as former rebels found themselves, consequent upon the wholesale land reallotment initiated in the 1650s, and the Article Men were those to whom special consideration should be given in determining their claims.

Ascendancy, The (Protestant)

The term 'Protestant Ascendancy' has a precise historiographical meaning, but does not appear to have been the creation of historians. It was in use as early as 1792, had a wide currency by 1840, and was used by GLADSTONE in 1868 to mean an identity of interest with the CHURCH OF IRELAND. In brief, the Ascendancy was made up of communicants of the Church of Ireland who, as a consequence of the political and religious settlement 1691, enjoyed total control of power and influence in Ireland subject only to the crown and government of England. The Ascendancy is not an expression of English exclusiveness in Ireland, but rather an exclusiveness of a section of the Irish population who appear to have considered themselves Irish rather than English, but were united by a common orthodox Protestantism. The Ascendancy rested upon the enforcement and mainte- nance of PENAL LAWS against Catholics, whether native Irish Catholics or OLD ENGLISH, and implicit in this was a continuing belief in the inherent threat of the Catholic religion to stability and well-being. The shift to regarding them- selves as Irish was gradual, and brought with it an expression of Irish patriotism (exemplified by men like GRATTAN and FLOOD) that frequently and forcefully regarded English interests as necessarily at variance with those of Ireland. The Irish PARLIAMENT was the domain of the Ascendancy, and Ireland's professional elite, largely educated at TRINITY COLLEGE, sought relentlessly to resist reforms that would reduce their authority in the Irish House of Commons. In this context, the very real concessions wrung from Britain by Grattan at the end of the eighteenth century were a successful assertion of Ascendancy power. Developing policies of toleration in England towards Cath- olics and DISSENTERS were viewed with suspicion by the Ascendancy, which sought to influence and to control the British government's executive arm in Ireland at the CASTLE. The survival of the Ascendancy was perceived to depend upon the continuing close links of Ireland with the English crown, the supremacy of which they acknowledged. Opposition to the Ascendancy was widespread and, by the 1790s, vocal. It came from moderate reforming Whigs of otherwise impeccable Protestant persuasion, from the refor- ming fervour of the CATHOLIC COMMITTEE, from the revolutionary republicanism of the UNITED IRISHMEN, and from the threat of rural unrest (see AGRARIAN OUTRAGES). As the application and enforcement of Penal Laws and disabling legislation was fundamental to the survival of the Ascendancy's power, measures such as the 1829 EMANCIPATION Act in favour of Catholics struck mortal blows to that power, and the LAND LEGISLATION of 1870 seemed to drive the Ascendancy into the cause of HOME RULE as a means of resisting the spread of reform. The cultural expression of the Ascendancy, seen in the massive rebuilding of DUBLIN in the eighteenth century and the spread of country houses, was an affirmation of a controlling interest in the future of Ireland. Since that interest rested upon laws designed to preserve exclusivity, once those laws were undermined or reformed, the basis of Ascendancy self- assurance began to give.

Ashe, Thomas (1885–1917)

Thomas Ashe, a schoolmaster by profes- sion, was born in County Kerry, and became involved in the republicanism of the GAELIC LEAGUE and a commander in the IRISH VOLUNTEERS. During the EASTER RISING of 1916, he commanded forces north of DUBLIN, was captured, and sentenced to life imprisonment. Upon his release in 1917 he undertook political campaigning for EAMON DE VALERA, and was arrested again. In prison, he organized and led a HUNGER STRIKE by SINN FÉIN prisoners, and died as a consequence. He was regarded by the republican movement in Ireland as a martyr for the cause of a free Ireland.

Askeaton Affair, The

The fight at Askeaton in County Limerick in August 1821 brought together in one confrontation various distinct elements and issues. A force of some 200 or so WHITEBOYS gathered to launch an attack on the house of a TITHE proctor, and were themselves assaulted by a small force of police. The Whiteboys suffered a defeat, and the prisoners were ordered to bury their dead in quicklime graves by the police commander, Major Richard Going. Going was notorious as a member of the ORANGE ORDER, and it was rumoured that not all of those buried were dead when they were thrown into the pits. The government took alarm at Going's behaviour, and replaced him, a move that led to a purge of Orangeism in the police. Going himself was waylaid and executed by ROCKITES seeking revenge for the Askeaton killings. The Askeaton Affair represented a direct confrontation between Catholics and Protestants, the latter representing the machinery of law enforcement, but apparently motivated by sectarian grievance. This aspect took precedence over the localized assertion of anti-tithe feeling, which was running high in Ireland, and heading towards the TITHE WARS of the 1830s. The Askeaton Affair also obliged the government to look at the infiltration of the police by Orange activists.

Assuring, Confirming and Settling of Lands and Estates, Act for (9 June 1657), *see* SETTLING OF IRELAND, Act for

Athlone

Athlone in County Westmeath came under siege in July 1690 by forces supporting King WILLIAM III in his struggle with the JACOBITE armies of King JAMES II. William laid siege to the town on 17 July, but resistance by Colonel Richard

Grace forced him to abandon his attempt to take it, on 25 July. In June 1691 troops under GINKEL advanced against Athlone and drove the Jacobites into the Irishtown area, where they surrendered on 30 June.

Aughrim, battle of

The battle of Aughrim, County Galway, was fought on 12 July 1691, and to the JACOBITE supporters of King James III was looked upon as 'the great disaster'. It was the last large-scale pitched battle to be fought on Irish soil. Following upon the fall of ATHLONE, GINKEL and his army advanced to meet the Jacobites under the command of the French General ST RUTH, who was killed in the ensuing engagement. Aughrim opened the way to Galway, which surrendered to Ginkel on 21 July. As late as November 1717, a certain Henry Luttrell was killed in DUBLIN by unknown assassins. He had been suspected of betraying the Jacobite army's dispositions to Ginkel on the eve of Aughrim.

Auxiliaries/Auxies

The Auxiliaries were formed on 27 July 1920 from among British Army officers who had served in Europe during the FIRST WORLD WAR. They were intended to reinforce the ROYAL IRISH CONSTABULARY in its struggle against the IRISH REPUBLICAN ARMY during the WAR FOR INDEPENDENCE that began in 1919. The bitterness of the fighting between the 'Auxies' and the IRA reflected the deliberate policy of terror that the Auxiliaries pursued against the civilian population, which caused their commander, Brigadier General Crozier, to resign in disgust. On 28 November 1920 an 18-man Auxiliary patrol was wiped out by a FLYING COLUMN of the IRA under Tom Barry at Kilmichael, County Cork. Martial law was declared on 10 December, and under its auspices the Auxiliaries murdered the parish priest of Dunmanway in Cork in reprisal for the Kilmichael killings. The activities of the 'Auxies' tended to unite Irish opinion, rather than to drive a wedge between the IRA and its civilian support.

B

B Specials *see* ULSTER SPECIAL
CONSTABULARY

Bachelor's Walk

Bachelor's Walk, DUBLIN, was the scene of
a violent confrontation between civilians
and British troops, supported by the
Dublin Metropolitan Police, on 26 July
1914. Having failed to disarm a column of
IRISH VOLUNTEERS returning to Dublin
with arms landed at HOWTH, the King's
Own Scottish Borderers opened fire on a
crowd, killing four and wounding 37 in a
brief fusillade.

Back Lane Parliament *see* CATHOLIC CONVENTION

Baggot-Rath, battle of

The battle of Baggot-Rath, known also as
the battle of Rathmines, was fought close
to DUBLIN on 2 August 1649. Irish royalist
forces under the Earl of ORMOND sustained a severe defeat at the hands of
MICHAEL JONES, who thus secured Dublin
for the arrival of OLIVER CROMWELL and
troops from England, prior to Cromwell's
campaign to bring the IRISH REBELLION to a
close.

Balfour, Arthur (1848–1930)

Balfour was a career politician who was
appointed CHIEF SECRETARY in Ireland in
1887 on the strength of his work as
Secretary for Scotland. In Ireland he
tackled head-on the NATIONAL LAND
LEAGUE, ordering its suppression, and
directed government policy against the
PLAN OF CAMPAIGN, the National Land
League's orchestrated rent strike against
landlords. Balfour was largely responsible for the creation of the CONGESTED
DISTRICTS BOARD, set up in 1891 to
purchase and redistribute land, one of
the more positive land measures adopted
under the UNION. Balfour served as
Conservative party Prime Minister from

1902 to 1905, and tended to favour
progress towards HOME RULE for Ireland.

Balliboe and Ballybetagh

The terms are anglicizations of Irish land
measures, which seem to have been
indicators of value rather than area. The
early seventeenth-century PLANTATION
policy interpreted a ballybetagh as a
defined area of 'tribal' authority, approxi-
mating to 16 balliboes of 60 acres apiece.
Subsequently, commissioners for allot-
ting land chose to see the ballybetagh as
equivalent to 1,000 acres, which was to be
the basic allotment to the ADVENTURERS of
1642 who advanced money towards the
suppression of the IRISH REBELLION in
return for forfeited lands.

Ballinamuck, battle of

The battle of Ballinamuck was fought on
8 September 1798 in County Longford
between the French expeditionary force
under HUMBERT which had landed in
Ireland in August to support the UNITED
IRISHMEN's rebellion, and government
troops commanded by CORNWALLIS. The
French and Irish were defeated, and the
loyal MILITIA perpetrated a vicious massacre of captured rebels on the instructions
of General LAKE. Humbert was treated as
a prisoner of war, but the Irishmen who
had come with him from France were
court-martialled and executed summarily. The battle marked the end of the
short-lived Republic of Connacht (see
RACES OF CASTLEBAR), which province the
French had controlled for a few weeks,
and marked also the turning-point of the
1798 rising in the west of Ireland.

Ballycohey, battle of

The affray at Ballycohey in County
Tipperary took place on 14 August 1868
in a period of heightened tensions over
the process of EVICTION and ejectment

10

that was hardening attitudes amongst the Irish peasantry in the LAND WAR. Tenants at Ballycohey united to resist by force the eviction procedures of the landlord William Scully, and in the process killed Scully's bailiff and a constable of the ROYAL IRISH CONSTABULARY, which force was backing up the bailiff. The affray indicated the degree of frustration felt as LAND LEGISLATION seemed nowhere near.

Ballynahinch, battle of

Fought on 13 June 1798 in County Down, the battle of Ballynahinch marked the end of the short-lived UNITED IRISHMEN rising in ULSTER. The rebels were commanded by Henry Munro, a linen draper from Lisburn and a PRESBYTERIAN. His forces took Ballynahinch on 11 June, and then faced the YEOMANRY and MILITIA under the command of General Nugent, fresh from suppression of rebellion in County Antrim. Munro was taken and beheaded at Lisburn on 15 June, and his followers slaughtered as they fled or surrendered.

Ballysadare, battle of

Scene of the defeat in County Sligo on 17 October 1645 of CATHOLIC CONFEDERACY forces by government troops commanded by Sir CHARLES COOTE.

Ballyveigh Strand, battle of

This confrontation in County Kerry on 24 June 1834 was less a battle than an encounter between rival factions (see FEUDS AND FACTION FIGHTING) remarkable for the numbers engaged. Some 3,000 adherents of the Cooleen faction and the Lawlor-Black Mulvihills faction fought it out, leaving more than 200 dead in the place. The battle was a massive explosion of gang warfare.

Bantry Bay

During the course of August 1796 discussions took place in Paris between representatives of the UNITED IRISHMEN, a revolutionary republican movement, and the French government with a view to bringing a French expeditionary force

into Ireland to support a rising. On 22 December 1796 such a fleet, commanded by Lazare Hoche and with WOLFE TONE in attendance, anchored in Bantry Bay off the coast of County Cork, some 43 ships carrying 15,000 men having set off from France. Disrupted by storms, the fleet split up, and the projected landing did not take place. Nevertheless, revolutionaries in Ireland saw it as a gesture of French good faith although, conversely, the failure of the Irish to take up arms to coincide with the French arrival led the French to see any future landing only as back-up to a rising which was already under way.

Bantry Bay was also the scene, on 1 May 1689, of a naval engagement between English and French fleets, during the JACOBITE war following the deposition of King JAMES II.

Barna, County Galway

Barna was the scene of a particularly horrific incident during the British campaign against the IRISH REPUBLICAN ARMY in 1920. On 15 November soldiers took Father Michael Griffin for questioning, and his body was subsequently found in a nearby ditch.

Baronies (*see also* ADMINISTRATIVE STRUCTURE)

Baronies were an English introduction into the administrative structure of Ireland, although ostensibly based upon earlier Gaelic territorial units, the 'tricha cét'. Baronies consisted of groups of adjacent parishes, but as late as 1840 the precise boundaries of such parishes were uncertain, as were the subdivisions of the various counties that went to make up the various provinces. The nearest English equivalent would be hundreds or wapentakes, the ancient subdivisions of English counties.

Battalion of St Patrick *see* IRISH BRIGADE OF ST PATRICK

Battle-Axe Guards

An honorary guard attached to the person and office of the LORD LIEUTENANT, purely ceremonial and equivalent to the Yeoman of the Guard in England. The 'battle-axes' convey an origin in the GALLOGLASSES mercenary soldiers whose vital role in sustaining feud and battle in Gaelic society, came to an end in the early seventeenth century.

Belfast

In 1600, during the English campaign against the Gaelic rebels in ULSTER commanded by the Earl of TYRONE, Belfast was little more than an isolated garrison with associated civilian dwellings. Incorporated by charter on 27 April 1613, and thenceforth returning MPs to the Parliament in DUBLIN, Belfast expanded rapidly until, by 1700, it ranked as the fourth port of Ireland. Within another 100 years it was a regional capital rooted in a valuable commercial life, looking as if it might ultimately eclipse Dublin in size and wealth. The first accurate census in 1841 showed a population of 75,000, which had grown to 387,000 by the census of 1911. The expanding city was clearly divided into religious or sectarian zones: in the mid-nineteenth century one-third of the city's population was Catholic, with concentrations in specific areas such as Divis Street (and equivalent Protestant enclaves around Sandy Row) that survive into the late twentieth century. As the city grew, outbreaks of sectarian violence associated with Protestant commemorative marches in July of each year, became commonplace. Belfast's role as the capital city of the SIX COUNTIES, all that remained of the Ulster province after PARTITION in 1921, is unchallenged.

Bellings, Richard (d. 1677)

Of OLD ENGLISH origin, Bellings was an historian of Ireland and served for a time as MP in the Parliament in Dublin. He became secretary to the Supreme Council of the CATHOLIC CONFEDERACY in 1642, and in that capacity undertook a mission to Europe to secure support for the Irish rebels. He returned to Ireland in October 1645 in company with the papal representative, RINUCCINI, but thereafter went over to ORMOND and the Irish royalists, and spent the 1650s in exile in France.

Benburb, battle of

The battle of Benburb, County Tyrone, was fought on 5 June 1646 between forces of the CATHOLIC CONFEDERACY under OWEN ROE O'NEILL, and an over-confident ROBERT MONRO with an ULSTER army. Monro's army was pushing south when O'Neill fell upon it and inflicted a decisive defeat which Monro chose to ascribe to a judgement of God. O'Neill then moved towards Clones in County Monaghan, mopping up resistance. The victory came as a godsend to RINUCCINI, who counted upon O'Neill's support in the political wranglings within the Supreme Council of the Catholic Confederacy.

Beresford, John (1738–1805)

Nicknamed in his own lifetime the 'King of Ireland', Beresford was a typical product of the ASCENDANCY, with a conventional education at TRINITY COLLEGE and rapid rise in the Irish administration. He became Chief Commissioner of the Revenue in 1780, with extensive powers of patronage, and foremost political adviser to William Pitt. Beresford was instrumental in gaining support for the UNION of Ireland and Britain which took place in 1801 through the manipulation of his patronage.

Berkeley, George (1685–1753)

Berkeley was born in County Kilkenny and received his education at TRINITY COLLEGE DUBLIN, thereafter following a career within the CHURCH OF IRELAND that earned him the bishopric of Cloyne in 1732. Berkeley was, however, preeminently a philosopher, whose *Principles of Human Knowledge* was published in 1710. He showed a fairly typical ASCENDANCY concern to promote the image of 'Irishness' that the identification of Irish interests with Ascendancy interests required, but coupled with this was a tolerance towards Catholics that was evidenced in his pastoral work. His other published works included *The Querist* of 1735 and *Maxims on Patriotism* in 1750.

Bessborough Commission

The Commission was established in 1880 by GLADSTONE's Liberal government, to make recommendations to be embodied in LAND LEGISLATION. The Commission was also, with its brief restricted to Ireland alone, an alternative to the Conservatives' RICHMOND COMMISSION. The commissioners carried out extensive interviews within the structure of Irish rural and agricultural society, and looked particularly into EVICTIONS or ejectments and the nature of tenancies. Gladstone took up the Commission's recommendations in the 1881 Land Act (see LAND LEGISLATION) which introduced security of tenure and an arbitration procedure but which critics believed inoperable and subsequent historians have seen as actually perpetuating the problem of uneconomic smallholdings.

Birmingham, George (1865–1950)

Birmingham was the pseudonym of the BELFAST-born James Hannay, a conventionally educated clergyman of the CHURCH OF IRELAND, who aligned himself with the movement for HOME RULE and associated himself with resurgent Gaelic cultural activity in Ireland. Under his pseudonym he wrote in advocacy of the objectives of the GAELIC LEAGUE, and produced outright Gaelic historical romances such as *Benedict Kavanagh* in 1907 which made the case for religious toleration, and *The Red Hand of Ulster* of 1912 which celebrated the defiance of the northern Gael. Nevertheless, the Gaelic League repudiated him when, in 1906, his ASCENDANCY origins became public knowledge.

Birrell, Augustine (1850–1933)

Birrell was appointed CHIEF SECRETARY in Ireland at a difficult time, in 1907, confronted by widespread agitation for HOME RULE and by the development of the republican SINN FÉIN. Birrell was deeply involved with measures such as the IRISH COUNCIL BILL of 1907 which anticipated a form of devolved power to meet the widespread enthusiasm for Home Rule, but he was criticized then and since for failing to perceive the drift towards armed uprising symbolized by the activities of republicans and the IRISH VOLUNTEERS. He dismissed the Commissioner of the Dublin Metropolitan Police (see CONSTABULARY) in the wake of the horrific killings at BACHELOR'S WALK in 1914, a gesture which probably did him more political harm than good amongst defenders of the UNION. He resigned his office in 1916 in face of the republican uprising.

Black Books of Athlone

Following upon the suppression of the IRISH REBELLION in 1653, the government in England pressed ahead with wholesale land forfeiture and the transplanting of thousands of Irish and OLD ENGLISH rebels and royalists into CONNACHT. The slowness of the removal led to the creation of a court of 'claims and qualifications' at Athlone in County Westmeath in 1654, backed up by court-martial powers in March 1655 to impose death sentences upon those who refused to transplant. The survey records and 'books of discrimination' used by the court at Athlone became known as The Black Books, in that they contained a record of evidences that dealt with the activities of individuals during the rebellion, and encompassed also documents of the CATHOLIC CONFEDERATION. These materials were used to determine who was liable to forfeiture and resettlement in Connacht.

Black List

The Black List was a schedule of those members of the Irish PARLIAMENT (see also GRATTAN'S PARLIAMENT) who were accused of selling Ireland into the UNION with Britain of 1801, in return for personal profit and preferment. It was published by Sir Jonah Barrington in 1833 in his *The Rise and Fall of the Irish Nation*, and listed some 140 persons including, for example, Mr J. Bingham who was said to have taken a peerage and £15,000 for his acquiescence.

Black Militia

The Black Militia was an element of Irish peasant folk lore and belief, although of uncertain origin. It was conceived of as an armed force that would, one day, be unleashed upon the Catholics to bring about their destruction. In the years around 1800 it was loosely identified with the militant Protestantism of the ORANGE ORDER, and frequently with the police in general. The BLACK AND TANS, who fought against the IRISH REPUBLICAN ARMY during the WAR FOR INDEPENDENCE in 1919/20 with particular savagery and animus, would also fit into the 'Black Militia' legend.

Black Oath, The

The Black Oath was a form of oath of ABJURATION, but applied specifically to the ULSTER Scots by proclamation of 21 May 1639. It was introduced by THOMAS WENTWORTH as a weapon against 'their abominable covenant', which was an undertaking by the Scottish PRESBYTERIANS to resist innovations in their church, which had spread to their co-religionists in Ulster. The Black Oath reflected Wentworth's (and the government's) view that the Presbyterians were potentially more dangerous than the Catholics, and it required them to abjure the Solemn League and Covenant and affirm their allegiance to King Charles I. It was enforced on all aged 16 or over, and the commissioners for the oath were accompanied by troops. The slaughter of Protestants that accompanied the outbreak of the IRISH REBELLION in 1641 was seen by some as a judgement of the Lord upon the oath-takers.

Black and Tans

The Black and Tans began recruitment on 2 January 1920 from amongst ex-British Army regular soldiers, as a reinforcement for the ROYAL IRISH CONSTABULARY engaged in the war with the IRISH REPUBLICAN ARMY since 1919. They were commanded by Major General Tudor, and began to arrive in Ireland from England in March 1920, quickly earning their nickname from their uniform of dark green or black caps and khaki tunics. On 28 April 1920 they went on the rampage in Limerick in the wake of an IRA attack on a police barracks, destroying personal property and assaulting civilians. The

technique was repeated in Cork on 11 December, when £3 million worth of damage was done after an IRA attack on the Victoria Barracks. Their ferocity was sanctioned by the British government, but, as in the case of the AUXILIARIES, proved counter-productive, merely strengthening support for the IRA. Popular perception of the years 1919 and 1920 has lumped together the excesses of the Auxiliaries and the Black and Tans, and made the term 'Black and Tan' one of universal opprobrium in Ireland.

Black Tom Tyrant *see* THOMAS WENTWORTH

Blackfeet

An agrarian secret society, ostensibly Catholic, particularly active in the 1830s. They were condemned by a Catholic bishop as a 'brutal canaille composing the Trades Unions and Blackfeet confederacies', from which it is clear that they arose from and represented exclusively the Irish peasantry, and belong to the tradition of AGRARIAN OUTRAGE and unrest directed at landlords, large farmers and issues such as TITHES and tenancies.

Blood's Plot

Colonel Thomas Blood (1618–80) was an English Protestant soldier who obtained property in Ireland following the suppression of the IRISH REBELLION of 1641–53. He seems to have lost all or part of his property following the land settlement under King Charles II, and in 1663 led or became involved in a conspiracy to seize Dublin Castle by embittered former soldiers. The conspiracy failed, but in 1670 Blood was involved in a kidnap or murder plot against the Duke of ORMOND which also failed. He is usually and chiefly associated with an attempt in 1671 to steal the crown jewels of England, which exploit led him to find favour with Charles II.

Bloody Sunday

On 21 November 1920, during the WAR FOR INDEPENDENCE, IRISH REPUBLICAN ARMY leader MICHAEL COLLINS carried out the killing of 14 members of British Intelligence in DUBLIN, who had been identified through infiltration. As a direct act of retaliation, the BLACK AND TANS opened indiscriminate fire into the crowd at a football match at Croke Park and killed 12 civilians. The incident was known as Bloody Sunday. The AUXILIARIES, in further retaliation, murdered IRA prisoners held in Dublin.

On 30 January 1972, 13 civilians in DERRY were shot down by British Paratroops, an incident also referred to as Bloody Sunday.

Board of Erin

The term occurs in ULSTER in the 1830s, and alludes to a secret national organization intended to unite all the various lodges of the RIBBONMEN, a Catholic secret society that had developed out of resistance to Protestant (see ORANGE ORDER) violence.

Boate, Gerard (d. 1650)

Boate was a Dutchman and physician to King Charles I, who became prominent in bringing Dutch investment into Irish land as part of the colonization process facilitated by the English Parliament in 1642 through the ADVENTURERS. Boate's book, *The Natural History of Ireland* was published posthumously in 1652 with a dedication to OLIVER CROMWELL, and was intended to 'sell' the idea of Irish land and PLANTATION to would-be colonizers.

Bogland Act, The

The Bogland Act of 2 June 1772 marked a breach in the rigidly enforced PENAL LAWS which had limited Catholic tenurial rights, by allowing them to take leases of blocks of bogland or waste of up to 50 acres, on realistic 61-year leases. If reclaimed and worked, bogland could be made productive.

Bonnaghts/Bonaghts

Bonnaghts or Bonaghts were, specifically, mercenary soldiers in GAELIC IRISH society, ordinarily of native origin, unlike the GALLOGLASSES who were introduced from Scotland. An alternative name is 'delonies' from the Gaelic 'diolmhaineach' meaning mounted troops or irregulars. Bonnaghts fought under TYRONE in the rebellion which ended at KINSALE in 1603.

Booleying

Booleying is an anglicization of a Gaelic agrarian term best understood as transhumance, and regarded by the English in the sixteenth and seventeenth centuries as barbarous and too convenient for prosecuting rebellions. In effect, it meant the movement of herds of livestock to upland pastures or to remote bogland pastures in the summer months, with the attendant creation of seasonal settlements or 'booleys' that might have some arable land attached to them. The practice was primarily to be found in Connacht and Ulster, but was virtually finished by the end of the seventeenth century.

Borlase, Sir John (1576–1648)

Appointed LORD JUSTICE in Ireland in 1640, having previously, given his military background, served as Master of the Ordnance there. In conjunction with the more active Lord Justice PARSONS, Borlase virtually ruled Ireland after the departure of THOMAS WENTWORTH until he was dismissed in 1644. It appears to have been to Borlase that word of the imminent IRISH REBELLION was broken in October 1641 by Owen O'Connolly. Borlase, like Parsons, was identified with the Parliamentary party in England, in opposition to the policies of King Charles I.

Borough Parliament

The term 'borough parliament' was used by GRATTAN as a contemptuous description of the Irish PARLIAMENT of the eighteenth century. It drew attention to the fact that of the 300 members of the House of Commons no fewer than 200 represented 'close boroughs', that is, boroughs where individuals or tiny oligarchies controlled the selection and election of MPs. Grattan himself, though he professed to despise it as a Parliament of time-servers, made no attempt to change the composition, which change occurred only with the act of UNION between Ireland and Britain in 1801. Thenceforth only 100 Irish MPs sat at WESTMINSTER, and of that number only 20 or so came from 'close' boroughs.

Bottle Riot

With the rise of militant Protestantism in the ORANGE ORDER, veneration of the memory of King WILLIAM III by decorating his statue at COLLEGE GREEN, DUBLIN, on 12 July had become part of a ceremonial. This was prohibited in 1821, on instructions of the LORD LIEUTENANT to the Mayor and Corporation of Dublin. In 1822 Orange demonstrators proceeded with their ceremony, and there was a running fight with Catholic onlookers. On 4 November troops were used to disperse a ceremony held to mark William III's birthday. A month later the Lord Lieutenant attending a theatrical performance in Dublin, was pelted with bottles. The instigators were arrested and charged with conspiracy, but the GRAND JURY resisted the charge, and when the case did come to trial, the perpetrators were acquitted. The 'bottle riot' seems to have occasioned some mirth amongst Catholic observers.

Boycotting

Boycotting was a weapon used effectively by the Irish peasantry in their campaigns for land reform, and during the LAND WAR of the late nineteenth century. The principle of having no social or economic intercourse with 'offenders' had been practised by RIGHTBOY agitators in the 1790s, but the use of the word 'Boycott' derived from the specific case of the land agent Captain Charles Cunningham Boycott (d. 1897) who was ostracized in County Mayo in 1880. PARNELL in September 1880 had called for a 'moral Coventry' against opponents of the LAND LEAGUE, and the pressure against Captain Boycott was sustained by the League. The Catholic bishop of Limerick denounced boycotting in 1888 as against 'the moral law of charity and justice'. The ORANGE ORDER retaliated against boycotting by organizing relief groups to move into areas to help victims by assisting in their harvesting and other agricultural work. Between late 1880 and September 1881 relief groups were active in 19 Irish counties, and the landlords feeling themselves under threat also set up a Property Defence Association with similar objectives. Captain Boycott had drafted in labourers from County Cavan in 1880, but had to provide almost 1,000 police to protect them whilst they worked.

Boyne, battle of the

The battle of the Boyne, fought on 1 July 1690, was a decisive defeat for the JACOBITE forces supporting King JAMES II at the hands of the army of King WILLIAM III. The Jacobite army of 25,000 men was defeated by 36,000, both armies being somewhat cosmopolitan in their makeup, with Frenchmen, Germans, Danes and Dutch fighting alongside English and native Irish troops. James II fled to DUBLIN after the defeat, and on 4 July left for France from the port of Kinsale. The action at the Boyne rapidly entered Irish historical consciousness, to be seen both as a combat between Catholic Ireland and the coming ASCENDANCY, and simply as a battle between Protestants and Catholics. Historians have gone to great lengths to stress the international nature of the battle, and its part in a general European war for which Ireland was in some respects a sideshow. But the significance of the popular perception had, and continues to have, impact. ORANGEISM exulted in the Boyne victory just as later nationalists saw it as a bitter blow against the people of Ireland. Republicanism in some instances has disdained both sides in the battle, seeing it as a struggle having little to do with Irishmen and much to do with alien monarchy.

Break of Dromore, battle of

The battle at the Break of Dromore was fought on 14 March 1689 in County Down between a JACOBITE army under Richard Hamilton and an ULSTER Protestant army under Lord Mountalexander. Hamilton had come into Ireland in January 1689 on behalf of King WILLIAM III to negotiate with the Earl of TYRCONNEL, but had changed sides and taken a Jacobite command. The defeat of Mountalexander's army gave the Jacobites considerable leeway in eastern Ulster, and made the Protestant garrison at DERRY, loyal to William III, crucially important as a bastion.

Brehons and Brehon Law

The word 'brehon' is an anglicization of the Gaelic 'brithemin', a plural referring to legal scholars who, in traditional Gaelic society, enjoyed exalted social status and acted as arbitrators in disputes. The English colonists of the sixteenth century perceived the brehons as 'families' or 'clans' of 'lawyers' whose speciality, inimical to English law, was negotiated justice. The process of ANGLICIZATION involved a direct attack on the brehons, introducing Assize Courts and other colonial procedures from England to replace them. To no small extent the task was aided by Gaelic chiefs and nobles such as TYRONE, who rid himself of the brehon system, largely in his own interests. The brehon law system or 'cin comhfhocuis' held families and clans responsible for the misdeeds of group members, on which negotiated justice was based, and recognized 'éraic' or blood money as a recompense for homicide. The whole structure was regarded by the English as unethical, but many of the OLD ENGLISH who gradually became assimilated by native society, endorsed brehonism. The brehons were virtually eradicated by the late seventeenth century.

Broghill, Roger Boyle Lord (1621–79)

Broghill was the son of the 1st Earl of Cork, and a second-generation NEW ENGLISH settler in Ireland. Created Lord Broghill in 1627, and educated at TRINITY COLLEGE as well as in England, Broghill was commissioned as a commander against the CATHOLIC CONFEDERACY after the outbreak of the IRISH REBELLION of 1641. His youthfulness might account for his evident disdain for the Irish: 'a people given to destruction, who ... let themselves be deluded by ridiculous things,

and by more ridiculous persons'. He commanded for the English Parliament against the Irish royalists under ORMOND, and sat as an MP in England in the 1650s. He chose to support the restoration of King Charles II in 1660 and received the earldom of Orrery, Derry and was appointed as LORD JUSTICE in Ireland.

Brotherhood, The

A euphemism for the IRISH REPUBLICAN BROTHERHOOD revolutionary movement.

Brunswick Clubs

The first clubs were founded in August 1828 as part of the alarmed reaction amongst Protestants to the successes of O'CONNELL and the move for Catholic EMANCIPATION. The clubs were ultra Tory in the new sense of that word, largely aristocratic and marked by a pronounced anti-Catholicism, and took their name from the Duke of Brunswick who had presided at a banquet where the notion was first mooted. Some 200 clubs in all sprang up, dedicated to the defence of the Protestant constitution, by which was meant, the ASCENDANCY. Some have seen the clubs as bringing into the open the people who had long secretly encouraged and sustained the ORANGE ORDER.

Buckingham Palace Conference

Following upon a House of Lords amendment to the HOME RULE legislation in May 1914, the conference was summoned to work out the details for the proposed PARTITION of Ireland, with the exclusion of ULSTER from the proposed government of Ireland. Present at the conference were irreconcilables, CARSON and Craig from Ulster, and REDMOND and DILLON on behalf of the Home Rule movement. Impasse followed, in July 1914, but the outbreak of the FIRST WORLD WAR caused all legislation to be shelved for the duration.

Burke, Edmund (1729–97)

Burke's career lay primarily in England, although he was born in DUBLIN the son of an attorney, and educated at TRINITY

COLLEGE in the conventional ASCENDANCY tradition. Yet he has been seen as the most original, perceptive and prescient thinker and writer to emerge from the Ascendancy in Ireland. His Whig enemies in the English Parliament regarded him as an 'adventurer', and his tolerant attitude to Catholics (his marriage to a Catholic led to her conversion to Protestantism, however) went side by side with rejection of republicanism and revolutionary movements. He spoke on behalf of the American colonists in their dispute with Britain, and championed EMANCIPATION for Catholics as early as the 1770s. His *Reflections on the French Revolution* published in 1790 were written before the events in France turned into a bloodbath, but foresaw it and warned against it. He advocated war against France with sustained vigour, but found time to support and to assist the foundation of a Catholic college at Maynooth in Ireland (see ST PATRICK'S COLLEGE).

Butt, Isaac (1813–79)

Butt may be regarded as the founder of the movement for HOME RULE in Ireland as a structured political programme and party. He was born, however, in the ASCENDANCY tradition in County Donegal, and proved himself an intellectual Tory whose innate conservatism remained with him all his life. From 1836 to 1840 he was Professor of Political Economy at TRINITY COLLEGE, DUBLIN, and, as a member of the Irish bar, defended the YOUNG IRELANDERS of 1848 and the FENIANS of 1865–68, whose demeanour and courage moved him towards seeing Home Rule as a necessary safeguard for the future of Ireland. Between 1852 and 1865 he was a Conservative MP for Youghal, but in 1869 headed the AMNESTY ASSOCIATION the object of which was to secure the release of Fenians held in British gaols after the 1867 uprising. He subsequently sat as MP for Limerick on a Home Rule platform from 1871 to 1879, arguing for Home Rule and the restoration of a Parliament to Dublin to deal with Irish affairs. He appears to have envisaged some kind of federal political structure for the United Kingdom, with Ireland playing an equal part, and certainly applied his mind more closely to definition of terms than O'CONNELL had done with the movement for repeal of the UNION of 1801. At Butt's death the single-minded constitutional nationalism which he had represented, ended.

C

Cabinet, The Irish

A term for the group of Irish politicians who, in the 1780s, identified closely with the British administration in opposition to the PATRIOT following of GRATTAN. They included John Parnell, the great grandfather of CHARLES STEWART PARNELL, who was Chancellor of the Irish Exchequer in 1785, and JOHN FITZGIBBON, arguably the most powerful and influential man in Ireland in the 1790s and an architect of the UNION of 1801. Their influence was based upon their usefulness to the administration of the LORD LIEUTENANT, but they exercised no governmental responsibility, although they had access to the patronage and sinecure system which they controlled in their own interests. Their cohesion was largely a reflection of the long ministry of William Pitt as Prime Minister in Britain, which gave an unusual stability to the government of Ireland.

Cairo Gang, The

A British intelligence system established in DUBLIN in 1920 by the implacable Unionist and Chief of the Imperial General Staff, Henry Wilson (who was to be assassinated in 1922). The Cairo Gang was destroyed by MICHAEL COLLINS in an IRISH REPUBLICAN ARMY action in the autumn of 1920 (see BLOODY SUNDAY).

Callan

A fortified town in County Kilkenny which, on 8 February 1650, was stormed by troops of the NEW MODEL ARMY, with considerable slaughter of the defenders in two fortified strongpoints.

Callan was also the scene of the first protection society for tenant farmers, established 14 October 1849 (see TENANT LEAGUE).

Camden, William (1551–1623)

Camden was an eminent historian and antiquary of the Elizabethan age, largely known for his massive work *Britannia* of 1586 which went into several editions in his lifetime. Camden introduced to a wide audience the important work of Giraldus Cambrensis, *Topographia Hibernica*, and the *Expugnatio Hibernica*, which fed the developing interest of the English in the colonization and exploitation of Ireland. Camden was noted for a virulent anti-Catholicism rooted in the events of his early life.

Camperdown, battle of

The naval engagement of Camperdown was fought on 11 October 1797 between the British fleet and a Dutch fleet en route to France. The Dutch were intending to collect forces that the UNITED IRISHMEN expected to be landed in Ireland as a signal for a republican uprising. The British victory was a major setback to United Irishmen hopes.

Canting

The Cant or Cent was a public auction, and an issue in agrarian discontents in the eighteenth century. Auctions of land, or tenancies, were held in which the bids were sealed. It was not unusual for the canting for lands in CONNACHT or MUNSTER to take place in DUBLIN or places well away from the locality, and the successful bidders were regarded as 'incomers'. Both the HOUGHERS and the RIGHTBOYS endeavoured to impose punitive money fines on such incomers, for the benefit of the sitting tenants who had been unable to match the successful bid and who enjoyed no right of compensation at termination of their tenancy, or reimbursement for improvements undertaken (see also ULSTER CUSTOM).

19

Capel, Henry Lord (d. 1696)

Lord Capel, widely known for his extreme hostility towards Catholics in England, and a prominent figure in the deposition of King JAMES II in 1688, was appointed LORD DEPUTY in Ireland in 1695 after serving for two years as LORD JUSTICE. Under his influence a compliant Irish House of Commons annulled the acts of James II's Parliament, and affirmed the legality of King WILLIAM III and of the WILLIAMITE land settlement which was the root of Protestant ASCENDANCY power in the ensuing century.

Captain Rock *see* ROCKITES

Caravats and Shanavests

In the simplest terms, the Caravats and Shanavests were rival gangs or factions (see FEUDS AND FACTION FIGHTING) whose rivalry came to a head in the first decade of the nineteenth century. But the extent of the rivalry, spreading through and assimilating gangs in Tipperary, Waterford, Kilkenny, Limerick, Cork, Carlow, Wexford, Clare and Kerry, with outbreaks in Queen's County and in Kildare, is itself significant and suggestive of something other than purely gang activity. Evidence for this has been adduced particularly in the case of the Shanavests (from the Gaelic Sean-Bheisteanna and meaning 'the old waistcoats'). Their most prominent leader, Patrick Connors, nicknamed 'Sharp Paddy' (Paudeen Gar), may well have been implicated in the UNITED IRISHMEN rising of 1798, which sought to overthrow British rule and set up an Irish Republic. Some of his reported rhetoric indicated at least superficial nationalist sentiments. The Shanavests, also known as 'Paudeen Gar's Boys', 'St Peter's Corps' and 'Dingers' came from amongst the slightly better-off in native peasant society, small farmers rather than labourers or cottagers. Their rivals, the Caravats (Carabhaiti) whose name meant 'cravats' or neckerchiefs, were largely labourers and industrial workers, and fit more firmly into a tradition of agrarian unrest manifested by the far more political WHITEBOYS, under which name (among

others) they sometimes went or were described. Other names for the Caravats were 'Blue Belts', 'Moll Doylists' and 'Dowsers'. Their most prominent leader, Nicholas Hanley, was hanged at CLONMEL in 1806 largely as a result of a successful Shanavest prosecution. The conflict between the two gangs is symptomatic of the tensions in peasant society between the landless and frequently jobless, and the farmers who clung on to small tenancies and tried to exploit their land for a living. To the Caravats, such men were the immediate face of the landlord system which had expropriated the land of Ireland in the interests of a religiously and socially acceptable few.

Carberry, Hugh (d. 1899)

A hero of the Irish nationalist and republican movements, Carberry was an Armagh Catholic who espoused the cause of the Boers in the Boer War (which broke out in October 1899) and was killed fighting against the British army on 30 October of that year.

Carders

The Carders, also and variously known as 'Threshers' or 'Shakers', were a rural protest movement who first came to notice in 1805 in County Mayo. Their threat – to use carding combs such as weavers used in their trade, on their enemies' flesh – indicates the small cottager origin of the movement, and the discontent of weavers faced with mechanization of the craft. They resorted to direct action in protest also against TITHES and dues paid traditionally to the Catholic clergy as well: the movement was not inherently sectarian. On 2 September 1806 a gang of 30 or so 'Threshers' was active in County Sligo, presaging violent outbursts that spread through Leitrim and Longford counties. A pitched fight with the MILITIA took place in November 1806 which went against the rioters, and the movement subsided, but appeared again in 1812 in protest against the price of bread and inflation. By February of the following year there were gangs operating in Westmeath, Waterford, Tipperary and

Limerick, and between 1813 and 1816 they were active in much of eastern Leinster.

Carolan, Turlough (d. 1738)

Carolan, born blind in County Meath, has been considered the last of the traditional wandering harpists and bards of Gaelic society. His work, amongst other things, lamented and lauded the departed Catholic gentry, banished by the land settlement and the PENAL LAWS, or reduced to poverty. After his death in County Roscommon in March 1738, interest in his music and poetry was sustained, not least by a collection of his songs that had been published in 1724. His work was marked by a lyrical but not sentimental sadness, and stark awareness of the passing of an old order.

Carrickfergus, County Antrim

In the midst of the TYRONE rebellion, which ended at KINSALE in 1603, Carrickfergus was the single most important town in ULSTER, and a major military base for the English forces opposed to Tyrone. The first Presbytery (see PRESBYTERIANISM) was established at Carrickfergus by Scottish troops under ROBERT MONRO sent over to oppose the Gaelic rebels of 1641. It was close to Carrickfergus that King WILLIAM III landed on 14 June 1690 to conduct the military campaign against his rival King JAMES II. The town was to be seized on 21 February 1760 by French forces under Thurot, who was later killed in action on 28 February. Its importance except as a military base was rapidly eclipsed by BELFAST in the course of the seventeenth century.

Carson, Sir Edward (1854–1935)

Carson was by birth a Dubliner and a true ASCENDANCY figure in the conventional nature of his education, at TRINITY COLLEGE, and his background. He had no strong anti-Catholic feelings, but was motivated by a consistent and resolute belief in the UNION of 1801. The shift of Liberal opinion in favour of HOME RULE and divisions over the issue in the Conservative party, pushed Carson towards militant Unionism. His legal training had brought him to some prominence: he had headed the prosecution of the leaders of the PLAN OF CAMPAIGN in 1889, and served as Solicitor-General in the Conservative administration of 1900–5. Leader of the Unionist party from 1912, he gave his support for the exclusion of ULSTER (see PARTITION) from the proposed Home Rule legislation of 1912 and set his hand to the ULSTER COVENANT which pledged to resist Home Rule and implied resort to arms in defence of the Union. The amendment of 1912 to the Home Rule Bill had looked to exclude four of the Ulster counties, but in 1913 Carson resolved upon total Ulster exclusion. From his own pocket he advanced £10,000 to help arm the ULSTER VOLUNTEER FORCE raised to defend the Union and in 1914 claimed to have organized the provision of arms for the UVF. Carson's developing militancy was saved from its ultimate expression in armed rebellion by the intervention of the FIRST WORLD WAR, which caused Home Rule legislation, and therefore Ulster exclusion, to be deferred until the war should end.

Case of Ireland Being Bound by Acts of Parliament in England Stated

This important document was written by WILLIAM MOLYNEUX and appeared in 1698. The argument it contained was virtually a revival of that of PATRICK DARCY put forward in 1643, objecting to the subservience of the Irish PARLIAMENT to that of England in matters of legislation and the initiation of bills (see also POYNINGS' LAW). Molyneux's case rested upon the assertion of the existence of a contract between the Irish people and King Henry II of England in the twelfth century, and that this contract took precedence over subsequent legislation by which the English Parliament arrogated supremacy to itself. Molyneux, in true ASCENDANCY style, saw the Protestant NEW ENGLISH as the 'people' of Ireland, representing the continuation of that contract. The English Parliament condemned Molyneux's argument in June 1698, and, as if to ram home the message, in May 1699 passed legislation prohibiting the export of woollen goods from Ireland into any country other than England, from which they were anyway more or less barred by high duties on imports. This virtual strangulation of an Irish industry in the interests of its English rival was precisely the case that Molyneux and others saw as a necessary consequence of English parliamentary supremacy.

Casement, Sir Roger (1864–1916)

A member of the British diplomatic service from 1892, Casement associated himself with nationalists in Ireland in 1904 when he became a member of the GAELIC LEAGUE. In 1913 he joined the IRISH VOLUNTEERS, and in 1914 travelled to Germany where he endeavoured to recruit forces from amongst Irish prisoners of war, with a view to a rising in Ireland. His return to Ireland on 21 April 1916 seems to have been an attempt to stop the rising planned for Easter, but he was apprehended by British forces when he landed on the Banna Strand in County Kerry from a German submarine. He and Julian Bailey were seized, their companion Monteith escaped. He was sentenced to death for treason on 29 June 1916, and the government revealed forged diaries intended to present him as a homosexual, to undermine sympathy for him. Casement was hanged on 3 August 1916 at Pentonville Prison in London. In 1965 his body was disinterred and returned to Ireland for burial.

Cashel, Rock of

On 12 September 1647 the garrison of troops of the CATHOLIC CONFEDERACY was attacked, taken and massacred by government forces under MURROUGH O'BRIEN in a particularly savage action.

Cashel was taken again by siege by OLIVER CROMWELL from its royalist defenders in April 1650.

Cashel, Thomas Croke archbishop of (1824–1902)

Despite the equivocation of the Roman Catholic hierarchy in Ireland towards land agitation, Archbishop Croke proved an active supporter of the LAND LEAGUE, seeing the movement as a legitimate vehicle for Irish nationalist aspirations. In later years he became patron of the GAELIC ATHLETIC ASSOCIATION which existed to encourage ancient Irish sports and games. The archbishop's association with the land agitation earned him the suspicion of many Catholic clerics, who regarded its association with moves towards HOME RULE as evidence of Protestant-inspired sedition, and Pope Leo XIII was obliged to remonstrate with the archbishop over his too active involvement in secular matters.

Castle, The

The machinery of British administration in Ireland was based at Dublin Castle, hence the term 'Castle' is used to denote that administration in its entirety, as well as to indicate the origin of political power in Ireland. The head of the British administration was the LORD LIEUTENANT, or, in his absence, the LORD DEPUTY or LORDS JUSTICES, but, as the eighteenth century evolved, the most powerful single figure at the Castle was to be the CHIEF SECRETARY. The Castle was the immediate identifiable presence of British authority, controlling or seeking to control in British interests, the workings of the Irish PARLIAMENT. Even after UNION in 1801 which brought the Irish Parliament to an end, it remained as the executive of decisions taken in London, and the Irish civil service in consequence survived as a distinctive bureaucracy. The ASCENDANCY clustered about the Castle, which represented its guarantee of stability, and its last achievement was to transfer its expertise from DUBLIN to BELFAST following upon PARTITION in 1921 and the independence of the FREE STATE of Ireland. The weakness of the Castle hierarchy was that appointments and their duration reflected more or less accurately the ups and downs of ministerial changes in Britain: a period of governmental stability such as that prevailing in the 1770s could encourage a Lord Lieutenant to seek to develop a political grouping in Ireland identified with and reliant upon the Castle, as in the case of TOWNSHEND.

The Castle was, naturally, identified

with repression and the maintenance of inequalities within Ireland. Catholics and others were confronted in the early nineteenth century with a 'Castle-ORANGE' link that can only be understood in terms of defence of an existing system and fear of the pressures for legislative reform. On the other hand, the Castle was sufficiently independent of sectarian interests as to be able, under a Chief Secretary such as DRUMMOND, to wield its influence in favour of equality and in the interests of reform to benefit the Catholic majority. That in itself demonstrated the extent to which the administration assumed its political colour from attitudes in Britain.

Castle Chamber, Court of

The Court was set up in DUBLIN and was used by THOMAS WENTWORTH to harry the NEW ENGLISH and PRESBYTERIAN colonists and planters by calling into question their titles to the land that they held. Its draconian powers, King Charles I felt, should be used more rigorously and he ordered more frequent sittings in September 1634.

Castlereagh, Robert Stewart Viscount (1769–1822)

Castlereagh was born in County Down of ASCENDANCY background, and first entered the Irish Parliament in 1790 where he was associated with the PATRIOT grouping which GRATTAN had led to victory in the 1780s. Created a viscount in 1796, Castlereagh was appointed acting CHIEF SECRETARY in 1797 on the eve of the republican uprising of the UNITED IRISHMEN. He endeavoured to forestall the rebellion by the tactical arrest of United leaders, and to avert the ferocity of repression by replacing the MILITIA with regular troops from Britain. By the time he became Chief Secretary in his own right, in 1799, he had already and perhaps as early as 1793, begun to favour the UNION of Britain and Ireland, and his commitment was crucial to the passage of the legislation which brought Union about in 1801. Castlereagh committed suicide in 1822, having in the previous year been elevated to the marquessate of Londonderry.

Catholic Army, The

A term used for the united forces of the GAELIC IRISH rebels of 1641 and the OLD ENGLISH with whom they formally joined: 'To all Catholics of the Roman party, both English and Irish'. The term was seized upon and applied as one of opprobrium by the parliamentarian leaders and propagandists in England to the northern royalist army raised by King Charles I in 1642 at the start of the ENGLISH CIVIL WAR.

Catholic Association, The

The first use of the title Catholic Association was in 1756, when Charles O'Conor (d. 1790) established it as a group to represent the interests of landed Catholic gentry, particularly in County Mayo.

On 25 April 1823 DANIEL O'CONNELL presided at a meeting held in DUBLIN to formulate plans for a campaign aimed at securing EMANCIPATION for Catholics. The Catholic Association inaugurated on 12 May was the result of those deliberations, but in itself a revival of an association that had arisen from the old CATHOLIC BOARD. The Association's objective was to secure emancipation by constitutional means, but O'Connell intended that it should have a broad basis in the Catholic community, and in 1824 introduced the subscription system known as the CATHOLIC RENT both to provide funds and to give poor Catholics direct involvement. The rent raised £20,000 in nine months. The majority support for the Association seems to have come from larger farmers, particularly graziers, who were favoured by O'Connell for economic reasons. The Association also undertook to acquire land for use of Catholics for burial of their dead. The great cemetery of Glasnevin, resting place of many later nationalist and republican dead, was acquired by the Association in September 1831. The Association did gain mass support in Munster and Leinster, and was regarded by the CASTLE as potentially dangerous. Following the Unlawful Societies Act of 9 March 1825, the Association dissolved itself, but reformed again in July, on a less ostensibly political platform. In January 1828 a parish meeting campaign was launched, with 1,600 meetings held simultaneously throughout areas of Association support. At the same time O'Connell endeavoured to gain the support of the DISSENTER interest in Britain for the cause of toleration and emancipation. The Catholic Rent was rationalized, churchwardens taking over its collection and raising £22,000 in 1828. The Association lost impetus following the emancipation legislation of 1829 which gave Catholics access to Parliament and to civil and military office. The Association was dissolved.

Catholic Board, The

The Catholic Board formed in 1811 developed from the older Catholic Committee which had first met in March 1760, founded in DUBLIN by John Curry, Charles O'Conor and Thomas Wyse. The Committee was at first aristocratic in makeup and constitutional in its approach to the problem of alleviating the PENAL LAWS against Catholics. Under these auspices, it showed itself less radical than many PRESBYTERIANS, for example in its opposition to the American colonists and their War for Independence from Britain. In 1783 a spokesman from the Committee told a convention of the VOLUNTEERS that the Catholic population was not interested in the franchise, as if that disclaimer would draw Protestant and Catholic closer together in the struggle for reform and allay Protestant fears. The Committee became radicalized, however, from about 1790, and from its leadership would emerge future leaders of the revolutionary UNITED IRISHMEN movement, including WOLFE TONE, who became secretary to the Committee in 1792. The objective of the Committee was immediate equality within the system, and the leadership fell to John Keogh (d. 1817). In February 1791 a petition was presented to King George III asking for relief for the Catholics 'from their degraded situation' that they should 'no longer suffer them to continue to live like strangers in their native land'. The Catholic relief act of 1793 (see EMANCIPATION) known as Hobart's Act, extended the franchise to FORTY-SHILLING FREEHOLDERS, and was probably a direct response to the united pressure of the

Catholic Committee and the Volunteer movement. Thereafter precious little else was achieved, and the Catholic Committee leadership moved closer to revolution and the rising of the United Irishmen in 1798. The Catholic Committee and the emancipation issue both revived again in 1809, the Committee aiming to petition the parliament at WESTMINSTER. This petitioning policy, decided upon on 9 July 1811, was crushed by government action in the form of a proclamation under the CONVENTION ACT which forbade the selection of representatives to a committee to petition for emancipation. In the wake of this studied harassment, DANIEL O'CONNELL set up the Catholic Board. The new Board was composed of named individuals, and so therefore excluded from the provisions of the law that had wrecked the Committee. Nevertheless, in June 1813, PEEL made it known that the government 'must crush the Board'. As it was, the essentially middle-class membership was splitting over the VETO issue, and when the Board was finally declared illegal in 1814, it was already virtually dissolving itself. With its departure, concerted pressure for emancipation fell away, though an attempt to reconstitute it was made in 1817.

Catholic Church, The

Although the doctrines of the Roman Catholic Church were subscribed to by the vast majority of the population of Ireland, both native and OLD ENGLISH, by 1600, the Catholic Church itself was by no means united. As well as being poorly organized and in desperate need of revitalization, it was regarded as degenerate in relation to the dynamic faith of European nations. Moreover, there was a notable distinction between Gaelic observance and that of the Old English, which historians have seen as a reflection of the Spanish Gallic wings of Catholicism, the latter a comfortable Catholicism of the Old English fostered by the Jesuits. Under the aegis of PETER LOMBARD, Catholic Primate of All Ireland, reform measures were undertaken, with provincial synods to address the problem of pluralism. To make this successful, the church was dependent upon the influential and as yet politically confident Old English, with the consequence that an anti-Gaelic emphasis crept in. On the other hand, the very fact of Catholic numerical majority in Ireland served to lessen the internal dissensions within Protestantism, that were fragmenting the reformed faith in England. Catholics in Ireland were seen as an identifiable and dangerous enemy, and there was a concerted Protestant suspicion of them that for much of the seventeenth and eighteenth centuries remained firm. The failure of the IRISH REBELLION of 1641–53 and the ensuant repression and mass forfeiture of land, made the Catholic Church vulnerable to a vengeful Protestantism which acquired security and power in the settlement following upon the overthrow of King JAMES II in 1688 by WILLIAM III. A long series of measures aimed at depriving the laity of their clergy was ushered in in 1697 (see CATHOLIC CLERGY, PROCLAMATIONS AND LEGISLATION AGAINST) reinforced by further measures seeking to deprive Catholics of status and participation in Irish society, now being reshaped on a distinctly exclusive Protestant model. The process of expropriation and suppression took account of all Catholics, paying no respect to distinctions between native and Old English, to which WILLIAM PETTY had drawn attention in the seventeenth century: between the poor Gaelic Catholics and the 'richer and better educated … such Catholics as are in other places', in other words, known and to an extent tolerated. Throughout the eighteenth century the Catholic clergy struggled to minister to and preserve the faith of the believers. Increasing toleration began to make itself felt even in Ireland, where sympathy for the plight of Catholics and concerted efforts by Catholics themselves to secure EMANCIPATION gradually peeled away the years of repression. The Catholic Church in the form of its clergy proved crucial to galvanizing support for the CATHOLIC BOARD and CATHOLIC ASSOCIATION, despite divisive issues such as the VETO CONTROVERSY. Although the church hierarchy attempted to keep aloof from violence and sedition, deploring, for example, the activities of overtly Catholic

defence organizations such as the DEFENDERS and the RIBBONMEN, the connotation of Catholicism with nascent nationalism was inevitable. One nationalist leader, Denis Moran, claimed 'the Irish nation is de facto a Catholic nation', and the parochial clergy by and large showed themselves more sympathetic towards revolutionary republicanism than their bishops approved of. Indeed, the Catholic clergy of the nineteenth century were markedly more 'liberal' and 'democratic' than their counterparts in Britain, and the majority of them had been educated within Ireland. PENAL LAWS signally failed to root out Catholicism, but they were not intended to: they were designed to intimidate and overawe the majority of the people of Ireland, and because they offered no relief or alternative, merely drove commitment to the old religion deeper and firmer than before. When concerted efforts at conversion finally came in the early nineteenth century, they came at a time of movement towards emancipation, and so accounted for little. Moreover, attempts to tie in FAMINE relief in the 1840s with Protestant missionary zeal merely added to the resentment felt towards the long-dominant reformed religion.

Catholic Clergy, Proclamations and Legislation Against

The English assault upon Gaelic Ireland and the Catholic OLD ENGLISH was essentially two-pronged. Expropriation of land for resettlement with religiously and politically acceptable colonists, and the suppression of the Roman Catholic religion, that had given Gaelic society and Old English society a coherence. In July 1605 the government ordered all seminary priests and Jesuits to quit Ireland, an edict reissued in July 1611. In October 1617 provision was made for the banishment of priests who had been educated abroad, in European seminaries, and in January 1624 a proclamation required all Catholic clergy to leave the country, although this was rescinded for political reasons a month later. The reign of King Charles I was marked with moves towards more toleration (see MATTERS OF GRACE AND BOUNTY), but following the final suppression of the IRISH REBELLION in 1653 and the wholesale expropriation of Catholic lands, an edict was issued to expel all Catholic priests. In 1673 measures were taken for the closure of religious houses in Ireland and the expulsion of bishops and regular priests, reinforced by a further proclamation in October 1678. In 1697 following the political settlement after the deposition and flight of the Catholic King JAMES II, a banishment act was passed requiring clergy to leave Ireland by 1 May 1698. The Registration Act of 1704 required remaining clergy to register with the authorities at Quarter Sessions, and in 1709 an oath was imposed upon all such registered priests requiring them to abjure papal authority. In 1719 the Irish Privy Council recommended that all unregistered priests found in Ireland should be castrated; the English Privy Council moderated that to branding, but the measures did not in the end become law. There were measures (in 1726) to prevent Catholic priests from marrying Protestants, and a priest was executed under that act in 1727. In 1746 an act annulled all marriages that might subsequently be performed by Catholic clergy involving couples of mixed religion. A turn in the tide may be noted in the failure in 1756 of a bill for restricting Catholic priests and expelling their bishops, a measure which failed to gain a hearing again in 1757. Thereafter enforcement of the laws became laxer, as was the case with the PENAL LAWS, part of a general intellectual shift in attitudes throughout much of Protestant Europe. Catholic priests continued to suffer under disabilities, but they did not, for the most part, go in fear of their lives unless for political reasons.

Catholic Committee *see* CATHOLIC BOARD

Catholic Confederacy, The

Within a few weeks of the outbreak of the Irish REBELLION in ULSTER in October 1641, an alliance was formed between the rebels and the OLD ENGLISH Catholics of the PALE. This alliance was and is referred to as the (Irish) Catholic Confederacy. On 7 June 1642 a ruling council or Supreme Council was established at Kilkenny, made up of Catholic laity and clergy with Lord MOUNTGARRET as its President. The members of the Confederacy took an oath of association, and the four provinces of Ireland (see ADMINISTRATIVE STRUCTURE) were given military commanders: PRESTON in Leinster, Barry in Munster, OWEN ROE O'NEILL in ULSTER, and Edmund or Edward Burke in Connacht. A form of 'parliament' was developed called the General Assembly of the Confederacy, to which members were sent by those areas under the direct control of the rebels. The Assembly first met in October and November of 1642 when it elected a Speaker, and there were subsequent meetings in May and June and November and December 1643, July and August 1644, May to August 1645, February and March 1646, January to April 1647, and again in November of that year, with the last meeting held from September 1648 to January of 1649. Under its motto or slogan '*Pro Deo, rege et patria Hiberni*' the Confederacy claimed loyalty to King Charles I, even though troops loyal to the Earl of ORMOND fought against the Confederacy in the name of the king, as did forces under the control of Parliament in London, this disparity reflecting the great civil war then raging in England and Wales. Despite the Gaelic origin of the rebellion of 1641, the business of the Assembly and of the Supreme Council was conducted entirely in English. Divisions within the Confederacy's Supreme Council arose from the direct involvement from 1645 of the papal envoy RINUCCINI, whose single-minded concern for the Catholic Church in Ireland caused him to resist and to disrupt attempts at rapprochement and alliance between the Confederacy and the Ormond royalists (see ORMOND TREATIES, CESSATIONS). On 18 September 1646 Rinuccini arrested his opponents on the Supreme Council, backed by the armed force of Owen Roe O'Neill, and a new Council was set up on 26 September to reflect Rinuccini's control. In the last meeting of 1648/9 the Council declared O'Neill a traitor for entering into negotiations with the Scots, now allied to the royalist supporters of Charles I (who was executed in London on 30 January 1649).

The Confederacy broke up under the military onslaught of the NEW MODEL ARMY from 1649, and the rebellion came to an end in 1653.

Catholic Convention, The

The Catholic Convention, also known to contemporaries as the Back Lane Parliament, was a manifestation of the Catholic Committee (see CATHOLIC BOARD), and met between 3 and 8 December 1792 in DUBLIN. Membership was by election from areas where the Catholic Committee was influential, and delegates were chosen to present a petition to King George III demanding EMANCIPATION for Catholics. One of the delegates was the future revolutionary leader WOLFE TONE. The petitioning process bypassed the role of the LORD LIEUTENANT as intermediary between Ireland and the British government, and seriously alarmed the CASTLE administration, which seems to have orchestrated hostile reaction to the Convention.

Catholic Defence Association (of Great Britain and Ireland)

The Defence Association was an extra-parliamentary body formed by Irish MPs at WESTMINSTER to generate popular opposition to the ECCLESIASTICAL TITLES ACT, which aimed to prevent the re-establishment of a Catholic Church hierarchy in Britain. The Association's objectives broadened through alliance with the TENANT LEAGUE, although there was little in common other than a shared constituency support, the Association being chiefly landlord and gentry based. The passage of the Ecclesiastical Titles Act was hardly obstructed, but it proved to be meaningless. The Association folded.

Catholic Rent

Known also as the 'Repeal Rent' or the 'O'Connell Tribute', the Catholic Rent was a masterly move by DANIEL O'CON-NELL in broadening the basis of support for the CATHOLIC ASSOCIATION, which was seeking EMANCIPATION by extra-parliamentary agitation. In 1824 the

membership fee for the Association of one guinea per annum, which essentially narrowed the possible membership, was boosted by a penny a month subscription which gave associate membership to the poor of rural Ireland. Collected on Sundays in Catholic churches throughout the country, within a year the Association had a steady income of at least £1,000 a week. The rent demonstrated O'Connell's perception of the importance of the parochial clergy as organizers, and showed also the willingness of the clergy to associate themselves with a largely political cause. Following the great emancipation legislation of 1829, the rent was renamed the 'O'Connell Tribute', but in the wake of the legislation, enthusiasm waned and the income declined. O'Connell revived the idea yet again as the 'Repeal Rent' in 1842 to whip up support for the repeal campaign he was leading against the UNION of 1801 (see REPEAL ASSOCIATION). The story of the Catholic Rent illustrates O'Connell's political ability.

Catholic Union of Ireland

The Catholic Union was launched on 26 November 1872 by Lord Granard in DUBLIN, with a programme of resistance to the persecution of Catholic religious orders, not only in Ireland, but chiefly on an international basis. It was a reflection of the sustained attacks on the temporalities of the CATHOLIC CHURCH, particularly in Italy, but it also championed the cause of church authority in educational matters relating to Catholic laity.

Catholic University *see* UNIVERSITY COLLEGE

Cattle Acts

The late seventeenth-century resistance in England to the import of Irish cattle on the hoof, which received strict legislative expression in the House of Commons, is an example of the type of interference with Ireland to which contemporary writers such as WILLIAM MOLYNEUX drew attention. The Cattle Acts were in line with the kind of legislation that imposed restrictions upon Irish economic activity, of which the 1662 Act forbidding the export of wool was an earlier example. The Cattle Acts began with seasonally restrictive legislation in July 1663, banning imports between July and December. The Great Cattle Act of 18 January 1667 was pushed through against the wishes of the government, and was draconic in its ban on the import of cattle, sheep, pigs, beef and pork, and bacon, the ban to last for two years. The export of cattle from Ireland was well established by the 1640s, and was centred upon the port of Youghal, which, it was claimed, suffered a severe decline as a consequence of the 1667 measure. Historians have argued that the impact was less severe than appeared; that it forced diversification, for example into butter and dairy products, exported into Europe and to the colonies. Indeed, in April 1667 within three months of the legislation, an act was passed permitting the Irish to export produce in time of war to the king's enemies. The legislation also speeded up a process of regional specialization in Ireland, with breeding and fattening becoming the primary husbandry of Connacht, for example. Failure to renew the Act in 1679 led to a sudden upsurge in the old trade, but it was shortlived, for further legislation in 1681 made the restriction permanent, and added butter and cheese to the list of prohibited imports. Irish agriculture therefore became heavily reliant upon European and colonial trade. Not until 1759 were the Cattle Acts suspended, and imports into Britain again permitted; one consequence of this was an increase in pasture farming in Ireland, rural unemployment and the emergence of secret societies such as the WHITEBOYS, representative of the increasing number of poor. In 1776 an act was passed that prohibited the export of Irish beef, butter and pork to anywhere other than Britain and its colonies. The legislation of the seventeenth and eighteenth centuries in its role of influencing changes in agricultural practice, contributed to the agrarian unrest that characterized Ireland from the 1760s onwards.

Cattle Driving *see* DOWNS POLICY

Ceannt, Eamon (1881–1916)

Ceannt was born in County Galway where his father was an officer in the ROYAL IRISH CONSTABULARY. By 1900 he was involved in the nationalist politics of the GAELIC LEAGUE, and became a prominent member of that organization. He became a member of, successively, SINN FÉIN and the IRISH REPUBLICAN BROTHERHOOD, thus associating himself with PHYSICAL FORCE separatist ideology, and was involved in the establishment of the IRISH VOLUNTEERS in 1913. As a member of the ruling council of the IRB, he was involved in the plans for an armed uprising in Easter 1916, and when it came, set his signature to the PROCLAMATION OF THE IRISH REPUBLIC. He was captured and shot to death on 8 May 1916.

Céitinn, Seathrun (Geoffrey Keating) (d. 1644)

Céitinn, as the English version of his name shows, was born of OLD ENGLISH family in County Tipperary. His life illustrates the fusion of Old English and native Gaelic values that typifies the 'degeneracy' complained of by Protestant NEW ENGLISH colonists of the early seventeenth century. Catholicism was at the root of Céitinn's commitment to the IRISH REBELLION which broke out in 1641. He was the author of *Foras Feasa ar Éirinn*, completed between 1620 and 1634, which translates as 'The Basis of the Knowledge of Ireland' and which circulated in manuscript form until 1857 when the FENIAN writer JOHN O'MAHONY translated it for publication.

Cessation, The (*see also* CATHOLIC CONFEDERACY, Earl of ORMOND)

The Cessation in which the Earl of ORMOND was closely involved, was the attempt by Ormond on behalf of his king, Charles I (then at war with his Parliament in England) to reach a peace with the CATHOLIC CONFEDERACY, with a view to releasing troops for service in England. The military situation in Ireland was complex in the 1640s. The Confederacy's CATHOLIC ARMY was at war both with Ormond, and with government troops loyal to the English Parliament, as well as with Scottish PRESBYTERIAN forces operating predominantly in ULSTER. The Confederacy, which repeatedly reiterated its loyalty to Charles I, was willing enough for a cessation with Ormond, for it would both materially assist the king, and give them a freer hand in prosecution of their campaigns in Ireland. Ormond was instructed to talk with them in January 1643, and a meeting followed at Trim, County Meath, in March. The king instructed Ormond to reach a cessation in April, and a year's peace was signed at Sigginstown in County Kildare. This paved the way for a delegation from the Confederacy to journey to Oxford to meet with the king, where they arrived in March 1644. Negotiations with Ormond reopened in September without success, and were broken off to reopen again in April 1645. King Charles' military predicament in England was growing increasingly more serious, and by the time peace was concluded, on 28 March 1646, the Irish forces (some of which had joined the royalist armies in England in late 1643) were of no use, for the king had been conclusively defeated by his Parliament. The terms of the 1646 peace were proclaimed in July, but at once met with opposition from the papal envoy to the Confederacy, RINUCCINI, who succeeded in forcing the Confederacy to disown the peace on the grounds that it carried no guarantees for the Catholic Church. Only after Rinuccini's departure was a second and firm peace agreed, on 17 January 1649, and the history of the 'Cessation' is an example of mutual suspicion defeating mutual self-interest.

Charter Schools

The Charter Schools were, and were seen to be by Catholics, a direct attempt by missionary Protestants to wean children away from Catholicism through education. They were established by the Incorporated Society for Promoting English Protestant Schools in October 1733 by charter, hence their name. An Act of Parliament of 11 April 1746 provided government grants towards their maintenance. Their achievement was negligible, but foreshadowed subsequent attempts at religious conversion, particularly in the early nineteenth century.

Chichester, Arthur (1563–1625)

Chichester first came to Ireland in 1597 as a commander operating against the rebel forces of the Earl of TYRONE in ULSTER. Following Tyrone's surrender in 1603, Chichester became LORD DEPUTY, a post he occupied from 1604 until 1614. Although a vigorous soldier intent upon destroying the basis of Tyrone's strength, he was nevertheless conscious of the importance of gradual ANGLICIZATION and actually resisted the strict enforcement of laws against Catholics, whether Gaelic or OLD ENGLISH. That attitude led to his resignation in 1614 shortly after his elevation as Lord Chichester of BELFAST, as failing to reflect the policies favoured by the fiercely Protestant NEW ENGLISH.

Chief Secretary, The

The Chief Secretary, based in DUBLIN at the CASTLE, was subordinate, in theory at least, to the LORD LIEUTENANT or his deputy. Through the exercise of the responsibility for supervising the machinery of government, the Chief Secretaries were the immediate face of British administration, particularly in the Irish House of Commons where they represented government policy. Whilst the Chief Secretaries could come and go with some frequency as ministries came and went in England, periods of ministerial stability gave the Chief Secretary opportunity to establish himself, and with the increasing residency of the Lords Lieutenants as the eighteenth century wore on, so the importance of the Secretary grew. He headed an 'office' in which the Under Secretary exercised control, and from 1777 that office was provided with two Under Secretaries with responsibility for civil and military affairs respectively; in 1800 a third Under Secretary appeared to oversee the YEOMANRY. The Chief Secretary's importance lay in his relationship with the Lord Lieutenant, executing Lieutenancy decisions, and with emphasis upon law and order. The political colour of the administration run by the Chief Secretary did not always reflect the attitudes of the ASCENDANCY milieu in which he worked. Indeed, under men such as THOMAS DRUMMOND the administration could effectively work against that interest, most particularly after the UNION of Britain and Ireland in 1801. (See Appendix 2 for a list of Chief Secretaries.)

Childers, Erskine (1870–1922)

Robert Erskine Childers was born in London but brought up in County Wicklow, and is chiefly remembered in England as the author of the novel *The Riddle of the Sands*, published in 1903. From 1908 he was active in the HOME RULE movement in Ireland, and was implicated in the shipment of arms from Germany to the IRISH VOLUNTEERS in 1914. Nevertheless, and like many nationalists (but unlike the already committed republicans), Childers served during the FIRST WORLD WAR in the British army and won the DSC in 1916. By 1919 he had become a republican, committed to wresting control of Ireland from Britain by military force. He was a minister under the first DÁIL ÉIREANN, but when SINN FÉIN and the IRISH REPUBLICAN ARMY split over the ANGLO-IRISH TREATY of 1921, Childers sided with the anti-Treaty IRA and produced their newspaper *Irish Bulletin*. He was arrested and shot to death by the FREE STATE forces in 1922.

Church Cess

The church cess was a rate levied, regardless of religious persuasion of the payers, on a parish basis for the maintenance and upkeep of CHURCH OF IRELAND churches. In view of the fact that in the 1830s there were no more than 850,000 communicants of the established church as compared to some 6½ million Catholics, in Ireland, the issue was a major contributing factor in the move towards DISESTABLISHMENT of the Church of Ireland.

Church Education Society *see*
KILDARE PLACE SOCIETY

Church of Ireland, The

The Church of Ireland was a reflection of the established Church of England, but in the Irish context was far more crucial to the maintenance of Protestant authority. Its origins lay in the Tudor colonization of parts of Ireland, and as colonization and PLANTATION spread, so the influence of the Church of Ireland spread with it, narrowly exclusive in its membership, but intimately linked to the rising Protestant and NEW ENGLISH power in Ireland. Not that this precluded its representation as the proper and lineal continuation of the church founded in Ireland by St Patrick. The seventeenth-century church was heavily Calvinist, and, at the same time, Erastian: this latter emphasis upon the right of the state to determine the religion of its people, made it easily conformable to the LAUDIAN reforms of the reign of King Charles I. That the Church of Ireland experienced no rifts comparable to those within the Church of England at the same time, is a reflection of its 'frontier' consciousness, surrounded by a mass population of Catholics who presented a more immediate threat than any doctrinal differences within the church itself. Puritanism and Episcopalianism flourished side by side. WILLIAM PETTY in the 1670s reckoned there were no more than 50,000 communicants to be found outside the New English dominated urban centres of Ireland, where the church was at its strongest, drawing for its intellectual content upon the graduates of TRINITY COLLEGE DUBLIN, for the most part. Its rural organization was defective, often pluralistic, and largely ineffectual. In the political and religious settlement ensuant upon the defeat of the JACOBITES in 1691, the church became crucial to the establishment and maintenance of the ASCENDANCY: indeed, the two were seen as inseparable, a challenge to the one being a challenge to the other. But the church's claims to be *the* church of Ireland came under progressive assault as the eighteenth century wore on. The CHURCH TEMPORALITIES ACT of 1833 removed 10 bishoprics, undermining the settlement of 1661 which had re-established the church structure after the CROMWELLIAN period, and paved the way for DISESTABLISHMENT in 1869, whereafter the church was governed by a synod, with its finances to be administered by the Church Body.

Church Temporalities (Ireland) Act, The

The Church Temporalities Act of 14 August 1833 went some way towards remedying the evident abuse of an established church barely representative of anything other than a small and exclusive element in the Irish population, yet drawing upon the resources of the nation at large. Organizationally, it reduced the number of bishoprics from 22 to 12 and appointed a board of ecclesiastical commissioners to reorganize livings and to use the revenues from the suppressed bishoprics to augment the stipends of the parochial clergy and maintain the churches. The CHURCH CESS was abolished, which had been a major grievance amongst the noncommunicant Catholics (and DISSENTERS), and a tax was imposed upon all clerical incomes in excess of £200 per annum. Of far more importance to the numerous tenants of church lands was the legislation that enabled them to convert their leaseholds into virtual freeholds by the payment of a reserved rent based upon the old leasehold rent and an average of renewal fines (see LAND TENURES).

Citizen Army, The

The Citizen Army, also referred to as the Irish Citizen Army, was established on 19 November 1913 by JAMES CONNOLLY and the ULSTER Protestant nationalist J.R. White. The army's origin lay in the ideas of 'Jock' White who, in the wake of the great LOCK-OUT, believed that the workers needed to be disciplined in preparation for the coming struggle with capitalism. 'The ownership of Ireland, moral and material, is vested of right in the people of Ireland' expresses the Marxist thinking behind the emergence of the Citizen Army, which at full strength did not number more than 200 men. Nevertheless, it took up arms in the EASTER RISING 1916 in support of the republican attempt to wrest Ireland from Britain by force of arms. Sean O'Casey (d. 1964), the playwright, served on the Council of the Citizen Army, and wrote its semi-official history which was critical of the leadership of James Connolly.

City of the Broken Treaty see
LIMERICK, Treaty of

Civility

The doctrine of 'civility' (current from the 1500s to around 1700) is inseparable from that of ANGLICIZATION, but has less to do with the changing of the structure of Gaelic society into something resembling and reflective of England (a policy keenly pursued by the English government in the sixteenth and seventeenth centuries) than it has to do with a perceived need to 'civilize' the native Irish by a reform of their values and manners. An instance of this might be the proposal, that came to nothing, in the 1650s to send Irish children into England as servants, there to imbibe 'civility'.

Clan na Gael

Clan na Gael was founded in New York on 20 June 1867 by Jerome Collins, and was rooted in the Irish immigrant community which remembered the oppressive poverty of rural life in Ireland. A revolutionary organization, from 1877 affiliated to the IRISH REPUBLICAN BROTHERHOOD, the Supreme Council of which Clan na Gael recognized as the legitimate provisional government of Ireland. Clan na Gael had already demonstrated its commitment by employing the ship *Catalpa* in 1876 to rescue six FENIAN prisoners from Australia (see TRANSPORTATION) and take them to America. A rival organization to Clan na Gael was set up in 1880 by O'DONOVAN ROSSA under the name of the UNITED IRISHMEN. Clan na Gael continued to flourish, however, and was largely responsible for acquiring German guns for the IRISH VOLUNTEERS in the build-up to the EASTER RISING of 1916.

Clanricarde, Ulick de Burgh 5th Earl of (1604–57)

Clanricarde was of Catholic OLD ENGLISH stock in CONNACHT, and came into confrontation with English PLANTATION policy when THOMAS WENTWORTH the LORD DEPUTY moved against Clanricarde's territory in County Galway. When the IRISH REBELLION broke out in 1641, Clanricarde endeavoured to remain neutral, but his influence diminished to his lands in Galway. The CATHOLIC CONFEDERACY offered him supreme command of their army in return for his alliance, but he remained aloof, being essentially a royalist. On 11 December 1650 he assumed command of the forces of the Earl of ORMOND when the latter left for France, and became LORD DEPUTY in the service of the exiled King Charles II. Defeated at Meelick Island on the Shannon by English government troops on 25 October 1650, he managed to survive for a further two years, but on 28 June 1652 after a well-executed raid into Donegal, Clanricarde surrendered to Sir CHARLES COOTE at Carrick. Clanricarde went into exile in England where he died.

Clarke, Thomas (1857–1916)

Thomas Clarke was born in England of Irish parents, but emigrated to America where he joined the CLAN NA GAEL movement. He returned to England under the assumed name of Henry Wilson to take part in the DYNAMITE WAR organized by the Clan and the IRISH REPUBLICAN BROTHERHOOD. He was arrested and gaoled in 1883, but released in 1898 and returned to America where he took out citizenship. Back in Ireland in 1907 he began to organize the IRB under cover of a newsagency, and joined its Supreme Council in 1915. Forward in the establishment of a Military Council to prepare for armed insurrection, Clarke held a command during the EASTER RISING of 1916, and his was the first signature on the PROCLAMATION OF THE IRISH REPUBLIC. He was captured and shot to death on 3 May 1916.

Clogher, Heber MacMahon bishop of (d. 1650)

MacMahon was promoted to the bishopric of Clogher in 1643 from that of Down and Connor, and acted as principal Catholic advisor to OWEN ROE O'NEILL in the army of the CATHOLIC CONFEDERACY, and an associate of RINUCCINI the papal envoy. His religion and politics were extremely pro-Spanish, and this generated mistrust among potential French support. The bishop became Commander-in-Chief of the forces under O'Neill on the latter's death, and was defeated in battle at SCARRIFHOLLIS in County Donegal in 1650. He was captured and executed by English government troops.

Clones, battle of

The battle of Clones, County Monaghan, was fought on 13 June 1643 between forces of the CATHOLIC CONFEDERACY commanded by OWEN ROE O'NEILL, and Scottish PRESBYTERIAN troops under Robert Stewart. O'Neill did not want to fight, intending to withdraw his forces into Connacht to train and drill them, but was pressured into it and was defeated. He nevertheless completed his withdrawal into Connacht.

Clonmacnoise

A synod of the Catholic bishops of Ireland met at Clonmacnoise on 13 December 1649 to call upon forces of the CATHOLIC CONFEDERACY to unite with the royalists of the Earl of ORMOND against English government forces under CROMWELL. In August of 1650 at Jamestown in County Antrim the bishops withdrew their support.

Clonmel

Clonmel, County Tipperary, was held by Hugh O'Neil against the siege army of OLIVER CROMWELL from 27 April 1650 to 10 May. IRETON, Cromwell's son-in-law, with wide experience gained in the Civil War in England, reckoned the fight for Clonmel to be the hardest he had ever been in. After a strenuous defence in which at least one storm attempt was beaten off, O'Neil and his army slipped away under cover of darkness, unbeknown to the besiegers, and the town surrendered on terms. Clonmel was also the scene, on 28 September 1848, of the trials of the YOUNG IRELAND revolutionary leaders SMITH O'BRIEN, MEAGHER and others.

Clontarf (*see also* UNION)

Clontarf, scene of the great battle of 1014 where Brian Bóruma was killed in the hour of victory, was chosen by O'CONNELL for a massive public meeting that was to mark the high point of his 'Year of Repeal' campaign, part of the pressure for an end to the UNION of Britain and Ireland of 1801. The meeting was scheduled for 7 October 1843, and followed upon equally major demonstrations of popular support at Trim on 9 March and at Tara on 15 August. O'Connell, aware of the growing disaffection in the YOUNG IRELAND, revolutionary wing of the Repeal movement, was keen to make shows of strength, but the government proclaimed the meeting unlawful, and O'Connell cancelled it rather than risk a military confrontation. At the time, the Young Irelanders supported his decision.

Clontarf was also the location for a massive AMNESTY ASSOCIATION meeting called by ISAAC BUTT in September 1873, when 250,000 gathered to support the campaign for the freeing of FENIAN prisoners.

Coercion Acts

Between 1800 and 1887 no fewer than 65 Coercion Acts or renewals were imposed upon Ireland by the British government. A Coercion Act, such as that of 2 April 1833, gave the LORD LIEUTENANT power to proclaim parts of Ireland disturbed areas, where public meetings could be declared unlawful, and court martials be imposed. That of 1833 was a response to the agitation and unrest of the TITHE WARS, and the frequency of such legislation testifies to the endemic unrest in the Irish countryside over issues of tithes, rents, tenancies, and all issues related to the land problem.

Coffin Ships

The Coffin ships were emigrant vessels, chiefly converted cargo ships, sailing from Irish ports and from Liverpool to North America and elsewhere (see EMIGRATION). The year of 1847, in the midst of the FAMINE, was a particularly bad year, when of 100,000 that embarked for Quebec in Canada, more than one-sixth died en route or upon arrival, a fact which made Canada a less favoured destination for subsequent emigrants. Landlords, busy clearing their lands of 'surplus population', were held responsible for the conditions on board the Coffin ships, for they invested money in sending people out of Ireland. Enthusiasm amongst landlords for this procedure underwent change in the 1850s in the light of the horrors of the previous decade.

Coleraine

Although for 300 years Coleraine has been only a major County DERRY town on the banks of the River Bann, the county known as Derry or Londonderry originally took its name from the town of Coleraine, which was incorporated by charter on 28 June 1613 and returned members to the Parliament in Dublin. The county of Coleraine came to be known as The Derry, which was not exclusively a reference to the city of Derry, and then as Londonderry (see DERRY).

College Green (*see also* IRISH PARLIAMENT)

College Green, DUBLIN, was synonymous with the Irish Parliament, as the CASTLE was with British administration. Historiographically, the name College Green appears as an alternative to the word Parliament. In February 1728 work began on a new Parliament house at College Green which was finished in 1731. The last meeting of the Irish Parliament took place there on 2 August 1800 to prepare the way for UNION in 1801. The symbolic importance of College Green was not lost on the IRISH VOLUNTEER leaders who paraded men there on 17 March 1916, on the eve of the EASTER RISING.

Collins, Michael (1890–1922)

Michael Collins was born in County Cork and worked for a time in London before returning to Ireland and joining the ultra-nationalist GAELIC ATHLETIC ASSOCIATION and the IRISH REPUBLICAN BROTHERHOOD. He took up arms during the EASTER RISING of 1916 and was captured and briefly interned by the British. He rapidly became Commander of the IRISH REPUBLICAN ARMY during the WAR FOR INDEPENDENCE which broke out in 1919, and held the posts of Minister for Home Affairs in the provisional republican government of 1918, and then for Finance from 1919 to his death. Collins infiltrated and outfought the British intelligence service in DUBLIN (see BLOODY SUNDAY, CAIRO GANG). Named as one of the commissioners from DÁIL ÉIREANN to negotiate with the British government in London in December 1921, Collins' natural pragmatism accepted what he saw as the necessity for compromise and he accepted, therefore, the perhaps temporary expedient of PARTITION and loss of the SIX COUNTIES of ULSTER in return for separation of the rest of Ireland from the British connection. Once he had taken the view he held to it firmly, but the IRA split around him, and in 1922 he was shot and killed by soldiers of the anti-Treaty IRA or Executive IRA in an ambush in County Cork.

Colonization *see* PLANTATION

Commission for the Remedy of Defective Land Titles

The Commission, set up in London on 22 July 1606, provided the machinery for enquiring into the suitability of GAELIC IRISH to continue to hold land after the defeat of the TYRONE rebellion in ULSTER in 1603. It formed part of the PLANTATION mechanism for introducing new settlers of Protestant stock into former rebels' lands. It was revived in June 1634 and established in DUBLIN, where the LORD DEPUTY, THOMAS WENTWORTH, used it against the NEW ENGLISH settlers themselves, offering secure titles to their lands

at a price. In the projected plantation of CONNACHT in 1635 the Commission was used to confiscate land for the crown.

Conacre

The term 'conacre' applies both to a plot of land allowed to rural labourers to cultivate, usually with potatoes, and the system of labour services given in return for it. Precise practice varied from area to area: sometimes it was taken on a seasonal basis, and there were instances of landlords assigning waste in conacre lots to labourers and then reclaiming it in return for other waste once the land had been worked and made productive. The system of 'conacre' contributed heavily to the labourers' dependence upon the potato crop at the onset of the FAMINE of the 1840s. Almost a million of the Irish population as recorded in the census of 1841 (see POPULATION) lived in relative poverty, there being precious little distinction between labourers with their 'conacre' plots and smallholders subsisting on holdings of an acre or less, of which there were perhaps 65,000.

Confederate Catholics (*see also* CATHOLIC CONFEDERACY)

The term 'Confederate Catholics' was used of themselves by members of the Catholic Confederacy.

Confederation, The Irish

The Irish Confederation was a breakaway movement from the constitutional REPEAL ASSOCIATION of DANIEL O'CONNELL, and was founded on 13 January 1847 by SMITH O'BRIEN and JOHN MITCHEL (although Mitchel left at the end of the year). The Confederation was made up of Confederate Clubs established throughout DUBLIN and other parts of Ireland by the YOUNG IRELAND dissident movement within the Repeal Association. The Confederate Clubs proliferated in England, too, where there were strong links with the Chartist reform movement. The Confederation was revolutionary and republican, drawing upon the tradition of the UNITED IRISHMEN of the 1790s. In 1848, following the return of two Confederate MPs in the

General Election of August 1847 to WESTMINSTER (as compared with 36 MPs of the Repeal movement). O'Brien publicly advocated a resort to PHYSICAL FORCE in pursuit of the Confederation's ends. The Young Irelanders were inspired by the revolution in France, to which country O'Brien had travelled in February 1848 to offer congratulations to the revolutionary leadership. On 21 July 1848 a War Directory was set up, presaging the abortive rising of that year. After the arrest of the Young Ireland element in the Confederation, Confederate Club leaders came to the fore, and a merger with the Repeal Association was agreed upon, to form the IRISH LEAGUE. The most significant of the Confederate Clubs was that led by THOMAS MEAGHER in Dublin, which called itself the 'GRATTAN Club'.

Confederation of Kilkenny

Historiographical term applied to the CATHOLIC CONFEDERACY, the Supreme Council of which sat at Kilkenny.

Confession of Faith (of the Church of Ireland)

The first national convocation of the CHURCH OF IRELAND was held in St Patrick's Cathedral, DUBLIN, between May 1613 and April 1615. The 104 articles of its Confession of Faith, largely the result of the work of James Ussher archbishop of ARMAGH, were formally adopted. In December 1634, against little resistance, the 39 Articles of the Church of England were imposed in Ireland by THOMAS WENTWORTH, part and parcel of the spread of LAUDIAN reform from England into Ireland.

Congested Districts Board, The

The Congested Districts Board was mooted and introduced by ARTHUR BALFOUR in 1891. A Congested District was one in which the rateable value was less than 30 shillings (£1.50) per head of population assessed in terms of the POOR LAW unions. This applied largely to western Ireland, and specifically to much of Connacht, and the counties of Donegal, Kerry and western Cork. The Board's

purpose was to facilitate the creation of larger land holdings by direct government intervention and funding. The personnel of the Board were appointed by the LORD LIEUTENANT, and included as permanent members the CHIEF SECRETARY and the relevant Under Secretary at the CASTLE, the centre of British administration. The Board came into existence as part of the Purchase of Land Act (see LAND LEGISLATION), and in 1909 its funds were drastically increased. By 1923 it was estimated that the Board had expended £10 million redistributing 2 million acres of land, as well as investing in agricultural improvements and acquiring untenanted lands for allocation to larger holdings.

Connacht, Plantation in the Province of

The PLANTATION and settlement of Connacht had been going on quietly under the auspices of OLD ENGLISH landlords for a generation or more before THOMAS WENTWORTH turned his attention to the province in 1635. Royal claims to the province dating back to the reign of King Edward IV were resurrected and submitted to the consideration of GRAND JURIES in the respective counties. Roscommon, Mayo and Sligo conceded the royal title but the jury in Galway, where the Earls of CLANRICARDE were all-powerful, resisted. It was claimed that the title of the earls and other Old English was confirmed by King James I and its recognition was implicit in the MATTERS OF GRACE AND BOUNTY negotiated between the Old English Catholics and King Charles I. The Galway jury was subjected to intimidatory investigation by Wentworth, and submitted in December 1636 conceding the royal title to its territory. This threw Connacht open to resettlement from 1637. The treatment of the Old English in Galway alarmed their fellows throughout Ireland, and contributed both to increasing hostility towards Wentworth, and to future willingness of many Old English to collaborate with Gaelic rebels in 1641. Following the suppression of the IRISH REBELLION that began in that year, in 1653 CROMWELL introduced new and far-reaching proposals for the future of

Connacht, by requiring that all delinquents elsewhere in Ireland on lands allotted to the ADVENTURERS and soldiers who had completed the defeat of the rebels, should be compelled to resettle themselves in Connacht. The scheme received statutory standing in the Act of SATISFACTION (see also BLACK BOOKS OF ATHLONE).

Connolly, James (1868–1916)

Connolly, in the historiography of the EASTER RISING of 1916 and in the traditions of the Irish republican movement, occupies a special niche. It may be due partly to the callous brutality of his execution, but is largely a reflection of his doctrinaire revolutionary socialism, which distinguished him from his fellow signatories of the PROCLAMATION OF THE IRISH REPUBLIC. Born in Edinburgh of Irish descent and wholly self-educated, he established in 1896 the Socialist Republican Party and founded in 1898 the journal *Workers' Republic*. He first rose to prominence, however, as the organizer in ULSTER of the Irish TRANSPORT AND GENERAL WORKERS' UNION in 1910 and became involved in the long and bitter industrial dispute known as the LOCK-OUT. His experience led him to help form the CITIZEN ARMY, intended to prepare Irish workers for the armed defence of their rights. He brought the Citizen Army into the Easter Rising, having joined the Military Council of the IRISH REPUBLICAN BROTHERHOOD early in 1916. At this point he was, or allowed himself to be, swept up in the revolutionary nationalism of the Brotherhood, less than a year after verbally denouncing PHYSICAL FORCE republicanism in favour of emphasis upon socialism. Connolly exercised a command in DUBLIN during the rising, was captured, badly wounded, and shot to death tied to a chair in Kilmainham Gaol on 12 May 1916.

Conscription 37 *see* FIRST WORLD WAR (1914–18)

Constabulary and Policing (*see also* ROYAL IRISH CONSTABULARY

For much of the eighteenth century, police work in Ireland reflected the practice in England, reliance upon unpaid local constables backed up, when necessary, by the Justices of the Peace and the use of regular troops, MILITIA and YEOMANRY units. Reform of the police system in Ireland, however, came before that in England, primarily as a consequence of the need to cope with widespread and sustained periods of agrarian unrest. District or baronial (see BARONIES) constables were created by Act of Parliament in May 1787, and in 1814 a PEACE PRESERVATION FORCE was created. The crucial legislation came in 1822, in the Irish Constabulary Act of 1 August, which created a permanent police force of constables and sub-constables, with chief constables in each county and inspector-generals for each province. Although directed by the magistracy, 50 per cent of its salaries and costs came from central government. Further legislation was passed in 1836, largely thanks to the reformist enthusiasm of the Under Secretary THOMAS DRUMMOND at the CASTLE in DUBLIN. Drummond, determined to introduce equity into policing and to rid the force of its Protestant and ORANGE associations, merged the constabulary and the Peace Preservation Force and gave it authority everywhere in Ireland except for BELFAST, DERRY and Dublin. A quasi-military structure and discipline was introduced, and a force of 10,000 men enrolled, which would form the basis for the ROYAL IRISH CONSTABULARY as the new force was redesignated in 1867. A Dublin Police Act followed in July 1836 setting up the metropolitan police in the city under the authority of two magistrates. In 1846 the costs of policing were transferred to central government, and subsequent legislation, such as that in December 1847 in the Crime and Outrage Act, allowed for the appointment of additional constables in times of emergency, thus increasing the reserve force. In 1865 Belfast's city police were merged with the national constabulary, and in 1870 the Derry police were also merged with the national force. Despite Drummond's intentions, which were to produce a police force that would be seen to be impartial, the constabulary became closely associated with Protestantism especially in ULSTER, where the ORANGE influence was never eradicated entirely.

Constitution of 1782 *see* GRATTAN'S PARLIAMENT

Convention Act, The

The Convention Act of 16 August 1793 was aimed at the increasingly successful agitation for EMANCIPATION of Catholics orchestrated by the Catholic Committee (see CATHOLIC BOARD). The Act outlawed all gatherings or assemblies of delegates or representatives claiming to be gathered together by nomination or election, with a view to preparing petitions to Parliament or to the crown. Such legislation has to be seen in the context both of the popular enthusiasm for a petitioning procedure that effectively by-passed the administration of the LORD LIEUTENANT in Ireland, and of the alarming events in France where revolution had overthrown the monarchy and seemed to be plunging Europe into a major war. The government was concerned to forestall the development of mass movements that might develop similar revolutionary tendencies. A second assault on the Catholic Committee came with the order of the CHIEF SECRETARY in 1811 to Justices of the Peace and sheriffs to take action against activist Catholic delegations. The Act was not finally repealed until 1879.

Convert Rolls

Convert Rolls were documents compiled during the eighteenth century of those former Catholics who converted to and became communicants of the CHURCH OF IRELAND, as a means of escaping the rigours of the PENAL LAWS, particularly the 'property act' of 1704. That Act prohibited Catholics from purchasing land or from entering into leases of more than 31 years' duration. It provided that at the death of a Catholic landowner, the estate was to be divided up among his heirs unless the eldest son converted to Protestantism, whereupon he inherited the whole. Courts had powers to appoint guardians to safeguard the interests of such an heir. An amendment to the Act in 1709 encouraged the proliferation of informers or 'discoverers' who, in return for revealing evasions of the law, were rewarded with possession of the property in question. The pressure for conformity with the established church was only too real.

Convicting, Discovering and Repressing of Popish Recusants, Act for

The Act for Convicting, Discovering and Repressing of Popish Recusants was essentially an enforcement of an oath of ABJURATION, and was passed into law in England on 26 June 1657. Persons suspected of popish sympathies were required to swear that they renounced the doctrine of papal supremacy and fundamental doctrinal matters such as the mystery of transubstantiation, or risk the loss of two-thirds of their property. Recusants were, in England and in Ireland, those who declined to observe the services and communion of the established church. Under the CROMWELLIAN regime of the 1650s, when neither the Church of England nor the CHURCH OF IRELAND existed (having been suppressed), the term 'Recusant' had a specifically political meaning, equated with Catholicism (which narrow application the word recusant did not originally bear) and so with potential rebellion.

Cook Street, Dublin

On 1 April 1629 the LORD DEPUTY in Ireland, Lord Falkland, issued a proclamation requiring the closure of all religious houses of the Catholic religion and the suppression of public priestly functions. Implementation was ordered throughout Ireland, and in DUBLIN alone 16 religious houses were suppressed. However, on 26 December 1629 when the archbishop of Dublin and an armed force moved into Cook Street to close down a Franciscan house there, they were met with concerted resistance and forced to withdraw. This token resistance did not prevent the full carrying out of Falkland's proclamation, however, and it was claimed that nowhere in Ireland was public celebration of the mass to be found.

Coote, Sir Charles (d. 1661)

Sir Charles Coote was a second-generation NEW ENGLISH settler in Ireland of firm Protestant beliefs, whose father was killed in action in 1642 fighting the forces of the CATHOLIC CONFEDERACY in the IRISH REBELLION which had broken out in 1641. Sir Charles Coote was Governor of Dublin at his father's death, and soon became a field commander against the rebels. In 1645 he was appointed PRESIDENT of Connacht by the Parliament in England. He fought alongside the NEW MODEL ARMY from 1649, and took the surrender of Athlone in July 1650. With the termination of the Presidency system, Coote was appointed Commissioner for Connacht, and in 1659 was appointed to the governmental commission to rule Ireland. With the restoration of King Charles II looking inevitable, Coote executed an about-turn, and was instrumental in the peaceful acceptance accorded to the restoration in Ireland. He was rewarded with the earldom of Mountrath and confirmation in the revived Presidency of Connacht.

Cork, Richard Boyle 1st Earl of (1566–1643)

In many ways Boyle exemplified the Tudor adventurer who made good in Ireland and out of Irish land. He arrived in Ireland in 1588, embarking upon a dubious career in the civil service, out of which he put by sufficient to purchase the Irish estates of Sir Walter Raleigh. Knighted and appointed to the government of the province of Munster in 1603 and 1606 respectively, he was created Baron of Youghal in 1616 and achieved his earldom in 1620. Dignified as the 'great earl', he represented the very NEW ENGLISH assurance and arrogance that THOMAS WENTWORTH as LORD DEPUTY made strenuous efforts to undermine and to curb. The earl is seen as Wentworth's main adversary, and it has been argued that he was primarily responsible for the Lord Deputy's downfall and ultimate trial and execution in London in 1641. The earl was made LORD JUSTICE of Ireland in 1629 and Lord High Treasurer in 1631, evidence of the meteoric rise of a single-minded and singularly gifted self-seeker who without the opportunity of Ireland might have amounted to nothing.

Cornwallis, Charles, 2nd Earl and 1st Marquess (1738–1805)

After a distinguished career as a soldier in North America, India and Europe, Cornwallis was appointed Commander-in-Chief and LORD LIEUTENANT in Ireland in 1798 in the midst of the uprising of the revolutionary republican movement, the UNITED IRISHMEN. His preference for clemency towards the rebels and his abhorrence of the excesses of the government forces came too late to make much difference, but he espoused the cause of Catholic EMANCIPATION on the grounds that the UNION of Britain and Ireland, which he favoured, would be meaningless without it. He perceived that such a Union would merely be a closer association of the powerful ASCENDANCY interest with Great Britain, and he resigned from office when it was clear no gesture would be made towards the Catholics. He returned to and died in India.

Corry's Act *see* DISSENTERS

Council Bill, The Irish

The Irish Council Bill was proposed by AUGUSTINE BIRRELL, British CHIEF SECRETARY in Ireland, in 1907, and was introduced into the House of Commons on 7 May. The proposal offered a measure of devolved government through a national council, but for the nationalists intent upon HOME RULE it did not go far enough, whilst the revolutionary republican movements would settle for nothing less than full separation from Britain. A nationalist convention rejected the measure within a fortnight and the bill was dropped in June 1907.

Council of Three Hundred

The Council was DANIEL O'CONNELL's alternative Irish government, and another aspect of his great campaign for the Repeal of the UNION in 1843. The REPEAL ASSOCIATION designated the year 1843 as the 'Year of Repeal', and had divided the country into districts in which Association members would select delegates to sit in DUBLIN in the Council of Three Hundred to work on the draft of a Repeal Bill. It seems that O'Connell hoped the mass support for the Council would induce the British government to acquiesce in its formation, and perhaps in its assumption of parliamentary powers. The British government, however, intended to proclaim and repress the Council should it ever meet, and O'Connell himself seems to have been wary of the potential for revolutionary action that the creation of the Council represented. The number of 300 Council delegates also drew attention to the fact that such a figure was two-thirds larger than the number of MPs from Ireland sitting in the British House of Commons since the Union in 1801.

Counsellor, The

Affectionate nickname for DANIEL O'CONNELL.

County Cess

The County assessment or cess (also referred to as the County Tax), was levied in the various Irish counties at the discretion of the GRAND JURIES, for which reason it is occasionally referred to as the 'Grand Jury Cess'. The rate was paid by occupiers of property, not by owners, and consequently fell upon poor tenants as well as upon the better off. The UNITED IRISHMEN revolutionary movement of the 1790s targeted the County Cess as a cause of grievance amongst the Irish, but it had been an issue of agrarian unrest (see AGRARIAN OUTRAGES) since the 1750s, and figured particularly in the agitation of the OAKBOY movement. In that instance, it seems to have been the use to which the cess was put as much as the collection itself, that aroused hostility, through a massive expansion of road-building reliant upon local labour.

Court of Claims *see* SETTLEMENT, ACT OF

Crawford, Robert Lindsay (1868–1945)

Crawford, born in County Antrim, a Protestant and member of the ORANGE ORDER, represented, in his political development, a return to the radical and nationalist PRESBYTERIANISM that lay at the root of the foundation in the late eighteenth century of the UNITED IRISHMEN movement. Crawford identified with a class-based community of interest in Ireland, and, as Grand Master of the radical INDEPENDENT ORANGE ORDER, advocated unity with Catholic nationalists. He attacked the conventional stance of the ULSTER UNIONIST COUNCIL in the MAGHERAMORE MANIFESTO, which sided with Catholic land reformers. His adoption of HOME RULE led to his expulsion from the Orange Order in 1908, whereupon he withdrew to Canada. During the 1920s he was an influential representative of the new Irish FREE STATE in America.

Creaghting

The word 'creaght' is an anglicization of the Gaelic 'caoruigheachta', meaning herds of livestock, whether cattle or horses or both, which represented the portable wealth of prominent chiefs and nobles. This central feature of Gaelic society was still evident in the seventeenth century, and posed a major military threat to English expansion, since such herds were moved with armies as a source of foodstuffs. The use of the word 'creaghting' by the English alluded to a pastoral economy, particularly but not specifically in ULSTER, in which the herds wandered, under guard, across wide territories to find fresh pastureland to support them.

Crofty, Hill of

The Hill of Crofty, also referred to as Knockcrofty, near DROGHEDA, was the location chosen for the important meeting between the leaders of the IRISH REBELLION which had broken out in ULSTER in October 1641, and the representatives of the OLD ENGLISH. At the meeting, on 3 December 1641, agreement was reached to form an alliance against the government in DUBLIN. A second meeting, on 7 December at Tara, sealed the alliance, to the great alarm of the Earl of ORMOND who summoned the Old English to meet him and explain themselves at a conference in Dublin. It was too late, the meeting at Crofty having made the rebellion a national movement rather than provincial.

Croker, John Wilson (1780–1857)

Croker came of the Protestant ASCENDANCY in County Galway, passed through TRINITY COLLEGE, and sat as MP in the Parliament at WESTMINSTER. Briefly, in 1808, he was CHIEF SECRETARY, and became a close friend of Sir ROBERT PEEL. It was Croker who first applied the word 'Conservative' to the Tory party. His 1808 work *The State of Ireland Past and Present* was a remarkably pro-Catholic history of his country, and he had sharply satirized DUBLIN Ascendancy society in his *An Intercepted Letter from Canton* of 1804. Croker was at odds with the Whig historian Macaulay, a dispute arising from Croker's edition of Boswell's life of Dr Johnson. He was a notable orator comparable to GRATTAN.

Crommelin, Samuel-Louis (1652–1727)

Crommelin was an important figure in the development of the ULSTER economy. A Huguenot, he fled France in 1685 and was invited by King WILLIAM III to take charge of the linen industry in Ireland in 1700, and, with government financial help, he established a manufactory in Ulster, at Lisburn. The subsidy came to him from Irish revenues, administered by the LORDS JUSTICES. Crommelin's individual significance is representative of the important role played by French Huguenot Protestants in Ireland during the eighteenth century. Henri de Ruvigny, Earl of Galway, set up a colony at Portarlington, and DUBLIN became the chief centre of settlement. Crommelin's influence extended throughout Ireland, where he endeavoured to develop the manufacture of sail cloth for shipping. His *Essay on Linen Manufacture in Ireland* was published in 1705.

Cromwell, Henry (1628–74)

The son of OLIVER CROMWELL, Henry's military career began and ended in Ireland during the suppression of the IRISH REBELLION which had begun in 1641, by his father. He became an MP from Ireland in the Parliament of 1653, and was appointed Major-General in Ireland in 1654, where he acquired forfeited estates around Meath and in CONNACHT. Although Henry Cromwell favoured the transplantation of Catholics as part of the pacification process, he did not favour the imposition of oaths of ABJURATION, and his appointment as Governor-General in 1658, though short-lived, gave him a chance to apply his own political ideas. He fell from power with the restoration of King Charles II, to which he declined to give his support, and the confiscation of his English property made him reliant upon that in Ireland, which was taken over by trustees on his behalf.

Cromwell, Oliver (1599–1658)

By the time that Cromwell arrived in Ireland on 15 August 1649, he had emerged as the single most powerful man in England, a soldier of more than ordinary competence and occasional brilliance, and committed to the crushing of the Catholic and royalist forces still operative in Ireland. The brutality of his campaigns, most marked at DROGHEDA and Wexford, merely added to the total of human misery without seriously denting rebel morale. He remained in Ireland only until May 1650, although his commission as Governor-General from the Council of State in England (the supreme authority after the abolition of monarchy) was for a three-year period commencing in June 1649. Under his regime in England, the policy of transplanting Catholics into CONNACHT and resettling their lands with former soldiers was carried out with strong resolution. His successors in the Irish government, FLEETWOOD and then his son HENRY CROMWELL, exercised authority through parliamentary commissioners appointed in England. The Irish PARLIAMENT ceased to meet, and 30 MPs were returned to sit at WESTMINSTER in the English House of Commons, creating a brief UNION of the two countries not to be tried again until 1801. Apologists for Cromwell, some of them historians, have implied that his military excesses in Ireland were necessary to bring a long war to an end, and have been exaggerated. To the Irish, the Gaelic and OLD ENGLISH Catholics, he was nothing more than yet another particularly brutal and vindictive foreign invader, and that is predominantly how he is remembered there.

Croppies

Broadly, the 'croppies' were the rebels of 1798 who rose in support of the revolutionary republican programme of the UNITED IRISHMEN. The term was derived from the fashionable haircut assumed by some United Irishmen in imitation of a style prevalent in revolutionary France. In contemporary parlance, a 'croppy-hole' was a burial pit filled with quicklime into which the bodies of rebels, who were not always even dead, were thrown by government troops. An 'Orange croppy' was an actual or potential rebel who changed sides, and draws attention to the fact that the 1798 rising was made up of both Catholics and PRESBYTERIANS; government repression on the eve of the rebellion was particularly severe in ULSTER, where the movement was essentially Presbyterian, and where most of the side-changing took place in face of the severity of the authorities.

Cross Tipperary

The county of Tipperary assumed its present area in 1637, for prior to that date it was divided into two distinct counties of Tipperary and County of the Cross of Tipperary, which was a large block of church lands. The merger was pushed through by LORD DEPUTY THOMAS WENTWORTH, bringing an end to the peculiar jurisdiction of the church.

Crowbar Brigade, The

The term was coined by the British newspaper *The Times*, to refer to the gangs of men employed to enforce EVICTION orders of landlords, by the simple expedient of demolishing the houses around the ears of the ejected tenants and depriving them of shelter should they seek to return. Their activities were particularly marked in the 1860s and 1870s, and created considerable rancour in Ireland and some moral indignation in Britain, too.

Cuba Five, The

On 5 January 1871 the British government, in face of the campaign of the AMNESTY ASSOCIATION, released from prison the FENIAN revolutionaries O'DONOVAN ROSSA, Charles O'Connell, JOHN DEVOY, John McClure and Henry Mulleda. They were the Cuba Five, named from the ship which carried them to America and which arrived on 19 January 1871 to widespread enthusiasm.

Cullen, Cardinal Paul (1803–78)

Paul Cullen, archbishop of Armagh in the Catholic hierarchy since February 1850, was raised to the dignity of cardinal in June 1866, the first Irishman to attain that rank.

He was born in County Kildare, and educated at the College of Propaganda in Rome where he was ordained to the priesthood in 1829. Throughout his life Cardinal Cullen put the interests of the CATHOLIC CHURCH, as he saw them, before all other political considerations in Ireland but was himself, and encouraged his clergy to be, fundamentally nationalist. His main concern was that the church should not be contaminated or used by parties or persons striving through purely secular means for Irish freedom. His position as Primate of All Ireland coincided with an explosion of Catholic enthusiasm in the 1850s, in the wake of the devastation of the FAMINE of the previous decade. Under Cullen the church harnessed the intensity of the new devotions, and maintained links with EMIGRANT Catholics, Cullen himself influencing the development of Catholic worship in America and the antipodes. The problem that most beset Cullen was the involvement of parochial clergy in political activity, first manifested to any degree during O'CONNELL's agitation for EMANCIPATION, creating a tradition of involvement which the church hierarchy had to handle gently. Cullen's temperate nationalism, an expression of suspicion of England and of Protestantism, gave him a sympathy for the priesthood modified only by the need to ensure that the church was not compromised by association with secular movements: he was, for example, a vehement critic of the FENIAN movement, which was fundamentally revolutionary in its posture, and committed to PHYSICAL FORCE politics to rid Ireland of British domination. He was aware, ultramontane as he undoubtedly was, that the Irish military support for the papacy in 1859/60 (see IRISH BRIGADE) owed a lot to the militant assertion of Irishness in preceding decades, encouraged and facilitated by the priesthood. Nevertheless, Cullen's NATIONAL ASSOCIATION founded in 1864 to press for DISESTABLISHMENT of the CHURCH OF IRELAND and to seek land reforms was almost certainly a deliberate attempt to push aside the Fenian agitators. That it failed to do so was due to the growing irrelevance of constitutional methods.

Cumann na mBan

A force of female auxiliaries founded in April 1914 by CONSTANCE MARKIEVICZ to assist the IRISH VOLUNTEERS. Cumann na mBan provided messengers and support for the IRISH REPUBLICAN ARMY during the EASTER RISING of 1916, and, after the rising's failure, became progressively more radical and revolutionary in its nationalism. The Cumann rejected the ANGLO-IRISH TREATY with its PARTITION of Ireland, and assisted the anti-Treaty forces of the IRA during the ensuant civil war of 1922. This militant women's organization preserved in its ideology the pure republicanism that they saw the Treaty of 1921 as abandoning.

Cumann na nGaedheal

The Cumann na nGaedheal was founded in September 1900 by ARTHUR GRIFFITH on a dual programme of opposition to the Boer War (there was much Irish sympathy for the Boers) and the achievement of political autonomy for Ireland. There were links with FENIANISM, the revolutionary movement that had emerged effectively in the 1860s, but there was a good deal of emphasis too upon the Gaelic aspect of nationalism, a concern for the survival and spread of the Irish language, which sat somewhat uneasily beside a constitutionalism that took GRATTAN'S PARLIAMENT of the 1780s as a model. Nevertheless, from the Cumann na nGaedheal emerged SINN FÉIN, the political movement that was to bring the nationalist struggle to a triumphant conclusion in the wake of the failure of the EASTER RISING of 1916.

Cumann na Poblachta

Cumann na Poblachta was the name given by DE VALERA to the staunchly republican party which he formed following his resignation as President of the Irish Republic in 1921, in opposition to the terms of the ANGLO-IRISH TREATY which PARTITIONED Ireland and left SIX COUNTIES of ULSTER in British hands. Cumann na Poblachta represented the split within SINN FÉIN over the Treaty, but itself achieved little and seems merely to have faded from the scene as a recognizable political party.

Curragh Mutiny/Curragh Incident

The Curragh was a British army base in County Kildare from which, on 20 March 1914, troops were assigned to move up into ULSTER. Precisely what then happened is not altogether clear. The commander at the Curragh appears to have represented the order as evidence that the troops would be used to coerce Ulster into accepting HOME RULE, legislation for which was nearly completed. They expected to be used to suppress the Protestant ULSTER VOLUNTEER FORCE, formed to defend the UNION with Britain. It is estimated that 57 out of 70 officers offered to resign their commissions rather than go into Ulster, and this 'mutiny' has been seen as the factor which forced the British government into conceding Ulster's right to remain aloof from a self-governing Ireland. In fact, there seems to have been no intention to use the troops in a coercive role against the Protestant Unionists, and the whole 'incident' (rather than a mutiny) was the result of over reaction to rumour.

Curran, John Philpot (1750–1817)

Curran came of ASCENDANCY stock in Ireland, was educated at TRINITY COLLEGE, and from 1783 to 1800 sat as MP in the Irish House of Commons where he was a prominent supporter of GRATTAN, FLOOD and the PATRIOT party. In the REGENCY CRISIS he refused (at some personal cost) to align himself with William Pitt's attempts to limit the powers of the Prince Regent, showed himself an advocate of EMANCIPATION for Catholics, and in the 1790s defended, in his legal capacity, UNITED IRISHMEN arrested by the government. He does not, however, seem to have sympathized with their revolutionary republicanism; his whole background would have gone against that. Curran's bitter dislike for the UNION of Britain and Ireland in 1801, to the support of which he could never be won, expressed itself in sympathy for the attempted insurrection of ROBERT EMMET in 1803, to whom Curran's daughter was engaged. The Whig ministry in Britain in 1806 made him a Privy Councillor and he secured appointment as Master of the Rolls. Curran's volatility – he fought between five and six duels with political opponents including the administration man FITZGIBBON (they thenceforth cordially detested each other) – and his outstanding powers of oratory, coupled with his espousal of 'reform' and 'toleration' and his earnest 'Irishness' make him a typical example of the Patriot tendency within the Ascendancy evident in the late eighteenth century.

Curry, John (d. 1780)

Co-founder of the Catholic Committee (see CATHOLIC BOARD), Curry was an historian and physician who wrote, and published in 1775, the important *Historical and Critical Review of the Civil Wars in Ireland*. The book challenged the accepted and long-propagated Protestant interpretation of the IRISH REBELLION of 1641–53, and was an attempt at recovering Irish history for the Irish people, or perhaps Catholic history for the Catholic Irish.

D

Dáil Éireann

Dáil Éireann translates from the Gaelic as the 'parliament of Ireland', and emerged from the SINN FÉIN *ard-fheis* (congress or conference) of October 1917 which put as its priority the gaining of independence from Britain, the precise form of the future government of Ireland to be decided upon thereafter. In the General Election of 14–28 December 1918 Sinn Féin returned 73 MPs, all of whom, by the policy of ABSTENTIONISM, declined to take up their seats in WESTMINSTER, 36 of them being in prison anyway. The Sinn Féin MPs met in the first Dáil Éireann in the Mansion House, DUBLIN on 21 January 1919, and declared independence from Britain. The first acting President was Cathal Brugha, appointed on 22 January, but he was replaced on 1 April by EAMON DE VALERA the first real President of the Dáil. De Valera's appointment marked the opening of the second session of the Dáil, and on 4 April MICHAEL COLLINS, the Minister for Finance, authorized the issue of 'republican bonds' to raise £250,000. The British government responded on 4 July with a proclamation to suppress Sinn Féin, the IRISH VOLUNTEERS, CUMANN NA MBAN and the GAELIC LEAGUE on the grounds that they were illegal organizations. The Dáil continued with its deliberations, and on 20 August determined that an oath of allegiance to the Irish Republic be imposed upon its members and upon the Irish Volunteers. On 12 September the British administration declared the Dáil to be an illegal assembly. The first shots in the WAR FOR INDEPENDENCE had already been fired at Fermoy, County Cork on 7 September when Volunteers attacked regular soldiers. The Dáil met in secret in June 1920 to vote funds for the prosecution of the war: the loan floated by Michael Collins in April 1919 was over-subscribed by more than one-fifth. Under the terms of the GOVERNMENT OF IRELAND ACT of 23 December 1920, a Parliament for southern Ireland and one for northern Ireland were to be established, and, on 13 May 1921, 124 Sinn Féin candidates and only four independents were returned unopposed for the southern Parliament. These MPs met in Dublin on 16 August as the second Dáil Éireann, one month after the signature of a truce between the British armed forces and the IRISH REPUBLICAN ARMY. From the Dáil, delegates were appointed to attend a conference with Prime Minister Lloyd George to negotiate a settlement and on 6 December 1921 the ANGLO-IRISH TREATY was signed in London. Henceforth, the Dáil Éireann was to be the Parliament of the FREE STATE and of the Irish Republic.

Dangan Hill/Dungan Hill, battle of

The battle of Dangan or Dungan Hill near Trim in County Meath was fought on 8 August 1647 between an army of the CATHOLIC CONFEDERACY and English government troops commanded by MICHAEL JONES. The Confederates were decisively beaten and their commander THOMAS PRESTON's plans for the investment of DUBLIN brought to nothing. Instead, OWEN ROE O'NEILL's army had to be brought south to defend Leinster against the resilient English garrison.

Darcy, Patrick (1598–1668)

Darcy came of OLD ENGLISH Catholic stock, and sat as an MP in the DUBLIN Parliament of 1634 and again in 1640. He devised and developed into a printed *Argument* (1643) the claim that the Irish PARLIAMENT enjoyed an authority quite independent of that of the English Parliament (see WILLIAM MOLYNEUX): that no English statute could be binding upon the Irish Parliament unless that Parliament itself caused it to be enacted and made law. This was a frontal assault on the dictum of POYNINGS' LAW. A committee from Dublin presented a memorial to King Charles I on 17 May 1641 arguing the case, and on 9 June 1641 Darcy himself presented his case before the House of Lords. Not surprisingly, at the outbreak of the IRISH REBELLION in October 1641, Darcy associated himself with the rebels and served as a member of the Supreme Council of the CATHOLIC CONFEDERACY at Kilkenny. His view of the role of the Irish Parliament was one that was to be endorsed by many Protestant NEW ENGLISH politicians long after Darcy's death, but he was the first to enunciate the sovereignty of the Irish Parliament under the monarchy of England.

Daunt, William Joseph O'Neill (1807–94)

William Daunt was born of Protestant parentage in County Offaly (King's County) but converted to Catholicism and sat as MP for Mallow in 1832 in the Parliament at WESTMINSTER. He helped found the REPEAL ASSOCIATION in 1840, which worked for the ending of the UNION of the Parliaments of Britain and Ireland of 1801, and was close to its leading spirit DANIEL O'CONNELL. He played a crucial role in developing the atmosphere for DISESTABLISHMENT of the CHURCH OF IRELAND, and in 1870 served as secretary to the HOME GOVERNMENT ASSOCIATION campaigning for HOME RULE. He published his memoirs of O'Connell in 1848.

Davies, Sir John (1569–1626)

Davies was an English civil servant who became, in succession, Solicitor-General for Ireland in 1603 and then Attorney-General from 1606 to 1619. He was a strenuous advocate of the PLANTATION policy for Irish land, arguing that since Gaelic usage did not recognize inheritance, the land was there for the taking. He regarded the reconciliation of the Earl of TYRONE after the Treaty of MELLIFONT in 1603 as potentially disastrous for English interests, and did as much as he could to break what was left of the earl's power. In 1608 he was involved in plans in England for the plantation of ULSTER, and ran into

confrontation with ARTHUR CHICHESTER over his emphasis upon the expropriation of the Irish. He was the author of *Discovery of the True Causes Why Ireland was Never Entirely Subdued until the Beginning of His Majesty's Reign* (1612). Davies sat in the Irish PARLIAMENT in DUBLIN in 1613 and became Speaker, representative of the NEW ENGLISH settlers although he was not strictly one of them. He sat in the English Parliament in 1614 and again in 1621.

Davis, Thomas Osborne (1814–45)

Historians have tended to see Davis as the single most powerful influence on Irish nationalism from the standpoint of the PHYSICAL FORCE principles of the YOUNG IRELAND movement of the 1840s, which broke with the constitutionalism of O'CONNELL's REPEAL ASSOCIATION. Born a Protestant in County Cork, and educated at the ASCENDANCY bastion of TRINITY COLLEGE DUBLIN, he did not convert to Catholicism but came to regard it as a legitimate expression of Irishness against the alien element of Protestantism. This did not make him primarily a religious nationalist, however, for his first concern lay in unity as a necessity for an independent Ireland. Nevertheless his convictions were as emotive as they were rational, evidenced by his anthemic *A Nation Once Again*, for generations a popular republican song. His intellect was a match for that of O'Connell, and his early death robbed the Young Irelanders of a charismatic but unofficial leader.

Davitt, Michael (1846–1906)

Michael Davitt was born in County Mayo, emigrated to England and was crippled by an industrial accident. An early member of the revolutionary FENIAN movement, and closely involved in the IRISH REPUBLICAN BROTHERHOOD after the failure of the 1867 uprising, he was arrested by the British and gaoled until 1877. He was partly responsible for the new strategy of the nationalist movement, which sought to link the demand for land reform with projected HOME RULE, and the restoration of self-government to Ireland. He thus became involved in the LAND LEAGUE established in 1879. Although initially a supporter of PARNELL and an influence upon him, Davitt, MP for County Meath since 1882, continued to sit for the constituency as a vigorous anti-PARNELLITE after the scandal which broke Parnell and almost broke Home Rule with him. He came to regard Parnell as dictatorial, and, perhaps in reaction to that, placed considerable emphasis upon democracy in the struggle for a free Ireland. The son of a family driven to EMIGRATION by EVICTION, Davitt's profound belief in the efficacy of land nationalization was rooted in his boyhood experience, but was rationalized in the context of the long-vanished BREHON law of Gaelic society. His book *The Fall of Feudalism in Ireland* was published in 1904.

Deasy's Act

The Landlord and Tenant Law Amendment Act of 28 August 1860 was known as 'Deasy's Act' after Richard Deasy the then Attorney-General for Ireland. It was remarkable for its introduction into landlord and tenant relationships of the doctrine of free trade, which was anathema to previous concepts of landholding. The legislation, although it did not seem to do so, worked in favour of the landlord by introducing the idea of a contractual relationship between the landlord and the tenant, although it has to be said that Irish lawyers disagreed markedly over the precise interpretation to be put upon the Act. It is also true that the Act dealt a blow to the idea of tenant right (see ULSTER CUSTOM) and simplified the process of EVICTION for the landlord. Historians have pointed out that landlord-tenant legislation subsequent to Deasy's Act abandoned its free market principles in favour of statute law.

Declaration, The (30 November 1660)

The Declaration was preliminary to the Act of SETTLEMENT, and was a short-term response by government to the problem of forfeited land in Ireland and the grievances of the dispossessed. The Declaration appointed commissioners to examine cases, but they lacked statutory authority and proved ineffective. It also guaranteed Cromwellian soldiers' and ADVENTURERS' lands whilst at the same time promising to redress the wrongs of innocent Catholics. Its intentions were good, but it amounted to little more than a statement of intent.

Declaratory Act of 1720

The Declaratory Act of the British House of Commons of 7 April 1720, known also as the 'Sixth of George I', reaffirmed British parliamentary supremacy over the PARLIAMENT of Ireland by denying the appellate authority of the Irish House of Lords. This measure, to 'secure the dependency of Ireland' upon Britain was a direct affront to the power of the developing Protestant ASCENDANCY, which, from its essentially colonial origins, was beginning to represent itself as 'Irish' and making claims consistent with the assertion of national identity. In 1719 the British House of Lords (where Irish peers did not sit) reversed a judicial decision of the Irish House of Lords and so precipitated the kind of crisis that men such as WILLIAM MOLYNEUX had foreseen a generation earlier. The Act reimposed POYNINGS' LAW with emphasis upon the requirement that all legislative proposals had to receive prior approval in Britain. The Declaratory Act provided the developing PATRIOT party in the Irish House of Commons with a specific target later in the eighteenth century. In February 1782 GRATTAN claimed that there was no legal basis for the Act of 1720 but his move for its repeal failed, and the Irish Attorney-General was dismissed from office for supporting Grattan's viewpoint. Nevertheless, through the developing agitation of the VOLUNTEER movement particularly in ULSTER, and the willingness of the Whig party in Britain to facilitate reform, the Declaratory Act was finally repealed on 21 June 1782. The Patriot MP HENRY FLOOD claimed that the repeal did not prevent Britain from passing further such legislation at a later date, and pressed for, and got, a renunciation of such a right in April 1783. The repeal of the Declaratory Act ushered in the period of GRATTAN'S

PARLIAMENT in Ireland, often represented as a triumph of Irish national assertion, but in fact a victory for the Ascendancy's view of what the Irish national interest was. The UNION of Britain and Ireland in 1801 effectively deprived the Irish of their own legislative Parliament for 120 years.

Defenders and Defenderism

The Defenders were a Catholic secret society originating in ULSTER to counter concerted Protestant intimidation at the end of the eighteenth century. So effective was the secrecy of the movement that little is known about its leadership, but its ideology, a complex mixture of agrarian agitation and revolutionary republicanism, has an important role in the emergence of militant Irish nationalism. The Defenders appear to have emerged in County Armagh around 1784, perhaps encouraged by the constitutional developments of GRATTAN'S PARLIAMENT. Opposition to taxation (the COUNTY CESS) and to TITHES blended with a backward-looking JACOBITE tendency. Over the years a general militant Catholicism rooted in hatred of English rule came to the fore, and in 1794 the Defenders (denounced by some Catholic politicians as 'unthinking oppressed people') articulated their objective as 'To quell all nations, dethrone all kings, and to plant the true religion that was lost at the Reformation'. Their primary enemies, the Protestant PEEP O'DAY BOYS, like the Defenders a largely Ulster movement based upon sectarian rivalry, were deeply involved in the developing violence of 1791/2. In the latter year, Defender contacts seem to have been made with revolutionary elements in France. Such a connection facilitated the merging in some areas of Defenders with the revolutionary republican movement of the UNITED IRISHMEN, although since the latter was avowedly non-sectarian, there was friction, and the religious crusade element of the 1798 rising may have owed not a little to the fact that, as in County Cork, the United Irishmen were often Defenders under a new name. Government legislation, such as that to establish the MILITIA, gave the Defenders opportunity to infiltrate peace-keeping forces with an eye to securing arms and training, and by the time the 1798 rising broke out, many Militia units were reckoned by their commanders to be politically unreliable. There seems little doubt that in Connacht to which many Catholics fled, particularly from Armagh in face of Protestant violence, Defenderism was the predominant factor in the 1798 rising. The collapse of Defenderism was inherent in the failure of the United Irishmen's rebellion of 1798 and the subsequent assertiveness of ORANGEISM which had a vehicle for repression in the government-formed YEOMANRY force that had behaved with appalling brutality in the suppression of the rising.

Derry, City and County of

Derry, like BELFAST, developed as a strategic point of particular importance to the English government in its suppression of the ULSTER rebellion of the Earl of TYRONE which came to an end in 1603. A charter of incorporation making Derry into a city was issued in July 1604, and reincorporation took place in 1613 when the name of the city was altered to Londonderry. In 1610 agreement had been reached between the English Privy Council and the City of London by which the London merchants undertook the PLANTATION and settlement of the new city, hence the change in its name, and the county of COLERAINE which became known as the County of Londonderry (or Derry). Dominated by Scottish traders, the city of Derry developed its own wool staple and undertook massive fortification work, its great walls being completed by 1618, marking it out as a colonial bastion in an area otherwise not entirely subdued. The London companies fell foul of the government of King Charles I in 1635, and were brought before the Court of Star Chamber in England and forced to surrender their patent and submit to a fine of £70,000 for failing to keep to the terms of the original agreement for settlement. In 1637 the city's charter was cancelled. It was to be granted again by Charles II in 1662. Later events (see DERRY, Siege of) gave the city a particular place in the Protestant memory in Ireland, and in its refusal from foundation to allow Catholics access, but to permit the development of Catholic settlement adjacent to the Bogside outside the walls, it symbolized the vigorously enforced sectarian differentiation that was the hallmark of plantation theory.

Derry, Siege of

The waging of the struggle between the deposed King JAMES II and his JACOBITE supporters on the one hand, and the Protestant King WILLIAM III developed in Ireland and not in England. In December 1688 a Jacobite army under the Earl of Antrim advancing on Derry, found the gates closed against it by the APPRENTICE BOYS. No immediate move was made against the city, which began to harbour refugees from areas where the Jacobite forces were dominant: there were some 30,000 isolated in Derry by the time a siege was launched. Governor LUNDY fled rather than try to defend a city he regarded as untenable, and command fell to Major Henry Baker and the CHURCH OF IRELAND clergyman George Walker (who was later killed in action at the battle of the BOYNE). When King James II was denied entry on 18 April 1689, siege was laid under Conrad von Rosen the Jacobite commander, but the defenders held firm, and on 28 July 1689 were relieved by sea. Three days later the besiegers abandoned the siege and withdrew their forces into Donegal. Derry had both withstood a major siege, and tied down for critical months an important Jacobite army.

Derryveagh Evictions, The

In 1861 John George Adair, landlord, issued EVICTION notices to 47 families on his property at Derryveagh, despite the fact that the rents were up to date. Adair (who in the 1850s had associated himself with the campaign for tenant rights) brought in the police to enforce the eviction process, and refused to be dissuaded by them from carrying it out. The Derryveagh incident became known throughout Ireland as a classic example of an all too prevalent obsession with eviction by landlords.

Despard, Colonel Edward Marcus, (1751–1803)

Historiography has dismissed Despard for the most part as an insane Irish career soldier in British service who, from a real grievance against the government, engaged himself in conspiracy to overthrow it. Recent research has shown that Despard was both a member of the revolutionary republican movement the UNITED IRISHMEN in 1797 and perhaps earlier and, following the failure of the United Irishmen's rebellion of 1798, maintained close links with ROBERT EMMET who led his own insurrection in DUBLIN in 1803. In that same year Despard was tried before a Special Commission in London for his own revolutionary plots and was executed 21 February 1803. He appears to have co-ordinated liaison between the United Irishmen survivals of 1802 and the UNITED BRITONS and UNITED ENGLISHMEN movements based in Britain. It is also likely that Despard was supposed to rise in England in 1803 to coincide with Emmet's rising in Dublin. The spread of Irish revolutionary politics into England was facilitated by Irish immigration, but the groups based in England were not exclusively Irish in their composition.

De Valera, Eamon (1882–1975)

De Valera was born in New York, but grew up in County Limerick and was educated in Ireland. His significance grew in the wake of the failure of the EASTER RISING of 1916, in which he fought, having been a member of the IRISH VOLUNTEERS since 1913. He was the last rebel commander to surrender to British troops. Released from gaol in June 1917, he was returned as SINN FÉIN MP on an ABSTENTIONIST platform for East Clare. In the same year he was both President of Sinn Féin and of the Irish Volunteers, and was arrested and gaoled by the British on the grounds of his alleged involvement in a spurious plot with Germany. He escaped from prison, and in April 1919 was elected President of the first DÁIL ÉIREANN which had proclaimed itself the government of the Irish Republic. He opposed the PARTITION clauses of the ANGLO-IRISH TREATY of 1921, and led the political struggle of the purist republicans in the ensuant civil war against the FREE STATE, although he was not, apparently, as committed to the anti-Treaty cause as he seemed to be. De Valera went on to form the political party Fianna Fáil in 1926, and in 1937 succeeded in deleting all references to the British monarchy from the Irish constitution. He was President of the Irish Republic from 1959 to 1973. His severe repression of the IRISH REPUBLICAN ARMY in the 1930s evidenced his distancing himself from the PHYSICAL FORCE principles of those who sought to reunify Ireland by armed might.

Devlin, Joseph (1871–1934)

Devlin was of Catholic parentage in BELFAST and, until 1914 and the outbreak of the FIRST WORLD WAR, pursued a conventional nationalist political career. He served as secretary of the UNITED IRISH LEAGUE in 1902, and sat as MP at WESTMINSTER for West Belfast from 1906 until 1918, on a HOME RULE platform. He was involved in the establishment of the potentially revolutionary IRISH VOLUN- TEERS in 1913, but constitutionalists found it expedient to seek to influence and direct extra-parliamentary movements, and when war broke out with Germany in 1914 Devlin was an active recruiter of Irishmen for the British army. His subsequent political career developed within the Northern Irish state, and he was MP for Fermanagh and Tyrone at Westminster from 1929 until his death.

Devon Commission, The

The Devon Commission, which took its name from the PRESIDENCY of the Limerick landowner the Earl of Devon, was set up on 20 November 1843 by the government to investigate and make recommendations concerning the practices of landholding in Ireland. The Commission was made up predominantly of Irish landowners. It reported in February 1845 and, almost as an aside, testified to the 'patient endurance' of the Irish rural labourer 'under sufferings greater ... than the people of any other country in Europe have to sustain'. The Commission considered the implications

for property law of the tenant right known as ULSTER CUSTOM which they recognized as beneficial but declined to recommend legislation for its further extension in Ireland. On the other hand, it recommended some system of reward or compensation for improvements to property carried out by tenants, but when an attempt was made in 1845 to introduce legislation into the House of Commons in favour of tenant compensation, it was defeated by the landlord interest. The Devon Commission drew the government's attentions to conditions in Ireland, but had no immediate impact. Indeed, an increase in emphasis on the free market, inimical to safeguards for the tenant, postponed remedies for the land problem. The Commission had merely made a start.

Devoy, John (1842–1928)

Devoy was an important FENIAN activist, who had undergone military training in the French Foreign Legion in 1861/2. As part of the Fenians' revolutionary programme, Devoy was given the task of infiltrating the Irish in the British army, in consequence of which he was gaoled in 1866. Released amongst other Fenians during the period of AMNESTY ASSOCIA- TION agitation in 1871, he went to America where he quickly established himself as the most powerful Fenian leader in exile, heading up the CLAN NA GAEL revolutionary organization. He remained, except for brief visits to France and Ireland in the late 1870s, an exile in America, publishing journals such as *The Gaelic American* and involving himself in fund-raising for the revolution in Ireland. He was certainly involved in seeking German support for an armed uprising on the eve of the FIRST WORLD WAR. He was ultimately buried in Ireland.

Diamond, Battle of the

The Battle of the Diamond, fought on 21 September 1795 at Loughall, County Armagh, was less a 'battle' than an affray and confrontation between Catholics and Protestants that was to have an impact well beyond its localized occurrence. In June of 1795 there had been a risk of a fight between the two sides, but it had been avoided or postponed. The battle of 21 September is presented as a clash between the Catholic DEFENDERS movement and the intimidatory PEEP O'DAY BOYS representing Protestants. In the fighting, which the Catholics lost, some 16 to 48 Catholics were killed: precise figures cannot be arrived at. Out of this fight was to emerge the ORANGE ORDER, the definitive movement for the assertion of Protestant supremacy in ULSTER, and the action itself is comme-morated in the town centres of many Ulster towns known as 'the diamonds'. The battle probably occurred over an intensely local confrontation, but it symbolized the increasing assertion of Protestant domination and the militant response of Catholics to that domination.

Dillon, John (1851–1927)

Dillon was born near DUBLIN and was an early associate of the revolutionary JOHN MITCHEL during the latter's election campaign of 1875. He himself sat in the Parliament at WESTMINSTER from 1880 to 1918, initially as a supporter of PARNELL in the struggle for HOME RULE, and latterly as a convicted anti-PARNELLITE and in 1896 leader of the anti-Parnellite parliamentary party of Irish MPs. In 1898 he founded the UNITED IRISH LEAGUE with WILLIAM O'BRIEN and MICHAEL DAVITT which helped to reunify the parliamentary party. Dill-on's constitutional approach to the Irish problem led him to endorse REDMOND and Redmond's emphasis upon devolved Home Rule. He favoured the legislation for devolution in 1914 and attended the fiasco of the BUCKINGHAM PALACE CONFER-ENCE. By the time that he secured the leadership of the nationalist MPs himself in 1918, events had overtaken them, SINN FÉIN had swept the electoral board in Ireland, and the WAR FOR INDEPENDENCE, a negation of constitutional nationalism, was about to break out. He was ousted from his seat in parliament by DE VALERA.

Dineley, Thomas (d. 1695)

Dineley was the author of *Observations on a Voyage through the Kingdom of Ireland* written in 1681 and published post-humously.

Discoverers (*see also* CONVERT ROLLS)

The 'popery act' of 4 March 1704 was backed up by an amendment act of 30 August 1709 which introduced the prin-ciple of the 'discoverer' who, if he could demonstrate Catholic evasion of the draconic anti-Catholic inheritance laws of 1704, was entitled to possession of the property in question. The Act of 1704 had drastically cut down the terms by which Catholics might lease land, and had introduced legally-enforced partibility of inheritance.

Disestablishment (of the Church of Ireland)

The Irish census of 1861 (see POPULATION) revealed that in a population of 5¾ million, 4½ million were adherents of the CATHOLIC CHURCH. The CHURCH OF IRELAND, which had from its inception enjoyed a narrow and exclusivist base, accounted for around 500,000 commu-nicants, a good half of whom were resident in the province of ULSTER. The inherent inequality of the churches in Ireland, with full state backing given to that which represented only a tiny minority of the population, had been given legislative justification from the early seventeenth century onwards. Indeed, the Church of Ireland was the single most important element of the narrow Protestant ASCENDANCY which had enjoyed control of Ireland, subject to the British crown, from the reign of King WILLIAM III onwards. The bulk of the population carried the church structure on its back, through monetary payments such as the CHURCH CESS. The need for reform within the body of the church had been partially met by the CHURCH TEMPO-RALITIES ACT of 1833, which, if nothing else, had shown that the institution was not wholly inviolable. The Disestablish-ment Act of 26 July 1869 marked the culmination of a long campaign both by Irish Catholic organizations and the Whig consensus in British politics. The General Election of 1868 was fought over the issue of Disestablishment, and gave Prime Minister GLADSTONE clear mandate to press ahead with contemplated legisla-tion to remove the privileges of the church. It was enacted that as from 1871 the church was to be a voluntary body controlled by commissioners with a synod to oversee the administration and a separate body to look after the church's revenues. The Act also made grants both to the Catholic ST PATRICK'S COLLEGE, and to the PRESBYTERIANS to replace the ancient REGIUM DONUM. Provision was also made for the tenants of church lands, already legislated for in 1833, by making it possible for them to purchase their holdings outright, and the Glebe Lands Act of August 1870 provided grants or loans of up to two-thirds of the overall cost involved. Within a decade of the Act's enactment, more than 6,000 tenants had taken advantage of the option, and the importance of this land transfer in the context of the Irish land question cannot be ignored, offering evidence of the way in which the state could facilitate land redistribution.

Dissenters and Dissent (*see also* PRESBYTERIANISM)

Dissenters were Protestants who, by reason of their specific faiths, dissented from the doctrines and ritual of the established CHURCH OF IRELAND (and, of the Church of England). The PRESBYTERIANS were the most numerous and so the most powerful element in Dissent, which embraced also Baptists, Quakers, Congregationalists and other, more exclusive, communions. In the atmosphere of late seventeenth-century Ireland, which almost exactly reflected the prevalent attitude in England, Dissenters were regarded with suspicion. SWIFT in his book *Tale of a Tub* viewed their practices as the 'corruption of religion', and long memories were fed on their role in the anarchic religious world of the mid-seventeenth century after the ENGLISH CIVIL WAR. In consequence, Dissenters were subjected to some of the disabling legislation that was imposed upon Catholics. In the Act of 1704, for example (see PENAL LAWS) the sacramental test, requiring candidates for public office to give evidence of communion with the Church of Ireland, hit as much at Dissenters as at the primary targets, Catholics, and this was intentional. Unlike the Catholics,

however, the Dissenters experienced relief legislation in 1719, and in 1780 and 1782 when the sacramental test was lifted for them and marriages performed by Presbyterian ministers were validated. It was the separateness of the Dissenting congregations, as much as their doctrine, which marked them out for suspicion: in their Protestantism, for example where the Presbyterians were concerned, they seem to have been regarded as natural opponents of the more numerous Catholics. The Presbyterians, for their part, looked upon themselves as a true national religion, and regarded fellow Dissenters as separatist and anarchic. There was some community of interest between Dissenters and Catholics in the face of the laws against them, and the UNITED IRISHMEN revolutionary movement of the 1790s drew heavily upon Protestant dissenters, particularly in its ULSTER organization, but for the most part the government bought the Dissenters off, and their role in the spread of militant ORANGEISM, intolerant of and intimidatory towards Catholics, was considerable.

Dolly's Brae, battle of

The affray at Dolly's Brae, County Down, on 12 July 1848 was a clash between the Catholic RIBBONMEN and the militant Protestants of the ORANGE ORDER, and occurred after the lapse of legislation against PARTY PROCESSIONS, introduced to prevent the fighting that was increasingly occurring in the sectarian province of ULSTER. The Ribbonmen, who had assumed some of the defensive role of the older DEFENDERS, launched an attack on an Orange procession and were beaten off.

Don Espagne

Don Espagne was the nickname of the rebel Donal Kavanagh of Carlow who, having been in arms with the Earl of TYRONE in the ULSTER rebellion which ended with Tyrone's capitulation in 1603, took to the hills and maintained a guerrilla war against the English army and settlers.

Down Survey, The

The Down Survey took its name from the mapping 'down' in the process of a survey of Irish land by WILLIAM PETTY on behalf of the English government in the 1650s. It was one of three surveys resolved upon by the Council of State in London in June 1653: a civil survey based upon the evidence of empanelled juries, instituted on 14 April 1654; a 'gross' survey which was an assessment based on precious little other than guesswork and which commenced in June 1653; and the more systematic and scientific 'down' survey which commenced in 1654. The purpose of all three surveys was to facilitate the allotment of forfeited lands in Ireland after the suppression of the IRISH REBELLION, to satisfy the ADVENTURERS of 1641/2 who had advanced money to finance the war effort in return for promises of real estate, and soldiers who were to have land in lieu of arrears of pay.

Downs Policy, The

This development in the Irish land question took its name from a speech delivered by Laurence Ginnell MP at Downs in County Westmeath in October 1906. His speech reflected the old tensions of pastoral graziers versus farmers, grass versus tillage, the long expansion of the former being held to be at the expense of the rural population who suffered by increasing unemployment. The shift from arable to livestock husbandry was marked by the end of the Napoleonic Wars in 1815, when the shift to large pastoral farms got under way, with significant increases in the export of animals on the hoof as a consequence. This development was contributory to EVICTIONS and general rural distress. The unofficial 'Downs' Policy advocated 'cattle drives' to intimidate large-scale graziers to revert to some arable cultivation. By the summer of 1907 more than 300 such farmers had police protection, and prosecutions of cattle drivers increased, particularly in County Clare. SINN FÉIN in principle opposed the policy, but local branches of the party became involved in it, and in the midst of the WAR FOR INDEPENDENCE from Britain there was a massive drive in County Westmeath followed by enforced redistribution of land. Elements of the IRISH REPUBLICAN ARMY were involved in that incident. Sinn Féin's equivocation was due to the fact that as a party it endorsed, though for purely Irish economic reasons, British government requirements during the FIRST WORLD WAR that at least 10 per cent of grassland be turned over to provide crop-growing arable. The chief area of cattle driving was to be in Connacht in areas where the work of the CONGESTED DISTRICTS BOARD was particularly evident, seeking to resolve the problems of tiny holdings. The 'Downs' Policy in one form or another flourished in the early years of the FREE STATE, and, during the civil war that followed the ANGLO-IRISH TREATY of 1921, seems to have been encouraged by the anti-Treaty IRA.

Drapier's Letters, The

The drapier's letters came from the pen of SWIFT, and launched a popular campaign between February and October 1724 against the copper coinage patent granted to William Wood (see WOOD'S PATENT). The first letter, written by Swift when he was busy with his *Gulliver's Travels*, appeared under the title 'A letter to the shopkeepers and common people of Ireland, concerning the brass half pence coined by Mr. Woods' and was published anonymously in DUBLIN. Further letters, regarded by the administration and the British government as incendiary, appeared in August, September and October of 1724, in which latter month a proclamation was issued for information leading to the identity of the author. Swift appears to have been widely suspected of producing them. The non-existent Dublin draper used the letters to condemn Ireland's subservience to the British legislature, emphasized in the recent DECLARATORY ACT and, more importantly, made the equation between the Irish Protestants and the people of Ireland that was to become a feature of the ASCENDANCY outlook.

Drogheda

The fortified town of Drogheda in County Louth stood on the mouth of the River Boyne, its development due to the English campaign against the Earl of TYRONE's rebels in ULSTER which had ended in 1603. At the outbreak of the IRISH REBELLION in 1641, Sir Henry Tichborne, the English Governor, had defended the town successfully against a rebel assault. In 1649 Drogheda fell into the hands of MURROUGH O'BRIEN, who garrisoned it, and on 2 September OLIVER CROMWELL advanced against the town, with 12,000 men. It was defended largely by refugee royalists from the ENGLISH CIVIL WAR under the command of the Catholic Sir Arthur Aston. Cromwell stormed the walls on 11 September, breached them, and permitted the slaughter of more than 2,000 of the garrison of 3,000 – apparently whilst the townsfolk remained largely unmolested. The slaughter was directly approved by Cromwell in order to terrify remaining rebel garrisons in Ireland. The Governor, Aston, was beaten to death with his own wooden leg when he had been disarmed.

Drogheda was a JACOBITE stronghold which was captured after the battle of the BOYNE in 1690.

Drumbanagher

The deliberate attack by VOLUNTEERS on Catholics at Drumbanagher, County Armagh on 23 June 1789 was organized by a local Protestant landlord, John Moore, to disrupt Catholic religious observance of the eve of the Feast of St John the Baptist, Midsummer Eve. There were many Catholic casualties, and incidents such as this helped galvanize active support for the DEFENDERS, the Catholics' defence movement. On 12 July the Defenders similarly disrupted a Protestant Boyne rally and provoked a pitched fight.

Drummond, Thomas (1797–1840)

Drummond, a Scotsman, was Under Secretary in Ireland from 1835 to 1840, dying in office on 15 April. WILLIAM O'BRIEN said of Drummond 'He knew the country, he loved the people, he felt the cause of the nation'. Through the CONSTABULARY Act of 1836 he sought to rid the police of their sectarian, ORANGE associations, to implant trust in the Catholic community – although in doing so he, unawares, created a quasi-military force that could be a weapon of repression. He abhorred government by coercion, and particularly set his face against the Orange Order which previous administrations at the CASTLE had sometimes seen fit to use against Catholic agitation for reform. The ASCENDANCY tried to be rid of him but a commission of enquiry into his office endorsed his actions in 1639. He earned the approval and support of O'CONNELL, much to the alarm of the landlord interest in Ireland.

Dublin

Dublin, with its surrounding PALE, had been the centre of an expanding English administration in Ireland since the early Middle Ages. At the time of the surrender of the rebellious Earl of TYRONE in 1603, it was a largely timber-built Tudor town, clustered about its ancient castle, and much inferior to English ports which served it across the channel. The 'royal city of Ireland' based its importance in its administrative and governmental role, and control of it was sought in successive rebellions against British authority. Although the plot to seize the CASTLE on the eve of the IRISH REBELLION of 1641 was probably wholly fabricated by the LORDS JUSTICES, the rebels certainly anticipated gaining control after their alliance with the OLD ENGLISH of the Pale. The royalist Earl of ORMOND handed it over to parliamentarian troops in June 1647, and CROMWELL, upon his arrival in Ireland in 1649, made it his campaign headquarters. In the wake of the defeat of the JACOBITE supporters of King JAMES II in 1691, Dublin began to settle down as the centre of the Protestant ASCENDANCY culture that was to develop its own specifically Irish expression in the course of the eighteenth century. Massive rebuilding and street-widening programmes were undertaken, turning Dublin into a city fit to rival anything on the British mainland, a solid expression of the confidence of the ruling elite in Ireland. The UNION of Ireland and Britain in 1801 took from Dublin its role in government. The Irish PARLIAMENT ceased to meet at COLLEGE GREEN, its building being turned over to the use of the Bank of Ireland. Dublin society henceforth revolved around the visits of the LORD LIEUTENANT and the British administration retained in the Castle. Virtually a provincial city henceforth, but with a recent glory that was not forgotten, Dublin declined: but new, middle-class suburbs grew up around it, commensurate with the growth of slums and tenements as Catholic peasant labourers drifted in from the countryside. The city corporation came to be dominated by nationalists, and identified itself with the popular HOME RULE and Repeal movements, as the former corporation had been identified with the PATRIOT party of the last years of Irish Parliament. Devolution of power envisaged by the Home Rule legislation of 1914, and the re-creation of a Parliament in southern Ireland, would have given back to Dublin its accustomed significance. But it was as the capital of a FREE STATE won by the soldiers of the WAR FOR INDEPENDENCE 1919–21 that it regained its importance.

Dublin Philosophical Society (The Dublin Society)

The Dublin Philosophical Society was founded in 1684 by WILLIAM PETTY and others, and met in the residence of Robert Huntingdon, Provost of TRINITY COLLEGE. Petty was the first President, and WILLIAM MOLYNEUX the first secretary. The Society's origins appear to have lain in Molyneux's contact with and experience of the Royal Society in London. There was an early concentration upon the encouragement of the study of Irish history and antiquity. The vast majority of the members and fellows were Protestants, and the Society was, in effect, a product of the developing ASCENDANCY.

Developing interest in scientific enquiry distanced it from the conservatism of Trinity College.

Dublin Protestant Operatives' Association

The Operatives' Association was founded in April 1841 by the Reverend Tresham Gregg (d. 1881) a CHURCH OF IRELAND clergyman educated at TRINITY COLLEGE and author of *Protestant ASCENDANCY Vindicated* published in 1840. Gregg seems to have been motivated by a fierce hostility towards DANIEL O'CONNELL and his campaign for repeal of the UNION of Britain and Ireland in 1801. His attempt to organize Protestant artisan opinion was directed also against the hierarchy of his own church, which had taken measures against him for his violently extremist religious doctrines. The Operatives' Association developed branches beyond DUBLIN, but it was essentially a Dublin-based organization conscious of the increasing Catholic working-class population of the city. Gregg's movement and opinions were influential amongst most sections of the Protestant working class, linked as they were to fear of the consequences of repeal.

Dublin Society for Improving Husbandry *see* ROYAL DUBLIN SOCIETY

Duffy, Charles Gavan (1816–1903)

Duffy was born of Catholic parents in County Monaghan and at the age of 23 undertook the publication of a weekly journal representative of northern, ULSTER, Catholic opinion. He trained as a lawyer and by 1847 was involved with the YOUNG IRELAND revolutionary movement through its Confederate Clubs and its IRISH CONFEDERATION. He was also editor of the journal *NATION*, which originated in 1842 as the vehicle for the views of the Young Irelanders. He does not seem to have been involved in the 1848 rising, but was briefly gaoled. He diverted his energies to the TENANT LEAGUE and sat as MP at WESTMINSTER in that interest from 1852 to 1855. He thereafter emigrated to Australia, where he was Prime Minister of Victoria state in 1871/2 and was knighted in 1873, his early youthful revolutionary enthusiasm having dissipated, although he seems always to have placed hope in the Catholic middle

classes. He also viciously defamed O'CON-
NELL's memory, a reflection of the fact
that the Young Irelanders emerged in
reaction to O'Connell's constitutionalism.
But in the end, O'Connell's contribution
to the Irish people was more profound
and more single-minded than Duffy's.

Dunfermline Declaration

The Dunfermline Declaration was issued
by King Charles II at Dunfermline on 16
August 1650 as part of his price for military
and political alliance with the Scottish
PRESBYTERIANS, in his campaign to establish himself on the English throne. For the
royalist interest in Ireland led by the loyal
Earl of ORMOND the declaration was a
major blow; in it the king repudiated his
alliance with Irish Catholics (supporters of
the CATHOLIC CONFEDERACY) which
Ormond had been trying to organize. In
the face of this abandonment by the king,
Ormond likewise abandoned his own
command and left Ireland for Europe on
11 December.

Dungannon Clubs, The

The Dungannon Clubs, which harked
back to the VOLUNTEERS of the 1780s and
1790s (see DUNGANNON CONVENTIONS),
were formed in 1905 by BULMER HOBSON,
the first such appearing in BELFAST on 8
March. They were intensely disciplined,
revolutionary, republican organizations,
conscious of their presence in the midst of
Protestant dominated ULSTER with its
Unionist militancy. There were links with
ARTHUR GRIFFITH and with CUMANN NA
NGAEDHEAL, Griffith's prototype for SINN
FÉIN. Another important figure in the formation of the Dungannon Clubs was
Denis McCullough who in 1915 was President of the revolutionary IRISH REPUBLICAN
BROTHERHOOD, and had been associated
with the IRB around the time of the
Dungannon Clubs' formation. The Clubs
were never extensive – no more than 60 to
80 members in the whole of Belfast.

Dungannon Conventions

The Conventions held at Dungannon in
1782 and 1783 were demonstrations of the
strength and political awareness of the
increasingly numerous VOLUNTEER
movement, an extra-parliamentary agitation movement which took encouragement from the successful struggle of
the PATRIOT MPs to secure legislative
independence of the Irish PARLIAMENT
from the British. The first of the Conventions held on 15 February 1782 was an
assembly of some 242 delegates sent by
more than 140 local Volunteer Corps in
ULSTER; they passed a resolution that 'the
claims of any other than the King, Lords
and Commons of Ireland to make laws to
bind this kingdom is unconstitutional'
(see also DECLARATORY ACT). A Convention
of Dublin Volunteers on 1 March
endorsed the view and resolved to dis-
obey laws that did not have their origin in
the Irish Parliament. The second of the
Dungannon Conventions met on 8
September 1783 with representatives from
almost 300 Ulster Volunteer groups, and
promoted a radical programme of
demands including parliamentary reform
(see BOROUGH PARLIAMENT), an annual
Parliament and voting by ballot. Subsequent conventions held in Connacht and
Munster subscribed to the Dungannon
demands, but the Volunteers in Leinster
adopted a more constitutional line. The
Dungannon Conventions favoured repeal
of the PENAL LAWS against Catholics, and
the increase of Catholic involvement in
the Volunteer movement was reflected in
the Reform Convention held at Dungannon on 15 February 1793, essentially a
Catholic rally. The Reform Convention
rejected republicanism (in the light of
developments in France and the genesis
of the UNITED IRISHMEN movement in
Ireland) but passed resolutions calling for
equality in the franchise, and voicing concerns about the government's MILITIA
legislation. From 1793 the Volunteer
movement came increasingly under republican influence, which interestingly
spread from the PRESBYTERIAN influence
rather than the Catholic, and there were
no further Conventions. Dungannon had
been the first of the new boroughs to be
incorporated by charter in 1612 in the
wake of PLANTATION in Ulster.

Dunraven Conference

The Dunraven Conference, taking its
name from its chairman, Lord Dunraven,

met in December 1902 at the prompting of the British administration at the CASTLE. It was a discussion between landlord and tenant representatives (the latter led by REDMOND) arising from dissatisfactions with the LAND LEGISLATION of 1891 and 1896. The conference, in its January 1903 report, recommended treasury advances to facilitate tenant land purchase which, among other things, was to be incorporated in legislation known as WYNDHAM'S ACT of that same year.

Dwyer, Michael (d. 1825)

Dwyer was a commander during the 1798 UNITED IRISHMEN republican rebellion who, in the wake of the rebellion's defeat, took to the Wicklow hills outside DUBLIN and conducted a sustained guerrilla war until his surrender in December 1803. The Wicklow and Dublin mountains had a tradition of harbouring rebels and fugitives which dated from the seventeenth century, and Dwyer became the most celebrated of them. He was TRANS-PORTED to New South Wales in Australia where he ended his life as High Constable of Sydney.

Dynamite War, The

A campaign launched in Britain, specifically in London, Glasgow and Liverpool, by FENIAN revolutionaries financed and assisted by the SKIRMISHER and CLAN NA GAEL movements based in America. The war lasted from 1880 to 1887, with major explosions at London Bridge in December 1884 and at the Tower of London, Westminster Hall and the House of Commons in January 1885. TOM CLARKE, future signatory of the 1916 PROCLAMATION OF THE IRISH REPUBLIC, was apprehended as a bomber in 1883. The recent development of dynamite as an explosive lent itself to the bomber's campaign, but there were some revolutionaries critical of its use, and the IRISH REPUBLICAN BROTHERHOOD held itself largely aloof from the mainland campaign.

E

Easter Rising of 1916

From the moment that HOME RULE legislation was shelved with the outbreak of the FIRST WORLD WAR in 1914, certain leaders of the IRISH VOLUNTEERS and of the IRISH REPUBLICAN BROTHERHOOD looked to armed insurrection as a means of securing Ireland's independence from Britain. Those leaders were not disenchanted Home Rulers, but rather committed republican revolutionaries who saw their chance in the collapse of the Home Rule movement on the very eve of its triumph. The rising brought together visionaries such as PADRAIC PEARSE and hitherto hard-headed revolutionary socialists such as JAMES CONNOLLY, blending the Irish Volunteers with Connolly's CITIZEN ARMY, to take on the British army. A rising had been contemplated for 1915 by the leadership of the Volunteers, but was postponed. The Military Council of the IRB determined upon Easter 1916, with Connolly as a full member and by now fully committed to the dream of an Irish republic, Gaelic and Catholic, which was the sole objective of Pearse and SÉAN MAC DIARMADA. It has been argued that for these two, and probably others as well, the principle of a blood sacrifice was essential to the awakening of Ireland; that even in failure, if the British government reacted as it was expected to react, the inevitable triumph of the ideal would be guaranteed. Such a perception proved right. Divisions within the IRB and Volunteer movement over the wisdom of the rising are exemplified by EOIN MACNEILL who tried to cancel Volunteer manoeuvres on the eve of the rising and thereby, unwittingly, fragmented the effort of the rebels, for the IRB decided nevertheless to press ahead for 24 April. Some 1,600 men occupied the GPO building in O'Connell Street, DUBLIN, and other strong points, and inflicted a defeat on British troops sent against them at Mount Street Bridge. The PROCLAMATION OF THE IRISH REPUBLIC was read from the steps of the GPO by Pearse, and then the British army moved in. General Lowe took command of the troops on 25 April pending the arrival of General Sir John Maxwell. Martial law was imposed. By 27 April there were 12,000 British troops deployed in Dublin. Risings in the countryside beyond the city came to nothing. Heavy shelling reduced the rebels' strongholds one by one, until EAMON DE VALERA at Bolands Mill was the last rebel commander resisting, holding off the Sherwood Foresters regiment with 17 men. Some 64 rebels were killed and 120 reported wounded, against British losses of 132 killed and 397 wounded. More than 300 civilians died in the intensive shelling, which included a gunboat firing from the River Liffey. Some 90 death sentences were passed by the British, of which 75 were commuted. The following were executed between 3 and 12 May 1916: Pearse, TOM CLARKE, MACDONAGH, JOSEPH PLUNKETT, Edward Daly, Michael O'Hanrahan, William Pearse, SEAN MAC-BRIDE, Con Colbert, EAMONN CEANNT, Sean Heuston, Michael Mallin, Thomas Ceannt (in Cork City), James Connolly and Séan Mac Diarmada. In December 1916 some 600 internees were released from prisons in Wales and Sussex, and in June 1917, 120 were freed including De Valera. The bishop of Limerick told General Maxwell on 17 May 1916 'I regard your action with horror ... it has outraged the conscience of the country'. In less than five years Britain conceded Irish independence.

Ecclesiastical Titles Act

In September 1850 Pope Pius IX (1846–78) re-established the Roman Catholic Church hierarchy in Britain, part of a papal policy that saw the creation of more than 200 episcopates and apostolic vicariates throughout the world. Throughout his pontificate, Pius IX strengthened control from Rome. Protestant opinion in Britain regarded the re-establishment of the hierarchy as evidence of papal political ambition, and in February 1851 the Prime Minister sought leave to introduce legislation into the House of Commons that was to be the Ecclesiastical Titles Act, made law on 1 August 1851. It prohibited Catholic prelates in Britain from assuming the titles and dignities inherent in the papal decrees. Catholic opinion in Britain and Ireland was united against the legislation, and the CATHOLIC DEFENCE ASSOCIATION was formed to unite their protest. In fact, the act meant precious little and was repealed in 1871. Its importance lies in the manifestation of government-inspired Protestant xeno-phobia that, for the Catholic Irish, seemed further proof that nothing much had changed in attitudes despite EMANCIPATION.

Ejection Act

The Ejection Act, made law in Parliament on 26 June 1816, was an attempt to enable landowners to cope with the agricultural depression and economic crisis after the end of the French wars in 1815. It allowed EVICTIONS to be pushed through the county court system to facilitate the consolidation of farm-holdings and the termination of smallholdings. The attack on small tenants in Ireland was sustained for much of the nineteenth century, creating in time the LAND WAR and widespread agitation for land reform.

Emancipation of Catholics Before the Union of 1801

The Catholics in Ireland, irrespective of social standing, suffered under severe PENAL LAWS which, whilst restricting Catholic rights and freedoms, underpinned the exclusive Protestant ASCENDANCY domination of Ireland and Irish affairs. Movement towards alleviation of the anti-Catholic laws grew out of a general development of religious tolerance during the eighteenth century in Britain, but in Ireland came up constantly against the vested interest of the Ascendancy in legalized intolerance. In the Irish context,

therefore, emancipation was a political issue rather than a religious one, for the extension to Catholics of the franchise would threaten Protestant control. King George III regarded the whole process of emancipation as reeking of revolutionary French Jacobinism, and his attitude was not peculiar to him. There were isolated reform moves before 1789. In June 1772 Catholics were permitted to take leases of BOGLAND on more generous terms, and in 1774 it was made possible for Catholics to take the Oath of Allegiance to the crown, but this should be seen in the context of the generous concessions made to Catholics in Canada through the QUEBEC ACT of the same year. Essentially, legislation favouring Catholics was forced out of WESTMINSTER, and the PATRIOT aspect of GRATTAN'S PARLIAMENT in Ireland from the 1780s showed no great enthusiasm to legislate for their fellow Irish. There were concessions over the leasing and inheritance of land in 1778 in Luke Gardiner's Act, but all this early emancipatory legislation was given renewed impetus with the advent of Grattan's Parliament. Not because the members of that Parliament were necessarily emancipationists, but because in the atmosphere of renewed expectation that the Parliament symbolized, pro-repeal and pro-emancipation extra-parliamentary agitation developed, particularly through the VOLUNTEER movement. In May 1782 Catholics were allowed to purchase and inherit freehold land outside parliamentary boroughs, and in July were permitted to become schoolmasters and to possess riding horses worth more than £5. The need to pacify Catholic opinion deepened. From April 1791 they were to be permitted to practise law, and Langrishe's Act permitted them to become barristers and solicitors. HOBART'S ACT of April 1793, it has been said, 'fundamentally altered power relationships in Ireland' and despite concerted efforts against it, gave to Catholics the right to bear arms, to attend TRINITY COLLEGE, and to enter the British administration's civil service and conceded a parliamentary franchise. Thereafter reaction set in. The MILITIA ACT was interpreted as an anti-Catholic measure because it was clearly intended to weaken the militant Volunteer movement, and in 1795 Grattan's proposals for further reform were defeated, a defeat that encompassed the downfall of the sympathetic LORD LIEU-TENANT, FITZWILLIAM. The approach of UNION of the British and Irish Parliaments, effective in 1801, left the Irish Catholics entitled to vote (by the 1793 Act) if they had forty-shilling (£2) freeholds or more, but without the right to be represented by Catholic MPs. Half a battle had been won, largely due to organized agitation beyond the Irish House of Commons.

Emancipation of Catholics After the Union of 1801

All future moves to liberate Irish Catholics further would come from the Parliament at WESTMINSTER where 100 Irish MPs – none of them Catholics – sat. It was to be a major struggle leading to the significant legislation of 1829. A petition on behalf of the Catholics was presented to Parliament in March 1805 and debated in the Commons. Debate and dispute over Catholic presence in the army led to the downfall of Lord Grenville's government in March 1807, and the consequent General Election was concerned with, and dominated by, anti-Catholic rhetoric. In the ensuing vacuum, extra-parliamentary agitation increased. GRATTAN's motion for emancipation in 1813 was thrown out of the Commons, as happened again in 1817 and in 1819. The first positive development came in 1825, when the radical Sir Francis Burdett introduced a bill which would give parliamentary representation but disenfranchise the FORTY-SHILLING FREEHOLDERS who had been given the vote in 1793. Parliament decided against the legislation, and Prime Minister Canning, who favoured it, died, and was replaced by the anti-emancipation Duke of Wellington. Burdett tried again in May 1828 and won support in the Commons, only to be defeated – as before – by the entrenched hostility of the House of Lords. From London, discontent in Ireland looked ominously like impending rebellion. The fear of such rebellion induced Wellington to support PEEL's measure of March 1829 which passed into

law as the Act for the Relief of His Majesty's Roman Catholic Subjects, thus opening up the posts of Parliament and government officers to Catholics. At the same time, taking up Burdett's earlier proposals, it raised the franchise qualification from forty shillings to £10. Many Irish Catholics saw this as retribution, on the one hand giving them the right to be represented by co-religionists in parliament, while on the other, depriving the majority of them of their right to vote. It cut the county electorate from 216,000 to 37,000, and the heavily Protestant boroughs remained untouched by the legislation.

Emerald Isle

This commonplace and whimsical euphemism for Ireland was first coined by William Drennan, a BELFAST UNITED IRISHMAN, in his *Fugitive Pieces* (1790–1800). Drennan was a militant revolutionary, enthusiastic supporter of the revolution in France and the execution of the French king, but also a somewhat elitist Protestant.

Emigration

Emigration to British colonies from Ireland was a feature of Irish life on a significant scale from the eighteenth century, though it had an earlier origin. There was connection with America in the early and mid-seventeenth century, and some enforced emigration in the wake of the suppression of the IRISH REBELLION of 1641–53. Land hunger and sectarian violence in the eighteenth century made emigration an inviting proposition, particularly in ULSTER, from which sometimes entire communities removed themselves and set up again across the Atlantic. Trading ships operating out of American ports returned home with cargoes of emigrants, and the place of disembarkation often dictated the areas of Irish settlement. Between 1770 and 1774 it has been estimated that some 30,000 persons arrived in America, and by 1790 that there were some 450,000 Irish there of whom at least 300,000 originated in Ulster. But emigration from all parts of Ireland was a common phenomenon, and it was very mixed in terms of religious background. Between 1815 and 1845 between 1 and 1½ million emigrated from Ireland, and between 1845 (at the height of the FAMINE) and 1870 a further 3 million persons in all. The traffic was not all one way, and the development of important settlements of the 'Irish overseas' had an impact on the 'old country' in two important ways. Firstly, it has been estimated that between 1848 and 1864 Irish-Americans remitted to dependents in Ireland in excess of £13 million, a feature of the continuing familial links across the Atlantic. Secondly, the 'nationalist' and emotive links remained. Irish-American revolutionary organizations dedicated to getting the British out of Ireland supported, and continue to support, PHYSICAL FORCE struggles to that end. They backed the mainland DYNAMITE WAR of the 1880s, and provided funds to arm the IRISH VOLUNTEERS of the pre-EASTER RISING period. The majority of nationalists in Ireland regarded emigration as an obscenity and a weakening of Ireland, but this was largely a response to deliberate landlord emigration policies whereby surplus people were given financial inducements to leave Ireland. It was a policy that suited government, too, because it alleviated pressure on the land and permitted consolidation of farms from abandoned holdings to proceed. The 'Tuke Committee' of March 1882 expended £70,000 charitably raised to send 9,500 emigrants to America.

Emmet, Thomas (1764–1827)

Emmet, born in County Cork and educated at TRINITY COLLEGE, represented the UNITED IRISHMEN leadership in the trials of 1793/4. He subsequently joined the movement and was secretary to its Supreme Council, being arrested in 1798 on the eve of the uprising organized by the movement. Exiled, Emmet spent time in France seeking to arouse French enthusiasm for support of a rising, and his failure to do so seems to have disillusioned him. He settled in America and pursued a career in law and was Attorney-General for New York in 1812.

Emmet Monument Association

The Association was the direct forerunner of the revolutionary FENIAN movement, and was founded in 1853 in New York by JOHN O'MAHONY as a deliberately military organization dedicated to Irish independence. In its title it looked back to the example of the EMMET REBELLION of 1803. By 1859 the Association had been transformed into the Fenian Brotherhood.

Emmet's Rebellion

Robert Emmet (1778–1803) was involved in the revolutionary republican UNITED IRISHMEN movement of the 1790s, and after the failure of the 1798 rising, was prominent in efforts to try to arouse French support for a further rising, being present in Paris in 1800 and in negotiation with Napoleon. He had links, also, with revolutionary organizations in England (see UNITED ENGLISHMEN). Emmet's rising, when it came, on 23 July 1803, was an abject failure. With Michael Quigley and Thomas Russell, both former United Irishmen, he proposed to seize DUBLIN CASTLE and barracks in the city, and to proclaim a provisional government, confidently expecting a French invasion in support, although it must be said that Emmet had doubts about that. His men were poorly armed, possessing mostly pikes, and expecting to arm themselves with muskets from captured stores. Support from outside Dublin melted away, and the rising began with 80 men. The Lord Chief Justice was assassinated in a chance encounter in the streets, and there was some fighting near Maynooth in County Kildare, but the Dublin action, centred upon Thomas Street, petered out and Emmet fled to the Dublin mountains where he was captured on 25 August. He was tried, hanged and beheaded, and Russell likewise. The government seem also to have executed a wholly innocent man, John Killen, for the specific charge of murder. Between 2,000 and 3,000 were arrested in the wake of the rising and interned. Emmet's rebellion marked the end of what was left of the United Irishmen, but inspired later generations of revolutionaries, particularly PADRAIC

PEARSE who rescued the rebellion from historical neglect and advocated it as an example to his generation.

Encouraging Protestant Strangers in Ireland, Act for

This Act, of 27 September 1662, was really an economic measure to encourage industry and manufactures by introducing into Ireland skilled, Protestant, craftsmen who might be Dutch, French Huguenots or English Quakers. An existing Dutch community in Dublin was expanded, and there was an increase of immigration into cities such as Cork where the newcomers developed goldsmithing. Further legislation of November 1692 threw open a million or so acres of forfeited Catholic JACOBITE land for settlement, and guaranteed toleration for various forms of Protestant worship, at the same time as extensive PENAL LAWS were being prepared against native Catholic Irish.

Encumbered Estates Act

The Encumbered Estates Act of 28 July 1849 was a landlord measure, designed specifically to assist them. Many landlords had gone into chronic debt in the wake of the agricultural depression from 1815 (the closing of the French wars) and were restricted in what they could do with their land by legal encumbrances such as mortgages. The Act established a court to facilitate sales of land, as a result of which, during the 1850s, some £20 million in lands moved from landlords to more flourishing landlords, or, as often as not, to speculators who looked for a profit from racking up the rents of the tenants. It has been estimated that by 1860 one-third of Irish land had changed hands, but for the most part, participation was beyond the reach of the tenants. The Landed Estates (Ireland) Act of August 1858 replaced the original court with a Landed Estates Court enjoying the same powers. For the peasantry, the workings of the Act led to increasing EVICTIONS in the quest for profits.

England, The Irish in

EMIGRATION into England had been a feature of Anglo-Irish contact since the Middle Ages, but emigration en masse became a consequence of declining employment in Ireland and the expansion of the manufacturing industries in England. The Irish tended to concentrate in expanding towns such as Manchester, Bolton, and Macclesfield, and there was a major community in Glasgow. Harvest failures, land-hunger and the FAMINE of the 1840s increased the flow. The government set up a Royal Commission to look into the problem of the Irish poor in 1836, and the 1841 census revealed an immigrant population of 419,000 which by 1851 had risen to 730,000. Alongside this, were the seasonal migrant workers who worked in the harvest fields, returning to Ireland at the end of the season. The success of the Industrial Revolution in Great Britain owed a good deal to this reservoir of manpower, and the developments in canal and railway construction depended upon the Irish navvies. The presence of Irish emigrants in Britain facilitated the spread of revolutionary UNITED IRISHMEN doctrines into England in the 1790s and there were corresponding radical groupings such as the UNITED BRITONS which were largely, though not exclusively, Irish in membership. Curiously, concerted nationalist enthusiasm came from emigrants to America rather than to England, but in England the Irish were, and long remained, a poverty-stricken working class.

English Civil Wars, The

The English Civil Wars were fought between 1642 and 1651, and, like the concurrent IRISH REBELLION of 1641–53, were marked by political realignments. The first civil war, which ended in 1646, was fought between the royalist supporters of King Charles I and his Parliament, aided by the Scots PRESBYTERIANS. But in 1648, when the next fighting broke out, the royalists and Presbyterians were allied against the Parliament, and such was the case in the fighting of 1650/1. 'The English Civil Wars' is in a sense a misnomer: fighting spread throughout

Wales and Scotland, and had its reactions in American colonies, whilst in Ireland the success of the rebels of 1641 in maintaining their struggle against the English government was facilitated by civil war divisions within the government forces opposed to them, the royalist element and that which looked to Parliament in London. It is arguable that the English Civil Wars were precipitated by the Irish Rebellion in 1641, and it is certainly true that that rebellion led Parliament to arrogate powers to itself that were a direct infringement of the royal prerogative. Historians debate precisely how far King Charles I was implicated, if at all, in the genesis of the Irish Rebellion, whilst it is true that the rebels themselves repeatedly asserted their loyalty to him and, ultimately, ended up allied to royalists against the king's enemies. The NEW MODEL ARMY which defeated Charles I was brought in to Ireland to deal with the rebellion in 1649 and did so with a thoroughness and savagery that left its mark. The Army was as much a religious as it was a political weapon. Consideration of the English Civil Wars requires awareness of the important Irish dimension, which made it rather a War of Three Kingdoms.

English Interest, The

The English interest can be defined only in relation to circumstances in Ireland. For most of the seventeenth century, the English interest was to impose stability and enforce ANGLICIZATION and PLAN-TATION to reduce Ireland to the state of political and economic dependency that would best safeguard England's interests. From the accession of King WILLIAM III and the consequent overthrow of the Catholic and JACOBITE cause by 1691, the English interest must be seen in relation not to the native Catholic Irish (amongst whom must be grouped the disinherited and expropriated Catholic OLD ENGLISH), but to the Protestant ASCENDANCY rooted in NEW ENGLISH settlement which increasingly took it upon itself to identify with 'Irishness' and a form of nationalism. The English interest in contrast to the 'Irish' may be exemplified by Hugh Boulter, bishop of Bristol (d. 1742), who became Primate of all Ireland and archbishop of Armagh in 1724. He controlled enormous influence and patronage, and dominated the Irish House of Lords, where he followed a consistent policy of subordinating the interests of the colony in Ireland to those of the English (and, since the Union with Scotland) British government. This explicit tendency to regard Ireland as a subsidiary of Britain, a colony like the colony in America, helped to create the reaction of the PATRIOTS in the Irish House of Commons which reached its triumph in GRATTAN'S PARLIAMENT, but which itself gave way to a re-assertion of the British interest in the UNION of the Parliaments of 1801. Briefly, if the Catholic Irish identified the Protestant Ascendancy as an alien dominant power block, that Ascendancy identified threats to itself not in terms of dispossessed and disenfranchised Catholics, but in terms of the pretensions to dominance of the British government in London.

Ensignmen

The Ensignmen were a specific category of persons entitled to consideration in respect of forfeited Irish lands, under the terms of reference of the Act of SETTLEMENT of 1662. They were those who had been in the service of King Charles II in Europe. Few applied.

Everard, Sir John (d. 1624)

Everard, for a brief moment in 1613, symbolized the Catholic OLD ENGLISH interest that the government in England had resolved to crush in terms of its political influence in Ireland. The Parliament that met in Dublin in 1613 was, by the creation of new boroughs particularly in ULSTER, weighted in favour of the NEW ENGLISH Planter interest, returning 132 Protestant MPs to 100 Catholics, who had previously controlled the House of Commons. The Catholic members selected Everard as their Speaker whilst the Protestants busily deliberated to appoint Sir JOHN DAVIES. Everard was seated in the Speaker's chair when the Protestants forcefully dumped Davies onto his lap. A fight ensued and Everard was obliged to quit the chamber, taking the Catholic

MPs with him who refused to sit further, thus nullifying the Parliament entirely.

Evictions

Evictions of tenants by landlords took two distinct forms, the official and the unofficial. In the case of the official, the CONSTABULARY (later the ROYAL IRISH CONSTABULARY) was present, and kept records of ejectments, as evictions were also termed. The deliberate destruction of small landholdings in the period following 1815 to make possible both larger farms and pasture farms, gathered impetus in the years of the FAMINE and its aftermath. Official police records show that they were present at the ejectment of 13,384 families in 1849; some 14,500 in 1850, and 8,800 in 1851. Between 1849 and 1867 some 558,000 individuals were evicted, representing 109,500 families. Evictions where no police presence was requested may have amounted to a further ½–1 million individuals. Landlords were supposed to give 48 hours warning of impending evictions to POOR LAW Guardians, and were forbidden to evict on Christmas Day or at Easter. The DERRYVEAGH case, when 47 families were ejected in one go by a single landlord in 1861 became a notorious example of the dreadful business.

Explanation, Act of

The Act of Explanation of 23 December 1665 followed upon the Act of SETTLEMENT of July 1662, which had sought to deal equitably with the claims of expropriated Irish landowners and tenants who had been forced from their property in the 1650s after the suppression of the IRISH REBELLION. One of the categories of persons to be heard under the 1662 Act were the 'innocents', those who had taken no part in armed insurrection, and the Act of Explanation served to confirm all decrees of innocency henceforth issued, whilst barring the hearing of further claims. The Act also required soldiers and ADVENTURERS to yield up one-third of their holdings to compensate civilian settlers who had lost land to meet the demands of claimants under the Act of Settlement.

F

Famine of 1845–49 (*see also* POTATO BLIGHT; FAMINE, Remedies for)

Agricultural disruption following the ending of the French wars in 1815 was felt in Britain as well as in Ireland, but in Ireland the impact was the more severe for the marginal nature and way of life of the vast majority of country people, the Irish Catholic peasantry, labourers and smallholders. Between 1816 and 1842 there were at least 14 partial failures of the potato crop, the staple element of the peasantry's diet, with consequent high death rates. In the famine of 1845–49, between 1 and 1½ million people died, either from starvation, or from cholera and other famine-related diseases. Death from fever was most severe in April 1847, with 2,500 deaths recorded in the workhouses (see POOR LAW) in one week. A particularly vicious winter in 1846/7 exacerbated the situation. The British attitude to the famine was mixed. There were, for example, increasing outbreaks of anti-Irish feeling in England, the proliferation of racist diatribes and caricatures of the Irish, redolent of the contempt often manifested in the seventeenth century. Intellectual British opinion tended to the view that the famine was the product of Irish fecklessness, and that it was entirely their own fault, an attitude which influenced the role British government played in alleviation. With remarkable restraint, the government allowed itself to be diverted from too radical an intervention, and its chief famine administrator, CHARLES TREVELYAN, saw the famine as a justification of the Malthusian doctrines of population. Much relief work fell to private initiative, of which there was plenty, although some Protestant relief organizations tied conversion from Catholicism to their charitable work. The Quakers were a notable exception to a rule that long rankled in the Irish memory. The failure of the potato crop was reported to the government by the LORD LIEUTENANT in October 1845, and in that same month DANIEL O'CONNELL made strenuous representations to the Lord Lieutenant that action must be taken. Every estimate reckoned that only three-eighths of the total crop would be available for consumption in November. The Irish were aware, however, of the sustained export of grain from their country, and saw in its retention and distribution a means of feeding people. That was why several people were shot dead in County Cork in 1846 when they tried to prevent a grain ship from sailing. Historians have chosen to dismiss the Irish nationalist view that the famine was engineered as policy by Britain to rid Ireland of surplus mouths, but it is certain that British relief efforts were inadequate and often callously indifferent, and the decline in population whether by death or EMIGRATION certainly would have been seen as economically beneficial, by landlords as well as by the government.

Famine of 1845–49, Remedies for

Prime Minister Lord John Russell admitted in October 1846 that 'we cannot feed the people'. The first outside effort happened in America, where a relief meeting was held in Philadelphia in November 1845. Three days later, on 20 November, a British government Relief Commission met. In February of 1846 POOR LAW commissioners refused to act in view of the fact that the structure of the Poor Law in Ireland was not fitted to cope with such an emergency, being workhouse and indoor-relief based, whereas the emergency required outdoor-relief measures. Overall direction of relief efforts was passed to the economically doctrinaire CHARLES TREVELYAN, Under Secretary of the Treasury in London, and in March 1846 a Board of Works was set up to administer relief in the countryside, and a Temporary Fever Act required Poor Law Guardians to establish hospitals, but this measure lapsed in August of the same year. ROBERT PEEL had acquired quantities of Indian maize in 1845 on the eve of the famine for relief purposes, and in May 1846 the depots in Ireland began to release this onto the market, but Trevelyan ordered the closure of the depots in August 1846 and the cessation in public works in face of increasing disease. The Poor Employment (Ireland) Act of that same month made Treasury loans available to fund public works (state- or council-funded projects), the loans to be repaid by the districts in which they were expended, in time. The £50,000 advanced was compared by Catholics with the millions poured into the emancipation of slaves in the West Indies, and drew unavoidable conclusions. By November 1846 some 300,000 were employed in public works programmes, and the Quakers' Central Relief Committee was at work in the countryside. At the end of 1846 food stores were made available at current market prices, which were beyond the pockets of the poor. The British Association for the Relief of Extreme Distress in Ireland was formed early in 1847, and as a fund-raising body, accrued £500,000 in aid. Prime Minister Russell (Peel had resigned in June 1846) took some remedial steps. Corn import duties were suspended for the period from January to September in the hope that the potato crop would recover in the autumn, and in February the Soup Kitchens Act (the Destitute Poor (Ireland) Act) made outdoor relief, at last, a reality. The Act lapsed in September, and further funding for relief was to be met from local rates. The Soup Kitchens disappeared in October 1847. In face of continuing distress, Trevelyan developed a rate-in-aid scheme whereby prosperous Poor Law Unions would subsidize those in distressed areas of the country and a further £100,000 was advanced by the government. The Chief Commissioner of the Poor Law in Ireland resigned in protest at the measure. In point of fact the famine eventually ran its course, remedial measures, such as they were, neither speeding up that process nor particularly softening it.

Famine Fever

Famine fever was typhus, which raged in epidemic alongside the FAMINE of 1845–49, the disease being carried by lice. Typhus spread beyond the areas of worst famine conditions as the wandering poor carried it with them. Precise mortality figures cannot be arrived at, but it is believed that typhus was a major contributory factor to the deaths of the famine years.

Famines

The Great FAMINE of 1845–49 was no isolated occurrence (see also YEAR OF SLAUGHTER). There were severe food shortages in Ireland in 1728/9, 1740/1, 1744/5 and 1756/7 that were part and parcel of periods of dearth throughout western Europe. In that of 1740/1 some 400,000 people died after the rigours of the savage winter of 1739/40. In August 1816 the potato crop failed and widespread famine followed, the worst since 1741, coupled with a spread of typhus (see FAMINE FEVER). Some 50,000 died between 1817 and 1819. Famine conditions prevailed in 1822 as well, followed by an outbreak of typhus that lasted until December of that year.

Féiritéir, Piras/Piaras (d. 1653)

Féiritéir, his name Gaelicized from Piers Ferriter, is an example of an OLD ENGLISH settler gone native, a process which the NEW ENGLISH of the PLANTATION period and the English in general affected to despise. He was born in County Kerry and became an accomplished and venerated poet in the Gaelic language, with a profound Catholicism that led him into political commitment. He joined the CATHOLIC CONFEDERACY after the outbreak of the IRISH REBELLION in 1641 and served as a commander throughout the wars, until his capture in 1653 when he was peremptorily and, it is said, treacherously, hanged by government troops.

Fenians/Fenian Brotherhood

Historiographically the Fenians tend to be synonymous with the IRISH REPUBLICAN BROTHERHOOD, but the origin of the Fenian revolutionary PHYSICAL FORCE movement seems to be much earlier. The first 'Fenian' military action may have been the attack on 16 August 1849 on the Cappoquin Police Barracks directed by FINTAN LALOR. That would certainly tie in the movement with the YOUNG IRELANDERS whose revolt in 1848 had been overcome. The name 'Fenian' for an already existing, if tenuous, movement was applied by JOHN O'MAHONY, along with formal foundation in New York in 1859, and alludes to the Fianna army of the medieval Irish hero Fionn Mac Cuchail. The Fenians were a military revolutionary republican movement, started in 1849 or 1859, dedicated to driving the British out of Ireland. There were links with the Catholic RIBBONMEN. Research has shown that the membership was middle class, consisting of farmers, shopkeepers, artisans and, to a large extent, schoolteachers, and was both rural and urban based, but with a developing emphasis in towns. JAMES STEPHENS established them in Dublin at the same time as the American foundation. There is an added difficulty in that the term 'Fenian' came to have a generic meaning and was often applied to nationalists otherwise unconnected with the Brotherhood proper. James Stephens became the most prominent leader of the movement, strenuously advocating revolt and becoming head centre or leader by May 1866. The Fenian invasions of Canada mounted from America showed the strength and resolution of the Irish-American movement, but Stephens twice postponed military insurrection in Ireland, leading to his deposition as head centre in December 1866. The rising of 1867 (see SIXTY-SEVEN, the) was promoted by Colonel Thomas Kelly, and in fact represented only a part of the Fenian movement. After its collapse, the Fenian movement was soon reorganized, in or before 1873, but on a less doctrinaire physical force basis. O'DONOVAN ROSSA was head centre of the movement in 1877, but it seems to have been more a spirit to conjure with than anything else.

Feuds and Faction Fights

The feud was endemic in Irish peasant society, rarely, if ever, rising above localized differences and grievances to become a politicized force comparable to the WHITEBOYS, for example. An exception may be made for the feud of the CARAVATS AND SHANAVESTS of the early nineteenth century, where there appears to have been, on one side at least, some revolutionary associations connected with the UNITED IRISHMEN movement and its rebellion of 1798. Historians cannot ascribe a beginning to the feuds and faction fights, which spread in scale and intensity as the eighteenth century wore on, and seemed always to be rooted, or to have their first cause, in individual rivalries or inter-family disputes. Religious sectarianism played no part, for Catholicism was the religion of both sides. Fairs and suchlike public gatherings were the often-chosen battlegrounds, where pitched fights were expected and frequently took place between hundreds of men and women. Membership of one side or of the other seems to have been determined by place of habitation or kinship links. The 'battle' at BALLYVEIGH STRAND fought in 1834 was the most spectacular outbreak of the feuding phenomenon, involving several thousand combatants and causing hundreds of casualties, many fatal. County Donegal was disrupted for a long time by the dispute between the Gallaghers and the McGettigans. The feud, at least on the grand scale, died away as the nineteenth century moved on, probably due to the intensive rural disruption of the FAMINE, EMIGRATION and EVICTIONS and consequent dispersal of populations.

Firm, The

The 'Firm' was an expression used by its members, to refer to the IRISH REPUBLICAN BROTHERHOOD, the movement which dominated Irish revolutionary activism between the 1860s and 1916.

First World War (1914–18), The

The outbreak of the First World War in August 1914 had an immediate impact upon Ireland in that it caused the deferring of HOME RULE legislation that was ready for enactment. The Irish nationalist leadership, primarily in the person of REDMOND, recognized the emergency and concurred in it, and committed Ireland to support of the British war effort. That support split the IRISH VOLUNTEER movement, and demonstrated how far removed constitutional nationalism was from the widespread republicanism which had mistrusted Home Rule with its in-built PARTITION of Ireland to preserve a Unionist minority in ULSTER. Thousands of Irishmen did volunteer for the British army: the Protestant Ulster VOLUNTEER FORCE, raised to defend the UNION with Britain, was virtually shot to pieces as the 36th (Ulster) Division on 1 July 1916 at the Somme. But conscription was withheld from Ireland, where JAMES CONNOLLY had established the Irish Neutrality League in September 1914. Germany saw in the encouragement of Irish national aspirations, a means of extending its war against Britain, but apart from supplying firearms to the Irish Volunteers, did very little else. But on 9 April 1918 Lloyd George introduced the Irish Military Service Bill to bring conscription into Ireland which became law on 18 April. The Home Rule MPs withdrew from the Commons in protest at this step. Having done as much as anyone to persuade Irishmen to volunteer, they were aware of the discontent the measure would create. On 23 April a national one-day strike took effect (except in Ulster) to protest at the law and to register opposition. Anti-conscription pledges were drafted by DE VALERA and distributed. LORD LIEUTENANT Viscount French made it known that 50,000 Irishmen were required immediately to make good the wastage in the Irish divisions at the front, and then some 3,000 a month would be needed to maintain numbers. Ernest Blythe of the IRISH REPUBLICAN BROTHERHOOD denounced conscription as a 'crime against us', but the end of the war in November 1918 averted potentially serious unrest over that issue.

FitzGerald, Lord Edward (1763–98)

Lord Edward FitzGerald was a younger son of a former LORD DEPUTY of Ireland, James duke of Leinster (d. 1773). Lord Edward served in the British army during the AMERICAN WAR FOR INDEPENDENCE, and then sat as an MP in the Irish House of Commons in association with the PATRIOT interest. In 1792 he was dismissed from the army after a visit to revolutionary leaders in France, where his democratic principles were broadened, and he came to believe in the possibility of French help for a revolution in Ireland. He joined the UNITED IRISHMEN republican movement in 1796, apparently persuaded that French backing for them was a strong probability, after further negotiations on his own part or on behalf of the DEFENDERS, a Catholic resistance movement with which he appears to have been associated. In the 1798 rising he was betrayed to the authorities by Francis Magan, and mortally wounded during the attempt to arrest him on 19 May. He died on 4 June 1798.

FitzGibbon, John (1749–1802)

FitzGibbon was perhaps the most powerful ASCENDANCY politician to emerge in the decades leading up to the UNION of Britain and Ireland of 1801. FitzGibbon was born in Ireland and educated at TRINITY COLLEGE DUBLIN and at Oxford. By 1783 he was Attorney-General in Ireland with a flourishing legal practice of his own, in which year he abandoned his PATRIOT politics and sat as MP for Kilmallock in the Irish Commons as a government man and supporter of the British administration. He was appointed Lord Chancellor in 1789, a post he held until 1801, and was, successively, Viscount FitzGibbon (1793) and Earl of Clare (1795) and entered the British House of Lords after the Union. A bitter opponent of Catholic EMANCIPATION, he pushed through repressive legislation aimed at the widespread WHITEBOY agrarian movement, and became the leading pro-Union politician in Ireland in the 1790s. He has been credited with single-handedly forcing Union through the Irish House of Commons by adroit manipulation of patronage and purchase of votes.

FitzWilliam, William Wentworth 2nd Earl of (1748–1833)

Earl FitzWilliam inherited substantial Irish estates in County Wicklow in 1782. In July 1794 a political alliance of Tories and Whigs in Britain led to his appointment on 4 January 1795 as LORD LIEUTEN-ANT of Ireland. He came into office amidst high expectations based upon his favourable attitude to Catholic EMANCIPA-TION. But FitzWilliam moved too fast in the matter, alienating the powerful ASCENDANCY grouping in the IRISH CABI-NET by selective dismissals, and seeking to increase Whig power. His motive seems to have been a profound suspicion that unless emancipation was carried through, Ireland would be faced with massive unrest and rebellion, a fear that proved wholly justified in 1798. But the political reaction against him was so ferocious that he was dismissed from the Lieutenancy on 23 February 1795 after barely seven weeks in the office.

Fleetwood, Charles (1618–92)

Fleetwood was Lieutenant-General of cavalry under OLIVER CROMWELL in 1650, having risen in the ranks of the parliamentarian forces during the ENGLISH CIVIL WAR. His reputation as a religious Independent (one opposed to state-directed religion and favouring separate congregations united by a shared, Protestant, belief) and bitter antagonist of Catholics was well established by the time he was appointed Commander-in-Chief in Ireland in 1652 in succession to IRETON whose widow, Cromwell's eldest daughter, he married. From 1654 to 1657 he was LORD DEPUTY in Ireland, and under him the land re-settlement and expropriation of Catholic landholders was at its height, although his excessive favour towards Baptists led to his recall to London.

Flight of the Earls of 1607

On 4 September 1607, in a ship arranged by Cuconnacht Maguire, 99 persons including Hugh O'Neill, Earl of TYRONE and Rory O'Donnell left Lough Swilly in County Donegal for exile in France. Their departure, self-imposed but probably depriving the English government of an opportunity to degrade them anyway, marked the end of Gaelic ULSTER. Tyrone's earlier rebellion had come to an end in 1603 at the Treaty of MELLIFONT, which opened the way to full-scale imposition of English administration in the province of Ulster but theoretically endorsed Tyrone's authority there in his capacity as an earl, rather than as a great Gaelic chieftain. It seems improbable, given the extensive land expropriation programme involved in PLANTATION, administered by the English government, that Tyrone and his allies would have been left alone for very long. In the interests of the English, it would be better if they were gone. Consequently, the administration in Ireland encouraged rivalries within Ulster, such as that between Tyrone and Donal O'Cahan, and that between Rory O'Donnell, 1st Earl of Tyrconnell, and Sir Niall Garbh O'Donnell. The extent to which these rivalries within Ulster had come to develop into a conspiracy by Tyrone and his supporters to reassert their independence is debatable. It does seem that Rory O'Donnell entered into negotiations for Spanish military help, and upon the death of MOUNTJOY the LORD LIEUTENANT in 1606, Tyrone moved against O'Cahan. O'Cahan, Tyrone's son-in-law, had the official backing of Sir JOHN DAVIES, the virulent advocate of Plantation and the reduction of Ulster to the status of the other Irish provinces, headed by a government-appointed President. Davies may have led O'Cahan to believe that his own power in the DERRY area would be maintained by the English at his father-in-law's expense. Tyrone by-passed Davies and the Dublin authorities and had his dispute with O'Cahan referred to London, hoping to trade upon the good relations he enjoyed with King James I. In the meantime Rory O'Donnell and Cuconnacht Maguire pursued their own plans to go over into Europe to serve the Spanish crown. Those plans were viewed by the English authorities as a general conspiracy to elicit foreign, Spanish help for a rising to be headed by Tyrone. The choice confronting the Earl of Tyrone was therefore one of either remaining in Ulster and enduring whatever should befall, conscious of the implacable hostility of the authorities in Dublin, or taking the risk of flight. He opted for flight, to the delight of Davies and his associates. In December Tyrone was declared a traitor and his property forfeited to the crown. In 1613 the Irish Parliament attainted him and confirmed royal title to the lands in Ulster. As for O'Cahan, the pliant tool of the English politicians, he was arrested and imprisoned until his death in 1626. The same fate befell Sir Niall Garbh O'Donnell, the government-backed rival of Rory O'Donnell, Earl of Tyrconnell. Neither Tyrconnell nor Tyrone ever returned to Ireland.

Flood, Henry (1732–91)

Flood was the bastard son of a prominent ASCENDANCY lawyer, was educated at TRINITY COLLEGE and Oxford, and first sat in the Irish House of Commons in 1759 as MP for Kilkenny. His personal affluence was based upon a successful marriage, and his political career upon a curious mixture of PATRIOT values and rivalry with the great Patriot leader, HENRY GRATTAN. He identified closely with Irish interests, as far as they were consistent with the interests of the Protestant Ascendancy, as early as 1773 when he advocated a tax on absentee landlords who were held responsible for draining money out of the country and offering no return. He joined the VOLUNTEER movement and served as an officer, but between 1775 and 1781 was a 'government' man in respect of his office of Vice-Treasurer in Ireland. His acceptance of government office in 1775 opened the way for Grattan to assume the role of foremost orator of the Patriot interest, and the rivalry between the two men was expressed in their differing views on Catholic EMANCIPATION, which Flood opposed, and the function of the Volunteer movement which Flood wished to see maintained. He represented two constituencies, sitting for Kilbeggan in the Irish House of Commons and, from 1783, for Winchester in the Parliament in London, whilst at the same time proving himself able to reaffirm his Patriot principles at the expense of Grattan. This was seen particularly in the repeal of the long-resented DECLARATORY ACT when Flood moved for a subsequent renunciation by the British Parliament of its right to legislate in the future for Ireland, a crucial legislative move that made the repeal more effective. In 1783 Flood, a competent duellist, came close to shooting it out with Grattan. The latter benefited politically from Flood's death in 1791.

Flying Columns

The WAR FOR INDEPENDENCE waged between the IRISH REPUBLICAN ARMY and the British government from 1919 until the ANGLO-IRISH TREATY of 1921 was an uneven struggle. To prosecute it successfully, the IRA had to resort to sustained guerrilla warfare, the most effective element in which was the highly mobile, lightly armed, disciplined 'flying column'. The most famous of them was that commanded by Tom Barry of the 3rd West Cork Brigade of the IRA, which wiped out a force of AUXILIARIES on 28 November 1920, at Kilmichael, County Cork.

Fortescue, Chichester (1823–98)

Fortescue (or Parkinson-Fortescue as he chose to be known from 1862) played an influential part in the development of LAND LEGISLATION under GLADSTONE. He served as CHIEF SECRETARY for Ireland in 1865/6 and again 1868–70. During this second term he proposed that the tenant right known as ULSTER CUSTOM be given legislative status, in the process of general legislative entitlement to compensation for tenants at EVICTION. He was also instrumental in the carrying through of the DISESTABLISHMENT of the CHURCH OF IRELAND. After taking a seat in the House of Lords as Lord Carlingford in 1874, he was involved in further land legislation in co-operation with Gladstone.

Forty-Shilling Freeholders, The

For a brief time between their enfranchisement in 1793 and their loss of the vote in 1829, the forty-shilling freeholders of Ireland, almost wholly Catholic, exercised political influence in their own country. They were those who, because the value of their holdings was estimated at forty shillings (£2), clear of rent, were arguably possessed of an 'interest' in their holdings. The franchise continued to have a property qualification in the eighteenth century. Their winning of the franchise was a concession to massive extra-parliamentary Catholic agitation, but in view of the fact that Catholics could not sit as MPs, the enfranchised freeholders had to cast their votes according to what they perceived to be the potential of candidates united by a common Protestantism. WOLFE TONE, one of the active leaders of the UNITED IRISHMEN republican movement, castigated the forty-shilling freeholders as 'the wretched tribe' who were 'driven to their octennial market (see OCTENNIAL ACT) by their landlords', a view that was not confined to impatient revolutionaries such as Tone. Theoretically the forty-shilling voters were at the mercy of their landlords, as were most tenants in Britain before the introduction of secret ballots. And, in Ireland, there was a definite proclivity amongst landlords to EVICT and dispossess tenants. But that said, and despite the fact that DANIEL O'CONNELL regarded them as landlord dominated, the forty-shilling voters united to break the ASCENDANCY hold in the Waterford election of 1826 when they turned out to vote for a strong pro-EMANCIPATION Protestant candidate, Henry Villiers Stuart. In 1828 they returned O'Connell himself as MP for Clare on 5 July, although O'Connell as a Catholic was barred from sitting in the House of Commons. The 1829 Emancipation Act, which permitted Catholics to take up seats in Parliament, at the same time broke the power of the forty-shilling voters, who had demonstrated they were capable of making their votes count after all, by increasing the franchise requirement to £10 and thus making the reforms of that year a two-edged weapon.

Foster's Corn Law

Foster's Corn Law of 14 July 1784 took its name from the Chancellor of the Irish Exchequer, John Foster (d. 1828), who in 1785 until the passage of the UNION, served as Speaker of the Irish House of Commons. The Corn Law was a vital legislative step in the policy of GRATTAN'S PARLIAMENT to encourage agriculture with expansion of arable and reclamation of waste lands. It imposed a sliding scale on grain prices, providing for subsidies to facilitate export at times of low prices, and prohibiting exports when the prices were high, a mechanism for which Foster had campaigned since the early 1770s. Historians see the Corn Law of 1784 as a prime example of PATRIOT policies pursued by the Irish PARLIAMENT consequent upon the repeal of the limiting DECLARATORY ACT of 1720.

Four Courts, The

The building in Dublin known as the Four Courts was built by James Gandon (d. 1820) to house the four courts of law, the courts of Chancery, King's (or Upper) Bench, Common Pleas and the Exchequer. Erected prior to the rising of the UNITED IRISHMEN in 1798, it had been seen as the manifestation of Protestant ASCENDANCY self-confidence. The building's strongest associations, however, arose from its being chosen as a strongpoint by IRISH REPUBLICAN ARMY troops opposed to the ANGLO-IRISH TREATY of 1921, who seized the building under the command of Rory O'Connor on the outbreak of the Irish Civil War of 1922.

Free State, The (Saorstat Eireann)

The ANGLO-IRISH TREATY of 1921 which brought to an end the WAR FOR INDEPENDENCE raging since 1919, provided for an independent government in 26 of Ireland's 32 counties, the other SIX COUNTIES remaining within the UNION of Great Britain and (Northern) Ireland. The Irish Free State Constitution Act and Consequential Provisions Act of 5 December 1922 gave legislative authority to DÁIL ÉIREANN's constitution and the Saorstat Eireann came into being on 6 December under its first Governor-General, HEALY. Purist republicans, opposed to the PARTITION inherent in the settlement between Britain and the Free State, were fighting a war against the new Free State government. The word 'Staters' came to be applied to the IRISH REPUBLICAN ARMY forces that supported the Free State and therefore the terms of the Treaty of 1921.

Friends of the Constitution

The Friends of the Constitution were a group of MPs in the Irish House of Commons, akin to the grouping in the English House of Commons of Whigs known as the 'Friends of the People'. They were radical reformers enjoying links with the extra-parliamentary reform movement of the Catholic Committee (see CATHOLIC BOARD and also with the proto-revolutionaries of the UNITED IRISHMEN.

Frightfulness

The English parliamentarian officer and theorist, Edmund Ludlow, advocated the need for 'extraordinary severity' in suppressing the CATHOLIC CONFEDERACY which had maintained the IRISH REBELLION since 1641. Frightfulness, essentially a policy based upon vengeance, was that pursued by the authorities in DUBLIN and by the NEW MODEL ARMY under, successively, CROMWELL and IRETON, in the military campaigns to defeat Irish rebels and Irish royalists between 1649 and 1653, the year of the rebellion's end. It tacitly permitted military reprisals and attacks on the civilian population.

G

Gaelic Athletic Association

The Gaelic Athletic Association was founded in Thurles, County Tipperary under the patronage of the Catholic archbishop of CASHEL, in November 1884. That it was an athletic association, endeavouring to spread interest in ancient 'Irish' sports and at the same time discouraging those denounced as non-Irish, was apparent, but its founding body included at least four FENIANS. The archbishop withdrew his patronage within three years because of the revolutionary republican makeup in the directing council, although Fenianism had mellowed somewhat since the 1867 uprising. Even so, the police kept an eye on the Association, especially during the 1890s, as it built up numerous local branches infused with nationalism and a strong sense of Gaelic resurgence. Officers in the IRISH VOLUNTEER force, armed and potentially revolutionary, tended to be drawn from the membership of the Athletic Association.

Gaelic Irish

The Gaelic Irish were the native population of Ireland. They were distinguishable culturally and linguistically, at least in the early to mid-seventeenth century, from the OLD ENGLISH (who shared the Catholicism of the native people) and the NEW ENGLISH introduced with PLANTATION. The latter shared nothing in common with the native Irish and precious little with the Old English, certainly not religion. The Old English had imposed upon Gaelic Ireland, or most of it (ULSTER was to be the preserve of the New English) English law, county administration and social structures with more or less success, and there had been some fusion of Gaelic and English peoples and values that the New English affected to disdain. The IRISH REBELLION of 1641, in its origin a Gaelic and almost nationalist uprising coming from Ulster,

saw, by the time it had come to an end in 1653, the wholesale destruction of a Gaelic 'gentry' and 'aristocracy', who were crushed militarily, persecuted in their religious observance, and deprived of their lands in massive expropriation to facilitate English resettlement of Ireland. Thenceforth the Gaelic Irish lived, as contemporaries observed, like strangers in their own land, a deprived and poverty-stricken peasantry for the most part, suffering under the same sustained repressive legislation as did the Old English who adhered to their Catholicism. The Gaelic Irish remained as an identifiable people largely because of the PENAL LAWS and other disabling legislation against them, and also because of their maintenance of their ancient religion. The very nature of Protestant ASCENDANCY power treated the Gaelic Irish as a race apart: a cultural, linguistic, religious and racial apartheid was enforced against them, but was counterproductive in that, under those restraints, Gaelicism survived and asserted itself, sometimes through agrarian unrest and sometimes through association with reform movements such as those led by DANIEL O'CONNELL. Resurgence of interest in Gaelic traditions and literature in the nineteenth century coincided with the development of militant nationalism and revolutionary republicanism, and not a few of the revolutionary leaders, themselves of Gaelic Irish origin, saw their struggle as a reassertion of an ancient and long-deprived people. In that political context, Old English distinctions were subsumed steadily in a gradual identification of interests, united by a common enemy, the Protestant Ascendancy and the British administration that sustained it (see also IRISH LANGUAGE).

Gaelic League (Conradh na Gaelige)

The Gaelic League was set up in July 1893 by EOIN MACNEILL and Douglas Hyde (its first President) dedicated to countering English cultural influences in Ireland by an emphasis upon the cultivation and spread of the IRISH LANGUAGE. It seems to have had a somewhat narrow, romanticized attitude to the future of Ireland, but was rapidly politicized. The Boer War which began in 1899 galvanized opinion in Ireland, and the membership of the League increased rapidly, with at least 400 branches by 1902. It was watched by the police, who noted its activism, as did the IRISH REPUBLICAN BROTHERHOOD, the revolutionary movement which began to take an interest in the League. In July 1915 at the League's annual conference or '*ard fheis*', Douglas Hyde stepped down as President in protest at revolutionary associations the League was developing, and control was taken by PADRAIC PEARSE who had edited the journal *An Claidheamh Soluis* (Sword of Light) since 1903. Pearse did not alter the purpose of the League, but rather, with MacNeill, gave it a political dimension.

Gaelic Revival *see* IRISH LANGUAGE

Gale Days

Gale days were, in Irish Gaelic society, rent-days. The term was used in Irish agriculture throughout the eighteenth and nineteenth centuries. Six months' credit in the matter of rent payments was called 'hanging-gale', for example, rents due on Lady Day (27 March) would be postponed until September, Michaelmas (29 September). The practice was also referred to as 'hanging half-year gale'.

Galloglasses/Gallowglasses (*see also* KERNS; SWORDSMEN)

The word 'galloglass' is an anglicization of the Gaelic '*galloglach*' or '*galloglaigh*' meaning, precisely, 'foreign soldier'. They were introduced into Ireland as mercenaries from north-west Scotland during the mid to late thirteenth century, to fight for various chiefs, predominantly in ULSTER. They established themselves as an hereditary fighting elite of 'picked and selected men' who chose 'rather to die

than to yield'. Their chief weapon was the formidable battle-axe (see BATTLE-AXE GUARDS), and they were heavily armoured. The English who came up against them thought them no match for concentrated musketry fire, but they were considered highly dangerous elements in a native population that was to be colonized and planted (see PLANTATION). They lived off the land, supported by a system of 'coynage and livery' which meant food for themselves and for their horses. Their last substantial fight was at the battle of KINSALE in 1601, serving under the Earl of TYRONE, who was an Ulster magnate. Thereafter, as a recognizable fighting force, they declined, and were swallowed up in the general armies of the CATHOLIC CONFEDERACY in the IRISH REBELLION of 1641–53.

Gavelkind

Gavelkind is an anglicization of the Gaelic word 'gabhailcine', and represents also an approximation of a known form of land tenure from England to a system of land tenures in native Irish society. The system of gavelkind in Ireland, which the English considered a cause of overpopulation, was officially suppressed in February 1606. It meant a tenurial and landownership system of partible and communal inheritance the precise application of which varied from region to region. It could refer to equal distribution of property between co-heirs, or to the distribution of land by a chief, which was sometimes annual. In their attempts to destroy the property-owning Catholics of Ireland in the early eighteenth century, the British reintroduced gavelkind as a PENAL LAW, requiring subdivision of property of Catholics between all sons unless the eldest assumed Protestantism, in which case the strict and English rule of impartible inheritance was applied.

German Plot, The (*see also* FIRST WORLD WAR, 1914–18)

The 'German Plot' was fabricated by the British authorities in Ireland in 1918 to provide an excuse for rounding-up and detaining leaders of SINN FÉIN and the IRISH VOLUNTEERS who were engaged in active campaigning against conscription of men into the British army. Its credibility was based upon the incontrovertible association of German arms with the EASTER RISING of 1916. Among those seized were DE VALERA and ARTHUR GRIFFITH. The plot was devised by the LORD LIEUTENANT, Field Marshal Lord French.

Ginkel, Godert de (1630–1703)

Ginkel, who in 1692 was created Lord Aughrim and Earl of Athlone by a grateful King WILLIAM III, was a Dutchman born in Utrecht. He came over to England in 1688 in the entourage of William of Orange, in the virtually bloodless coup that deposed King JAMES II. He fought at the BOYNE and, when William III returned from Ireland to England, succeeded as Commander-in-Chief of the WILLIAMITE armies in Ireland. He tried to adopt a placatory attitude towards the Catholics and JACOBITES, offering generous terms in May 1691 to those who would surrender themselves, and extending promises of religious toleration that angered and alienated the Protestant elements in Ireland as well as running contrary to William III's policy. They were promises Ginkel could not keep. He commanded the victorious army at the battle of AUGHRIM in July 1691 after the capture of Athlone, and went on to take LIMERICK. Thereafter he retired to Holland and fought as a commander in the Dutch wars against the French.

Gladstone, William Ewart (1809–98)

More than any other British politician of the nineteenth century, Gladstone recognized and addressed himself to the resolution of the chronic problem of Ireland as seen from the British viewpoint. His natural contempt for the Irish was subordinated to his political perception, which saw the 'Irish card' as a means of reuniting the Liberal party for the 1868 General Election. He remained throughout his life a committed friend to the Protestant ASCENDANCY, despite his pursuit of DISESTABLISHMENT of the CHURCH OF IRELAND, and his reform measures were intended to deprive the

enemies of British supremacy of weapons they could use for its termination. Something of a disciple of ROBERT PEEL, Gladstone early took an interest in Irish issues. He resigned from the Presidency of the Board of Trade over his failure to increase the government grant to ST PATRICK'S COLLEGE at Maynooth in 1845, and in 1851, as MP for Oxford University, opposed the extreme Protestant ECCLESIASTICAL TITLES legislation. He became the leader of the Liberal party in 1867 succeeding Lord John Russell and in 1868 pushed the legislation for the Disestablishment of the Church of Ireland. The act embodying Disestablishment was passed in 1869, Gladstone having been returned as head of a Liberal government in the General Election of 1868. Important LAND LEGISLATION was passed in 1870 and 1871 and, for the sake of the integrity of the British Empire, he favoured Irish progress towards HOME RULE, although he personally disliked it and preferred some kind of devolved autonomy, chiefly in domestic affairs. But Gladstone was by no means a thorough-going imperialist, and in the Midlothian Campaign of 1879/80 vigorously criticized Disraeli on that basis. His commitment to Irish Home Rule may have been partly due to the threat of FENIANISM, armed republican revolutionaries particularly strong in America, for Gladstone was conscious of the dangers inherent in an Irish-American preoccupation with Irish liberty. Becoming Prime Minister again in 1886, he pressed ahead with creation of a representative assembly in DUBLIN, but was voted out of office in the ensuant General Election in which Home Rule was the major issue between the parties. As Prime Minister for the fourth time from 1892 he introduced Home Rule legislation again, which passed the Commons but was rejected by the House of Lords in September 1893. Gladstone's failure to produce the changes that PARNELL and others had been pressing for, went a long way towards undermining the constitutional nationalist approach in Ireland, and encouraged the revolutionary movement, so that in his failure, Gladstone nevertheless gave ammunition to the PHYSICAL FORCE men of organizations such as the IRISH REPUBLICAN BROTHERHOOD.

Glamorgan Treaties

During the course of 1644, King Charles I, waging war against his Parliament (see ENGLISH CIVIL WAR) pressed for a CESSATION in the struggle in Ireland between the CATHOLIC CONFEDERACY and the government and royalist armies. Although securing such a cessation or truce, leading to a negotiated peace, was entrusted to the royalist Earl of ORMOND, the king also gave plenary powers to a Catholic royalist nobleman, the Earl of Glamorgan, on 1 April 1644, to act separately. His commission renewed on 12 March 1645, Glamorgan arrived in Ireland in June and came to terms with the Catholic Confederacy by treaty on 25 August 1645 by which, on behalf of the king, the earl conceded to the Irish their own Parliament and religious toleration. The secrecy of the negotiations was destroyed when documents relating to them were found on the body of the archbishop of Tuam, killed in action with government forces near Sligo in October. The Earl of Ormond arrested Glamorgan in December 1645 for treasonable activities, largely to protect himself, and then released him in January 1646 on bail put up by the Earl of CLANRICARDE. The Treaty of August, however, was already meaningless, because of the opposition of the powerful papal envoy to the Catholic Confederacy, RINUCCINI. King Charles found it politically necessary publicly to disown Glamorgan, which he did in March 1646. In September, the earl took an oath of allegiance to the papal envoy and formally associated himself with the rebellion of the Confederacy, several months after the king had surrendered himself to his enemies in England. Glamorgan served on the Supreme Council of the Confederacy, commanded in the field for it in the province of Munster, and then went into exile in France in 1648.

Glenmacquin, battle of

The battle of Glenmacquin was fought near Raphoe, County Donegal, on 16 June 1642 between forces of the CATHOLIC CONFEDERACY under Sir PHELIM O'NEILL and ALASDAIR MACDONNEL, and a Scottish PRESBYTERIAN army operating in ULSTER. The Confederates were defeated, and four days later O'Neill sustained a further defeat at the River Blackwater.

Gonne, Maud (1866–1953)

Maud Gonne was born and brought up in Hampshire, the daughter of a British army officer, and was sent into France to be educated privately. There she developed her Irish nationalist sympathies, and made her way to Ireland where she founded INGHINIDHE NA H'EIREANN, a feminist nationalist movement. Maud Gonne converted to Catholicism, worked closely with W.B. Yeats, and met and married SEAN MACBRIDE in 1903. She seems to have remained in Paris, where she was married, until 1917, returning to Ireland after the arrest and execution of her husband for his part in the EASTER RISING of 1916. She herself was arrested during the spurious GERMAN PLOT scare of 1918. Her autobiography, *A Servant of the Queen*, was published in 1938.

Government of Ireland Act, The

The move towards HOME RULE for Ireland came to an abrupt end with the outbreak of the FIRST WORLD WAR in 1914. In 1916 revolutionary Irish republicans rose in arms, and in 1919 the WAR FOR INDEPENDENCE broke out, the IRISH REPUBLICAN ARMY seeking to break the British connection by force of arms. The Act for the Better Government of Ireland of 23 December 1920 was devised by a British government anxious to get out of the conflict in Ireland, and it incorporated within its clauses the principle of PARTITION, whereby the SIX COUNTIES in ULSTER would be excluded from any separate Irish state. The Act allowed for two Parliaments in Ireland, one in the north for the six counties, and one in the south for the remaining 26. In the wake of General Election results, 124 of 128 southern Parliament seats were to go to SINN FÉIN and the other four to Independent Unionists. In the six northern counties, electoral contests produced 40 Unionist MPs, six Sinn Féin and six nationalists of the old Home Rule persuasion. Ulster was prepared for this development, and accommodated it, since it conceded to northern Unionists the partition which they wanted. Matters were not so simple in the south, for the new Parliament wholly ignored the creation of DÁIL ÉIREANN and consequently when, on 28 June 1921, the southern Parliament met, it was forced to adjourn itself because of the non-appearance of the 124 Sinn Féin MPs. This refusal to co-operate with the imposed system of government meant that the British must either bow to Irish pressure or endeavour to govern as if Ireland or the 26 counties of the south, at least, were a colony. The British preferred to negotiate, and the ANGLO-IRISH TREATY was signed in December 1921.

Grace, Court of

The Court was established on 18 February 1684 to enquire into titles to land in Ireland, and to dispose of those lands still in the king's hands. As such, it should be seen as the final stage in the land legislation ensuant upon the restoration of King Charles II in 1660 and the need to deal with the claims and grievances of the dispossessed Gaelic and Old English landowners whose lands had been ruthlessly taken from them in the 1650s. The Court made it possible for holders of possibly defective land titles to purchase confirmatory documents, the proceeds from which purchases would go towards the compensation of the remaining dispossessed. It enshrined the final land dispersal in Ireland, whereby only one-fifth was held by Catholics as against three-fifths held by them in 1641, but nevertheless, it was an improvement on the position prevailing in 1650.

Graces, The *see* MATTERS OF GRACE AND BOUNTY

Grand Juries

The Grand Jury system was an introduction of English county administration practice into Ireland, consequent upon the spread of settlement and PLANTATION. As in England, the county juries were empanelled from amongst the resident gentry, and required to sit and meet half-yearly during the holding of the Assizes, where the judges of the Common Law tried presentments of the Grand Juries. The jury system was crucial to the successful application of the county ADMINISTRATIVE STRUCTURE, dealing with civil and criminal matters, the setting of the COUNTY CESS and matters of law and order. The juries appointed the High Constables of the BARONIES, who were responsible for gathering in revenues, and paying them to the Grand Jury's permanent Treasurer. As well as presenting criminal offences and other matters to the judges of the Assize, Grand Juries could also authorize expenditure within their county, for such purposes as road construction or the maintenance of highways by directing subordinate units in the county structure to undertake works. The Grand Juries were, from the early seventeenth century, bastions of the Protestant interest, and remained so despite tentative reform, for example in 1836. In 1817 steps had been taken to give Justices of the Peace power to inspect presentments before they came before the Grand Juries, and by the legislation of 1836 expenditures ordinarily at the discretion of Grand Juries, were referred in the first instance to Barony committees of JPs and ratepayers for their approval. The Grand Jury system embodied the principle of unpaid public service, which the enactment of 1817 began to encroach upon, imposing restrictions on jurors' powers.

Grattan, Henry (1746–1820)

Henry Grattan's fame is reflected in the attachment of his name to a 20-year period of relative parliamentary independence enjoyed by Ireland until the UNION of 1801 brought the Irish Parliament to an end. Grattan belonged to the Protestant ASCENDANCY, a communicant of the CHURCH OF IRELAND, and educated at TRINITY COLLEGE. Yet he epitomized that PATRIOT and 'nationalist' aspect of the Ascendancy, which saw itself as fundamentally Irish and consequently concerned with the well-being of Ireland before the considerations of Britain. In

1778, returned as MP for Charlemont to the Commons in DUBLIN, Grattan urged an address to the king to represent the complaint that the 'condition of Ireland [was] no longer endurable'. Grattan made use of the developing extra-parliamentary agitation for reform, to promote his cause of legislative independence from Britain, and with the withdrawal of HENRY FLOOD from leadership of Patriot politics in the Commons, quickly assumed leadership of the reform grouping in the House. The repeal of the 1720 DECLARATORY ACT in 1782 (followed by the equally vital passage of a Renunciation Act) achieved victory for Grattan and his supporters. Thereafter, he wished to moderate the influence of extra-parliamentary movements such as the VOLUNTEERS, and his stance in favour of Catholic EMANCIPATION may have been due as much to his rivalry with Flood as to any profound commitment. In October of 1798 he was accused of involvement with, perhaps membership of, the revolutionary UNITED IRISHMEN whose rebellion had been crushed in that year. In February he fought a duel over the allegation with Isaac Corry, wounding his opponent in the process. As MP for Wicklow, although in ill-health, he spoke vigorously against the proposals for the Union of the two Parliaments of Britain and Ireland which came into law in 1801. He secured return to the Parliament at WESTMINSTER in 1805 for Malton in Yorkshire which he continued to represent to his death, but he never took government office.

Grattan's Parliament

Grattan's Parliament is a term for the Irish Parliament during the years from 1782, when it recovered legislative independence, until either 1797 when Grattan seceded from the Commons over reform, or 1800 when the legislation to create the UNION of Britain and Ireland marked the end of the Irish PARLIAMENT as a separate body. In effect, Grattan's Parliament was a reassertion of the Protestant ASCENDANCY, a triumph of the colonists who had come to see themselves as truly Irish. The repeal of the DECLARATORY ACT of 1720, which had

asserted the right of the British Parliament to supremacy over that in Ireland, forced through in 1782, marked the beginning of Grattan's Parliament, but the Irish Parliament had been restive for a long time. In November 1769, for example, the Commons had rejected a supply bill on the grounds that 'it did not originate in Ireland' but was to apply to Ireland. The eulogies of nineteenth-century historiography, fired by mass movements such as O'CONNELL's repeal campaign, created a mythology around Grattan's Parliament that, for the most part, later republicans and revolutionaries refused to subscribe to. Throughout the two decades at the close of the eighteenth century, the Parliament steadfastly resisted its own reform, and leaned towards Catholic EMANCIPATION only where it was wholly compatible with, or useful to, the Ascendancy. Moreover, legislative independence did not mean that the Irish Parliament was not subject to British supremacy, for the nature of the constitutional arrangement was such that the British administration centred upon the CASTLE and the person of the LORD LIEUTENANT had undergone little if any change. Ireland was for 20 years a self-governing colony, but nothing more than that.

Greenboys *see* OAKBOYS

Griffith, Arthur (1871–1922)

Griffith was one of the most influential republican revolutionary figures to emerge from the protracted HOME RULE campaign at the end of the nineteenth century. A proficient organizer, he founded CUMANN NA NGAEDHEAL in 1900, was active in the GAELIC LEAGUE and in the IRISH REPUBLICAN BROTHERHOOD from 1893, and launched SINN FÉIN in 1906. At that date, and probably as late as 1917, Sinn Féin was far more a constitutional movement than it was revolutionary, and Griffith himself more concerned with developing economic self-sufficiency for a future free Ireland than the achievement of freedom by armed insurrection. He had military experience – he had fought for the Boers against the British in

1899 – and he was active in the IRISH VOLUNTEERS and in securing guns from Germany, but he took no part in the EASTER RISING of 1916. Even so, he was arrested with hundreds of others and again in 1920 during the WAR FOR INDEPENDENCE. Griffith headed the delegation from DÁIL ÉIREANN that went to London to negotiate what emerged as the ANGLO-IRISH TREATY of 1921 and stood resolutely by its terms. He had, however, been eclipsed within Sinn Féin and the Dáil by DE VALERA.

Griffith's Valuation

On 26 May 1826 an act passed through Parliament to provide for a reform of local taxation through a thorough revaluation of land in Ireland. The task was allotted to Sir Richard Griffith (1784–1878) a trained geologist who had undertaken survey work in Leinster in 1808 and major road-building schemes in Munster. From 1830 Griffith's team covered Ireland commencing in Ulster, assessing values as if for a tenancy of 21 years. The survey, which made a major contribution to knowledge of Ireland, revealed that one-third of the total land area was classified as 'waste' but much of it (Griffith was an expert on land drainage as well) was fit for reclamation schemes which, if pushed on, would meet the demand for land. The Griffith Valuation provided the basis of rateable assessment for the rest of the century, but tended to be used for setting rents as well, for which it was not intended.

Grousset, Paschal (d. 1909)

Grousset was the French author of a seminal work on Ireland, *Ireland's Disease: The English in Ireland* published in English translation in London in 1887 under the pseudonym of Philippe Daryl. The book was based upon articles written for publication in France in 1886/7 in the newspaper *Le Temps*, for which Grousset had been correspondent in Ireland during the 1886 General Election. How far Grousset's book influenced GLADSTONE in his consideration of LAND LEGISLATION is not altogether clear, but Gladstone himself read 'the ... weighty and important inquiry' and met the author on a visit to Paris. Grousset made recommendations for reform and improvement in Ireland, and even suggested that, in the event of HOME RULE, ULSTER might well be linked politically and economically to Scotland.

H

Harry of Ireland

Nickname for HENRY CROMWELL.

Healy, Timothy (1855–1931)

Timothy Healy was born in County Cork and worked for a time on the railways and then as a writer in the *NATION*, journal of the YOUNG IRELAND movement, which in 1869 was resurrected by ISAAC BUTT as a platform for nationalist opinion. He worked as PARNELL's secretary for a short time in 1880, the year Healy entered the House of Commons, and quickly became influential. The 'Healy Clause' in the 1881 LAND LEGISLATION covered protection for improving tenants against consequent rent increases. He had turned against Parnell by 1891, isolating himself progressively and seeking to found extra-parliamentary groups such as the Peoples' Rights Association of 1897, which led to his expulsion from the IRISH PARLIAMENTARY PARTY in 1902. He acted for the employers in the DUBLIN LOCK-OUT of 1913 and was first Governor-General of the FREE STATE in 1922.

Hearth Tax, The

The Hearth Tax was an innovation in revenue raising in England and in Ireland, but its introduction into Ireland in 1662 is of interest in two respects. Firstly, because the recommendation for its adoption came from the Irish House of Commons, as a proposed bill for submission to approval in England; the Irish Commons were thus originating fiscal legislation. Secondly, and redolent of the seventeenth-century English obsession with ANGLICIZATION, it was hoped the tax would have a 'civilizing' effect in Ireland, although this aspect was a later emphasis. The rate was assessed at two shillings (10 pence) per hearth to be collected twice-yearly in half instalments. As in England, there were exemptions for the poor, but in 1666 an amendment provided that houses that did not possess a chimney – a thing in itself hinting at civilized living – would be charged double, as an inducement to have one fitted.

Hearts of Oak *see* OAKBOYS

Hearts of Steel *see* STEELBOYS

Hedge Schools

Hedge schools, also known as 'pay schools' and 'popular schools' were a token of Irish peasant resistance to PENAL LAWS and disabling legislation. Their appearance and popularity are evidence of the commitment of the Irish to learning and education, for the schools could not have flourished without popular support. And, as has been pointed out by historians, the schools, in their secrecy and mobility, were in effect a conspiracy against the government. That the masters taught their charges in hedge bottoms, with a lookout nearby, was true, but as the enforcement of the laws relaxed, room was found for the schools in barns and cottages. The teaching, originally undertaken in Gaelic shifted to the English language as the schools became less secretive. The parochial Catholic clergy connived at the system, by which parents paid small sums direct to the itinerant masters for their work, and there was some emphasis upon classics and Gaelic history and literature. By the 1820s it has been estimated some half-million Irish children were gaining an education through the hedge schools.

Hibernian Bible Society

The early nineteenth century witnessed a surge in Protestant missionary activities in Ireland, aimed at converting Catholics to the reformed religion. The context of that increased zeal lies in the legislation towards Catholic EMANCIPATION that came to a height in 1793 with the franchise being extended to the FORTY-SHILLING FREE-HOLDERS. The missionary activity was in direct proportion to the developing political influence of the Catholic majority. The Hibernian Bible Society was founded in DUBLIN in 1806, a direct counterpart of the London Hibernian Society. By 1923 both societies had distributed in Ireland some 200,000 Protestant Bibles, and had managed to establish schools in country areas. The educative principle lay behind the activities of the Baptist Irish Society set up in December 1814 which established 60 schools in the province of Connacht with a direct intention of making converts. The Religious Book and Tract Society for Ireland distributed over a million pamphlets between 1819 and 1832. The proliferation of printed materials and the expected readership does indirect credit to the level of Irish peasant literacy, almost entirely due to the HEDGE SCHOOL system. The missionaries must have supposed their output would be read by the peasants, because it was highly unlikely that Catholic priests or schoolmasters would read the pamphlets and bibles to their assembled flocks. How much impact the missionary movement made is hard to quantify, but probably very little. Government-sponsored educational programmes came with the KILDARE PLACE SOCIETY of 1811, although the original brief was for non-denominational education which, in itself, alienated the Catholic clergy. Within a short time that Society was actively seeking to convert, along orthodox Protestant lines.

Hibernianism

A term for the principles and doctrines of the ANCIENT ORDER OF HIBERNIANS, a revolutionary secret society formed in the 1880s. Historiographically it is sometimes used where RIBBANDISM would be better employed, alluding to the ideology of the RIBBONMEN earlier in the nineteenth century.

Hibernias

Hibernias were coins of small denomination – halfpence and farthings – produced by the JACOBITE authorities in the defence of LIMERICK in 1691 to meet the demand for small change. The coins were struck from melted down large and small shilling pieces.

Hobart's Act (*see also* EMANCIPATION BEFORE 1801)

Hobart's Act is the name given to the Catholic relief act of 9 April 1793, which gave the franchise to the rural FORTY-SHILLING FREEHOLDERS, the most far-reaching stage in emancipation legislation before the UNION of 1801. Hobart (1760–1816) was CHIEF SECRETARY in the Irish administration 1789–93, and introduced the measure in Parliament in February 1793. He succeeded his father in the earldom of Buckinghamshire in 1804. The Act was not inspired by any commitment to toleration, but by the developing crisis with France, and the need to make sufficient concessions to keep the Catholic majority in Ireland relatively docile. In view of the fact that Catholics were denied seats in Parliament on grounds of their religion, the newly enfranchised might vote only for a choice of Protestant candidates anyway. As an emancipatory measure, it was the last important step before the Act of 1829 which, ironically, deprived the forty-shilling freeholders of the vote even as it gave Catholics entitlement to sit in Parliament.

Hobson, Bulmer (1883–1969)

Bulmer Hobson was one of the most active republican organizers from 1901 when he joined the GAELIC LEAGUE. He was born in ULSTER and was educated by Quakers, but his Protestantism was not sectarian, as his early career demonstrated. He helped found a branch of the nationalist GAELIC ATHLETIC ASSOCIATION in County Antrim in 1901 and, after joining the IRISH REPUBLICAN BROTHERHOOD in 1904, formed the exclusive and militant republican DUNGANNON CLUBS in Ulster. Hobson's single-minded devotion to republicanism recommended him beyond Ulster. He became Vice-President of SINN FÉIN in 1907 but left the organization in 1910, and his political sympathies underwent change. Although he espoused and helped co-ordinate the acquisition of guns from Germany, by 1914 he had sided with the constitutional nationalist REDMOND and abandoned the IRB, taking no part in the EASTER RISING of 1916 and appearing to settle for semi-obscurity in the FREE STATE from 1921. Amongst his written works was a life of the UNITED IRISHMEN leader WOLFE TONE, published in 1919.

Home Government Association

The Home Government Association was founded in 1870 by ISAAC BUTT in DUBLIN as a political party aimed at self-government for Ireland by backing parliamentary candidates who held HOME RULE principles. Its first electoral success was in 1871 when John Martin was returned for Meath. The Association was seen by the landlord interest, predominantly Protestant, as a suitably moderate, constitutional grouping for them to be associated with. They had taken fright at the DISESTABLISHMENT of the CHURCH OF IRELAND in 1869, and looked to control the progression towards Home Rule that seemed, then, almost inevitable. Butt was motivated by the idea of a Federalized United Kingdom, taking courage and inspiration from British legislation that federated the provinces of Canada. In November 1873 the Home Government Association dissolved itself and re-emerged under the title Home Rule League. John Martin's successor as MP for Meath was PARNELL, the leading figure in the new League, which had seen the return of 59 MPs adhering to its principles in the General Election of February 1874 as compared to 33 Conservatives and only 10 Liberals. The League campaigned for a limited devolution of power from WESTMINSTER, for denominational education (as espoused by the CATHOLIC CHURCH hierarchy in Ireland) and for further LAND LEGISLATION. Various Home Rule-based organizations developed subsequent to the League, all tied by association to the IRISH PARLIAMENTARY PARTY of Home Rule MPs and their allies.

Home Rule Confederation (of Great Britain)

The Home Rule Confederation was established in Manchester as an extension within Britain of the Home Rule movement led by ISAAC BUTT in Ireland. It was set up in January 1873 under Butt's Presidency, and was intended to be an organization for the politicization of the Irish emigrant community in Britain. It was accused of FENIAN infiltration, even of being a front for that revolutionary republican organization which had risen in arms in 1867, but the Confederation was clearly respectable. PARNELL replaced Butt as its President in 1877. The term 'Home Rule' as an expression of the campaign for self-government, gained currency during the 1860s, the enunciation of an alternative but successor programme to the somewhat vaguer notion of repeal of the UNION of 1801 that had been championed by O'CONNELL.

Home Rule Legislation

The Home Rule movement, developed by ISAAC BUTT, was transformed politically by PARNELL who rose to prominence in the 1870s. Between 1885 and 1914 numerous attempts were made in Parliament to secure a devolved form of government for Ireland, particularly after GLADSTONE's conversion (for political reasons) to the principle, which was widely known by December of 1885. As recently as November Gladstone had declined to commit himself, but the General Election of December returning 85 Home Rule MPs from Ireland, gave Gladstone no alternative other than to work with Parnell, since the Home Rule bloc in the Commons precisely equalled the Liberal majority over the Conservatives. Gladstone became Prime Minister in February 1886 and on 8 April 1887 introduced legislation into the Commons which was defeated, thanks to Liberal defections, in June. The proposed measure included a Parliament in DUBLIN but the reservation of fiscal and military (defence) matters to the Parliament in WESTMINSTER. It was somewhat vague over whether or not there would be continued Irish representation in the

British Commons. Gladstone's second Home Rule Bill was introduced in February 1893 which, like that of 1886, envisaged a bicameral Parliament in Dublin in which the Upper House was to be wholly elective (that is, it would not be a House of Lords with peers sitting by right of title and inheritance), and allowed, too, for the presence of 80 Irish MPs at Westminster where external and monetary policy would be decided after devolution. In September 1893 the bill passed its third reading in the Commons but within days was thrown out by the House of Lords by a massive 419 votes to 41. Gladstone resigned on 3 March 1894, and with him went any prospect of securing Home Rule. His successor as Prime Minister, Lord Rosebery, expressed his reservations about the wisdom of Home Rule almost immediately. In 1905 Sir Henry Campbell-Bannerman met with the leaders of the Irish nationalist MPs, REDMOND and O'Connor, and gave them a promise that Home Rule legislation would be introduced again, but not until April 1912 was a new bill prepared and laid before the Commons. In the General Election of 1910 Redmond's nationalist group with 70 MPs returned from Ireland held the balance of power, and the proposals of 1912 were preceded by the Parliament Act of August 1911 which effectively deprived the House of Lords of the power to obstruct legislation for more than two years. This meant that any legislation voted by the Commons in 1912 could become law in 1914, if the Lords persisted in their resistance to Home Rule. If not, it might happen sooner. On 17 October 1911 the Primrose Committee recommended fiscal autonomy for Ireland. In an atmosphere of increasing Unionist hostility, fanned by Conservative politicians, Asquith laid the legislation of April 1912 before the Commons. The Liberal MP Agar-Robartes moved an amendment that the counties of Antrim, Armagh, DERRY and Down be excluded from the provisions of the bill, but the amendment was rejected by the House by 69 votes. The bill passed its third reading in January 1913 by 110 votes but was thrown out by the Lords on 30 January. The Lords did the same when the bill again passed the Commons in July with a similar majority in favour to that in January. Positions in Commons and Lords were now thoroughly entrenched, but time was on the side of the legislation, or so it seemed. Throughout this period opposition in ULSTER was growing, with more than tacit political support from the Conservatives and the Liberal party Unionists. In September 1913 the Ulster Unionist Council under CARSON was formed into a provisional government for Ulster in the event of Home Rule becoming law. In response to the threat from Ulster, on 23 June 1914 an amendment bill was introduced by the government allowing for the temporary exclusion of the Ulster counties for a period of six years, but the Lords in July amended the amendment to exclude Ulster permanently from the provisions of the Home Rule legislation. The Commons postponed consideration of that amendment by the Lords. On 4 August Britain declared war on Germany (see FIRST WORLD WAR), and in September the Commons voted to suspend the GOVERNMENT OF IRELAND ACT for the duration of the war. Redmond and the nationalists had, anyway, hurried to give their political support to the government's war effort, and were willing enough for deferral. In the aftermath of the republican EASTER RISING of 1916 in Ireland and the series of brutal executions of its leaders, Lloyd George was instructed by Prime Minister Asquith to reach a settlement of the Irish problem. From the Unionists, Lloyd George got approval for legislation that permanently excluded SIX COUNTIES of Ulster, whilst as far as Redmond and the nationalists were concerned, they had the impression that such exclusion would be temporary only. Lloyd George recommended immediate legislation, with continued Irish representation at Westminster, but the scheme foundered in the Commons in July 1916. Home Rule, in the altered circumstances of 1916 onwards, was a dead letter. The issue now was to be the creation of a FREE STATE, for which the Irish had already selected their members of an Irish PARLIAMENT (see DÁIL ÉIREANN) predominantly from the ranks of the republican SINN FÉIN party.

Home Rule Party, The

The terms 'Home Rule Party' and 'IRISH PARLIAMENTARY PARTY' are, during the campaign for Home Rule, interchangeable. Both apply to the MPs representing Irish constituencies in the British House of Commons, who were elected on a Home Rule platform. Their influence, and consequently government interest in pursuing Home Rule, depended upon their numbers and their unanimity. In the 1885 General Election the Home Rule Party were powerful enough to keep the Conservatives in office for two months whilst negotiations with the majority Liberals went ahead. The Conservative Prime Minister fell when the Home Rulers gave their support to GLADSTONE's Liberals. The Home Rule Party, since it could never form an administration by itself, depended upon consistency in numbers, and action as a distinctive grouping. It was also dependent upon the predominance of the Liberal party, which was by and large sympathetic to Home Rule. The Home Rulers were also designated as nationalists, a distinction in Irish political terms that became important only when they were challenged in their constituencies by the republican SINN FÉIN party and suffered significant loss of MPs in the Commons, particularly since the Sinn Féin MPs followed an ABSTENTIONIST policy and did not take their seats. For a period of some years, moreover, the parliamentary grouping was split between adherents of and opponents of PARNELL in the wake of the divorce scandal which blew up in December 1889. Initially there was widespread sympathy and continuing support for Parnell, the leader of the Home Rule Party in the Commons (see PARNELLITES) but Gladstone in November 1890 expressed himself unable to work further with the Parnell-led party leading to a split in the Home Rule ranks of 44 to 28 against Parnell's continued leadership. In the ensuing North Kilkenny by-election the two rival groups almost came to blows, but the anti-Parnell candidate routed the Parnellite by 2,500 votes to 1,350. Further anti-Parnell candidates were returned, making the pro-Parnell group a declining force in the Commons.

Parnell's sudden death in October 1891 theoretically made a resolution of the rift plausible, and the Parnellite leader RED-MOND kept his Waterford seat in the election of December 1891. Reunification came in 1900, with Redmond as leader of the Home Rule Party in the Commons and leader of the nationalist constitutional movement in the country. Nationalist/Home Rule presence in the Commons was maintained at 80 or so seats in 1900, and became increasingly significant as the government moved towards Home Rule legislation. Victory for the constitutional approach was denied to them by the FIRST WORLD WAR of 1914–18, and the shelving of legislation. It may be that Redmond's enthusiastic support for the British war effort, and the involvement of eminent Home Rule MPs in recruitiing volunteers for the British army and the slaughters in Europe, told against them with the popular vote. Certainly, the war saw the growth of Sinn Féin, the success of which party depended upon its defeat of the old, constitutional nationalist members. In the wake of the EASTER RISING of 1916, Sinn Féin challenged the nationalists outright. In the North Roscommon by-election of February 1917 Count Plunkett took the seat from the Home Ruler Thomas Devine with a substantial majority. Further such victories followed at South Longford (May 1917), East Clare (July) and Kilkenny (August). Awareness of the legislation which aimed at separation of the SIX COUNTIES of ULSTER in the event of Home Rule, enabled Sinn Féin to present the Home Rule Party and its remaining MPs as betrayers of the independence struggle. In the General Election of 1918 Sinn Féin returned 73 MPs on an Abstentionist platform, and the Home Rulers were confined to only 6 seats.

Houghers and Houghing

'Houghing' meant cattle-maiming, a recognized and traditional weapon of rural protest and agitation, not only in Ireland, but evidenced in England as well in the eighteenth and nineteenth centuries. In Ireland, the mutilation of cattle had an ancient origin, reflective of the importance attached to herds as portable wealth in Gaelic society. The 'Hougher' movement developed in Connacht around the early 1700s, and although ordinarily categorized as an 'agrarian' movement, it was nevertheless highly organized and seems to have had both gentry and native Gaelic and OLD ENGLISH 'outlaw' associations. In August 1710 government legislation against 'houghing' made areas where it took place responsible for recompensing the owners of victimized livestock. The authorities seem to have regarded the outbreak as incipient rebellion: orders were issued for Catholic priests in 'Hougher' areas to be arrested, and convicted activists were hung, drawn and quartered. The 'Hougher' leader (or leaders) passed under a variety of pseudonyms, the most frequent of which was 'Ever Joyce', who claimed to be a dead man come to life. The basis of the 'Hougher' agitation was opposition to the spread of grassland at the expense of arable (with consequent fall in demand for labour) and the exemption of grassland from TITHES, and thus represented the smallholder and rural labourer. The death sentence for 'houghing' was made mandatory in 1710: in 1711 the disturbances spread into Galway, and by 1712 there was widespread unrest in Counties Mayo, Sligo, Roscommon, Leitrim, Fermanagh and Clare. In 1713 a pardon was extended to all 'Houghers' who surrendered to the government before March, just as disturbances spread into King's County. The movement lacked any sectarian edge, although it was more or less confined to the Catholic peasantry: victims could be, and often were, relatively prosperous Catholic dairy farmers. The agitation died away after 1713, with occasional isolated revivals.

Howth Gun Running, The

On 26 July 1914 the ship *Asgard*, navigated by ERSKINE CHILDERS, arrived off Howth, north of DUBLIN Bay with 1,500 rifles for the IRISH VOLUNTEERS supplied by the German government. Unlike the similar episode at LARNE, where rifles were shipped into Ireland for the Protestant ULSTER VOLUNTEER FORCE in April 1914, the army turned out to interfere at Howth. Unable to prevent the landing and distribution, the troops attempted to harass a column of Irish Volunteers marching back to Dublin. The ensuing incident, known under the name of BACHELOR'S WALK, resulted in the deaths of uninvolved civilians. There was a subsequent successful gun running at Kilcoole, County Wicklow, on 1 August.

Humbert, Jean Joseph Amable

General Humbert commanded the French expeditionary force which landed on 22 August 1798 at Kilcumin in Killala Bay, County Mayo in support of the UNITED IRISHMEN rebellion of that year. Humbert had been deflected by contrary winds from landing in County Donegal. With his 1,000 men he soon took Killala, and the countryside began to rally to him. The British commander, LAKE, advanced against him, but was routed at the RACES OF CASTLEBAR on 27 August. Several hundred Irish volunteers rallied to the French, but the United Irishmen organization in Connacht was almost nonexistent, and the local people were undrilled and untrained, despite the efforts of the Mayo exile Henry O'Kane who gave them an example by his courage at Castlebar. Against them CORNWALLIS ranged 20,000 troops, regulars and MILITIA. Humbert pushed southwards, hoping to unite with several thousand rebels reported to be advancing towards him from Westmeath under Hervey Morres, and collided with the British and the Militia at BALLINAMUCK on 8 September 1798. The French and their Irish allies were routed. Humbert was taken to DUBLIN, he and his officers treated well, whilst the government troops exacted reprisals against the native Irish. Humbert was evidently perplexed by his reception in Ireland, not least by the appalling poverty of the Catholic Irish, and the rigid sectarian division which caused the Protestants to keep aloof from the rebellion.

Hunger Strikes

The hunger strike is a form of protest deeply rooted in Irish tradition, in Gaelic culture. To 'fast upon' an enemy was to sit before his door and to starve, thereby forcing him into arbitration and negotiation (see BREHONS). The English regarded the procedure as anathema. It has been resorted to by Irish republicans in the twentieth century as an additional weapon intended to shame their enemies. The British no more understand it now than they did in the seventeenth century and earlier.

I

Inchiquin, Earl of (see MURROUGH O'BRIEN

Independent Irish Party

In the General Election of 1847, in the midst of the FAMINE disaster, 36 MPs were returned from Ireland on the repeal of the UNION of 1801 platform pressed so hard by DANIEL O'CONNELL (who had died in Italy the previous May). O'Connell's death had deprived the Repeal movement of leadership, and the crisis of subsistence in the Irish countryside had changed the political emphasis. The YOUNG IRELAND activists of the REPEAL ASSOCIATION were developing their own political identity. The repealer MPs merged into a general Liberal stance in the Commons. During 1850 outside Parliament, a unification of tenant-right agitation in the TENANT LEAGUE occurred, which aimed to build up support for LAND LEGISLATION amongst sitting MPs, or else to campaign for the return of MPs who were favourable to the movement's aims. Within Parliament, a grouping of MPs known (to their friends) as the IRISH BRIGADE emerged to oppose the ECCLESI-ASTICAL TITLES legislation of 1851 and resorted to extra-parliamentary agitation in collusion with opponents of the bill from other parties (see CATHOLIC DEFENCE ASSOCIATION). The coming together of the Tenant League and the CDA forced a unity of purpose upon the Brigade MPs and the tenant-righters in the Commons. In the General Election of July 1852, 48 Liberal Independents were returned as MPs from Irish constituencies. Some 41 of them attended a conference in Dublin with the Tenant League to discuss a uniform policy to be pursued in the Commons, and agreed to pursue an 'independent' line 'in opposition to all governments' that failed to take the reform of tenant law into their legislative programme. Thus the Independent Irish Party emerged and went into action in November 1852, holding the balance of power in the House. Their resolution was broken in the first vote of confidence in the government, when they split 50/50 because the government appeared to be prepared to consider legislation. When Prime Minister Lord Derby disavowed any such idea, his government was forced out by the Independents' votes in December 1852. Lord Aberdeen's successor ministry, Liberal and Peelite, drew upon the natural Liberalism of perhaps half of the Independent Party, two of whose number – Keogh and Sadleir – accepted government office and their defection deepened the inherent rift within the 'party'. The remnant of the Independent Party settled into a steady opposition. A viable IRISH PARLIAMENTARY PARTY was not to emerge again until the HOME RULE campaign got under way.

Independent Orange Order (see also ORANGE ORDER)

The Independent Orange Order was founded in 1903 by Thomas Sloan (d. 1941) as a radical, working-class alternative to the established Orange tradition. Sloan was a shipyard worker who had fallen foul of the Orange Order for his criticism of Edward Saunderson, Deputy Grand Master and Conservative MP for North Armagh. The Independent Orange Order, through its Grand Master ROBERT LINDSAY CRAWFORD, adopted a policy of rapprochement with Catholics, a markedly positive policy which the official Orange Order had not pursued. The Magheramore Manifesto of 13 July 1905 sought to appeal to all working-class Irishmen irrespective of religious persuasion, who felt themselves Irishmen first and foremost, but its chief architect, Crawford, moved towards HOME RULE politics and was expelled from the order on 20 May 1908.

Infallible Subtle

Nickname for DANIEL O'NEILL.

Inghinidhe na hÉireann (Daughters of Ireland)

The Daughters of Ireland was a small, feminist group founded in 1900 by MAUD GONNE, with membership limited to women of Irish descent. As well as a strongly republican commitment to independence from Britain, the group's chief target was what was seen as deleterious English cultural influences in Irish life.

Inishbofin, Connemara

Inishbofin was the last royalist stronghold in Britain and Ireland to surrender to the government, on 14 February 1653.

Innocents

The Innocents were, in the context of the Act of SETTLEMENT of July 1662, those Catholic Irish (whether Gaelic or OLD ENGLISH) who had had no part in the waging of the IRISH REBELLION of 1641–53. They were to be entitled to special consideration for restoration of their forfeited lands, taken during the 1650s under the Cromwellian regime. To those who occupied such lands, the government extended no compensation for giving them up to the 'innocents'. A Court of Claims heard some 800 cases and found in favour of 700 or more, including the claims of more than 100 Protestants. But this barely touched the surface. There were several thousand petitions to the Court that were never heard, from people whose last chance, if they survived, to recover their lands came in the 1689 PATRIOT PARLIAMENT.

Instrument of Government

The Instrument of Government, by which the English constitution under the Protectorship of OLIVER CROMWELL was defined, was ratified by Cromwell on 15 December 1653. In March the Long Parliament at WESTMINSTER had voted that Irish representation at Westminster should be increased from six members to 30, and this was written into the Instrument. The independent Irish PARLIAMENT had ceased to exist, and the Irish, like the Scots, returned MPs to the Parliament of the three kingdoms. In reality, the majority of members so returned were serving army officers of the occupying forces. The first 'Protectorate' Parliament under the Instrument, met in September 1654. The Long Parliament dissolved itself in March 1660, and with the restoration of King Charles II, the Irish Parliament met again in 1661.

Insurrection Acts

The Insurrection Act of 24 March 1796 was the direct government response to the spread of Catholic DEFENDERISM, particularly in ULSTER. Its clauses imposed the death penalty for administering illegal oaths of association, and allowed for the imposition of curfews and arms searches in areas where the LORD LIEUTENANT recognized a state of disturbance. This was backed up by an act to suspend Habeas Corpus in such areas, passed in October 1796. The one-sidedness of the legislation's enforcement, being directed primarily against Defenders rather than against the ORANGE ORDER whose sectarian excesses had brought the Defenders into being, and the way in which the Act was enforced reflected the government view that the real enemy was the Defender movement and, as well, the republican UNITED IRISHMEN. The first victim of the draconic measure was William Orr, hanged on 14 October 1797 for administering a United Irishmen oath. On 1 August 1807 the 1796 Act was reinforced by a second act, which seems to have come to the statute book in face of CARDER disturbances. This second act empowered the Lord Lieutenant at the request of local Justices of the Peace, to proclaim disturbed areas where the normal processes of trial by jury could be suspended and TRANSPORTATION for illegal oaths, and possession of arms, be imposed. In June 1810 an Unlawful Oaths Act extended legislation against 'secret

societies'. The subsequent PEACE PRESER-
VATION FORCE legislation of 1814 was a
necessary corollary. In 1822, faced with
ROCKITE and RIBBONMEN disturbances, the
government passed a further Insurrection Act with the suspension of
Habeas Corpus to run from February to
August of that year. Unlawful Oaths
legislation followed in 1823 and, again, in
August 1839. The last Insurrection Act to
be applied to Ireland was made law in
August 1835, with the acquiescence of
DANIEL O'CONNELL, in face of the violence
of the TITHE WARS, but its powers were not
used and it expired in 1840.

Invincibles, The (National)

The radical revolutionary republican
movement known either as the Invincibles or National Invincibles, represented a continuity of revolutionary activism
in FENIANISM after the failure of the 1867
insurrection. They were responsible for
the PHOENIX PARK assassinations in May
1882 of the CHIEF SECRETARY and his
Under Secretary, killings which the broad
front of nationalists condemned. In
January 1883 17 'Invincibles' were
arrested, and by June five of them –
Brady, Curley, Kelly, Fagan and Caffrey –
were executed. James Carey, who had
informed against them, was himself
executed by an Invincible gunman on
board ship to Cape Town, South Africa.
His killer, Patrick Donnell, was hanged in
November 1883. There were no further
incidents attributed to the Invincibles.

Ireland as She Ought to be

'Ireland as she ought to be' was the
slogan of the UNITED IRISHMEN that
emerged as the Catholic element in the
revolutionary republican movement
spread its influence through the militant
DEFENDERS, in 1796/7.

Ireton, Henry (1611–51)

Henry Ireton was a comrade in arms of
OLIVER CROMWELL during the waging of
the ENGLISH CIVIL WAR, becoming Cromwell's son-in-law in 1646. He was
second-in-command of the cavalry
regiments of the NEW MODEL ARMY, and

became prominent in the political debates
of the period 1647/8, denounced as the
'chief of Machiavellians' by one political
opponent. In 1649 he went into Ireland
with Cromwell to suppress the royalist
and CATHOLIC CONFEDERACY forces and
bring to an end the IRISH REBELLION raging
since 1641. When Cromwell returned to
England, Ireton assumed overall command on 26 May 1650, having been
appointed in January, PRESIDENT of Munster, where he had been apportioned
lands in 1649. Ireton died of fever
contracted during the siege of LIMERICK in
November 1651, and was himself succeeded by FLEETWOOD. During Ireton's
brief period of control, civil commissioners were appointed to govern Ireland
in place of the old system of LORD
LIEUTENANT and deputies, but Ireton did
not live long enough to make any mark
beyond military conquest.

Irish Academy *see* ROYAL IRISH ACADEMY

Irish Brigades

The term 'Irish Brigade' has several
distinct meanings in Irish history. It first
appears as the designation of a cavalry
force expected to be raised in Ireland and
sent into England in 1643/4 to support
King Charles I in his struggle with
Parliament (see ENGLISH CIVIL WAR). It was
to be attached to the royalist army of the
Earl of Newcastle in northern England,
but was never formed, since its appearance depended upon negotiated CESS-
ATIONS between royalists and the
CATHOLIC CONFEDERACY involved in the
IRISH REBELLION of 1641–53.

The term is also applied to forces of the
French armies of the eighteenth century,
composed of Irishmen and of their
descendants who fled from Ireland (see
WILD GEESE) in face of the collapse of the
JACOBITE armies, 1689–91. These Irish
troops, whose prowess caused King
George II to observe on the eve of the
battle of Dettingen 'God curse the laws
that made these men my enemies', for the
most part disassociated themselves from
the French revolution, but were replaced
by Irish revolutionary republicans. In

1803 Napoleon I was offered the services of an Irish Legion, which was to be commanded by ARTHUR O'CONNOR. Dressed in green uniforms, the Irish troops fought in the conquest of Prussia, where they liberated fellow countrymen, prisoners after the UNITED IRISHMEN rising of 1798, who had been shipped to Germany to work in the mines. This 'Legion' or Brigade was disbanded in 1815.

A force known as the Irish Brigade in June 1819 served in South America under the command of Simon Bolivar.

FENIAN leaders in America created an Irish Brigade which fought on the Union side in the American Civil War of 1861–65 under the command of THOMAS MEAGHER. The Brigade was savaged at the battle of Antietam in September 1862, and was virtually destroyed in action in May 1863.

Beyond the military field, the Irish Brigade was a term that was applied to Irish MPs sitting at WESTMINSTER during the 1850s (see INDEPENDENT IRISH PARTY, CATHOLIC DEFENCE ASSOCIATION) who came together in a united front against the ECCLESIASTICAL TITLES BILL, an anti-Catholic measure that they sought to resist in the House of Commons and in the country at large by extra-parliamentary organization. The term 'Irish Brigade' was coined for them by the influential journalist FREDERICK LUCAS, and was meant to convey echoes of Ireland's military past and prowess.

Irish Brigade of St Patrick (Battalion of St Patrick)

The struggle in Italy in the 1850s between resurgent Italian nationalism and the temporal power of the papacy created, within Ireland and its Catholic community, a wave of sympathy for the Pope, Pius IX (1846–78). In 1859 the journal the NATION advocated military aid in papal defence, and during February 1860 almost £100,000 was raised by parochial collections in Ireland, and moves were afoot to recruit volunteers for an armed force to go into Italy. In May 1860 the LORD LIEUTENANT prohibited the recruitment of men for foreign service, but that made little difference. More than 1,000 volunteers known as the Irish Brigade of St Patrick or the Battalion of St Patrick, sailed for Italy. They fought under papal banners at Spoleto, and were involved in the defeat sustained by papal forces at Castelfidardo on 18 September 1860. The force had returned to Ireland by the end of November. The nationalist movement in Ireland affected to disdain the effort, and they were certainly embarrassed by its single-minded Catholicism, but the popularity of the volunteers amongst the Irish Catholic peasantry was immense.

Irish Commission, The (Whateley Commission)

A Royal Commission to investigate the state of the poor in Ireland, was established in September 1833 under the chairmanship of Richard Whateley archbishop of DUBLIN (hence Whateley Commission). The House of Commons debated the Commission's report in May 1836. The Commission's work was extensive and prolonged, and the burden of the report was that it was necessary to promote economic growth in Ireland as a solution to problems of poverty. To that end, the Commissioners advocated extensive government financial aid for reclamation of waste lands and drainage schemes, and financial support, too, for EMIGRATION out of Ireland. If this proposal to expend massive sums were not enough to alarm the Commons, the Commission also reported against the POOR LAW on the English system of indoor relief as unsuitable for Ireland, where poverty was so intense and so widespread. The report was thus debated and discarded, but aspects of its perceptive and far-reaching proposals found expression in later legislation, such as that for the CONGESTED DISTRICTS BOARD in 1891. Immediate implementation of 'outdoor relief' would have gone some way to limiting the disastrous effects of the FAMINE of 1845–49, had the Commons acted.

Irish Convention, The

In May 1917 Lloyd George introduced into the House of Commons proposals for a bill intended to provide either immediate HOME RULE or the establishment of a Convention to thrash out a programme for self-government in Ireland. The proposal came a year after the EASTER RISING of 1916, and the ensuant surge of support for SINN FÉIN and outright republicanism. Lloyd George's measure, however, was probably an attempt to smooth the way for the introduction of conscription into Ireland (see FIRST WORLD WAR, 1914–18) by taking steps to meet the national aspirations of the Irish people. On 21 May 1917 a Convention 'of Irishmen of all parties' was formally announced, and had its first meeting in DUBLIN at TRINITY COLLEGE on 25 July. Sinn Féin abstained from attending, but the declining Home Rule Party led by REDMOND attended, as did moderate Unionists from ULSTER. Deliberations ran on into January 1918, whilst Sinn Féin took the Kilkenny seat from Redmond's candidate, and THOMAS ASHE died from forcible feeding in Mountjoy gaol in September 1917. The nationalist position at the Convention was out of touch with shifting loyalties in Ireland at large. Redmond's own group split within itself in January 1918 over the question of fiscal autonomy, and the Convention came to an end in April 1918. Its published report recommended an Irish Parliament subservient to that at WESTMINSTER with exclusion of SIX COUNTIES of Ulster from its provisions. A minority report urged Dominion status within the British Empire (see also HOME RULE LEGISLATION; GOVERNMENT OF IRELAND ACT).

Irish Council Bill, The

In May 1907 CHIEF SECRETARY AUGUSTINE BIRRELL introduced into the House of Commons a proposal for an Irish Council which was intended to 'associate the people with the conduct of Irish affairs'. The nationalist response was uniformly hostile towards what amounted to a proposal for devolution and nothing more. The measure was something that might have found support and favour in the 1880s, but was out of date. The idea of a part-elected (82 members) part-nominated (25 members) Council was dropped by the government in June 1907.

Irish Felon, The

The *Irish Felon* was a journal first published in June 1848 by John Martin as a replacement for the UNITED IRISHMAN, and was named in token of respect for JOHN MITCHEL, the YOUNG IRELAND activist who had been transported (see TRANSPORTATION) for 14 years. The *Felon* became a vehicle for the ideas of LALOR, who saw the crucial importance of the land issue for the political development of Ireland and the cause of self-determination. Martin was gaoled in July 1848 and the journal ceased publication in the same month.

Irish Land Committee see LAND LEAGUE

Irish Parliamentary Party, The

The expression 'Irish Parliamentary Party' represents an identity of political interest shared amongst the vast majority of MPs representing Irish constituencies in the House of Commons at WESTMINSTER between 1801 (when the Parliaments of Britain and Ireland were merged) and 1921 when the ANGLO-IRISH TREATY established the mechanism for creation of the FREE STATE with its own DÁIL ÉIREANN. During that period of 120 years, the Irish MPs (from 1829 (see EMANCIPATION) with Catholics amongst them) moved between tacit support for Whigs or Liberals, Tories or Conservatives, and the formulation of specifically Irish programmes, such as the struggle for repeal of the UNION of 1801, and the quest for HOME RULE. In consequence, the Irish Parliamentary Party would also be conceived of as the HOME RULE PARTY, for example, or as the earlier INDEPENDENT IRISH PARTY. The power of the Irish Parliamentary Party depended upon its ability to influence government policy and opposition proposals by weight of numbers, holding the balance of power whenever possible. But it is also true to say that after the Union of 1801 there was no continuity nor cohesion that would justify the view of Irish MPs as always and specifically distinct from British parties. It was susceptible to dislocation by judicious offers of ministerial appointments from the government (such as effectively wrecked the unanimity of the Independent Irish Party) and to internal rifts, particularly the scandal surrounding PARNELL in 1890 which caused the Home Rule Party to divide along pro- and anti-Parnell lines, from which it did not recover until REDMOND reunited it in 1900. Thereafter, it arrogated to itself the role of 'nationalist' grouping, flirting with, but inherently too much a part of the Imperial political system to really countenance the revolutionary republican politics of organizations such as SINN FÉIN. The term 'Irish Parliamentary Party' should, therefore, not be taken as a specific. It is rather an amorphous concept within which more clearly defined campaigning purposes giving unity, emerged.

Irish People, The

The *Irish People* was a journal of the revolutionary FENIAN movement founded in November 1863 under the proprietorship of THOMAS LUBY and the editorship of John O'Leary. It circulated chiefly in DUBLIN where its editorial offices were, and directed its campaign against the constitutional nationalists and the political equivocation (as the *Irish People* saw it) of the CATHOLIC CHURCH. On 15 September 1865 police raided the offices (which were being used as a meeting place for Fenian activists) and suppressed the journal, arresting O'DONOVAN ROSSA.

The title of the journal was resurrected in 1899 for the journal of the UNITED IRISH LEAGUE.

Irish Rebellion, The (of 1641–53)

The Irish Rebellion, which broke out on Saturday 23 October 1641 in ULSTER, was the greatest and most sustained challenge to the process of English domination of Ireland. Although it began amongst the Catholic GAELIC IRISH in Ulster, within a brief time it had spread to encompass the Catholic OLD ENGLISH. Despite the enormous complexity of the issues: internal dissensions amongst the leadership, the questionable role of the papal envoy RINUCCINI, the added factor

of the ENGLISH CIVIL WAR and the consequent divisions within the loyal forces in Ireland, it can be seen as a national movement directed against NEW ENGLISH influence, PLANTATION and religious persecution by Protestants. In 1662 the Irish PARLIAMENT required that 23 October be observed in perpetuity, as a constant reminder of the terror that was unleashed by RORY O'MORE, Lord MAGUIRE and PHELIM O'NEILL and their fellow Ulster plotters. The rebellion spread rapidly from Ulster: by 31 October there was fighting in Counties Louth, Down, Fermanagh and Monaghan, that spilled over into Roscommon and Sligo in mid-November, and Carlow, Kilkenny and Waterford. It spread through Tipperary and reached Limerick by January 1642. The rebellion's spread was facilitated by the adherence of the Old English, whose influence in the counties of the provinces of Munster and Leinster was crucial. Although by no means a united front, the Old English transformed an Ulster particularist rising into a nation-wide struggle. Against them were pitted the inadequate forces of the English government commanded by the Earl of ORMOND, an Old English Protestant conspicuous for his enduring devotion to the crown. In time, the civil war in England (which began in 1642) led Ormond to seek and to eventually make alliance with the CATHOLIC CONFEDERACY, as the combined Gaelic/Old English struggle came to be known. Their common enemy then became the Parliament in England, its servants and soldiers operating in Ireland. The rebel/royalist alliance was slowly outfought, between 1649 when CROMWELL arrived in person, and 27 April 1653 when Philip MacHugh O'Reilly surrendered the last field army of the alliance. The English Parliament dated the official end of the rebellion to 26 September 1653. The memory of the rebellion lasted long. It was used, partly, to justify the draconian PENAL LAWS against Catholics that followed the overthrow of King JAMES II in 1691 in Ireland; it was commented upon by the reformer John Wesley when he toured Ireland in the mid-eighteenth century, and it was said that revolutionary UNITED IRISHMEN groups found difficulty in the 1790s in raising support in areas which had witnessed particularly brutal events of the rebellion of 150 years before. How true that is, is debatable.

If the rebellion of 1641–53 was the most massive counterattack launched against aggressive resettlement and restructuring of Ireland by the English, then its consequences were equally as profound. To finance the war effort against the rebels, the English government introduced the ADVENTURERS, who advanced money against future grants of forfeited Irish land. The government, and, from 1642, the English Parliament in particular, thus committed itself to wholesale confiscation of property and the dispossession of 'rebels' – in the broadest sense of that term. So it can be argued that the rebellion gave to the English the opportunity to do in one fell swoop what had been going on more or less legally since the mid-sixteenth century. The involvement of the Old English in the rebellion was, therefore, a bonus; some, like LORD JUSTICE PARSONS may have actively contrived to force that alliance. The acreage released by acts of defiance would further promote English interests in Ireland. It does not seem that the English ever seriously contemplated the possibility of being defeated. Thus their war effort was, in a strict sense, a war for territory, rather than a counter-strike against rebels who could be made to submit and then restored to their rights on certain conditions. The great expropriation of the euphemistically named Cromwellian Land Settlement of the 1650s, entailing as it did forced transplantation of Catholic Irish to less fertile and promising lands in Connacht, those who were not denied pardon for their misdemeanours, that is, had a long-term and unhappy consequence for Ireland. The land issues that dominated political activism in the nineteenth century were founded in the legalized theft of land in the 1650s, and that itself was but a continuation of an old process. The rebellion produced remarkable leaders on both sides, OWEN ROE O'NEILL the professional soldier, commanding for the Confederacy in Ulster, and the government General MICHAEL JONES who died on campaign in 1649. The stories of atrocities that circulated in England and in English-controlled Ireland from October 1641 were, as such

things are, gross distortions of a basic truth, and were also fabricated to whip up anti-Catholic fury. They were used by the English Parliament to try to blacken the person of the king himself, who was widely rumoured to have countenanced the Irish Rebellion as a weapon against his own racalcitrant subjects. Certainly, the rebel leaders repeatedly asserted their loyalty to the crown: but the precise link between the king and the leaders of 1641 remains to be established, if it is there. The years 1641–53 witnessed dreadful excesses in a war made all the more bitter both by religious antagonisms and the inherent English view of the Irish as savages needing to be reformed, repressed or slaughtered.

Nothing that the rebels and their Old English allies sought to achieve in the way of concessions from government, was realized. The rebellion left them infinitely worse off than they had been. That was virtually inevitable from the moment the rebellion began.

Irish Republican Army

The Irish Republican Army, the IRA, was the military organization that waged the WAR FOR INDEPENDENCE against Britain, 1919–21. The precise point at which the IRA emerged as a distinctive force is debatable. For example, in May 1866 FENIAN troops invading Canada under Colonel John O'Neill reportedly carried a banner adorned with the letters IRA. They engaged in two successful military actions before retiring into America. Some historians ascribe the first action of the IRA to the attempt, on 19 December 1919, on the life of the LORD LIEUTENANT Viscount French, basing their argument on the resolution in DÁIL ÉIREANN of 20 August 1919 moved by Cathal Brugha that all members and officials of the Dáil and of the IRISH VOLUNTEERS should swear allegiance to the Dáil and to the Republic of Ireland which it embodied. If that were strictly adhered to, then the Fermoy action on 7 September 1919 would be the first significant aggression by the IRA. It may also be argued that (as popular Irish imagery would have it) the IRA became a fact when the Irish Volunteers and the CITIZEN ARMY came together in the EASTER

RISING of 1916 to seek to overthrow British rule in Ireland, for at the commencement of that rising PADRAIC PEARSE read aloud a PROCLAMATION OF THE IRISH REPUBLIC signed by the *de facto* government of that republic, all of whom were shot by the British after the rising was over. Whichever view is preferred, the IRA emerged from the Irish Volunteers, or from that section of the Volunteers that in 1914 held aloof from the pro-war politics of the nationalists led by REDMOND. The IRA was a militant, revolutionary republican force dedicated to the violent overthrow of British government in Ireland. It was subordinate to the IRISH REPUBLICAN BROTHERHOOD and, after its formation, to Dáil Éireann as the army of the Irish Republic. The IRA fought a sustained guerrilla campaign against the British army, the ROYAL IRISH CONSTABULARY, the BLACK AND TANS and the AUXILIARIES and forced the British government to negotiate with Sinn Féin in 1920, from which negotiations the republican movement hoped an independent Irish republic would emerge. The ANGLO-IRISH TREATY, however, when its terms were known, split both Sinn Féin and the IRA. For the negotiators in London, sent by Dáil Éireann, had conceded PARTITION and the exclusion of SIX COUNTIES of ULSTER from a future independent Ireland. The purist and uncompromising republicans within the IRA disavowed the terms of the Treaty, and disdained to be bound by their allegiance to the Dáil to observe them, on the grounds that the Dáil, by voting the terms acceptable, had betrayed the republic. Thus the IRA split between, on the one side, the 'Irregulars' or 'Executive' anti-Treaty IRA, and the pro-Treaty IRA which believed itself to be the army of the Irish Republic, a major step towards which had been taken with the Treaty. DE VALERA was a somewhat equivocal leader of the anti-Treaty side, more representative of the diehard republicans being men like Rory O'Connor, Oscar Traynor and Liam Lynch. A bitter civil war broke out in 1922, in which the anti-Treaty IRA were outgunned and overcome. Nonetheless, the civil war of 1922 contributed to the resolution of diehard republicans, and the IRA as a fighting force, despite periods of intense repression and inaction, remained in being. The Provisional IRA of the latter half of the twentieth century is, despite its Ulster origins and the split within the IRA that led to the emergence of the Provisionals, in direct descent from the anti-Treaty IRA of 1922. The reunification of Ireland remains the primary objective, as it was then.

Irish Republican Brotherhood

The Irish Republican Brotherhood is, and was, often taken as one and the same as the FENIAN movement, but should perhaps be seen as the military directive of that movement, and a grouping which survived the 1867 Fenian uprising and the more moderate development in Fenianism thereafter. It appears to have been founded as the Irish Revolutionary Brotherhood in DUBLIN in 1858 by JAMES STEPHENS, dedicated to the achievement of an Irish republic by PHYSICAL FORCE. In August 1867 the IRB assembled in Manchester, appointed Colonel Thomas Kelly as head centre (leader) of the Fenian movement preparatory to the rising of that year, and after a breach with Stephens who was proving cautious in the implementation of his revolutionary doctrines. The IRB survived the failure of the rising, and in 1869 its Supreme Council drafted a constitution for the Irish Republic. Irish political activity was directed steadily in the 1870s towards HOME RULE and the resolution of the land question, and the IRB in 1873 gave tacit and conditional support to ISAAC BUTT's programme to achieve that end, but withdrew its support in 1876, occasioning a divergence within the IRB itself and the Fenian movement particularly in America, between those who would work with the constitutional approach and those who would not. Thus many Fenian activists and IRB men became involved in the vigorous LAND LEAGUE alongside PARNELL from 1879. Certainly the IRB became somewhat moribund, and remained so until the eve of the FIRST WORLD WAR in 1914 when the failure of the Home Rule campaign, the deferring of legislation until after the war should be over, gave to the revolutionary republicans reason, and the war itself opportunity, to resort to Physical Force in pursuit of its old and unchanged goal of an Irish republic. In 1910 it developed the journal *Irish Freedom* under SÉAN MAC DIARMADA and THOMAS CLARKE; PADRAIC PEARSE joined the IRB in 1913. The resurrection of the IRB as the 'Government of Ireland' – explicit in the movement's constitution – began. Between 1914 and 1916 the movement's membership increased to 2,000, predominantly drawn from the province of Leinster, as a direct result of a Supreme Council's decision to recruit taken in September 1814. A 'secret' Military Council was quickly set up with Pearse, JOSEPH PLUNKETT and CEANNT as its members, later joined by Mac Diarmada and Clarke. JAMES CONNOLLY was co-opted in January 1916, and Thomas MACDONAGH on the very eve of the proposed EASTER RISING in April. The collapse of the rising, and the execution of every member of the IRB's Military Council, did not destroy the organization. It was reconstructed by MICHAEL COLLINS in 1917, became active amongst the IRISH VOLUNTEERS (later the IRISH REPUBLICAN ARMY) and involved in SINN FÉIN's political campaigns. A new constitution was drafted committing the IRB afresh to a free republic and to the necessary military action to secure that, and equating Presidency of the IRB's Supreme Council with the Presidency of the proposed republic (inherent in the traditional constitutional structure of the IRB anyway). The ANGLO-IRISH TREATY of 1921 split the IRB as it did the IRA, the Brotherhood's Supreme Council (under Collins' influence) splitting 11 to 4 in favour of the Treaty, fully aware that in doing so they rode roughshod over their own declared objective of the free republic. Within the FREE STATE the role of the IRB declined.

Irish Republican Union

The Irish Republican Union was formed amongst the Irish emigrant population of New York in 1848 by Michael Phelan, with strong links to the YOUNG IRELAND organization. It was intended to be a military force, and in 1849 formed itself into companies which in time became the

formal 9th Regiment of the New York State Militia.

Irish Socialist Republicans

A political party formed by JAMES CONNOLLY in DUBLIN as an offshoot of his association with the Dublin Socialist Society, in 1896. The party was imbued with Connolly's then doctrinaire Marxism, which was later developed into perceiving the Imperialist connection with Britain as the first thing to be broken before a socialist republic could be inaugurated in Ireland. The Irish Socialist Republicans were always a small group, and seem to have been a vehicle for Connolly, who, as in the Irish Socialist Federation which he established in New York, promoted the international interest of workers that transcended state and national boundaries.

Irish Unionist Council *see* ULSTER UNIONIST COUNCIL

Irish Volunteers

In January 1913 the Unionists in ULSTER formed the ULSTER VOLUNTEER FORCE, the purpose of which was to provide a trained, drilled and disciplined body with which to defend the status of the province of Ulster against moves towards HOME RULE. In November EOIN MACNEILL recommended the formation of a similar force for the rest of Ireland, a national force of Volunteers intended to recruit also in Ulster – although that was not altogether realistic. A steering committee was set up to organize the Irish Volunteers, and in mid-November JAMES CONNOLLY led the way with his elite CITIZEN ARMY, the politics of which were more socialist than they were nationalist. For, essentially, the Irish Volunteers (as events were to show) had a strong constitutional nationalist element in line with the Home Rule movement and REDMOND's politics, despite the republicanism of the founders, MacNeill, PEARSE, MACDONAGH, HOBSON and others. The Irish Volunteers came into being on

25 November 1913 in DUBLIN, with MacNeill as their chairman. There is some evidence that Pearse, at least, may have envisaged a common cause between the UVF and the IV but the goals their leaders aimed at were diametrically opposed. The parliamentary Home Rule Party regarded the Volunteers with suspicion, and in June 1914 provision was made for 25 nominees of the party to represent its interests in the governing body of the Volunteers at the direct request of Redmond. With the outbreak of the FIRST WORLD WAR in August 1914, the majority of the Home Rulers in Parliament opted to support the government's war effort against Germany, and Redmond made his celebrated or notorious speech at WOODENBRIDGE in September when he called upon the Volunteers to offer their services to the British crown. He was very conscious, in the postponement of Home Rule necessitated by the outbreak of war, of the loyalty to the crown being demonstrated by the UVF in the north. His speech split the Volunteer movement between the republican leadership repudiating him and those Volunteers who acceded to his appeal. Redmond's following amongst the Volunteers assumed the name of the National Volunteers, and became a distinct organization some 150,000 strong. The surviving Irish Volunteers, or their leadership at least, seemed to be uncertain as to direction. In October 1914 MacNeill addressed their convention and represented them as both soldiers of Ireland, not to be made to fight for anyone else, and yet as guarantees of the eventual achievement of Home Rule, to which Redmond and the National Volunteers were likewise committed. The IRISH REPUBLICAN BROTHERHOOD, however, through its Military Council, looked to the Irish Volunteers as the fighting force which would wage war for the liberation of Ireland from British rule. In 1916 Pearse, organizational director of the Volunteers, ordered them to go on manoeuvres on Easter Sunday, and units of the Volunteers with the Citizen Army rose in arms in Dublin on 24 April. From the Volunteer movement emerged the IRISH REPUBLICAN ARMY, which subsumed it, in 1919.

Irregulars

The Irregulars were, to the pro-ANGLO-IRISH TREATY forces of the IRISH REPUBLICAN ARMY in 1921, those IRA men and units who opposed the Treaty and waged civil war to nullify it.

J

Jacobites and Jacobitism

Jacobites were the supporters of King JAMES II, driven from his throne in 1688 by a revolutionary clique in England who brought over William of Orange (WILLIAM III) as king. The Catholics of Ireland were, by choice or association through religion, Jacobites, and as Jacobites they suffered in their persons and estates following the defeat of King James' armies between 1689 and 1691. Jacobitism – both an expression of loyalty to James II, his heirs and the Stuart dynasty in general, and a nostalgic remembrance of the almost-achieved liberties for Catholics of his brief reign – was as much a literary and cultural movement as it was a political one. The Jacobite cause did not again bring men into the field in arms as it did in Scotland and England as late as 1745. Most active Jacobites in Ireland went into self-imposed exile to serve the Catholic kings of France, and never seriously contemplated or undertook attempts to reassert Jacobitism in Ireland.

James II, King (of England, Scotland and Ireland) (1633–1701)

Despite attempts to have James Duke of York excluded from succession to the throne because of his Catholicism, he became King James II in February 1685 following the death of his brother Charles II (who was also said to have died a Catholic). His accession aroused hopes in Ireland of some measure of redress for the Catholics. Initially, however, the king did not proceed as vigorously as he might. He appointed two impeccable Protestants as LORD JUSTICES and the Earl of Clarendon as LORD LIEUTENANT. Nevertheless, James' confidence in Ireland was vested in Richard Talbot Earl of TYRCONNELL who had command of the army in Ireland, and who was soon appointed LORD DEPUTY. From February 1687 Tyrconnell directed affairs, appointing Catholics to government office, selecting Catholics to serve as sheriffs in the counties, and redrawing borough charters to enforce Catholic representation, anticipating a House of Commons that would be predominantly Catholic. The promoted Catholics pressed for a redistribution of land, expropriated from them during the 1650s and only partially restored by Charles II (see Act of SETTLEMENT). Tyrconnell recommended that 50 per cent of the land held under the Cromwellian settlement be returned to its former owners or rightful claimants. James II consented, and the measure was to be laid before Parliament late in 1688. It was the birth of a male heir to the king that made the situation for Protestant opinion more than desperate, for it meant that his Protestant daughter Mary, married to William of Orange (see WILLIAM III) would not now succeed her father. A coup was prepared in England to bring William in as king. James II fled to France in December 1688 and made his way to Ireland in March 1689, landing in County Cork, with French backing, to dispute the issue with King William. The war that ensued ended with the complete subjugation of Catholicism, a subjugation maintained by rigorous PENAL LAWS. It also led to the elevation to supremacy in Ireland of a small but clearly defined Protestant population, subscribing to the doctrines of the CHURCH OF IRELAND, which enjoyed ASCENDANCY in Irish affairs for 200 years. James II initially entered DUBLIN in triumph, and summoned a Parliament to meet in May 1689 (see PATRIOT PARLIAMENT) that represented most of Ireland with the exception of those parts of Ulster under Protestant, WILLIAMITE control. The House of Lords was also attended by bishops of the Church of Ireland, though not all summoned, some put in an appearance. A subsidy of £20,000 a month for a year was voted, although it was far from adequate to meet the king's military costs, who resorted to producing currency of base metal to meet the shortfall. Meanwhile, DERRY city was resisting James' armies, and pinning them down. Although William III clearly did not wish to have to fight, he was unable to win over the Catholics with promises of toleration, and the confrontation between Jacobite and Williamite armies at the BOYNE on 1 July 1690 resolved the issue. On 4 July King James took ship for France, leaving his generals to continue the war. He never returned.

Johnston, William (1829–1902)

William Johnston of Ballykilbeg County Down, assumed the status of an ULSTER Protestant folk hero for his challenge to the anti-ORANGE ORDER legislation, the PARTY PROCESSIONS ACTS of 1832, 1850 and 1860. In July 1867 Johnston led a major Orange march from Newtownards to Bangor, for which he was tried and gaoled in February 1868. In the ensuing General Election of November, he was returned as MP for BELFAST, a seat he held for 10 years, revealing himself as a bitter antagonist of the LAND LEAGUE and of the HOME RULE movement, and equally as committed to female suffrage. He also wrote novels with a political message, particularly scathing of conciliatory Protestants.

Jones, Michael (d. 1649)

Michael Jones came of NEW ENGLISH settler stock in Ireland and fought for the royalists of the Earl of ORMOND against the CATHOLIC CONFEDERACY in 1641/2. He joined the parliamentarian side in the ENGLISH CIVIL WAR, became Governor of Chester and in 1647 was appointed Governor of DUBLIN. In that capacity he inflicted major defeats on the Confederacy at DANGAN HILL in 1647 and on his old commander, ORMOND, at Rathmines or BAGGOT-RATH in 1649. Admired by CROMWELL, Jones died in December 1649 on campaign.

Julianstown, battle of

The battle of Julianstown, near DROGHEDA, was fought on 29 November 1641 at the outbreak of the IRISH REBELLION, between rebel forces under RORY O'MORE and a column of 600 government troops en route to Drogheda. The defeat inflicted by O'More hastened the rapprochement of the rebels with the OLD ENGLISH that led to the CATHOLIC CONFEDERACY.

K

Kerns

The word 'Kern' is an anglicization of '*ceithearn*' and seems to translate simply as 'troop' or 'trooper'. The 'Kernety' were light troops, and the meaning seems to refer to spearmen or skirmishers who fought in association with the heavily-armed GALLOGLASS. The household kern (ceithearn tighe) was an official of a Gaelic nobleman's household, not only fulfilling military duties, but acting as an official for seizing wrongdoers. The 'Kerns', like the Galloglass and other groups of old Gaelic society, disappeared during the seventeenth century, but the word survived in 'Woodkern', outlaws expropriated by PLANTATION, taking to the hills and wastelands and pursuing guerrilla warfare against their transplanters. The expression was familiar in 1610, and later came to be applied not only to outlaws but to wandering vagabonds and beggars.

Kilcoole, battle of

The battle of Kilcoole, County Wicklow was fought on 1 December 1641 between government troops under Sir CHARLES COOTE and Irish rebels (see IRISH REBELLION), Coote having shortly before relieved Wicklow Castle. The rebels were defeated.

Kildare and Leighlin, James Warren Doyle bishop of (1786–1834)

Doyle became Catholic bishop of Kildare and Leighlin in 1819. He was an Augustinian monk who had fought for the Spanish in the Peninsular War and was an interpreter for the British in Spain who were commanded by the future Duke of Wellington. As bishop of Kildare, Doyle championed the cause of EMANCIPATION for Catholics, and became involved in the extra-parliamentary movement the CATHOLIC ASSOCIATION, whilst at the same time preserving a political stance that tended to favour the UNION of 1801. He was not a supporter of repeal, although he died before it became a major political issue. He wrote widely under the initials J.K.L., his most significant work being his *Vindication of the Irish Catholics* of 1824. Bishop Doyle gave evidence to various commissions of inquiry on Ireland, and sided with O'CONNELL in denouncing the spurious KILDARE PLACE SOCIETY and its role in Irish education.

Kildare Place Society (Society for Promoting the Education of the Poor in Ireland)

The Kildare Place Society was established in 1811, largely through the efforts of PEEL, to promote non-denominational educational opportunities in Ireland. It appeared at a time of increasing Protestant missionary activity, and its non-denominational posture was crucial to it, since it sought to avoid overt Catholic hostility. From 1815 it received government grants towards providing schools for the 'lower classes' in Ireland, and by 1820 there were some 380 schools. In that same year complaints about the nature of the education became frequent, the Society being accused of coming under the influence of evangelizing elements in the CHURCH OF IRELAND (see SECOND REFORMATION). DANIEL O'CONNELL, who had been on the Society's management board, demanded an inquiry into the functioning of the Society and its adherence to its first principles, but was refused. He disassociated himself, and by 1830 the Catholic hierarchy was openly hostile to yet a further example of Protestant missionary activity directed through education. The same problems beset the less significant Church Education Society of the Church of Ireland, which likewise abandoned whatever objectivity it had had.

Kilkenny Confederation

An alternative, historiographical term for the CATHOLIC CONFEDERACY which made its base at Kilkenny in 1642. Kilkenny was the single most important inland city of Ireland by 1600, almost all other major urban centres being coastal. It was in Kilkenny that the Confederacy maintained its Supreme Council, and where its representative assemblies met. It was noted that within the city there were no distinctions between the GAELIC IRISH and the OLD ENGLISH, 'they walk in loyal and warrantable ways' it was reported. Kilkenny fell to CROMWELL on 27 March 1650.

Kilmainham Treaty, The

During the course of 1880, LAND LEAGUE agitation increased in its intensity in its pursuit of the dual objects of land reform and HOME RULE. In September PARNELL urged 'boycotting' as a weapon against landlords and their agents, and immediately afterwards his call for a 'moral Coventry' was translated into the action against Captain Charles Boycott in County Mayo, which gave its name to the entire ostracizing system. In the same month Lord Mountmorres was assassinated in County Galway. The government launched proceedings against Parnell and others for conspiracy in November but the ensuant trial ended in disagreement amongst the jurors. In January 1881 the Irish MPs at WESTMINSTER, convened by Parnell and DAVITT, considered withdrawal from the Commons to form a convention, but decided instead to launch the NO RENT campaign. Following the introduction of a land bill (see LAND LEGISLATION) into the Commons in April, a Land League Committee in County Limerick was arrested in its entirety, leading to widespread unrest in the countryside, and further arrests. The Land Bill promoted by GLADSTONE passed into law in August, and the Land League resolved to test its effectiveness by using its provisions. Within a month Parnell himself was arrested, and the arrests of WILLIAM O'BRIEN, JOHN DILLON and others followed by 16 October. From their prison at Kilmainham, the arrested leaders issued the No Rent Manifesto requiring tenants to withhold payments to their landlords or the agents, intended to draw attention to the vast numbers of tenants with accumulated rent arrears for whom no provision had been made in the 1881 legislation. The CHIEF SECRETARY denounced the Land League as a 'criminal association'. It seemed that a great trial of strength between the Land League and the government was about to be joined, but Parnell, in April 1882, on parole from prison, entered into discussions with fellow leaders to find a way of extracting himself from the position he was in. He would undertake to stop the No Rent Manifesto and to curb agrarian unrest, if alteration could be made to the 1881 Act, and its provisions extended also to leaseholders. On 2 May Gladstone's cabinet accepted the terms, and the Land League leaders were released, by virtue of this Kilmainham Treaty. Some Land Leaguers saw the compromise as a betrayal of principle by Parnell, but Gladstone had been only too glad to come to terms. The internal Land League dispute was soon dwarfed, however, by the INVINCIBLES' attack on and assassination of the new Chief Secretary in PHOENIX PARK, whose immediate predecessor had resigned in protest at the Kilmainham Treaty.

Kilrush, battle of

The battle of Kilrush, County Kildare, was fought on 15 April 1642 when the Earl of ORMOND, commanding a government army on campaign against the CATHOLIC CONFEDERACY, collided with rebel troops under RORY O'MORE and LORD MOUNTGARRET. Ormond was returning to the PALE after a successful advance into Kildare, and his victory at Kilrush though minor, was made much of by the London propaganda machine.

King, William (1650–1729)

William King is an interesting example of a thoroughgoing Protestant and Whig who regarded himself as Irish and the British interest as inherently inimical to Ireland. He was born in County Antrim and educated at TRINITY COLLEGE, and moved in intellectual circles in DUBLIN where he was gaoled in 1689 for his support for WILLIAM III. His loyalty was rewarded with appointment to the bishopric of DERRY in 1691, and he wrote and published a massive eulogy of King William and the revolution of 1688 entitled *State of the Protestants of Ireland under the late King James's Government*. His orthodox theology led him to regard PRESBYTERIANS as only marginally preferable to Catholics, and he regarded Ireland during the reign of King Charles II as 'flourishing' where even the Catholics, where their 'rancour, pride or laziness' did not get in their way, shared in a general prosperity. It was the impression of a man moving within a limited social and intellectual milieu, but his writing fitted the time, and became the staple of ASCENDANCY historical perceptions long after his own death. King was appointed archbishop of Dublin in 1703, but he never achieved the primacy, because he was, as was remarked, 'to a ridiculous extravagance, national' and outspoken about the intrusion of Englishmen into places of profit and honour in Ireland. He also, in 1703, advocated the UNION of England and Ireland as a guarantee of the future prosperity of both kingdoms, recognizing that otherwise Ireland would remain subsidiary to the English interest.

King of Ireland

The title of King of Ireland was assumed in 1541 by King Henry VIII, and its adoption indicated that henceforth rule of Ireland from England would be total and the extension of English power and influence would be pressed. Previously, Ireland had been a 'lordship', but Henry VIII's assumption of regal dignity made it into a kingdom. King Henry VIII's arrogation of sovereignty was also part and parcel of his challenge to the papacy, since the lordship of Ireland had always been exercised in submission to papal overlordship. Henry's assumption of the crown did not preclude subsequent generations of IRISH GAELIC rebels from offering the 'crown' to others in return for support. It was offered, for example, in 1595 to Philip II of Spain by the ULSTER rebels under TYRONE.

The term 'King of Ireland' was also a nickname applied to JOHN BERESFORD.

Kinsale, battle of

On 21 September 1601 a Spanish fleet arrived at Kinsale, County Cork, under the command of Don Juan del Aguila, to support the ULSTER rebels under their leader, the Earl of TYRONE. English troops at once began to move towards Kinsale, whilst Tyrone marched south to effect a junction with the Spaniards. On 24 December the battle of Kinsale was fought, and resulted in a resounding defeat for the Irish and Spanish at the hands of MOUNTJOY. The battle of Kinsale broke the back of Tyrone's rebellion: in March 1603 he submitted to Mountjoy at MELLIFONT, Queen Elizabeth I having promised her pardon, although it was to Mountjoy as representative of King James I that Tyrone unwittingly surrendered. Elizabeth had died on 24 March 1603, and Tyrone's submission came on 30 March. Historians have seen the battle of Kinsale as marking the end of all hopes of Gaelic assertion and revival in Ireland, Tyrone's necessary surrender clearing the way for the PLANTATION of Ulster and the consequent subjection of the last Gaelic province of Ireland.

Knockanoss/Knockanuss, battle of

The battle of Knockanoss, County Cork was fought on 13 November 1647 between MURROUGH O'BRIEN heading government forces, and the Munster army of the CATHOLIC CONFEDERACY commanded by Lord Taafe and ALASDAIR MACDONNELL, who was killed. Murrough O'Brien's victory made it clear to the Confederacy leadership that an alliance with the ORMOND royalists would be essential if the outcome of the war was to go in their favour. RINUCCINI, the papal envoy to the Confederacy's Supreme Council, had doggedly resisted such an alliance, backed by the power of OWEN ROE O'NEILL and his largely Gaelic forces. Knockanoss obliged him in principle to pursue either royalist allies, or to look to Europe for the support of a powerful prince.

L

Labourers' Act, The

The Labourers' Cottages and Allotments Act of 25 August 1883 was a response to the pressure of the Irish Labour and Industrial Union formed by PARNELL in 1882, and the NATIONAL LEAGUE's involvement in calling for legislation to alleviate the labourers' poverty. The Act was primarily concerned with housing. Cottages with a half acre of land attached were to be built and offered at a low rental, the full rent to be met by government subsidy. Responsibility for the enforcement of the Act was given to the POOR LAW Guardians. In 1892 the specified half acre was increased to one acre per cottage, and by 1921 some 54,000 cottages had been built.

Laggan Army, The

The Laggan army was a Scottish force operating in ULSTER by 1643, against the forces of the CATHOLIC CONFEDERACY. It was commanded by Robert Stewart, and was officered by Scottish soldiers experienced in the European wars. It defeated OWEN ROE O'NEILL at Clones in County Monagahan on 13 June 1643. In 1647 the Laggan army received a new commander, George Monck, sent from London to direct its operations against rebels and royalists. Sir CHARLES COOTE's forces were added to it, but it proved difficult for Monck to control as the Scottish PRESBYTERIANS moved towards an alliance with the royalists.

Lake, Gerard (1744–1808)

Gerard Lake, from 1807 Viscount Lake of Delhi, was a British professional soldier who took over from Sir RALPH ABERCROMBY in February 1798 as Commander-in-Chief in Ireland, on the eve of the UNITED IRISHMEN uprising. He had previously enjoyed command in ULSTER, where he had directed official repression against potential rebels, and virtually broken the back of revolutionary activity in the province. He permitted his soldiers to indulge in brutal excesses, and made a point of purging MILITIA units of United Irishmen and their sympathizers. Four such, from the Monaghan Militia, were made to stand beside their coffins into which they fell when they were shot at Lake's command. Lake was also responsible for the rigged trial and execution of William Orr, a farmer and PRESBYTERIAN gaoled in 1796 for administering the United Irishmen's oath to new recruits. The jury felt unable to convict Orr on the evidence shown, the witnesses against him were discredited, but nevertheless, Lake went ahead with the man's execution on 14 October 1797, a 'judicial murder' that aroused bitterness amongst the republican movement, along with additional terror in Ulster which he had set out to create. He commanded the army which defeated the rebels at VINEGAR HILL in June 1798 and took the surrender of HUMBERT and the French expeditionary force at BALLINAMUCK in September 1798. By 1800 he was on active service in India.

Lalor, James Fintan (1807–49)

Lalor, born in Queen's County, the son of a farmer who, briefly, was a radical MP at WESTMINSTER on behalf of O'CONNELL's repeal campaign, was amongst the most perceptive and important political thinkers of his time. To Lalor, repeal was unachievable and offered no solutions to what he perceived to be the most crucial of Ireland's problems, the land and the need for reform in its ownership and usage (see LAND LEGISLATION). A convinced nationalist, he advocated a policy of passive insurrection, by the withholding of rents to force the government to act on behalf of the tenants of Ireland. PARNELL took up this idea later in the nineteenth century, but hesitantly and without commitment. It was never really tried. Lalor moved towards PHYSICAL FORCE nationalism by 1847, embittered by the FAMINE and regarding the landlords and the government as devoid of any lgitimacy henceforth. To Lalor, the land was a communal asset, however, it was parcelled up into private property, and he recognized the need for a new contract between landowners and tenants which was more equitable than that which prevailed. He wrote in the radical *NATION* journal, where he exerted influence on JOHN MITCHEL, and was for a time associated with the *IRISH FELON* journal which began publication following Mitchel's TRANSPORTATION. In 1848 he was arrested and then released on the grounds of his health, and in September 1849 he led an attack on the Cappoquin police barracks. Lalor died at the end of the year. His theories found practical expression in the policies of the LAND LEAGUE.

Land League (The Irish National)

The Land League (from 1881 the Irish National Land League and Industrial Movement – reaching out to urban and industrial workers) was founded in DUBLIN in October 1879 by DAVITT and others to bring together the struggle for HOME RULE and agitation for land reform. The prototype of the League had been founded in County Mayo in August of the same year by Davitt. Through PARNELL, the Land League looked to American-Irish financial backing, to which end the Irish National Land and Industrial League of the United States was formed in New York by Parnell in November 1880. There is no doubt that to Parnell the Land League was part and parcel of the move towards Irish independence, and Parnell's Presidency of the League gave him the means to assert himself as leader of the HOME RULE PARTY in Parliament. The land League was from its inception intended to be a mass movement, rooted in the townships and BARONIES of rural Ireland, in principle eschewing PHYSICAL FORCE but resorting to intimidation (see BOYCOTTING) to register its case. It developed and grew with the violence of the LAND WAR that

began in 1879, although Parnell distanced himself and the movement from the AGRARIAN OUTRAGES that became more frequent and widely reported in the press. The British government, however, chose to see, or professed to see, in the League's agitation something conspiratorial and revolutionary. Whilst it was true that FENIAN involvement was identifiable, to the more purist of the Fenian revolutionaries, the League was by no means as vigorously nationalist as they might desire. This partly reflected the fact that within the League, hitherto disparate interest groups came together, however tenuously at times: dairy and grassland farmers and small arable farmers, their common cause being their tenant status. Tenancy standing and virtually complete identification which Catholicism were the common factors of the membership. The remarkable thing about the League was that it brought together old enemies, and gave them a coherent and specific goal. It looked like Catholic Ireland, Irish peasantry, on the march, and that was what concerned and bewildered the government. Landlords and ORANGE lodges also found themselves co-operating against the League for these very reasons, again by no means a natural alliance of interests, but based upon a perception similar to that of the government. When the Land League was proclaimed in 1881 as a 'criminal association' and its leaders gaoled, the Ladies' Land League (founded in 1880 in America and in January 1881 in Ireland) with its radical executive, took over direction of events, which in itself revealed the potential for rifts within the movement between its various group interests. Support for non-payment of rents, pushed as far as it was possible to go without risking EVICTION, was neither uniform within the movement, nor applied uniformly in the countryside. Indeed, to the radicals of the Ladies' League, evictions were necessary to further radicalize the League's campaign, a doctrinaire view that did not gain wide currency within the rank and file of the membership. Tenants did not, for example, question the justice of rents as such, but only the scale of them and the way in which they were arrived at. The tenants were not so radical as to believe the land was theirs by right (something even LALOR had not gone so far as to suggest) but just radical enough to hold back payments and thus create the maximum of nuisance for the landlords and their agents. The truth was, tenants would pay if they could pay. They needed a reform of the system which would give to them the means to pay. The League's membership were not the stuff of revolution that the Ladies' League hoped they were or may have led themselves to think that they were. For the same reason, ideas of land nationalization did not gain currency outside the 'intellectual' levels of the League. The government's LAND LEGISLATION of 1881, following the proposals of the BESS-BOROUGH COMMISSION, went some way towards meeting tenant grievances over security of tenure and rent arbitration. The League asserted itself again in 1886/7 but disputed within itself about the proposed PLAN OF CAMPAIGN urged by radical members. Further land legislation in 1887 extended the terms of the 1881 Act, and there was a marked downward trend in rent levels for the rest of the century. The Land League as constituted in 1879 was no longer a significant movement.

Land Legislation

As the nineteenth century developed, the British government moved on the land issue in Ireland, legislating to meet the demands and necessities of landlords and tenants (often mutually incompatible groupings) and thereby redressing grievances arising from the land settlements of the seventeenth century and the virtual inertia of the eighteenth. Land legislation evolved around basic problems: the difficulties of landlords with heavily encumbered estates and bankruptcies, tenants seeking security for their tenures, safeguards against EVICTIONS, compensation for their improvements on their holdings (see ULSTER CUSTOM) and safeguarded rents, and the perennial problem of poverty and distress in the countryside amongst labourers and smallholders. Movements such as the LAND LEAGUE and TENANT LEAGUE developed to press for reforms: they

galvanized public opinion outside Parliament and, through sympathetic or representative MPs in WESTMINSTER, applied pressure upon the government. The role of the IRISH PARLIAMENTARY PARTY, under its various guises (see INDEPENDENT IRISH PARTY, HOME RULE PARTY) was crucial in concentrating ministerial minds upon the land issue, chiefly, when they had the numbers, by acting as power brokers within the House of Commons. The progress of legislation was neither uniform nor always coherent; the FAMINE of 1845–49 revealed the appalling consequences of doctrinaire free market principles when applied to a situation such as that prevailing in Ireland. There was a constant grudging British attitude towards alleviation of Irish problems, particularly if the pressure for reform could be presented as tied up in some way with quasi-revolutionary programmes and 'secret society' republicanism. Nevertheless, there was a steady progression from the 1860s onwards. The Land Improvement Act of May 1860, for example, in providing loans for the erection of cottage dwellings for labourers, anticipated the more far-reaching legislation of the LABOURERS' ACT of 1883. DEASY'S ACT – the Landlord and Tenant Law Amendment Act of August 1860 – established the principle of government intervention in the relationship between landlord and tenant, although in this instance, motivated by doctrinaire free trade ideas, in favour of the landlord by in fact appearing to deny that tenant right such as then existed in parts of Ireland, could be legislated for. The first major legislation came in 1870 with GLADSTONE's first venture into the land law, in the Landlord and Tenant (Ireland) Act of 1 August. It was wide-ranging, recognizing the tenant-right principle inherent in Ulster Custom and providing for compensation at eviction for improvements made by the tenant on his holding. It established entitlement to compensation for eviction if the eviction were for causes other than rent arrears. Tenants seeking to purchase their farms could be advanced two-thirds of the price from the Commissioners of Public Works repayable, with interest, over a 35-year period. Against these positive aspects, the Act failed to legislate for rent controls, and the government failed to realize that most tenants could not raise the one-third of the purchase price needed to acquire their holdings. Take-up was, therefore, low. Leaseholders of leases of more than 31 years were exempted from the Act's provisions, and landlords began to shift towards leases in lieu of tenancies 'at will', of which some 77 per cent of landholdings in Ireland were composed before the 1870 Act. Implicit in the Act was Gladstone's acceptance that the Irish land system was thoroughly inequitable, that the Irish people had been methodically robbed of their land and rights for several hundred years, and that to redress the balance an attack upon landlord rights was unavoidable. Certainly the 1870 Act was seen as a direct interference with property rights. The Shaw-Lefevre Commission of 1878 recommended to the government that greater facilities be made available to tenants wishing to purchase their holdings. (The 1869 Act for DISESTABLISHMENT of the CHURCH OF IRELAND and the ensuant Glebe Lands Act of 1870 had extended the principle of tenant-assisted purchase to holders of church lands). The BESSBOROUGH COMMISSION, set up in 1880 to look into the working of the 1870 Act, reported in 1881 and laid emphasis upon the THREE F's – Fair Rent, Free Sale and Fixity of Tenure. The Land Law (Ireland) Act of 22 August 1881 incorporated the Bessborough recommendations in its provisions. Gladstone's second major land legislation, the 1881 Act, established a Land Commission and Land Courts and ensured that tenant improvement did not result in increased rents, providing an incentive for the conscientious tenant. Tenants might apply to the courts to have rents fixed for 15 years, and would enjoy security of tenure whilst their rents were paid up to date. This Land Act has ben viewed as more of a political measure aimed at the Land League, and PARNELL, its leader, was keen to have its measures tested in the new courts. Certainly, there were important omissions from its terms. The Arrears of Rent Act of 1882 extended the 1881 Act to cover 130,000 tenants estimated to be in arrears, entitling them to retrospective rent reductions, a move

that whilst it met Land League criticism, carried interference with landlord property rights so far that it has been seen as a death blow to the landlord interest. Ashbourne's Act, the Purchase of Land Act of 14 August 1885, provided £5 million to make it possible for tenants to borrow the entire purchase money for their holdings, with interest pegged at 4 per cent over 49 years. Some 950,000 acres changed hands in the ensuing years. In 1887 the Land Law (Ireland) Act extended the terms of the legislation of 1881 to leaseholders, enabling them to use the land courts to have their rents fixed. The Purchase of Land (Ireland) Act of 1891, known as Balfour's Act, provided £33 million towards tenant purchase through government stock, but was so bound up with complexities that the take-up was nowhere near the funds available. The same act saw the establishment of the important CONGESTED DISTRICTS BOARD which redistributed land in specific areas of Ireland and funded improvements. Legislation in 1896 empowered the land courts to sell some 1,500 bankrupt estates to their tenants. Wyndham's Act of 1903 (Wyndham was CHIEF SECRETARY in Ireland) dropped the government loan stock idea, legislated for the government to advance purchase monies at 3.25 per cent interest over 68½ years, and offered landlords a bonus for sale of their estates. It also made sale of estates to tenants where three-quarters of them required it, automatic. Wyndham's Act represented a further assault on the landlord position, and since for the most part the landlord and the ASCENDANCY were one and the same, it is clear the British government was undoing the structure by which power had been exerted in Ireland since 1691. Between 1906 and 1908 there were more than 100,000 land transactions attributable to the terms of Wyndham's Act, and by 1914 it was estimated that almost three-quarters of Ireland's farmers owned their own land. It was a complete transformation of the land system that had been established between 1641 and 1691. The introduction in 1909 of compulsion on landlords (Birrell's Act) coupled with the 1907 Evicted Tenants' Act which allowed reinstatement and the compulsory purchase of land for victims of eviction, affirmed the direction of legislation. When, in 1909, a further act extended the powers of the Congested Districts Board and added compulsory purchase powers, the legislative achievement of various British ministries was accomplished. The principle of purchase aid was inherited by DÁIL ÉIREANN and applied in its legislative programme of 1919.

Land War, The

The Land War, a prolonged intensification of violent rural unrest, is ascribed to the period 1879–82, with a brief outburst again in 1886/7. It arose from a variety of causes that came together in a general agricultural depression (not confined exclusively to Ireland). There was an atmosphere of expectation in the HOME RULE campaign and in the development of the LAND LEAGUE: debt-ridden landlords and the just plain greedy pitted against tenants who found their rents impossible to pay; the consequent widespread EVICTIONS with all their associated injustices; and the poor harvests creating near-FAMINE conditions in Connacht, where the Land War had its roots and its first expression. The targets of the Land War activists were landlords, their agents, their bailiffs, and those tenants who took advantage of the times to increase their holdings at the expense of their less successful neighbours. In April 1878 the notorious landlord the Earl of Leitrim was assassinated in County Donegal in what seemed like an isolated incident of local vengeance, but the killing was not compatible with the actions of earlier generations of agrarian agitators (see WHITEBOYS, ROCKITES). During February 1879 religious disturbances in Connemara directed at Protestant missionary activity contributed to increasing instability and in April in County Mayo there was a major demonstration of land agitation, followed by further meetings, one of which, addressed by PARNELL in June, was urged to let the landlords see the tenancy intended to keep a 'firm grip' on their 'homesteads and lands'. In October the first expression of what became known as BOYCOTTING was voiced, and the Land League came into being in October. All

political activism within Ireland now appeared to turn around the land question, 'the question of questions', and in November Parnell led 8,000 country people to prevent an eviction in County Mayo. The degree of distress apparent in rural Ireland led even the wife of the LORD LIEUTENANT to organize relief, raising £135,000 within 12 months in Britain as well as in Ireland. In January 1880, 3,000 peasants rallied to drive off a force of police come to support a bailiff in the eviction of a family at Carraroe, County Galway. The government took immediate remedial measures, empowering POOR LAW Guardians to provide seed potatoes for the destitute, and making provision for outdoor relief; on the other hand, the ROYAL IRISH CONSTABULARY was equipped with large supplies of cartridges for shotguns to use against crowds. Violence was rife in Kerry, Galway, Leitrim and Westmeath, and radiating out from there. Another landlord, Viscount Mountmorres, was assassinated in County Galway in September 1880. The government moved against Parnell and the Land League leadership, and against local branches, such as that at Kilmallock, County Limerick where, amongst those arrested, they seized Father Sheehy, a local priest. The government signally failed to distinguish between Land League agitation and rural violence rooted in the issues that had given rise to the Land League. The League certainly attempted to restrain violent outbreaks by seeking to channel outrage into a national campaign, and through its activities in Parliament, to be seen to be pressing the peasantry's case. Government repression of the League merely enhanced its reputation, and at the same time helped generate further unrest. The 1881 LAND LEGISLATION was the only positive long-term measure adopted by the government. The Protection of Person and Property Act of March 1881 which allowed for imprisonment without trial of those suspected of offences, more properly reflected British attitudes.

Landlord Absenteeism

'The landlord system' said JOHN DEVOY 'is the greatest curse inflicted by England on Ireland', a view held by many in the eighteenth and nineteenth centuries, often in relation to the absentee. Absenteeism fuelled the suspicion of, and hostility towards, England that became marked in ASCENDANCY attitudes during the eighteenth century, and was inherent in PATRIOT concerns for Ireland. Absentees were those landlords who, enjoying estates in Ireland, resided more or less permanently elsewhere (usually in England) and so drew the revenues of their property out of Ireland. Thomas Priors' *A list of the absentees of Ireland, and the yearly value of their estates and incomes spent abroad* compiled in 1729 (when some £326,000 was reckoned to have been drained from the Irish economy), went into six further editions before 1783, indicative of the widely-accepted view that absenteeism was prejudicial to the Irish economy in a major way. ARTHUR YOUNG writing in 1779 estimated that some £732,000 poured out of Ireland every year to landlords he condemned as 'lazy, trifling [and] negligent', for the revenues would have financed much-needed improvements, as Young saw them, in Ireland's agriculture. None of these early estimates are wholly reliable. The first accurate statistical survey, that of 1870, showed that 97 per cent of all Irish land was managed in the interests of landlords who lived off the rents, though not all were absentee. Research has indicated that in the years prior to the FAMINE of 1845–49 between one-third and one-half of landowners were unquestionably absentees. The 1870 statistics revealed 49.3 per cent of landlords were ordinarily absentee, but that 36 per cent merely lived away from their estates whilst remaining in Ireland (in urban centres for the most part). One of the consequences of absenteeism was the employment of the universally detested land agents, who managed the estates, set the rents, undertook contractual negotiations and, for the most part, moved in the bailiffs and the police to EVICT. That absenteeism was so marked in Ireland was entirely due to the way in which Irish land had been allotted to English and Scottish speculators during the mid-seventeenth century, creating a landowning class whose interest was largely pecuniary. LAND LEGISLATION from

1870 onwards effectively destroyed the landlord interest, and rid Ireland of the absentee phenomenon.

Language, The Irish

The history of the Irish language is well documented. Modern Irish, developing in the seventeenth century out of Irish Gaelic or Goedelic is the fourth development in the language recognized by philologists, preceded by Middle Irish which is ascribed to the period from 1600 BC to AD 900. The survival of the language under English colonization, PLANTATION, ANGLICIZATION and the spread of CIVILITY, was due firstly to its exclusivity – a means of communication of which the vast majority of the English were ignorant – and secondly to the survival of a strong Gaelic literary tradition. The language was, for its users, an expression of anti-Englishness, one of the few weapons left to them after the suppressions of the mid and late seventeenth century which in many respects destroyed native Gaelic cultural and social forms. WILLIAM PETTY writing in the 1670s remarked upon the proficiency of native Irish in the use of the Latin tongue, which points towards another factor in the language's survival: not only the proficiency of the Irish in languages, but their delight in the use of them, remarked upon by English people in the eighteenth and nineteenth centuries when seasonal Irish migrant labourers came among them. In short, the Irish could talk and express themselves volubly. Amongst the English there was division in attitudes towards the Irish language. Some saw it as a barrier to the Anglicization process, others were content for the peasantry to use it so long as the formal life of the country was conducted in English. This was the norm by 1641: the Supreme Council of the CATHOLIC CONFEDERACY conversed, published and communicated generally in English. In time native Irish retreated to the west and south-west of the country, a language of the dispossessed, of the peasantry and the fallen Gaelic gentry. Parallel with this was a scholarly interest in it, akin to that for Latin, which regarded the Irish language as an accomplished form to be studied as any other dead language might be studied. De Montbret, a French traveller in Kerry in the 1790s, noted that though a good deal of Irish could be heard spoken, precious few of its speakers could read it. There is no doubt that the massive dislocation of the FAMINE, with consequent EMIGRATION and dispersal, undermined the language and its continuity. Quite incidentally, Protestant missionaries aiming to convert Catholics perpetuated its use. John Richardson's *A proposal for the conversion of the popish natives of Ireland* of 1712 advocated using their language to influence them. Thomas Price, CHURCH OF IRELAND archbishop of Cashel 1667–85 advocated the use of Gaelic in formal worship. The 1818 missionary society, 'Society for Promoting the Education of the Native Irish', was designed to promote its ends through Gaelic. The ASCENDANCY-dominated TRINITY COLLEGE instituted a chair in Irish in 1838. A nationalist spokesman in 1892 said 'if HOME RULE be carried … the Irish language … shall be placed on a par with – or even above – Greek, Latin and modern languages in all examinations held under the Irish government'. The nationalist surge of the late nineteenth century led to a parallel development of interest in the preservation and promotion of the native tongue: indeed, so much emphasis was placed upon matters cultural in opposition to pervasive Anglicization, that some historians have seen the cultural revival as filling a vacuum in political activism, without perceiving they were one and the same thing. PADRAIC PEARSE the leader of the EASTER RISING of 1916 was, not coincidentally, an accomplished Gaelic scholar, fluent in the language. To many nationalists and revolutionary republicans, the Irish language was an expression of Irishness, a thing in itself undefiled by colonization, expropriation and dispossession. But it is also true that the use of English as a recognized international language of communication, meant that its associations with conquest and oppression had to be ignored. From the deliberations of the Confederacy in 1641 to the meetings of the Military Council of the IRISH REPUBLICAN BROTHERHOOD in 1916, the language

of active Irish assertiveness was the language of the enemy.

Larkin, James (1876–1947)

Liverpool-born of Irish parentage, Larkin developed and made into an effective weapon, the unionization of dock labour in Ireland. An organizer of the National Union of Dock Labourers, Larkin organized and led a strike in BELFAST dockyard against the Belfast Steamship Company in May 1907, all the more effective for managing to subsume sectarian differences within a working-class action. He worked effectively with the INDEPENDENT ORANGE ORDER, and managed to undermine the resolution of the ROYAL IRISH CONSTABULARY. His tactics were directly confrontational, but he could not sustain the unity of Catholics and Protestants and by 1908 the strike had collapsed. In that year he founded the Irish TRANSPORT AND GENERAL WORKERS' UNION. Larkin never espoused or adopted 'nationalism', he was interested solely in the development of socialism and the principle of industrial action to improve working conditions. On 26 August 1913 the tram workers in DUBLIN struck under his leadership, police and strikers clashed violently (see Dublin LOCK-OUT), and Larkin was gaoled for seven months for sedition. He went to America on his release, and in 1921 condemned the ANGLO-IRISH TREATY. Gaoled in America for syndicalism, 1920–23, he returned to Ireland and remained active in labour politics.

Larne Gun Running, The

In April 1914 at Larne, Donaghadee and Bangor some 35,000 firearms and between 2 and 3 million rounds of ammunition were unloaded to supply and equip the ULSTER VOLUNTEER FORCE, which had been raised to defend the UNION with Britain in face of mounting likelihood of HOME RULE being imposed on Ireland from London. The landing was organized by Major F.H. Crawford on behalf of the UVF Commander, General Sir William Adair, and had the active complicity of EDWARD CARSON the Unionist spokesman in the Commons. No effort was made by the British authorities to interfere with the landing (see also HOWTH). Carson gave the Larne incident full publicity within the House, intending it as a warning from ULSTER to the British government. In fact, the exclusion of the SIX COUNTIES of Ulster from Home Rule had already been determined.

Laudianism

Laudianism derives its name from the archbishop of Canterbury, William Laud (1573–1645), and refers to the policy adopted by Laud (in compliance with King Charles I) of reform within the Church of England. That reform movement was extended to the CHURCH OF IRELAND under the auspices of THOMAS WENTWORTH the LORD DEPUTY. Basically, Laudianism represented a return to ritual in the established Protestant Church, and a break with the emphasis on Calvinist doctrine that had been prevalent during the late sixteenth century. It meant the return of altars to the east end of churches, and the abandonment of the idea of them as 'tables' around which the congregation gathered. Laudianism restored observances such as that of bowing at the name of Christ. Laudianism in the Church of Ireland encountered less resistance than it did in England: the archbishop of ARMAGH, Ussher, by no means a Laudian, made no effort to resist the appointment of Laudians to episcopal office, nor to the imposition of the 39 articles of Anglican doctrine observed in the Church of England. Laudianism, like the established churches, was crushed and abolished by the Long Parliament of 1641–60 as part of its reform measures during the ENGLISH CIVIL WAR. The Laudian tendency, however, re-emerged in both England and Ireland at the restoration of Charles II in 1660.

Lavelle, Father Patrick (1825–86)

Father Lavelle is an example of the kind of political Catholic priest who exercised the concern of the Catholic Church hierarchy. Born in County Mayo and educated at ST PATRICK'S COLLEGE, Maynooth, he became a parish priest in 1858 after a period lecturing in Paris. One historian has described Lavelle as a 'crank', apparently on the grounds that his 1870 book *The Irish landlord since the revolution* (of 1688) argued that landlordism was essentially immoral and that security of tenure was an essential. The book was a wide-ranging survey of tenurial custom throughout Europe, offering comparative remarks intended to point the way forward for Ireland. Lavelle's preference for smallholdings with fixity of tenure was a recognition of the poverty and distress caused by farm consolidation ensuant upon the FAMINE of 1845–49, but already a feature of Irish agriculture from long before. Lavelle ran into trouble with Cardinal CULLEN and other church leaders, who took exception to his association with revolutionaries, and particularly to his *Catholic Doctrine of the Right of Revolution* of 1862.

League of North and South *see* TENANT LEAGUE

Leases for Lives

The holding of land by lease for three specified lives was a normal tenurial practice in England which became increasingly popular in Ireland, amongst landlords, during the eighteenth and nineteenth centuries. A leaseholder would take the tenancy of a property which (provided the rent was paid) was guaranteed to him for the duration of the lives of three named persons whose exact ages were known. The landlord's income from the rent over the duration of a lease of this kind was boosted by 'fines', lump sum payments made at the conclusion of the contract, and levied whenever it was necessary to replace a life, for example, if one or two of the three specified should die. Theoretically the lease was thus renewable in perpetuity, and, moreover, the tenant was able to sell his interest to an incoming tenant, provided the landlord ratified the changeover. It was a far more secure tenure than those based upon yearly renewal, and those tenancies held at the 'will' of the landlord. Leases for lives also suited middlemen, who could rent out the land at rents profitable to them, and covering their annual rent and the fine to the landlord.

Leinster, Plantation in (*see also* PLANTATION)

Leinster, of all the ancient provinces of Ireland, was the most ANGLICIZED, with a dominant OLD ENGLISH gentry and nobility and little GAELIC IRISH presence. The process of PLANTATION, therefore, was less rigorous and more peacefully accomplished. Leix and Offaly (Queen's and King's Counties) were 'planted' in 1556. Wexford presented an obstacle. It was an area with Anglicized Gaelic landowners, and, following the usual practice, surrender was made of existing titles to land in expectation of regrant by the crown. The NEW ENGLISH settler element made the most of a technicality in the procedure to intrude themselves. The government in DUBLIN expropriated freeholders enjoying less than 100-acre holdings and turned them into leaseholders, in this way freeing between a quarter and a half of the land for plantation. Protests to London led to TRANSPORTATION to the Americas for the more persistent. In 1611 there were surrenders and regrants in Wicklow, Wexford and Carlow, and patents for plantations in Leitrim, King's and Queen's and Westmeath were issued. All regrants involved diminution of the old holdings, setting aside territory for crown-sponsored plantation and resettlement. A survey in 1622 revealed that the new landowners were predominantly absentee (see also LANDLORD ABSENTEEISM) drawing rents from the native Irish occupiers of their lands.

Leinster Army, The

The Leinster Army of the CATHOLIC CONFEDERACY was the last of the Confederacy's armies to surrender itself to the government, when its commander, CLANRICARDE, submitted to Edmund Ludlow in May 1652. The Confederacy's armies had been based in each of the four provinces of Ireland following the alliance of the ULSTER rebels of 1641 with the OLD ENGLISH.

Leinster Lease

The term 'Leinster Lease' enjoyed a common currency in the nineteenth century, meaning a one-sided agreement or bargain. It arose from tenurial practice on the estates of the Duke of Leinster in County Donegal, where tenants were obliged to sign away any entitlement to compensation for any improvements made on the property by them if they were evicted unless with the lessor's prior agreement. This procedure was intended to enable the Duke of Leinster to circumvent the LAND LEGISLATION of 1870. Leinster himself was assassinated in 1878 by his tenants.

Levellers

An alternative name for the WHITEBOYS.

Liberal Clubs

The Liberal Clubs began to appear and to spread in the 1820s as localized political organizations of the CATHOLIC ASSOCIATION in its struggle for EMANCIPATION. Membership was not exclusively Catholic: the middle-class orientation of the clubs included liberal Protestants sympathetic to reform. Their significance lay in the way that the clubs represented local opinion to the central organization, and organized that opinion on its behalf. The clubs survived the emancipation victory of 1829 and became more radicalized, moving towards republicanism, sometimes refounded as 'Independent Clubs'.

Liberator, The

Affectionate nickname for DANIEL O'CONNELL.

Lichfield House Compact

The General Election of 1835 saw 34 liberal repeal candidates returned for Irish seats, alongside 34 Liberals and 37 Conservatives. The Repealers, or O'Connellites, met in February at Lichfield House in London with other Liberals and radical MPs from British seats. The result was the Lichfield House Compact, by which the Repealers agreed to co-operate with the other anti-Conservative groupings within the House of Commons. Amongst the consequences of this alliance was the Poor Relief Act of 1838 (see POOR LAW) and the MUNICIPAL REFORM ACT of 1840. The appointment of the Liberal THOMAS DRUMMOND as Under Secretary in Ireland was a reflection of the Compact, introducing into a crucial administrative post a man sympathetic to the Catholics and intent upon challenging the ORANGE ORDER and its power in ULSTER and within the Irish police (see CONSTABULARY). The compact lasted effectively for six years, and during that time, Ireland was administered with a view to meeting Catholic grievances.

Limerick, Siege of

The city of Limerick, on the estuary of the river Shannon, was a major city by the seventeenth century, probably the third largest in Ireland, divided into 'English' and 'Irish' towns, the English being heavily fortified and standing upon an island. It was a city of strategic importance during the JACOBITE wars of 1689–91, and what happened there, apart from the military affairs, was of crucial importance for more than 200 years. On 9 August King WILLIAM III's forces laid siege to the city, harried by Jacobite troops who, on 11 August, destroyed the besieger's siege train at Ballyneety. The siege was raised on 30 August, and the city was open again. The Earl of TYRCONNELL arrived there in January 1691, and was joined by the French General SAINT-RUTH in May. Tyrconnell's death in the city in August of that year deprived the Jacobites of a leading General who might have made peace with William III. Defence of the city fell to PATRICK SARSFIELD, when the siege was rejoined by the Dutch General GINKEL in August 1691. By that time Limerick was the last stronghold of the Jacobites, who had been defeated in battle at the BOYNE (in 1690) and at AUGHRIM (in 1691). Morale was low, and the defenders offered to treat. Negotiations followed upon a truce on 24 September, and the Treaty of LIMERICK was formally signed on 3 October. The sorry consequences of that Treaty, which were to give to Limerick the euphemism 'City of the Broken

Treaty', dogged the Catholics of Ireland for generations. By the military terms, Sarsfield and his fighting men were permitted to go into France, the flight of the WILD GEESE that eventually gave the French kings a formidable, anti-British fighting force which they used for a century or more.

Limerick had also been besieged by HENRY IRETON in June 1651, and had surrendered to him in October of that year. Ireton died in the city within a month, from plague.

In March 1921 George Clancy, Mayor of Limerick, and the former Mayor Michael O'Callaghan, were murdered by British forces, during the WAR FOR INDEPENDENCE.

Limerick, Treaty of

The Treaty of Limerick was the formal declaration of the terms by which the JACOBITE city was surrendered to the Dutch General GINKEL on 3 October 1691. Ginkel wished to bring the war to an end as quickly as possible, for the Jacobite surrender would entail their abandonment of large areas of Cork, Clare, Kerry and Mayo. To this end, it was argued then and since, that Ginkel went further than he ought to have done. The military terms were straightforward and unexceptional, involving free passage of the soldiery under SARSFIELD to go into France. Sarsfield had endeavoured to make the terms as generous towards the Catholics as he could, and Ginkel had obliged him: there were vague references to such religious freedom as the Catholics had enjoyed in the reign of King Charles II, guarantees of pardon and security of property for those diehard Jacobites who surrendered themselves and swore allegiance to King WILLIAM III. The Treaty actually covered those 'in arms' for King JAMES II. Sarsfield pushed for, and achieved, a clause to the effect that those 'civilians' under the protection of the Jacobite forces would enjoy similar terms. Ginkel consented, and Limerick yielded. By the time the Treaty reached William III in London, the last clause had been omitted. Against advice, the king inserted it himself into the final draft of the Treaty. The Irish PARLIAMENT in October 1692, dominated by Protestants, protested at the clause, but as events turned out, the Treaty was meaningless beyond the fulfilment of the terms for the departure of the fighting men. From 1695 onwards PENAL LAWS, totally against the spirit and purpose of the Treaty of Limerick, were imposed upon Catholics in Ireland and enforced for a further 130 years. To many Irish Catholics years hence, the breaking of the Treaty symbolized the perfidy of the British and the institutionalized intolerance of the minority Protestant population.

Limerick Soviet, The

On 14 April 1919 a general strike was organized in Limerick by the Limerick United Trades and Labour Council, bringing out 15,000 workers. The strike leaders organized a workers' 'soviet' on the Russian revolutionary model, although their target was the martial law imposed upon the city on 6 April following an attempt to rescue the republican hunger-striker Robert Byrne. The soviet collapsed by 25 April. Another soviet was established by creamery workers in Knoclong County Limerick in May 1920, but this was broken up (and the creamery wrecked) by ROYAL IRISH CONSTABULARY action in August.

Local Government Act, The Irish

The Local Government Act of 12 August 1898 brought to an end the old GRAND JURY system, already much curtailed during the course of the nineteenth century. The legislation provided for elective county and district councils for urban and rural districts. Under the terms of the Act the LORD LIEUTENANT ordered that women be entitled to serve on the district councils, though they were prohibited from doing so on county (and borough) councils. In December 1911 the Local Authorities Act gave women access to those councils, as well.

Lock-Out, The Dublin

The DUBLIN Lock-Out, the 'revolt of the slums', was the consequence of employer reaction to the spreading unionization of labour within the city under the aegis of LARKIN and CONNOLLY. In August 1913 William Murphy, the employers' leader, dismissed 40 men for their membership of the TRANSPORT AND GENERAL WORKERS' UNION. An all-out strike of tramway workers was called for 26 August, which developed under Larkin's leadership into a general strike. Clashes between strikers and police within the city developed. A summer of industrial unrest, which had even involved pupils at the city's national schools, had come to a climax. At the instigation of the Dublin United Tramways Company, the city's Employers' Federation met on 3 September and agreed to require pledges from their employees not to join the union. Some 25,000 men refused to give such a pledge, and were 'locked-out' from their places of work by their employers. Larkin was arrested and imprisoned for 'sedition', and the confrontation in the streets between strikers and police (in which two strikers, James Byrne and James Nolan, were beaten to death by the police) led to the formation in November of the CITIZEN ARMY, intended as a disciplined defence force for use in future industrial conflicts. Food supplies for the locked out men were organized from charity efforts in England and America, but help from trade unionists in Britain was not forthcoming, its leaders responding with suspicion as to the motives of the Irish union leaders. A commission of inquiry into the lock-out in October 1913 recommended withdrawal of the pledge requirement for two years, to facilitate a return to work with a reciprocal agreement by the workforce not to strike for two years. In January 1914 Connolly was obliged to recommend a return to work provided the pledge was withdrawn, but the union action merely sanctioned the drift-back occasioned by hunger and the lack of support from union members elsewhere. The Builders' Labourers' Union actually agreed with its employer counterpart to exclude TGWU members from its ranks.

Loftus, Adam (Viscount Ely) (1568–1643)

Loftus was the nephew of the Adam Loftus, in turn archbishop of Armagh and of DUBLIN, who was involved in the foundation of TRINITY COLLEGE. Loftus rose rapidly in the Irish administration, becoming a Privy Councillor in 1608 and Lord Chancellor in 1619, after an earlier church career. Loftus headed one of the NEW ENGLISH political groups, that which opposed the LORD DEPUTY, Lord Falkland, in the 1620s, and which seemed to enjoy OLD ENGLISH confidence. When THOMAS WENTWORTH was appointed Lord Deputy, Loftus gravitated to his side as the best guarantee of further preferment. Since 1629 Wentworth had acted as LORD JUSTICE, virtually ruler of Ireland, alongside his political adversary the Earl of CORK, and under Wentworth's rule Cork became progressively isolated. Wentworth used Loftus as he used MOUNTNORRIS, whose fall and disgrace enabled Loftus to secure the Vice-Treasureship of Ireland under Wentworth's patronage. The Lord Deputy did not need New English support, and Loftus fell from power in 1637 and was gaoled for a time. His experience subdued him, but the incident was used in the articles of impeachment directed against Wentworth (as Earl of Strafford) by the Long Parliament of 1641, and which led to Wentworth's execution.

Lombard, Peter (1560–1625)

Peter Lombard was born in Waterford, and ordained in the CATHOLIC CHURCH. Archbishop of Armagh from 1601, he was a most influential advocate of, and representative for, the Earl of TYRONE during the latter's rebellion which ended in 1603. Lombard was based in Rome, where his enthusiasm for the Irish Rebellion and for Spanish intervention, brought him into conflict with other, like himself OLD ENGLISH, Catholic clergy who were more concerned with averting anti-Catholic measures from England. Lombard's *De regno Hiberniae sanctorum insula commentarius*, written in 1600 and eventually published in Louvain in 1632, was an evocation of Tyrone's rising as a defence of the interests of the Catholic Church, a means of urging the papacy to lend its support to the struggle. (The book was later suppressed in Ireland by LORD DEPUTY WENTWORTH). The written word secured Lombard his archbishopric (he never visited Ireland again however), and some other signs of papal favour, but Pope Clement VIII refused to require Irish Catholics to support Tyrone. Subsequent events persuaded Lombard of the need for the Catholics in Ireland to reach a compromise with King James I's government once Tyrone had abandoned the country in 1607 (see FLIGHT OF THE EARLS).

Lord Lieutenant, Lord Deputy and the Lords Justices

Definition of the functions of the Lord Lieutenant, the Lord Deputy and the Lords Justices is simplified if they are seen as 'Chief Governors' or 'Deputy Governors' representing the authority of the English or British crown in Ireland. The titles, which are often used confusedly, are in fact irrelevant when what is referred to is an exercise of power, directing the British administration in Ireland, enforcing legislation and, when necessary, directing the machinery of military repression. The use of terms such as 'Viceroy' and 'Governor' by historians is meant to convey that authority. From 1172 when Hugh de Lacy was appointed 'Justiciar', to 1921 when the last Lord Lieutenant was appointed (Viscount FitzAlan), Ireland was governed by either a single representative of the crown of England (those parts of Ireland which fell under or acknowledged English supremacy), or by Lords Justices (Deputy Governors) working in tandem, or (as in the 1650s) by commissioners answerable to the English Parliament. Beneath them, increasing in complexity as the centuries wore on, was a bureaucratic structure that by 1566 was headed by the CHIEF SECRETARY. The Lord Lieutenant was always an appointee of social standing and wealth, but, until the mid-eighteenth century, the office might be an honour that rarely involved a visit to, let alone residence in, Ireland. The role of Deputy, however, implied active involvement and presence in DUBLIN at the centre of the administration (see CASTLE), whilst the Lords Justices were ordinarily 'Irish' anyway (or saw themselves as such). Government by Lords

Justices was often an interim measure, as, for example, when in March 1643 King Charles I appointed John Borlase and Henry Tichborne Lords Justices, who executed the office of Chief Governor for a few months before the Earl of ORMOND was appointed Lord Lieutenant in November 1643. From the 1760s the Chief Governor was encouraged to reside in Dublin, and this development increased the influence of the CHIEF SECRETARY. At the UNION of Britain and Ireland which took effect in 1801, some doubt attached to the future role of the Chief Governor, but the Lord Lieutenancy was retained even though the Deputy Governorship ceased, the last appointees being the archbishop of Armagh and FITZGIBBON who took office in 1795. From the time of the Union, the Chief Governorship was always exercised by the Lord Lieutenant, although he no longer exercised the right to summon and to dissolve the Irish PARLIAMENT, which had ceased to function as a separate body at the Union. Following the ANGLO-IRISH TREATY of 1921 and the PARTITION of Ireland into north and south, a Governor-General was appointed to head the FREE STATE, symbolizing continued British sovereignty, whilst a Governor was appointed for the SIX COUNTIES of Northern Ireland. In 1937 the office of President of the Irish Republic came into being, with Douglas Hyde as its first holder. Thereupon the role and office of the Governor-General ceased, the last of the three men to have held that post being Domhnall Ua Buachalla. All three of the Governor-Generals had been native Irishmen. The Governorship of Northern Ireland was abolished in 1973 following imposition of direct rule from WESTMINSTER (a response to the vigorous campaign of the IRA in the north).

The Chief Governors of Ireland were intended to be reflective of policy originating in London, whether a powerful and single-minded Lord Deputy such as THOMAS WENTWORTH in the 1630s (who discovered he could not make royal policy, only implement it), or a dangerously thoroughgoing reformer like FITZWILLIAM who was Lord Lieutenant for seven weeks in 1795. FitzWilliam was answerable to the government of the day

in Britain. He, and others, were appointed chiefly because of their acceptability to the British ministries. The power of the Chief Governors and of the Deputy Governors was thus circumscribed from London. They headed an administration, but they were also part of it, and because of that, susceptible to pressures, decisions, policy changes and instructions from Westminster. (See Appendix 1 for a list of Chief Governors and Deputy Governors).

Lorraine, Charles IV, Duke of

In the DUNFERMLINE DECLARATION of 16 August 1650, King Charles II disowned and denounced royalist alliance with the CATHOLIC CONFEDERACY, under pressure from the bitterly anti-Catholic Scottish PRESBYTERIANS. In November 1650 an assembly of Confederate leaders met to consider the 'betrayal', and to require the royalist Earl of ORMOND to hand over his discredited authority to the Earl of CLANRICARDE. Clanricarde was, in the eyes of the Irish at least, LORD DEPUTY, and there were Confederate plans to invite into Ireland the soldier Duke of Lorraine, expelled from his duchy by the French in 1633, and based in the Netherlands in service of the Holy Roman Empire. Lorraine may have been approached by the Irish rebels as early as 1645, but definite approaches were made in the summer of 1650 when Ormond sent Lord Taafe to Brussels to negotiate the alliance. Subsequent talks were to be held in Ireland, but the Dunfermline Declaration and Ormond's departure, confused matters. The Confederacy sent two delegates back to Brussels, whilst Clanricarde dealt with Lorraine's envoy in Ireland.

Loyalists and Loyalism

In the Irish context, these words have a specific political and largely sectarian meaning. Loyalists regarded (and regard) themselves as loyal to the UNION of Britain and Ireland of 1801, which deprived Ireland of its separate Parliament. They were (and are) loyal to a Protestant dominance, rooted in the PENAL LAWS and suppressive legislation of the late seventeenth and early eighteenth centuries. Loyalism manifested itself in reaction to and in defiance of, the pressure for HOME RULE that took up where the movement for Repeal of the Union had left off in the mid-nineteenth century. Loyalism, somewhat qualified and almost contractual in its attitude to Britain, had long been part of the dogma of the ORANGE ORDER, but in the 1880s as the pressure for Home Rule seemed likely to pay off, given Liberal party support, the Conservative party saw in loyalty to the Union a political weapon to use against their political enemies at WESTMIN-STER. There was a proliferation of political, but not overtly sectarian, organizations using the word 'loyal' in their titles. In May 1885 Lords de Vesci and Castlehaven set up the Loyal and Patriotic Union, which performed disastrously in the 1885 General Election. In January 1886 conservatives in BELFAST founded the Ulster Loyalist Anti-Repeal Committee. GLADSTONE's third premiership began on 1 February 1886 and his commitment to Home Rule spurred the conservatives on. On 22 February Lord Randolph Churchill in a speech in Belfast gave approval to Loyalist militancy: 'Ulster will fight (and) Ulster will be right'. He saw the 'Orange card' as one that could be played to the detriment of Gladstone. The Loyalist platform attracted to it disenchanted liberals as well (just as Home Rule had an appeal for some radical Protestants, hence the Irish Protestant Home Rule Association founded in May 1886), and in June 1886 the Ulster Liberal Unionist Committee was formed. A rally of 12,000 delegates from local clubs was held in 1892 under the auspices of the Ulster Unionist Convention of Conservative and Liberal Unionists. In April 1893, 100,000 Loyalists paraded in Belfast to show their opposition to Home Rule. The problem of Loyalism was that it was only numerically significant in the province of ULSTER, and only in some counties of that province. It could not challenge the nationalism developing throughout the rest of Ireland and so, from its development as a mass movement, it was essentially defensive. Loyalism was an expression of the emotive principles that underlay Union-ism, and Unionism was the political expression of that reservoir of Loyalism. Unionism was given strength by its association with conservatism in British politics, and militant Unionism drew upon the traditions of the often denounced and suppressed Orange Order to demonstrate the long attachment of Protestant Irish to the British connection. In popular terms, the 'loyalist' was the epitome of Ulster Irishness, just as the 'rebel' symbolized the aspirations of nationalism for the majority of the Catholic Irish. (See REBELS.)

Luby, Thomas Clarke (1821–1901)

Luby was a Protestant nationalist, the son of a CHURCH OF IRELAND clergyman, educated at TRINITY COLLEGE and a product of the ASCENDANCY tradition. Attracted by the movement for repeal of the UNION of 1801 (which was by no means exclusively Catholic in origin or support), Luby gravitated to the YOUNG IRELAND wing of that movement and wrote for its journal NATION. Gaoled in 1849, he later became involved with JAMES STEPHENS and was a prominent leader of the IRISH REPUBLICAN BROTHERHOOD. Arrested again in 1865 he was released during the campaign of the AMNESTY ASSOCIATION for the freeing of revolutionary FENIANS in 1871, and went into exile in America.

Lucas, Charles (1713–71)

According to Lucas, a DUBLIN apothecary and political reformer, Protestant control of Ireland was entirely justifiable because the Protestants had the experience and the commitment to do the job. This was the view of an Irishman who, in 1749, was condemned as an enemy of his country by the Irish House of Commons and forced to flee into exile. Lucas, through his own paper the *Citizens' Journal* which first appeared in 1747, presented the case for Irish separation from Britain, and enunciated those principles of suspicion towards Britain that were later to be taken up by the PATRIOT Protestants of the 1770s and 1780s. Although described as the 'Wilkes of Ireland', Lucas was actually only a little ahead of his time. He articulated the 'Irish' Protestant view of themselves as the true Irish, capable of governing their own country and yet obliged to accept a secondary role in relation to the government and Parliament of Britain. Had he lived, GRATTAN's PARLIAMENT would have been an affirmation of his principles, and the Patriots who brought that Parliament about inherited Lucas's beliefs.

Lucas, Frederick (1812–55)

Lucas was brought up as a Quaker in England, but converted to Catholicism at the age of 18, and embarked upon a career in the law. His Catholicism was fiercely ultramontane. He published his *Reasons* for conversion, and in 1840 founded the *Tablet*, publication of which he transferred to DUBLIN in 1850. He sat as MP for Meath in the Commons after the General Election of 1852, where he was to be an important figure in the IRISH BRIGADE of MPs which developed in 1851 to resist the anti-Catholic ECCLESIASTICAL TITLES ACT. An active supporter of the TENANT LEAGUE outside Parliament, he was critical of the Catholic hierarchy's opposition to clerical involvement in the tenant struggle, and went to Rome to present his case to Pope Pius IX. The Pope asked Lucas to prepare a report on the situation in Ireland, but it was unfinished when Lucas died in 1855.

Lundy, Robert

To the Protestants of ULSTER from 1689, Lundy's name became a byword for treachery. He was a commander under King JAMES II in DERRY in that year, and accepted the Governorship of the city for King WILLIAM III. When JACOBITE forces of the Earl of Antrim moved against the city, Lundy advised surrender, but it was only he who left the city, its defence falling into more resolute hands.

M

MacBride, Sean (1865–1916)

Sean MacBride was a representative of the IRISH REPUBLICAN BROTHERHOOD in America in 1896 before emigrating to South Africa where, during the Boer War, he fought with the Boer forces against the British. In Paris he met and married MAUD GONNE in 1903, although they separated soon afterwards. He was appointed to the Supreme Council of the Irish Republican Brotherhood, but was not involved in the Military Council which planned and carried out the EASTER RISING of 1916. He fought in the rising under the command of THOMAS MACDONAGH, was captured, and shot to death on 5 May.

McCracken, Henry Joy (1767–98)

McCracken was a BELFAST Protestant of Huguenot descent, and a cotton-manufacturer by trade who, by default, became leader of the rising of the UNITED IRISHMEN in County Antrim in June 1798. McCracken's membership of the United Irishmen dated back several years: he was an associate of WOLFE TONE early on. But the military leadership in Antrim had devolved upon the Reverend Dickson and Robert Simms. Severe repression in ULSTER by General LAKE had virtually broken the resolution that would be needed for a mass rising, but after the arrest of Dickson, his successor, Simms, whilst appearing to be ready to rise, in practice hesitated. McCracken and Henry Munro realized if they hesitated they were lost for certain. On 7 June 1798 he commanded 4,000 men (predominantly PRESBYTERIANS), in an attack on Antrim town, which was fought off. McCracken was apprehended in July, tried and executed on 17 July.

Mac Curtáin, Tomás (d. 1920)

Tomás Mac Curtáin, Lord Mayor of Cork and commandant of the 1st Cork Brigade of the IRISH REPUBLICAN ARMY, was murdered at his home on 20 March 1920 by men of the ROYAL IRISH CONSTABULARY. One of their number, Inspector Swanzy, was himself gunned down in Lisburn by the IRA for his part in the murder.

Mac Diarmada, Séan (1884–1916)

Mac Diarmada (anglicized as Mac-Dermott) was born in County Leitrim but was involved in the ULSTER-based revolutionary republican DUNGANNON CLUBS. A signatory of the PROCLAMATION OF THE IRISH REPUBLIC in 1916, Mac Diarmada, crippled by polio in 1912, has been seen by some as the driving force behind PADRAIC PEARSE the leader of the EASTER RISING. He was a member of the republican GAELIC LEAGUE, ANCIENT ORDER OF HIBERNIANS, and the IRISH REPUBLICAN BROTHERHOOD, served in the IRISH VOLUNTEERS and was involved in the planning of the rising of 1916. He has been described as a 'visionary' whose republicanism was rooted in Ireland's history and who entertained a grave distrust of international socialism such as that presented by LARKIN and CONNOLLY. He was arrested after the 1916 rising, tried, and shot on 12 May. Detective John Hoey, who identified Mac Diarmada after his capture, was himself shot down in September 1919 outside the police headquarters in DUBLIN.

MacDonagh, Thomas (1878–1916)

MacDonagh was a signatory of the PROCLAMATION OF THE IRISH REPUBLIC in 1916, and a commander in the IRISH VOLUNTEERS during the EASTER RISING of that year. He was born in County Tipperary, was an early associate of PADRAIC PEARSE and, from 1901, a member of the GAELIC LEAGUE. He became a lecturer at UNIVERSITY COLLEGE, DUBLIN, in 1911. A founder-member of the Irish

Volunteers, he joined the IRISH REPUBLI-CAN BROTHERHOOD in 1915 and was involved in planning the Easter Rising. He was captured, tried and shot on 3 May.

MacDonnell, Alasdair/Alaster (d. 1647)

MacDonnell came of Catholic Scottish stock in ULSTER, and was a commander in the IRISH REBELLION of 1641. In June 1644 he sailed with Irish troops from Waterford to Scotland with the Earl of ANTRIM, to support the guerrilla war of the Marquess of Montrose on behalf of King Charles I against the Scottish PRESBYTER-IANS. He was present at the battle of Tippermuir (1 September) and Auldearn (9 May 1645) and at the defeat sustained by Montrose at Philliphaugh on 13 September 1645. MacDonnell returned to Ireland, and died on active service for the CATHOLIC CONFEDERACY in 1647.

MacManus, Terence Bellew (1823–60)

MacManus was involved in the YOUNG IRELAND uprising of 1848, captured, tried, and sentenced to death. The sentence was commuted to TRANSPORTATION and he was sent to Van Diemen's Land, from where he escaped on 5 June 1851 and reached America. He died in America on 15 January 1860 in poverty. His body was transported back to Ireland for a funeral intended to demonstrate the strength of the nationalist and republican movement. The reburial at Glasnevin was resolved upon amongst the Irish in America, found favour in Ireland, and received the support of the Young Irelanders. The organization fell to JAMES STEPHENS and THOMAS LUBY, who disowned a formal religious ceremony when Archbishop CULLEN called in question the purpose of the funeral. MacManus lay in state in November 1861 in DUBLIN, and on the 10th his body was conveyed to Glasnevin cemetery with an honour guard of some 8,000 marching men, and thousands more Dubliners lining the route in silence. It was a massive demonstration of nationalist feeling, and a Catholic priest was found to defy the

hierarchy and to perform a proper funeral. MacManus achieved more in his death than he had been able to achieve in his short life.

MacNeill, Eoin (1867–1945)

MacNeill was, from 1908, Professor of Early and Medieval History at UNIVERSITY COLLEGE, DUBLIN, and had been associated with militant nationalism since 1893 when he served as Vice-President of the GAELIC LEAGUE. He became Chief-of-Staff of the IRISH VOLUNTEERS but, when the Military Council of the IRISH REPUBLICAN BROTHERHOOD was set up in 1915, MacNeill was not involved, and knew nothing of the developing plans for a republican uprising which came at EASTER 1916. MacNeill's doctrinaire republicanism was certainly in doubt. In 1904 he had made it clear that he would settle for less than independence if he could get Irishmen influence over their own affairs. When PEARSE issued commands for Volunteer manoeuvres at Easter 1916, MacNeill cancelled some of the orders, with the consequence that the rising was crippled from the start. Nevertheless, he fought, was captured, and gaoled. In 1918 he was SINN FÉIN MP for the National University of Ireland, supported the ANGLO-IRISH TREATY of 1921, and held government office in the FREE STATE.

Macroom, battle of

The battle of Macroom was fought on 10 April 1650 in County Cork. The last of the CATHOLIC CONFEDERATE and royalist armies in Munster, commanded by Boetius MacEgan bishop of Ross, was defeated by government troops under Lord Roche. The bishop was captured and summarily hanged.

MacSwiney, Terence (1879–1920)

MacSwiney died on HUNGER STRIKE on 25 October 1920 after 74 days of protest. He was an accountant by profession and an amateur actor, and helped found the Cork units of the IRISH VOLUNTEERS in 1913. At the outbreak of the EASTER RISING of 1916 he was one of those Volunteer commanders who received instruction from EOIN MACNEILL countermanding the orders of PADRAIC PEARSE, and in consequence remained aloof from the rising. He was nevertheless gaoled. Elected as SINN FÉIN candidate, to the DÁIL ÉIREANN in 1919, he became Lord Mayor of Cork in 1920, and was holding that office when he was arrested by the authorities in August. MacSwiney's was the last hunger-strike death of the campaign, the IRISH REPUBLICAN ARMY gaining maximum publicity from it, but authorizing no others.

Magheramore Manifesto *see* CRAWFORD, Robert

Magistrates and Justices of the Peace (*see also* CONSTABULARY)

The Justices of the Peace, like the counties of Ireland in which they operated, were an English introduction, part and parcel of the ANGLICIZATION of Irish society and legal forms. By 1600, the JPs were largely ineffective, the counties (the 'shiring') of Ireland not yet fully organized even if their boundaries were more or less known and their names applied (see ADMINISTRATIVE STRUCTURE). JPs were unpaid gentry fulfilling the obligations of rank, the conduit by which legislation was passed on to the localities from central government, and their efficiency and co-operation was crucial to the central executive. The JP system was imposed upon ULSTER following the surrender of TYRONE in 1603. The JPs headed the system of local courts which were modelled upon those in England, Quarter and Petty Sessions – the one met quarterly, the other when a quorum of JPs met for extraordinary business. During the seventeenth century, as the OLD ENGLISH gentry lost political power, influence and, often, if they adhered to Catholicism, their estates, the JPs came more and more to be dominated by Protestants of NEW ENGLISH origin. The control of the JPs was essential for a government bent upon PLANTATION and resettlement, and yet within the ascendant Protestant gentry, rival families vied for the sometimes expensive honour of the office. With the coming of

PENAL LAWS against Catholics after 1691 on a massive scale, the role of the JPs in their enforcement – quite apart from their normal concerns with civil and criminal matters within their counties – was crucial. A proliferation of handbooks, based upon and revised in the light of new legislation, was aimed at keeping them informed of their powers and obligations, a phenomenon not confined to Ireland but to be found also in England during the eighteenth century. Two acts limited the authority of the JPs, that of 1705 which set a limit of £20 on the monies that could be authorized at a Quarter Sessions for public works (state- or council-funded projects) and that of 1728 which moved road construction decisions from the Sessions to the sitting of the Judges of Assize. But their power to supervise the GRAND JURIES was undiminished. Indeed, by 1817 their powers over the Juries were extended until they virtually supervised every aspect of Grand Jury procedure, but by that time the JPs had themselves been 'reformed' by the addition of professional barristers, appointed by the LORD LIEUTENANT, to 'assist' the JPs in their work, on a ratio of one barrister per county. The unpaid JPs were made to give ground to the more professional and paid magistrates by the late 1830s. Government purged them of clergymen and absentee gentry, and the number of magistrates correspondingly increased as part and parcel of law and order reforms (see CONSTABULARY, PEACE PRESERVATION FORCE). EMANCIPATION giving Catholics an entitlement to be appointed as JPs in fact produced very little change in the religious complexion of the commission of the peace in the counties. This was partly a reflection of the relatively few Catholics of sufficient 'means' to recommend them in the class context of appointments, and partly also, discrimination. Consequently the sectarianism of many JPs, most pronounced in their deference to the ORANGE ORDER in the 1800s – a fact remarked upon by less sympathetic, more liberal JP gentry – continued to bring the office into disrepute amongst Catholics. With the development of a paid magistracy, and particularly during the period of THOMAS

DRUMMOND's Under Secretaryship at the CASTLE (1835–40), there were deliberate appointments of Catholics and of Protestants friendly to Catholic grievances. This was important because with the magistracy went direction of the emerging police force, which likewise had shown pronounced sectarian sympathies, especially in Ulster. The decline of the JPs and the appointment of efficient magistrates, particularly when directed by liberals such as Drummond, was a major blow against the solidity of the ASCENDANCY domination of the dispensation of justice in the countryside. PEEL gave the system a serious start with the Peace Preservation legislation which became effective in 1814, when paid magistrates were put in control of police in disturbed areas of the country. The new magistrates ran into opposition from the local JPs because of the requirement that their salaries be met from local funds, but the principle was established nonetheless. It was magistrates who ran the Peace Preservation Force wherever it was employed, and their role was further clarified by the legislation of 1836, the Constabulary Act.

Maguire, Connor/Cornelius, 2nd Lord (1616–45)

Connor Maguire succeeded to the lordship of Maguire of Enniskillen in 1634, and was one of the few Gaelic peers in the province of ULSTER when the IRISH REBELLION of 1641 broke out. He was accused of implication in the spurious plot to seize Dublin CASTLE on the eve of the rebellion, and was amongst those immediately apprehended by the government. He had certainly been in contact with PHELIM O'NEILL in early October, and after his capture his brother Rory was in arms with O'Neill. Maguire escaped from custody in August 1644, was recaptured, committed for trial and executed in January 1645.

Mallow

At Mallow in County Cork soldiers of the IRISH REPUBLICAN ARMY under the command of Liam Lynch and Ernie O'Malley attacked and captured a barracks then in

the hands of British troops. The following day the discomfited soldiers went on the rampage in the town, plundering and looting. The same scenario was enacted on 31 September at Trim in County Meath, after a successful IRA attack on a police barracks in the town.

Manchester Martyrs *see* SMASHING OF THE VAN

Mandates, The

The Mandates, introduced by Sir ARTHUR CHICHESTER, the LORD DEPUTY, were designed to enforce anti-Catholic legislation by compelling leading DUBLIN citizens to attend the services of the CHURCH OF IRELAND in Chichester's company. It was intended that they should thereby set an example. Failure to obey the Mandates led to heavy fines and even imprisonment after judgement by the Court of CASTLE CHAMBER. The Mandates were issued on 13 November 1605, but were withdrawn in 1607 in response to pressure from London, where the Privy Council took alarm at Chichester's rigour.

Manifesto to the Irish People

The Manifesto, of 29 November 1890, was an attempt by PARNELL, in the wake of the O'Shea divorce scandal, to bypass the discontents within the HOME RULE PARTY in the House of Commons and to rally support for himself amongst the people at large. On 25 November, Parnell had been unanimously re-elected chairman of the party. Immediately thereafter, GLADSTONE made it known that he found Parnell's continued leadership made his own position untenable. Since the Home Rulers relied upon Gladstone's continued legislative commitment to Home Rule, the party split against Parnell, and by 6 December a large anti-Parnell group had emerged under Justin MacCarthy and others. The Manifesto, which was issued between these two events, was intended to stabilize Parnell's position, but it failed. In it he denounced Gladstone and the Liberals, asserting that English political parties were not to be relied upon to pursue objectives desired by Irishmen.

The struggle to re-establish himself broke Parnell's health. He died in October 1891.

Mansion House Conference

The Mansion House in DUBLIN was the scene of a meeting on 18 April 1918 of representatives of the nationalist parliamentary party (led by REDMOND), SINN FÉIN, the Irish Labour party and others, to discuss the CONSCRIPTION legislation of 9 April introduced by Lloyd George into the Commons. A meeting of the hierarchy of the CATHOLIC CHURCH took place at Maynooth at the same time, and the two meetings communicated. A one-day strike was called to protest at the Military Service Bill, for 23 April, which took effect everywhere outside ULSTER. Within a month the GERMAN PLOT had been concocted by the LORD LIEUTENANT to provide an excuse for the arrest of Sinn Féin leaders, including DE VALERA and the Countess MARKIEVICZ. The conference had ushered in concerted opposition to conscription (see FIRST WORLD WAR 1914–18).

Marat

Nickname given to the UNITED IRISHMEN leader WOLFE TONE during his career as a lawyer in Ireland, indicative of his sympathies for the French Revolutionary cause.

Markievicz, Constance, Countess (1868–1927)

Countess Markievicz was the most influential of the many women leaders who emerged in the republican cause during the 20 years or so before the EASTER RISING of 1916. She was born in London and educated there and in Paris, where she met and married Count Casimir Markievicz in 1900. An early member of SINN FÉIN, but not a great admirer of ARTHUR GRIFFITH (its founder), she launched Fianna Éireann in 1909, a republican movement that had been created by BULMER HOBSON in BELFAST in 1903. She joined the militantly feminist INGHINIDHE NA HÉIREANN, and when the CITIZEN ARMY was formed towards the end of the LOCK-OUT in DUBLIN, became an officer of that force. She fought during the Easter Rising of 1916 and was arrested and sentenced to death, but the sentence was commuted. Released, she became President of the radical CUMANN NA MBAN, a female republican movement that was to denounce the ANGLO-IRISH TREATY of 1921 and stand alongside the IRREGULARS of the IRISH REPUBLICAN ARMY in the civil war of 1922. Elected as MP for Dublin in the 1918 General Election, were it not for the ABSTENTIONIST policy pursued by Sinn Féin, she would have been the first woman MP at WESTMINSTER. Her republicanism was unequivocal, and although she was returned as a Sinn Féin MP to DÁIL ÉIREANN in 1923, she maintained her abstentionism.

Matters of Grace and Bounty

The Matters of Grace and Bounty, ordinarily referred to as the 'Graces' were an agreement arrived at between the OLD ENGLISH Catholics of Ireland and King Charles I intended to secure financial support for the king in return for concessions on grievances related to the Catholicism of the Old English. The 'graces' alienated the NEW ENGLISH Protestants and alarmed Protestant opinion in England, but they were neither uniformly enforced nor legislated for, the government proving hesitant and equivocal. The fact was, the king got more from the bargain than did the Old English. In 1625 they undertook to finance the military defence of Ireland in return for 26 'matters of grace and bounty', a term indicating that any concessions were at royal discretion, they were not 'rights' but rather 'privileges' extended by the sovereign. Amongst the 'graces' were included the suspension of recusancy fines (fines levied for non-attendance at services of the CHURCH OF IRELAND) and the lapsing of the requirement that heirs to property should take the oath of Supremacy which was a rejection of papal supremacy. In November 1626 Old English lords met in DUBLIN to discuss the proposals and to arrange for a delegation to go to England to confer with the king, which the LORD DEPUTY, Falkland, barred, but eventually conceded in June 1627. In January 1628 the delegation of eight Old

English and three New English spokesmen met King Charles and their discussions culminated in the issue by the king of 51 'instructions and graces' in return for three annual subsidies of £40,000 a year. The only major concessions the Catholics won involved their right to bear arms, and in matters of inheritance. The recusancy laws remained in place, and they were denied a militia force of their own to be based within the PALE. Parliament was to legislate for these 'graces', but a changing European situation rendered the matter less pressing. The king got his subsidies, the Catholics had secured only promises. In 1634 (largely due to THOMAS WENTWORTH) there was a statute of limitations that guaranteed land titles of 60 years standing or more (see PLANTATIONS), but within three years came the proposals for plantation in CONNACHT and the encroachment upon the Old English lands in County Galway. Legislation for the 'graces' was postponed or deferred until, in 1641, there was some indication from the king that they would be given statutory effect. The ENGLISH CIVIL WAR, which broke out in 1642, following upon the IRISH REBELLION of October 1641 in which the Old English became involved, brought the matter to an abrupt end.

Maynooth *see* ST PATRICK'S COLLEGE

Meagher, Thomas Francis (1823–67)

Meagher was a colourful exponent of the revolutionary republicanism of the YOUNG IRELAND movement, whose inspiration for revolution was less founded in the French experience than in the AMERICAN WAR FOR INDEPENDENCE. The sword, he said, 'at its blow' created 'a giant nation ... from the waters of the Atlantic, and by its redeeming magic the fettered Colony became a ... free Republic'. He moved from the constitutional Repeal movement of DANIEL O'CONNELL to the PHYSICAL FORCE principles of the IRISH CONFEDERATION of Young Irelanders with rapidity. He visited France in 1848 to congratulate the leaders there on their revolution, and returned to Ireland with a tricolour flag presented by the French to the Young Irelanders. After the 1848 rising, he was sentenced to death, but it was commuted to TRANSPORTATION to Australia. In January 1852 he informed the Governor of his intention to escape, and did so, making his way to America where he continued active in republican revolutionary movements and, at the outbreak of the American Civil War, commanded an IRISH BRIGADE in defence of the Union. He was killed in an accident after appointment as Governor of Montana.

Mellifont, Treaty of

The Treaty at Mellifont in 1603 (agreed to on 30 March, six days after the death of Queen Elizabeth) represented the submission of the Earl of TYRONE to the LORD DEPUTY, MOUNTJOY, who had deliberately withheld the news of the queen's death. Mountjoy's motive in so doing was to bring Tyrone to agreement, the news of the queen's death quite possibly would cause the earl to refuse to negotiate, hoping in the generosity of the new king, James I. Talks had dragged on for a year or more anyway, Tyrone refusing to concede military garrisons in his territory, and refusing to abandon his right to the exclusively Gaelic title of 'The O'NEILL'. At Mellifont, Mountjoy conceded to Tyrone recognition of his absolute authority in ULSTER, and Tyrone yielded on the spread of English administrative forms into his province. James I ratified the Treaty, and Mountjoy and Tyrone visited him together in May. The Treaty initially strengthened Tyrone's position in Ulster, confirming his power and authority over lesser Gaelic chiefs, and this was confirmed when the earldom of TYRCONNELL was granted to Rory O'Donnell in the same year. In fact, English administrators in DUBLIN after Mountjoy's death particularly, worked to overthrow the settlement by creating tensions within Ulster (see FLIGHT OF THE EARLS).

Mellifont itself was taken and burned by troops of the CATHOLIC CONFEDERACY in November 1641 at the start of the IRISH REBELLION, which had its roots in Tyrone's old territories.

Mere Irish

The term 'mere Irish' was employed frequently by the English in the seventeenth century, and was applied to those of pure Irish descent, the GAELIC IRISH. In the Irish PARLIAMENT of 1634 the 'mere Irish' were represented by eight MPs, as compared to 142 NEW ENGLISH and 94 OLD ENGLISH. 'The wild and, as I may say, mere Irish' as one Englishman wrote of the natives of Munster in the 1580s, gradually became the peasantry of Ireland, particularly after the war of the IRISH REBELLION of 1641–53 broke their territorial power (or what was left of it) and the PENAL LAWS enforced from 1691. The 'mere Irish' fell short of the ideals of English CIVILITY and civilization that the English determined, through ANGLI-CIZATION and PLANTATION, to bring to the Irish and their society.

Milesmen

Milesmen were part-time police, even vigilantes, who patrolled country roads at night to guard against highway robbery. They were active during the WHITEBOY insurgency of the eighteenth century, but they were themselves suspect. The Shanavest leader (see CARAVATS AND SHA-NAVESTS) Patrick Connors was a 'milesman'.

Militia, The Irish

The Act of Parliament of 9 April 1793 that set up a Militia in Ireland with an initial prescribed strength of 14,900 men, came on the same day as Hobart's Act which went some way towards EMANCIPATION of Catholics by extending the franchise. The government's Catholic legislation had come as a response, in part, to extra-parliamentary pressure and the need to placate it in the light of revolutionary changes in France. The Militia Act, in consequence, was seen as, and intended to be, coercive. It was primarily aimed at the increasing strength of the Catholic DEFENDER movement and at the spread of the non-sectarian UNITED IRISHMEN movement. The Militia was based on a county quota system: counties falling short of their quota were expected to subscribe £10 for each missing man. Selection was by ballot, which in itself led to local violence, and in time gave way to outright volunteering, the provision of substitutes by those who could afford to buy themselves out, and even the recruitment of men in England and Scotland. But the Militia, because of the way in which it was raised, rapidly became strongly Catholic in makeup, albeit poverty-stricken peasants, and because of that the government soon came to regard it as politically unreliable. To overcome this, units tended to be employed away from their localities, particularly during the 1798 rising of the United Irishmen. Intended to provide an alternative to the VOLUNTEER movement, the activities of which had put increasing pressure on government during the 1780s, the Militia was, in some areas, infiltrated by, and even controlled by, active Defenders. This was tackled by General LAKE in ULSTER on the eve of the 1798 rising by rigorous and brutal purges of the local Militia units. Despite this, the Militia did prove reliable during the 1798 rising: much of the callous and vicious behaviour of the government forces was due to the excesses of Militia forces. The Monaghan Militia virtually destroyed the United Irishmen movement in BELFAST, and in May 1798 the Wicklow Militia (in collaboration with the YEOMANRY) systematically murdered rebel prisoners at Dunlavin and other places. At the time of the 1798 rising its strength had risen to 21,660, entirely officered by Protestant gentry.

Mitchel, John (1815–75)

John Mitchel was brought up as a PRESBYTERIAN in County DERRY, educated at TRINITY COLLEGE, and became involved with the Repeal movement of DANIEL O'CONNELL, which sought to re-establish the Irish PARLIAMENT in some form or other. Mitchel, influenced partly by the economic theorist FINTAN LALOR, was instrumental in the development of the secessionist YOUNG IRELAND element within the REPEAL ASSOCIATION, and split from O'Connell over an article Mitchel wrote in the *NATION* journal advocating sabotage, in 1846. He was arrested and tried for sedition in May 1848, where a rigged jury found him guilty and he was sentenced to 14 years TRANSPORTATION, a miscarriage of justice that won him renown in Ireland and in America. He escaped from the penal colony in 1853 and made it to America, where he published his *Jail Journal* and set up the *Citizen* newspaper. He became involved with the FENIAN revolutionary movement and acted as its representative in Paris in 1866. He stood for Parliament for Tipperary in 1875, the year of his death, but was discharged from sitting as a convicted felon. He was nevertheless returned on a new writ, shortly before his death.

Mitchelstown Massacre

The Mitchelstown Massacre was a term coined at the time, to describe an incident at Mitchelstown, County Cork, during a public meeting to support the PLAN OF CAMPAIGN. The Plan of Campaign was a revival, rejected by PARNELL, of LAND LEAGUE agitation, the primary weapon of which was the withholding of rents. Police in the barracks at Mitchelstown opened fire on the crowd without provocation, killing at least three of those present, on 9 September 1887.

Molly Maguires

The Molly Maguires were considered by some observers to be the revolutionary ANCIENT ORDER OF HIBERNIANS under another name: this was the view of an American Catholic bishop commenting upon an outbreak of violence in the Pennsylvania coal field in 1875. They seem first to appear as an agrarian movement akin to the WHITEBOYS of earlier times, in the Leitrim, Roscommon and Longford areas in 1845, but are predominantly associated with Pennsylvania and the coal miners. In September 1875 in the course of several days' violence, they murdered a fellow miner and some mine staff at Schuylkill County. In June 1877 10 of the Molly Maguires were hanged, and a further 10 suffered between March 1878 and October 1879, which seemed to break the 'secret society'.

Molony, Helena (1884–1967)

Helena Molony, like MAUD GONNE and the Countess MARKIEVICZ, was a prominent and committed woman revolutionary who took an active role in the fighting for Irish Independence. She first joined the radical feminist INGHINIDHE NA HEIREANN in 1903 and was involved in SINN FÉIN activism by 1911. Her leanings were towards the international socialism of leaders such as CONNOLLY and LARKIN, and it was the CITIZEN ARMY, rather than the IRISH VOLUNTEERS, which she consequently joined prior to the EASTER RISING of 1916 in which she fought. She was gaoled until December 1916. When the ANGLO-IRISH TREATY of 1921 became known, she sided with the anti-Treaty forces of the IRISH REPUBLICAN ARMY. Her later political career within Ireland was involved with Trade Union work, and in the perpetuation of the beliefs of Connolly, who had been shot in 1916.

Molyneux, William (1656–98)

Molyneux's political argument for the separateness of the Irish PARLIAMENT, the *CASE OF IRELAND*, written in 1698 is in itself crucially important for the evolution of 'Irish' nationalism in its many forms. Molyneux was a typical Protestant intellectual, educated at TRINITY COLLEGE, based in DUBLIN, philosopher and political theorist of the developing Protestant ASCENDANCY which was guaranteed by the increasing number of PENAL LAWS directed against Catholic involvement in government and much else. Molyneux evolved a theory of a direct contract between the Irish people and the English crown as far back as the reign of King Henry II in the twelfth century, which, by its ancient nature, by-passed and had no relevance to the interpolation of the English Parliament, which claimed superiority over that of Ireland. Molyneux's contention of necessity implied that the English in Ireland were lineal inheritors of that original contract, that they had, in that sense at least, become the Irish. That attitude and belief fuelled the reasoning of PATRIOTS and nationalists of otherwise orthodox Protestant persuasion throughout the eighteenth century: because they believed it so, it was so, its weakest point always being the relegation of the Catholic Irish to a position of inferiority, almost of non-Irishness. Molyneux himself openly wrote on behalf of 'The great Body of the present People of Ireland who are the Progeny of the English and Britains'. His words were not for the 'mere handful of the Ancient Irish' (who, with the OLD ENGLISH Catholics made up the majority of Ireland's population). If, as Molyneux contended, Ireland were a separate kingdom, and if that kingdom was to be legislated for in WESTMINSTER, then, Molyneux's argument followed, the Irish should have members of that Parliament present. In that context, Molyneux would probably have welcomed UNION, which eventually came in 1801.

Monro, Robert (d. 1680)

A Scottish PRESBYTERIAN career soldier who had served in Europe, Monro was sent into ULSTER in 1641 to take command against the Catholic forces of the IRISH REBELLION and the subsequent CATHOLIC CONFEDERACY. Monro's military successes – the capture of the rebel Earl of ANTRIM (who later escaped), the occupation of BELFAST in 1644 among others – were brought to a sudden end by the massive defeat inflicted on him at BENBURB in 1646. His LAGGAN ARMY (deriving its name from the river valley) was to be placed under the command of the English government General, George Monck, and was to be fused with the English army of Sir CHARLES COOTE. Monro, like many Presbyterians, was shifting his allegiance in 1647 towards King Charles I, who had been defeated during the ENGLISH CIVIL WAR largely as a result of Scottish support for his enemies. That support was now moving towards the king, and in consequence Monro was arrested by the English government and sent prisoner into England. He was eventually released by OLIVER CROMWELL in 1654 and allowed to return to Ulster, where he settled.

Monstrous Evil, The

PEEL's colourful term for the nagging problem of the land issue in Ireland in the early nineteenth century.

Montgomery, Hugh 3rd Viscount (1623–63)

Hugh Montgomery, grandson of a Scottish Laird of Bradstone who undertook extensive PLANTATION in ULSTER in 1610, commanded troops in Ulster against the CATHOLIC CONFEDERACY during the IRISH REBELLION of 1641–53. Like many PRESBYTERIANS, Montgomery went over to the cause of King Charles I in 1647/8, and commanded royalist troops in 1649 in uneasy alliance with the Catholic Confederates, his former enemies. He surrendered to CROMWELL and went into exile in the Low Countries. In 1660 at the restoration of King Charles II he was created Earl of Mount Alexander.

Moonlighters

The Moonlighters were a shadowy rural secret society active during the LAND WAR of 1879–82, employing tactics earlier associated with the ROCKITE and WHITEBOY movements. They were, in the context of the Land War's mass agitation, less significant and soon faded.

Moral Economy

The Moral Economy is an historiographical term used to define the hierarchical structure of Irish society, and in its definition would be equally as applicable to rural society in sixteenth- or seventeenth-century England as to the Ireland of the eighteenth century. In the light of the idea of the moral economy, eighteenth-century Ireland is seen as essentially stable and conservative, with an established way of doing things consequent upon the settlement of political power defined by the PENAL LAWS against Catholics. Emphasis is placed upon the 'norm' of co-operation and mutual respect between the landlords and their tenantry, the system of hierarchical paternalism and deference towards it, which is occasionally disrupted by outbreaks of AGRARIAN OUTRAGE. Such outbreaks, in this context, are reactions to challenges to the order of things, whether it be creeping grassland at the expense of arable, or the intrusion of 'incomers' into established communities. The period of the dominance of the moral economy is defined by its explicit breakdown from the 1790s, where agitation for EMANCIPATION and other reforms represents a politicization of the hitherto apolitical Catholic majority, a process begun by Protestant 'nationalists' in the VOLUNTEER movement, and made permanent by government repression through MILITIA and YEOMANRY. The concept of the moral economy must rely upon something more positive than the mere acquiescence of the majority in a system which had been imposed upon them: it must rely upon a positive response to that system, in order to see outbreaks such as those of the WHITEBOYS, as aberrations and wholly defensive and protective responses to disturbance within the system. This view is rooted amongst contemporary writers at the end of the eighteenth century, but could also be classified as an ASCENDANCY attempt to justify a system from 1793 and the emancipation measures of that year, no longer tenable in its old form. The moral economy idea lies also behind the historiographical view that eighteenth-century cultural development, expressive almost wholly of a dominant minority, in some way redresses the balance and even outweighs the institutionalized repression on which it was based. Eighteenth-century culture and its concrete and plastic expression was financed from an expropriated peasantry, which occasionally hit out through agrarian violence, but did not find a political voice until the examples of the revolutions in America and France awakened the consciences, initially, of members of that dominant minority.

Moran, Denis (1872–1936)

Moran, a leading figure at the end of the nineteenth century in the revival of Gaelic literature and culture, subscribed to his own view that 'we can never beat England, can't even remain long in a fight with her, on her own terms'. The IRISH REPUBLICAN ARMY, if it was not in itself aware specifically of Moran's opinion, took the burden of it to heart, and during the WAR FOR INDEPENDENCE, steadily broke

down British resistance to Irish independence by waging guerrilla warfare. Moran's Gaelic enthusiasms were defeatist: he fiercely rejected ANGLICIZATION in all its forms, and he strove towards 'Irishness' as an expression that must be contained within political forms that cannot realistically be altered. Thus he denounced, among others, writers such as Yeats who, he considered, represented an Anglo-Irish culture and nothing specifically 'Irish'. He rejected, on the same grounds, nationalism, whether that of REDMOND and the constitutionalists, or that of the revolutionary FENIANS and their successors. Nevertheless, he was involved with and exercised a command over, the IRISH VOLUNTEERS from 1913 until 1916, but he played no part in the EASTER RISING of that year. His published work included *The Philosophy of Irish Ireland* of 1905.

Moryson, Fynes (1566–1630)

Fynes Moryson was a well-travelled observer throughout Europe and the Near East before he became, in 1600, secretary to MOUNTJOY the LORD DEPUTY in Ireland, a post he held until 1603. He was therefore involved in the campaigns to crush the rebellion of the Earl of TYRONE which ended with the earl's submission at MELLIFONT in 1603. Moryson was a stern advocate of thoroughgoing English control in Ireland: 'nothing is more dangerous than middle counsels'. He must have been out of step with his employer, Mountjoy, for Moryson's attitude was that of the PLANTATION pioneers like DAVIES. He wrote his *Itinerary*, volume two of which contained a detailed account of Ireland.

Mountgarret, Richard Butler 3rd Viscount (1578–1651)

From 1641 and the alliance of the ULSTER rebels with the OLD ENGLISH Catholics, Lord Mountgarret was President of the Supreme Council of the Confederacy established at Kilkenny. He was the son-in-law of the Earl of TYRONE who had fled from Ireland in 1607 (see FLIGHT OF THE EARLS) and had fought under Tyrone during the latter's rebellion which had ended in 1603 at MELLIFONT. Mountgarret, himself of Old English origin (and the great uncle of the government's commander, the Earl of ORMOND), had raised the Kilkenny area for the rebels in November 1641 and had sent troops into Munster to resist the PRESIDENT of the province, Sir William St Leger. He was defeated in action at KILRUSH in April 1642. He was still in arms against the government at his death, although the Confederacy of which he had been head, had already disintegrated.

Mountjoy, Charles Blount 8th Lord (1563–1606)

Mountjoy had an eventful military career, almost sharing in the disgrace of the Earl of Essex who was executed in 1601 for rebellion against Queen Elizabeth I. He was appointed LORD DEPUTY in Ireland in 1600 with command of the forces against the rebellious Earl of TYRONE, committed not merely to bringing Tyrone to submission, but to securing an abandonment of his sovereign power in ULSTER. Through Sir George Carew, President-designate of Munster, that province was rapidly overrun, and Mountjoy turned his attention to Ulster. Using a combined land and sea operation, the Deputy sent Henry Docwra to DERRY, where a garrison was established and alliances made with Gaelic enemies of the Earl of Tyrone. Mountjoy himself, however, proved unable to face Tyrone in the field and withdrew his army. He opted, rather, for thorough wasting of the countryside, destroying farming and crops and livestock to bring the rebels to their knees. Even his secretary, MORYSON, was astonished by the savagery. Tyrone fell back upon anticipated Spanish help which, in 1601, was forthcoming, but which was destroyed at the battle of KINSALE. Negotiations between the earl and the Lord Deputy opened soon afterwards, and led to Tyrone's submission at MELLIFONT, although it was not until 1607 (see FLIGHT OF THE EARLS) that it really dawned upon Tyrone that he had lost. Mountjoy was made LORD LIEUTENANT in 1603 and created Earl of Devonshire in reward for his efforts. He enforced bans on Catholic worship in public, but turned a blind eye to private devotions. His moderacy once the rebellion was crushed, had little opportunity to take effect. Mountjoy was replaced as Deputy by CHICHESTER, and under his successors, the PLANTATION policy was pursued vigorously.

Mountnorris Affair, The

Sir Francis Annesley, NEW ENGLISH settler in Ireland, raised to the barony of Mountnorris in 1628, fell foul of the LORD DEPUTY, THOMAS WENTWORTH, in a case illustrative of the Lord Deputy's general policy in Ireland. Mountnorris had been eminent in the English administration, with extensive estates in ULSTER, and experience as Vice-Treasurer and Receiver-General of Ireland before 1625. His elevation to a peerage in 1628 was a mark of royal favour, generally shown to the faction amongst the New English of which he was a member. An attempt to disgrace him in 1629 by the rival faction of the Earl of CORK, backed by the then Lord Deputy, Falkland, failed. When Wentworth assumed the Deputyship, Mountnorris was instrumental in securing OLD ENGLISH support for him, and the alliance with Mountnorris and with ADAM LOFTUS enabled Wentworth to assert himself against the New English interest headed by the Earl of Cork. By 1635, however, the Deputy denounced Mountnorris as dishonest and corrupt, alluding to his office of Vice-Treasurer and his management of financial affairs in Ireland. It was a political move, intended by Wentworth to rid himself of New English involvement in the vital area of financial administration, although initially he opted for another New English figure, Loftus, to replace Mountnorris. Wentworth then moved against him in his capacity as a military officer, for some indiscreet remarks made at a private dinner with Loftus, concerning the Lord Deputy. After a period of factional lobbying for influence – Mountnorris had powerful political friends in England – he was tried before a council of war accused of defaming his commanding officer, the Lord Deputy. He was sentenced to death. Loftus replaced him as Vice-Treasurer for the time being, and royal confirmation of the trial of Mountnorris was forthcoming in January 1636. The death sentence was never carried out, but Mountnorris did not recover his authority in Ireland. Nevertheless, Wentworth's venom against him contributed to the growing criticism of his Deputyship that would, eventually, bring him to trial and execution in 1641. Mountnorris became a Secretary of State in Ireland during the government of HENRY CROMWELL in the 1650s and died in 1686.

Moyle Rangers

The Moyle Rangers appear to have been a grouping of WHITEBOY elements in County Tipperary that took their name from the River Moyle, and in derisive allusion to the YEOMANRY. Their leader, Nicholas Hanley, appears also as a CARAVAT faction leader in the early nineteenth century.

Municipal Reform

The Irish Municipal Reform Act of August 1840 was one of the products of the LICHFIELD HOUSE COMPACT, which drew together in February 1835 the MPs returned to WESTMINSTER on DANIEL O'CONNELL's Repeal platform, and English liberals and radicals. The Repealers were able to demand, and to get, reforms in Ireland. On the eve of the Reform Act there were 68 corporations – cities and boroughs – in Ireland. By the 1793 EMANCIPATION Act, Catholics had the right to serve on municipal corporations, just as their share of the franchise had been extended to permit them to vote in parliamentary elections. Thus their admission to corporations was largely meaningless. In 1829 the Catholic franchise holders (see FORTY-SHILLING FREE-HOLDERS) had been drastically cut, commensurate with the extension of the right of Catholics to sit as MPs. The municipal corporations were major bastions of Protestant domination and effectively controlled the return of Tories to the Parliament at Westminster: a commission of inquiry into the Irish corporations in 1835 had revealed them to be, for the most part, 'of no service to

the community' and often positively 'injurious'. It was O'Connell's policy to force equitable treatment for Catholics onto the existing corporations: his Liberal allies in Parliament were unprepared to exchange Tory-dominated municipalities for potentially Catholic-dominated municipalities. Thus the legislation of 1840 did not reflect O'Connell's objective, even though its passage derived from the support of the Repealers. The Act was largely a product of the House of Lords, reflective of Tory opinion that instead of 'reform' there should be abolition. The Act abolished 58 corporations at a stroke: of the 10 that survived, including DERRY, BELFAST, Cork and Limerick, the electoral franchise was based upon £10 householders (unlike the English Act of 1835, which had impressed O'Connell, where the franchise was set at £5). O'Connell himself, on the strength of the Act, was returned as Lord Mayor of DUBLIN in 1841, the first Catholic to hold that office since 1688. There had been no legal bar to Catholics serving on corporations during the eighteenth century, but Protestant dominance had effectively kept them out. O'Connell's election, therefore, was important symbolically, but municipal reform had in no way reflected the policy of the Repealers, and that fact helped alienate the future YOUNG IRELAND dissident element in the Repeal movement.

Munster, Plantation in the Province of

The province of Munster was, by 1611, already extensively planted, with somewhat more than 5,000 NEW ENGLISH settlers established there. A widespread revolt – the Desmond wars (so named from the Earl of Desmond who came to lead the rebellion) – began in 1569, partly reaction to English policy of setting up a PRESIDENT in the province, and partly a Catholic rebellion against creeping Protestant conformity. The rebels possessed a charismatic leader in James FitzMaurice FitzGerald who gave to the revolt the aura of a Catholic crusade. The Desmond wars dragged on until they became merged in 1599 in the TYRONE rebellion which had spread from ULSTER. In the intermittent periods of peace, and in the wake of campaigning English armies, PLANTATION was forced through, with, from 1586, heavy reliance by the government in England upon the merchants and adventurers of south-west England. This created a link between Munster and that part of England that long remained vital. By the time that Munster was swallowed up in the Tyrone rising, some 12,000 or more settlers were spread across the province. The dispersed nature of much settlement made the planters easy prey for the rebels, especially for the GALLO-GLASS clan of the McSheehys who had been effectively dispossessed of thousands of acres of land during the resettlement. After Tyrone's submission, Munster was resettled, but the structure of landownership had changed in consequence of the rebellion. Some 20 or so major holdings in Munster changed ownership between 1604 and 1625, new New English supplanting earlier New English settlers. On the other hand, Munster was a province where the process of ANGLICIZATION was held to have been only partially successful. New English settlers were often 'strangely degenerated into Irish affections and customs', partly a reflection of the survival of many native and OLD ENGLISH landowners in the plantation areas.

Murphy, Father John (1753–98)

Father Murphy was the Catholic parish priest at Boolavogue, County Wexford in May 1798, when the UNITED IRISHMEN uprising broke out. The North Cork MILITIA, operating (as so many Militia units) outside their native locality, destroyed the church and houses at Boola-vogue on 26/27 May. Murphy raised the countryfolk in rebellion, a rebellion tenuously linked to the formal rising, and with strong religious overtones (see WEXFORD RISING). Initially victorious at OULART HILL on 27 May, Murphy's men defeated and killed Colonel Walpole at Ballymore Hill on 4 June. Defeated at Arklow soon after, Murphy fell back, was captured in the battle at Kilcomney Hill, and was tortured to death by the YEO-MANRY on 26 June 1798. Father Murphy rapidly achieved folk-hero status in County Wexford, and in the Irish nationalist tradition.

Murphy, William Martin (1844–1919)

Murphy was a DUBLIN entrepreneur and capitalist, whose fame is to be attributed to the fact that he chose to take on JAMES LARKIN and JAMES CONNOLLY, the forceful organizers of trade unionism in the city. Murphy had sat as a HOME RULE MP in the Parliament at WESTMINSTER from 1885 to 1892. As President of the Dublin Chamber of Commerce, he headed the Employers' Federation in 1913 and organized the LOCK-OUT against workers who refused to pledge not to join the TRANSPORT AND GENERAL WORKERS' UNION. In 1914 Murphy, like most constitutional nationalists, advocated support for the British war effort against Germany and expressed the view that able-bodied Irish workers who would not enlist themselves should be barred from their employment. He kept aloof from the EASTER RISING of 1916, but came out against the idea of PARTITION which would cut ULSTER off from the rest of Ireland in the event of Home Rule.

N

Nappach Fleet, The

The Nappach Fleet was a localized STEELBOY group founded in Markethill, County Armagh in 1784 after a relatively trivial incident rooted in a local FEUD. In a pitched fight between two Protestants, a Catholic bystander joined in on the side of the winner. A local PRESBYTERIAN seized upon this to form an anti-Catholic mob which raided Catholic homes and endeavoured to drive Catholics from the area. The actions of the Nappach Fleet spread far and wide, eventually becoming merged in developing ORANGEISM. In 1787 a 'captain' of the Fleet and four known DEFENDERS (a Catholic resistance group) were tried for a violent affray in which they had been involved. The Fleet man was acquitted, the Defenders were sentenced. This, and similar incidents, demonstrated the partiality of the Protestant magistracy in favour of the anti-Catholic campaign. The Fleet took its name from Edenknappagh, where it first met.

Nation, The

The Nation was a journal founded by dissident members of DANIEL O'CONNELL'S REPEAL ASSOCIATION, including THOMAS DAVIS and CHARLES DUFFY, who were becoming increasingly disillusioned with the constitutionalist approach to repeal of the UNION of Britain and Ireland of 1801. It was from the group of journalists and polemicists gathered about the Nation, that the revolutionary YOUNG IRELAND movement emerged. On 28 July 1848 the editorial offices were raided by police, and the production staff and the presses were seized. In September 1849 Duffy revived the title for a brief period. In 1869 ISAAC BUTT used the title 'Nation' for a new journal aimed at seeking to promote a new, united and nationalist movement in Irish politics.

National Association of Ireland

The National Association of Ireland did not, in fact, achieve the 'national' platform that it set out to promote. It remained a regional force with varying degrees of support in the provinces. It was founded in December 1864 by O'Connellite politicians and the CATHOLIC CHURCH hierarchy in the person of CULLEN, archbishop of DUBLIN. Its objects were to promote tenant interests, particularly in relation to their struggle for compensation for improvements made upon their holdings (see LAND LEGISLATION, TENANT LEAGUE), and to lobby for the DISESTABLISHMENT of the CHURCH OF IRELAND. The Catholic hierarchy also saw it as an attempt to counter the growing influence of the revolutionary FENIAN movement. The National Association faded during the 1870s, after disestablishment was secured.

The title 'National Association' was also used in 1840 by DANIEL O'CONNELL for what became the Loyal national REPEAL ASSOCIATION.

National Board of Education see
KILDARE PLACE SOCIETY

National Brotherhood of St Patrick

The National Brotherhood was a fairly amorphous association of Irish nationalists, which developed branches throughout the British Isles and in America. It was founded in March 1861 under the chairmanship of Thomas Neilson Underwood, to prepare for the funeral in DUBLIN of the YOUNG IRELAND activist TERENCE BELLEW MACMANUS in November 1861. It was in his capacity as Vice-President of the Brotherhood that the Catholic priest LAVALLE made his remarks about the Catholic doctrine of the justifiable revolution, which alarmed the Catholic hierarchy, and which, in its turn, denounced the Brotherhood. There were strong links with the revolutionary FENIAN movement, and the Brotherhood circulated its own journal, the *Irish Liberator*. In 1864 Fenian involvement was curtailed, and decline set in.

National Council

In January 1832 DANIEL O'CONNELL, nothing if not a gifted founder of political organizations, set up a National Council to work for the restoration of the franchise to the FORTY-SHILLING FREE-HOLDERS. These freeholders, predominantly Catholics, had received the vote in 1793 EMANCIPATION legislation, only to have it removed by the further Emancipation Acts of 1829. The National Council itself evolved from the short-lived National Political Union founded in 1831 as a cross-party alliance working towards the same objective. The campaign for restoration of the franchise failed, and the Council folded.

A 'National Council' was set up in 1903 to orchestrate protests to the visit to Ireland of King Edward VII. It merged with SINN FÉIN in 1907.

National Evening Star

The newspaper or journal of the DUBLIN UNITED IRISHMEN in the 1790s, founded and edited by W.P. Carey. Its masthead symbol represented three hands clasped in unity, the Catholic, the PRESBYTERIAN or Dissenter, and the Anglican or CHURCH OF IRELAND. In the latter case, it was wishful thinking. The United Irishmen rose in rebellion in 1798 and were defeated. The paper's title owed something to the BELFAST United Irishmen paper, the *NORTHERN STAR*.

National Federation, The Irish

The National Federation was founded as a rival HOME RULE constituency organization to the NATIONAL LEAGUE, following the split in the HOME RULE PARTY between supporters and opponents of PARNELL in 1891. Its founder members were JOHN DILLON and TIMOTHY HEALY, although Healy was subsequently expelled. It

developed its own newspaper, the *National Press*.

National League, The Irish

The Irish National League has been called the first organized Irish political party. The name itself was not new. It had been given in 1864 to an organization founded to promote the 'restoration of a separate and independent Irish legislature', but the National League of October 1882 bore no relation to that earlier, semi-revolutionary grouping. It was formed, with WILLIAM O'BRIEN as secretary, to be a constituency party of the HOME RULE PARTY in Parliament at WESTMINSTER, and came into being as a direct consequence of the suppression of the LAND LEAGUE. PARNELL exercised considerably more control over the new organization than he had done over the Land League. The object was to bring out the voters for Home Rule candidates, and by 1886 there were some 1,200 branches, the establishment of which was assisted by support from the CATHOLIC CHURCH and the active involvement of parochial clergy. Funds were channelled in from America for the payment of the MPs in Parliament. In July 1887, under the terms of the new Criminal Law and Procedure Act, the LORD LIEUTENANT proclaimed the National League illegal for its tendency to incite violence, and prosecutions followed wherever there seemed to be a link between its activities and rural unrest such as BOYCOTTING. The National League was shattered by the scandal surrounding Parnell in 1891.

National Volunteers *see* IRISH VOLUNTEERS

Navigation Acts

The Navigations Acts passed between 1660 and 1671 were direct interference in Irish trade by the English Parliament. In 1651, whilst the IRISH REBELLION was staggering towards its close, the English Parliament passed a Navigation Act requiring that all goods imported into Ireland should be conveyed on English merchant ships. An Act of September 1660, after the restoration of Charles II, treated England and Ireland as a single economic unit – excluding Scotland from its provisions – for the purposes of the Act. English shipping was to be interpreted as shipping built in English or Irish shipyards. Vessels carrying goods to the American colonies were required to bring back import goods to English or to Irish ports. Legislation in July 1663 'for the encouragement of trade' gave priority again to England, restricting direct imports from Ireland to the colonies to foodstuff, horses and servants. All other goods had to be shipped from English ports, and parity was given to Scotland with Ireland in the restrictions imposed. The Act also prohibited Irish cattle exports to England (see CATTLE ACTS). The 1663 Act did not rest upon repeal of that of 1660, with the consequence that until 1671 the attempt to enforce colonial goods to English ports exclusively was a relative failure. In 1671 the new Navigation Act directly prohibited imports of colonial goods into Ireland for 10 years, and was renewed in 1685. Historians have disputed the impact of the various acts on Irish ports and trade. The decline of BELFAST and Galway as ports, relative to the expansion of DUBLIN, has been attributed to interference with Irish colonial trade, and the decline of other ports linked to the restrictions on the import of cattle on the hoof into England. Though there was plenty of clandestine evasion of restrictions, many Irish merchants worked in consort with their English counterparts and a good deal of Irish trade was effectively anglicized.

Neilson, Samuel (1761–1803)

Neilson was the son of a PRESBYTERIAN farmer in County Down and entered trade as a draper. He became a member of the VOLUNTEER movement, and sympathetic to Catholic EMANCIPATION. Neilson became a member of the UNITED IRISHMEN movement and founded and edited the *NORTHERN STAR* newspaper, the journal of the BELFAST United Irishmen, in 1792. Neilson's activism led to his arrest in 1796 on a charge of treason alongside other prominent Belfast leaders. Released, Neilson continued his involvement, and

was part of the organizing committee for the uprising scheduled for 1798. During the rising he was captured, and apparently acted as an informer, or gave 'honourable information' to the government. He was released and went into exile in America where he died in 1803. He expressed himself in favour of the UNION of Britain and Ireland of 1801.

Nenagh, battle of

The battle of Nenagh, County Tipperary, was fought on 17 May 1652, between rebel Irish forces under Loghlen O'Mara, and government troops. The collapse of the CATHOLIC CONFEDERACY was now assured. FLEETWOOD had taken over as English Commander-in-Chief in Ireland in July, and the defeat for loyal troops at Nenagh had no long-lasting consequences, beyond a reassertion of Irish prowess.

New Departure

The 'New Departure' in Irish 'nationalist' politics, proposed in 1878, was the preliminary development prior to the setting up of the LAND LEAGUE of 1879. The phrase was first employed in American newspapers reporting the suggestion of JOHN DEVOY, made in New York, that the movement for self-government (HOME RULE) and the land agitation for peasant proprietorship should come together in a single movement (which LALOR 40 years before had believed should happen). The alliance proposed was an alliance of militant nationalists and the constitutional Home Rulers represented by PARNELL and his party in the British Parliament. The revolutionary CLAN NA GAEL favoured such an alliance, but the IRISH REPUBLICAN BROTHERHOOD was less enthusiastic: its Supreme Council decided against involvement in January 1879, although in reality IRB members did give support to the ensuant Land League, as did many in the FENIAN revolutionary tradition. To the mainstream IRB the land issue was potentially divisive, and must be secondary to the wresting of political power back to the Irish, from which reform would necessarily follow. Parnell, conscious of the importance of the land problem, welcomed the proposed alliance, of which the Land League was the powerful and influential expression.

New English

The New English were, according to LORD DEPUTY WENTWORTH in the 1630s 'a company of men the most intent upon their own ends that ever I met with', a view that would have been shared by the OLD ENGLISH and the GAELIC IRISH. But when Wentworth spoke, the New English were in Ireland to stay, and had been moving in since the 1520s. The most usual crucial distinction made between the New English and the inhabitants of Ireland they found when they arrived, has been that of religion. They represented Protestantism almost to a man. The Old English, whose roots in Ireland in most instances went back into the Middle Ages, remained – with a few, politically astute, conversions notwithstanding – Catholic, as were the Gaelic Irish or the Old Irish. The New English settlers, whose numbers increased during PLANTATION, and particularly during the land settlement of the 1650s following upon the suppression of the IRISH REBELLION of 1641–53, were never numerically dominant. It has been estimated that in 1600 they accounted for no more than 2 per cent of the population, which had risen to 27 per cent by 1700, and were best represented in Counties Wicklow, Wexford, Armagh and Cork. The expropriation and plantation of ULSTER following the submission and flight of the Earl of TYRONE (see FLIGHT OF THE EARLS) eventually made Ulster into a major area of New English expansion, alongside Scottish Protestant settlers (largely PRESBYTERIAN) with whom they shared a collective hostility towards the native Catholic Irish. The New English came to control Ireland – their ultimate expression was the powerful ASCENDANCY which enjoyed exclusive political power in the country for more than a century, and which fought a dogged rearguard action against diminution of its power during the nineteenth century. They were, for the most part, communicants of the CHURCH OF IRELAND, the touchstone of whether a man belonged to or stood outside of, the Ascendancy. Their intensive racism, particularly in the seventeenth century, caused them to disdain not only the native Irish but also those elements of the Old English who were considered to have 'gone native', to have merged with certain Gaelic social and cultural traditions. The New English were colonialists first and foremost: during the eighteenth century, as they discovered their Irishness, and came to see themselves as the true 'Irish' and to look upon England or Britain as a potential threat to Ireland, their essentially English outlook intensified and became rigid. When the English themselves were moving, for example, towards toleration of religious dissent or of Catholicism, the Anglo-Irish remained resolutely opposed to concessions. From their ranks emerged, of course, reforming elements: GRATTAN and FLOOD, and their supporters of the 1780s, had tendencies towards liberal attitudes. But they were also primarily concerned with the legislative independence of Ireland, by which they would secure their eminence.

Consideration of classifications such as New English, Old English or Gaelic Irish must raise the question of at what point these distinctions ceased to matter, a general 'Irishness' subsuming them all. There is no doubt that exclusivist attitudes survived longer than did the distinction between the Old English and the Gaelic Irish, a distinction that was almost legislated out of existence by the PENAL LAWS, and rendered more and more meaningless by New English attitudes. To the revolutionary republicans of 1798 (see UNITED IRISHMEN) religious differences should be relegated in order to produce a united Irish nation governing itself. The religious issue was, more or less, played down and disregarded by the Irish nationalist movement of the nineteenth and twentieth centuries. To the republican revolutionaries and to the constitutional nationalists, it was an irrelevance except in so far as it impeded unification of Irishmen. The Protestant Ascendancy in its decline, for the most part maintained the religious distinction, and their earlier tool, the ORANGE ORDER, which was avowedly and violently sectarian, preserved religious distinctions as a crucial prop for the continuation of UNION with Britain that had been made real in 1801. More important, perhaps, is the perpetuation of the religious issue as that of paramount importance in the late twentieth century, a view promulgated by observers of continuing struggle within Ireland. The issue is not religious but political, a struggle between 'nationalists' and 'unionists' that remains rooted in the events around the year 1801.

It could be argued that New English, Old English, Gaelic Irish and the Scottish settler element, became Irish by virtue of shared domicile. In that view, the political structure perpetuated distinctions that merely glossed over the reality of a shared involvement in the future of Ireland. It is a transition that is not yet complete. But the New English, transformed into the Ascendancy, positively perpetuated internal divisions in Ireland and it was the pressure of events, rather than change in attitude, that made those divisions gradually disappear.

New Geneva

New Geneva was a projected settlement intended to be created near Waterford in the 1780s. As its name implies, it owed much to Calvinist Protestant theology, and the settlement was seen as a deliberate planting of purist Protestant values and political democracy. It did not materialize. Its buildings, ironically, became a prison for UNITED IRISHMEN in 1798, and after that, a military barracks.

New Light

The New Light movement was a development within the PRESBYTERIAN Church in Ireland, which had always been susceptible to controversies in Scotland, as well as to English puritan developments. In organization, there were two Presbyterian groupings in Ireland, that in the south (southern association) and, in the north, the Synod of ULSTER. Fundamental to the exercise of the ministry within the church was the doctrinaire Westminster Confession of Faith. Early in

the eighteenth century some Ulster ministers, questioning the need for subscription to the Confession, formed the BELFAST Society under the leadership of the Reverend John Abernethy. Their 'new light' that doctrines were not essential for evidence of Christian faith, inaugurated a dispute that led, in 1725, to the creation of the Presbytery of Antrim which was designed to include all those of the 'new light' persuasion. There was some criticism of the Ulster Synod for this 'leniency', particularly in the 1730s when disputes within the Scottish Church began to spill over into Ulster as well, particularly concerning the issue of lay patronage. Religious revivalism (see SECOND REFORMATION) in the early nineteenth century had a direct impact upon the Presbyterians. For a long time the Ulster Synod had not enforced the orthodoxy of subscription to the Confession of Faith, but the emergence of the Reverend Henry Cooke (1788–1868) as an advocate of stricter theological orthodoxy came at a time when the former radicalism of some Presbyterians (evidenced by their involvement in the UNITED IRISHMEN movement in 1790s) was ebbing in the face of EMANCIPATION for Catholics. The tolerance of the Ulster Synod gave way before Cooke's assault, and the liberal Presbyterians were driven to establish their own remonstrant Synod under the direction of the Reverend Henry Montgomery (1788–1865) who had favoured and continued to favour emancipation for the Catholics. The old Ulster Synod became the General Assembly of the Presbyterian Church in Ireland.

New Model Army

The New Model Army emerged from the ENGLISH CIVIL WAR as, theoretically at least, the radicalized fighting force of the English Parliament, which defeated King Charles I in the field by 1646. Its radicalism was essentially religious rather than political, despite attempts to turn it into a political army. But it was also radical in that the legislation to create it had effectively barred peers of the realm and sitting MPs from commands (with the exception of OLIVER CROMWELL).

Regiments of the New Model accompanied Cromwell to Ireland in 1649 to campaign against the CATHOLIC CONFEDERACY and the Irish royalists, and were present and involved in the massacres at DROGHEDA and Wexford.

New Ross, battle of

The battle of New Ross, County Wexford, was a defeat for the rebels of County Wexford (see WEXFORD RISING) in 1798. It was fought on 5 June, between rebel forces commanded by Bagenal Harvey and government troops under Major-General Henry Johnson. In the fighting John Kelly, 'the boy from Killan', was killed, a rebel commander who rapidly entered Irish folk memory.

Newtownbutler, battle of

The battle at Newtownbutler was fought on 31 July 1689 between JACOBITE troops under Lord Mountcashel, and WILLIAMITE troops out of Enniskillen under William Wolseley. The Jacobites were defeated in a major engagement that inflicted heavy losses, and seriously hampered the siege operations being directed against the city of DERRY.

Ninety-Eight, The

In Irish tradition, the UNITED IRISHMEN uprising of 1798 is alluded to as the 'Ninety-Eight' (as the later FENIAN uprising of 1867 is referred to as the SIXTY-SEVEN). The rising of 1798 was republican in character, non-sectarian (especially in ULSTER, less so in Wexford) and looked to armed intervention from France on behalf of the rebels. Its failure was due to the successful repression instituted in Ulster before 1798, the lack of equipped and disciplined rebel armies, and the failure of the French to make more than a token appearance, under HUMBERT, in Connacht. There were reckoned to be some 300,000 committed men in the provinces of Ulster, Leinster and Munster, and an unknown element in Connacht that the French endeavoured to raise but were only partially successful in so doing. But the efforts of the rebels were localized, and were dealt with piecemeal by government troops that included the allegedly unreliable MILITIA and the heavily sectarian YEOMANRY, both of which formations committed calculated outrages against the rebels and their civilian supporters. In Ulster, the rising was largely confined to the efforts of HENRY JOY McCRACKEN and Henry Munro, since the effective actions of General LAKE in 1796/7 had dispersed or taken the United Irishmen leadership and purged the Militia of rebel infiltration. The Ulster rising was most purely in the United Irishmen mould, non-sectarian, largely PRESBYTERIAN in makeup, and republican in politics. By contrast the WEXFORD RISING (which is considered as a separate entry) was most markedly Catholic and anti-Protestant. In March 1798 the leadership in Leinster had been raided and broken up, and the LORD LIEUTENANT had proclaimed a state of rebellion on 30 March. The Leinster rising, however, won initial success at the battle of Prosperous on 23 May. As the rising spread there were rebel defeats at Tara and Meath, and the DUBLIN rebels were routed at Old Kilcullan and Rathangan. At the end of May the infamous CURRAGH massacre occurred, inflicted on surrendered rebels by government forces. The rising in Ulster took place in June and was over within a matter of days after the bitter fight at BALLYNAHINCH.

In view of the collapse of the insurgents, the Lord Lieutenant proclaimed a general pardon to those who would come in, but General Lake ignored it, and continued to exact retribution and to permit atrocities. The French invasion, which came in August and too late, created for a brief time the 'Republic of Connacht' after the victory known as the RACES OF CASTLEBAR. The French, however, were defeated and made prisoners in September at BALLINAMUCK. In October there was a naval engagement off Lough Swilly between French and English naval vessels, which the English won. By act, the British government offered the rebels still in arms in October the chance to surrender or be tried for treason when taken. The rebellion degenerated into combats between bands of rebel fugitives and increasingly confident regular troops backed with Militia and Yeomanry. Court martials were enacted by Parliament in March 1799 to provide for summary trials and executions. 'What have you got in your hand?' ran a known litany of the United Irishmen, to which the answer was 'A green bough. Where did it first grow? In America. Where did it bud? In France. Where are you going to plant it? In the crown of Great Britain'. The United Irishmen's rebellion was republican in purpose and separatist in intent. It was meant to wrest power back to Ireland from Britain, to create an independent republic, inspired by the models of America and France. The rebellion received its most powerful inspiration, not from Catholic nationalism, but from Presbyterian discontent, which later took on board, and was almost swamped by, Catholic activism. Support for the American revolution had been widespread in Presbyterian circles, where the concept of republicanism had been nurtured; the United Irishmen were the expression of that Protestant republicanism, extending towards Catholics the concept of an Ireland united through its Irishness. More than 30,000 were killed during the rising of 1798.

Ninety-Eight Clubs

The Ninety-Eight Clubs developed, more or less by imitation, in 1898 to promote remembrance and celebration of the UNITED IRISHMEN rising of 1798. They were largely FENIAN in origin, but encompassed all types of Irish nationalists who looked back to the principles of the NINETY-EIGHT rising with sympathy.

No Rent Manifesto, The

The No Rent Manifesto was PARNELL's response to what he considered to be the inadequate provisions of the 1881 Land Act (see LAND LEGISLATION). The Act, so far as Parnell was concerned, was a political measure and he, gaoled in Kilmainham, resurrected proposals for a national rent strike that had been agreed upon by the Irish MPs at WESTMINSTER. Tenants, who by the provisions of the 1881 Act were entitled to have their rents fixed by land courts, were urged to apply to the courts to test the efficacy of the legislation. Parnell, however, miscalculated: the rank and file supporters of the LAND LEAGUE did not regard the Act as necessarily defective, and the large farmers were, in particular, satisfied with it. Had the strike idea taken hold, the country may well have moved toward open rebellion. The LORD LIEUTENANT (Earl Cowper) proclaimed the No Rent Manifesto illegal, but there was little need for coercion, since there was no response to Parnell's call from the peasantry at large.

Non-Importation

Non-importation, or a 'buy-Irish' campaign, as a means of winning equality of trading rights from Britain, was first mooted by SWIFT in the early eighteenth century, but was taken up as a form of protest, by the militant VOLUNTEER movement from the 1770s onwards. In November 1779 a massive parade of Volunteers in DUBLIN demanded the easing of commercial restrictions on Ireland by the Parliament at WESTMINSTER: there had been proposals in 1778 for giving Ireland direct access to the import-export trade with the colonies but nothing had come of it. The Irish PARLIAMENT assembled in October 1779 with emphasis upon the issue of free trade, and, ominously, voted an address of thanks to the Volunteers. Following the Volunteer demonstration in November and subsequent rioting, GRATTAN persuaded the Irish Commons to vote against granting any further taxes, which effectively gave the British government warning that after six months had elapsed, there would be no revenues out of Ireland. The British Parliament hurriedly passed legislation permitting Ireland to trade with the colonies, and America, on equal terms with Britain. It represented a conclusive victory for the PATRIOT element in the Irish Commons which members of the British administration in Ireland regarded with foreboding. The 1780 Act was as important in its context, as the repeal of the 1720 DECLARATORY ACT for the immediate future of the Irish Parliament. How far the non-importation campaign was responsible for the change in British opinion is debatable: as an expression of the popular Volunteer agitation, it certainly gave encouragement to the MPs in the Irish Parliament seeking to assert that Parliament's legislative independence. Although Grattan would later try to moderate extra-parliamentary agitation, his influence rested upon it, and so did his achievement. The international situation would also have worked in Irish interests. France and Britain had been at war since the conclusion of a French alliance with the American colonists in February 1778: concessionary measures such as the EMANCIPATION Act of August 1778 had become necessary, and in June 1779 Britain and Spain had opened hostilities as well.

North King Street, Dublin

North King Street was the scene of an atrocity during the British suppression of the EASTER RISING of 1916, when regular troops indiscriminately murdered innocent residents. This, and the murder of Francis Sheehy-Skeffington whilst he was trying to prevent looting and excesses by the British troops, contributed to the growing hostility towards the British after the rising was put down.

Northern Star, The

The *Northern Star* was the newspaper of the BELFAST UNITED IRISHMEN movement, and was founded in the city in October 1791, its first issue appearing the following January. The founders were SAMUEL NEILSON and the brothers Robert and William Simms. It was primarily a Belfast Protestant publication, which on the one hand welcomed and gave approving coverage to the revolution in France, whilst on the other rejected the armed activities of the Catholic DEFENDER movement, which had arisen in response to intimidatory Protestant violence in ULSTER. That this editorial line reflected the opinion of Neilson seems likely. The United Irishmen originally emerged in Belfast as a strongly PRESBYTERIAN movement, despite its republican principles, and the future amalgamation of Defender and United Irishmen memberships prior to the 1798 rising, would come as a result of a shift towards an alliance with the Catholic. The *Northern Star* offices were raided by MILITIA on 19 May 1797, and the printing presses destroyed. It ceased publication.

The title 'Northern Star' was resurrected in 1837 by Fergus O'Connor the Irish Chartist leader in England, who had abandoned the struggle for repeal under DANIEL O'CONNELL and had immersed himself in English radical politics.

O

Oakboys (also Hearts of Oak, Greenboys)

The Oakboys were a largely non-sectarian agrarian secret society which sprang up in ULSTER in mid-1763. Its targets were the COUNTY CESS, the road-building activities of the GRAND JURIES which the cess financed, and the perennial grievance of TITHES. Compulsory road labour had been abolished by act in May 1760; the Oakboy movement, therefore, was not a protest against that so much as a protest against road-building programmes that seemed to them to favour the interests of the landlords. The Oakboys were engaged in a pitched fight in March 1772, the 'Battle of Gilford', when they were confronted by a local landowner, Richard Johnston of Gilford, and a body of troops. The movement died down and burst forth again in 1772 when Oakboys marched into BELFAST and attacked the home of a new lessee of the Lord Donegall, who was raising rents and entry fines (see LEASES FOR LIVES) beyond the levels at which the outgoing tenants could afford to compete. This action reveals the Oakboys as regulatory, concerned with a moral issue as they perceived it. Oakboy activity faded away from 1772.

Oblivion, Act of

The 'Act of free and general pardon, indemnity, and oblivion' passed by Parliament at WESTMINSTER on 29 August 1660, brought to an end the years of the ENGLISH CIVIL WAR and the short-lived English Republic. King Charles had made his formal entry into London on 29 May, and the Act of Oblivion was a necessary, urgent legislative measure to calm feelings in England. The Act was also used to reassure the settlers (soldiers and ADVENTURERS) in Ireland, for it expressly excluded from its terms all persons engaged in the IRISH REBELLION of 1641–53. In view of the ultimate alliance of Catholic rebels and Irish royalists which had led them all to be liable to sequestration and expropriation of their lands during the 1650s, the Act of Oblivion implied that there would be little tampering with the Cromwellian land settlement.

O'Brien, Murrough (Murchdah na Atoithean or Murchadh na dToitean) (d. 1674)

Murrough O'Brien, 'Murrough of the Burnings', was of GAELIC IRISH stock but a Protestant. Charles II created him Earl of Inchiquin in 1654. He was Vice-PRESIDENT of Munster when the IRISH REBELLION of 1641 broke out, and took the field against the rebels. The English Parliament, at war with King Charles I from 1642, confirmed O'Brien as President of Munster in 1645 (a post he had not been able to obtain from the king) and this confirmed his shift of allegiance from the royalist to the parliamentarian side. In 1648 he negotiated with the royalist Earl of ORMOND and declared for the king, and then operated in alliance with the CATHOLIC CONFEDERACY and the royalists against government troops. RINUCCINI and the Catholic bishops of the Confederacy regarded O'Brien with intense suspicion and denounced the Confederacy's association with him, which had chosen to overlook O'Brien's butchery of Catholics at the Rock of Cashel earlier in the wars. O'Brien left Ireland for France in 1650, served in the French armies, and converted to Catholicism.

O'Brien, William (1852–1928)

O'Brien, born in County Cork and a close associate of PARNELL, prepared the NO RENT MANIFESTO of 1881 which was devised by Parnell as a campaign against the provisions of the LAND LEGISLATION of 1881. He became secretary of the

NATIONAL LEAGUE of 1882, founded to organize in the constituencies for the HOME RULE PARTY in the Parliament at WESTMINSTER. Between 1883 and 1918 he sat as MP himself for three Irish constituencies, and was gaoled in 1887 for organizing a rent strike by tenants. When the Home Rule Party split between those for and those against Parnell, O'Brien, who was close to Parnell, tried to negotiate between the two sides. From 1890 there was no unified Irish party in the House of Commons, but O'Brien was amongst those who brought it together again under the leadership of REDMOND in 1900. For a brief period between 1904 and 1908 O'Brien was moving towards the republicanism of SINN FÉIN. His All For Ireland League, founded in 1910 in Cork, was rapidly infiltrated by republicans and came to little. O'Brien himself favoured the Home Rule proposals of 1914 but was resolutely opposed to PARTITION which would separate ULSTER (or SIX COUNTIES of it) from the rest of Ireland and this led him to vote against the bill as a whole. When the FIRST WORLD WAR broke out, he spoke frequently in favour of Irish enlistment into the British army. At the approach of the 1918 General Election he determined not to stand, his support in his constituency, Cork City, having swung decidedly towards Sinn Féin. He abandoned his political career and became a writer.

O'Brien, William Smith (1803–64)

Smith O'Brien was a Protestant landlord from County Clare who, as MP for Ennis from 1826, appeared as a firm government supporter. In 1828, however, he became or declared himself to be, a supporter of the CATHOLIC ASSOCIATION which was struggling for EMANCIPATION. O'Brien was essentially a conservative and alarmed by DANIEL O'CONNELL's espousal of radicalism, but he saw himself as a moderating influence, and was significant enough to lead the REPEAL ASSOCIATION in its campaign for repeal of the UNION of 1801 during O'Connell's imprisonment. O'Brien's dislike of O'Connell's radicalism seems to have propelled him towards the YOUNG

IRELAND dissidents of the Repeal Association, who were developing a commitment to armed rebellion as a means of securing Irish independence. From 1835 to 1848 O'Brien was MP for Limerick, fulfilling a constitutional role in politics whilst becoming increasingly appalled by the condition of the Irish peasantry. It may have been the experience of the FAMINE, or government inadequacy in dealing with it, that led O'Brien finally to countenance the kind of insurrectionary ideas for which he had frequently denounced JOHN MITCHEL, another Young Irelander. Arrested briefly in the spring of 1848, upon his release O'Brien helped plan the rising and, somewhat unwillingly, accepted the leadership of it. The revolt, at Ballingarry, County Tipperary, on 29 July 1848 was a failure, O'Brien was arrested, tried, and sentenced to execution, but the sentence was commuted to TRANSPORTATION. He was pardoned in 1856, and retired from political activity.

Ó Bruadair, Dáibhí (d. 1698)

Ó Bruadair was a fighting poet, a champion of JACOBITISM, who, born in Cork or Limerick in the 1620s, had lived through the mass expropriation of the Cromwellian land settlement in the 1650s. He combined in himself the mixture of Catholicism, Francophile attitudes, and Gaelic Jacobitism that were redolent of an older Ireland swept away by the wars of 1689–91. His greatest poetic work, the *Shipwreck* (*An Longbhriseadh*), was written probably after his experience in defence of Limerick and in the light of the 'broken' Treaty of LIMERICK by which the Jacobite war came to an end. Ó Bruadair's view of his contemporary Ireland as a purgatory that had begun in the 1650s implied expectation of some heaven to be arrived at once purgatory had been endured. He clearly believed there was little point left in struggling further, that the defeat of the Irish was accomplished and complete. He allowed himself to celebrate the accession of JAMES II as perhaps ushering in a new age, but he accepted the crushing of that hope with resignation.

Obstructionism

The policy of 'obstruction' of parliamentary business was advocated by PARNELL and pursued by MPs of the HOME RULE PARTY at WESTMINSTER following the 1874 General Election (60 Home Rulers had been returned from Ireland with 33 Conservatives and 10 Liberals). The function of obstructionism was to so make use of the procedures of the Commons as to impede and hamper legislation unconnected with the Irish problem, and to thereby draw constant attention to their presence and their objectives. It had more impact in Ireland than it did in England: in fact, as a measure for promoting the image of the Home Rulers as vigorous and committed men it was well designed for consumption in the constituencies. It also owed something to the complete failure of ISAAC BUTT to achieve anything at all through constitutional means.

Ó Cléirigh, Míchael (1575–1643)

His name is anglicized as Michael O'Clery. He was a Franciscan laybrother who collected Irish manuscripts on behalf of his House at Louvain. He was a prolific writer, often with associates, who produced, between 1623 and 1630, *Reim Ríograidhe* (The Royal List) and, amongst other things, *Felire na Naomh nÉrennach* (Martyrology of Donegal) of 1630, *Annála Ríoghachta Éireann* (Annals of the Four Masters) of 1636 and a vocabulary of 1643, *Focloir na Sanasan Nua*.

O'Connell, Daniel (1775–1847)

O'Connell's greatness may be evidenced by the passion with which he was regarded by his contemporaries. To the YOUNG IRELAND movement he was 'Next to Britain the worst enemy that Ireland ever had': many Catholics regarded him as their 'Liberator' in respect of the EMANCIPATION legislation that he was held to have forced upon the British government. He was somewhat ambiguous in his political objectives – it was said of him that although he campaigned for repeal of the UNION of 1801 it was never clear what he would do with repeal if he

got it – but he was also a gifted organizer of a myriad of groupings, movements and 'parties' that his own particular oratory galvanized into action. O'Connell was born in County Kerry, of a Catholic gentry family, familiar with Gaelic language and culture, but destined for a career in the law. He joined the Irish Bar in 1798, in which year, coincidentally, he appears to have served against the republican UNITED IRISHMEN in the rising they had organized. Before the Union came into force in 1801, O'Connell had publically denounced it on behalf of Catholics, and he became known as a proponent of emancipation as early as 1803. In 1823 he set up the CATHOLIC ASSOCIATION in succession to the CATHOLIC BOARD of 1811 to press for the redress of Catholic grievances, and in 1828 was returned as MP for Clare, but was unable to take his seat in the Commons because of his Catholicism, although O'Connell argued that the Act of Union did not directly prohibit him from doing so. When the Emancipation Act of 1829 enabled him to sit, he absolutely declined to be administered the oath of Supremacy which required him to abjure his Catholicism. In 1835 he negotiated the important LICHFIELD HOUSE COMPACT with liberals and radicals in the Commons, on the strength of which MUNICIPAL REFORM and other measures were to be passed, of mixed benefit to Ireland or the Irish Catholics. He formed the REPEAL ASSOCIATION to work towards the restoration of an Irish Parliament, but his constitutionalism alienated some of his support within the Association, which emerged later as the revolutionary Young Ireland movement. His massive 'Year of Repeal' campaign in 1843 came to a somewhat ignominious end at CLONTARF, where he acceded to a government instruction to cancel a monster meeting of several hundred thousand supporters. He had, at least, seriously frightened the government. He was gaoled in 1844 for sedition but the sentence was quashed by the House of Lords. In 1847 he died whilst on pilgrimage to Rome. O'Connell had possessed a gift for organizing opinion, but much that he achieved or attempted to achieve depended upon him: the movements were expressions of

O'Connell's energy, and the way in which he failed to use it is shown in his relative neglect of ULSTER. He seems never to have visited the province, and when his organizers began to operate there in 1828, there was severe sectarian reaction, particularly in Monaghan. But O'Connell's standing in Irish tradition is unquestionable and, since he disowned PHYSICAL FORCE nationalism, he worked admirably within narrow parameters.

O'Connell Tribute *see* CATHOLIC RENT

O'Connor, Arthur (1763–1852)

Arthur O'Connor was one of the most revolutionary of the UNITED IRISHMEN leaders, influenced by and ultimately loyal to, the French revolution for the principles which it enshrined. He sat as MP for Philipstown in the Irish House of Commons from 1791 to 1795, and seems to have been inducted into the United Irishmen movement by Lord EDWARD FITZGERALD, just as he was about to try to purchase a seat in the British Parliament, grown weary with Irish politics. O'Connor despite his name was not of Gaelic stock: he chose to add the 'O' himself, and was occasionally and not always kindly alluded to as 'The King of Connacht'. Historians debate as to who influenced whom, whether O'Connor was more influential over FitzGerald or vice versa, but they were both committed to a revolutionary position by 1796. In January 1797 O'Connor published his *To the Free Electors of the County of Antrim* which has been seen as tantamount to an opening of hostilities between the United Irishmen and the authorities. It was certainly one of the factors that induced the government to set out to repress the United movement in ULSTER, which was done vigorously and brutally by General LAKE. O'Connor was arrested in DUBLIN and charged with high treason, a proceeding the British government did not like, although the CASTLE authorities favoured it because of O'Connor's notoriety. They were overruled, and O'Connor set at liberty. Thereafter he was active in Europe rallying support for the Irish cause, and in 1798 was arrested in

England where he was in communication with radical revolutionary groups. Opposition politicians rallied to O'Connor's side, including Charles Fox, and he was again at liberty. He took no part in the rising in Ireland in 1798, and made his way to France where in 1804, he became a general in the army of Napoleon. His interest in fomenting revolt in Ireland remained, and in 1810 he was involved in the despatch of agents into Ireland, but French interest had waned and the circumstances were not propitious. O'Connor remained an exile in France until his death in 1852.

Octennial Act, The

The Octennial Act of 16 February 1768 limited the life of the Irish PARLIAMENT to eight years, a British government measure in response to the Irish Parliament's proposal for a septennial act. The argument was that since the Irish Parliament met in alternate years, an eight-year act was more reasonable. The Irish Commons welcomed the legislation. Theoretically, prior to this, a Parliament could last as long as the life of the monarch, convening in numerous sessions as and when required. The General Election campaign of 1760 following upon the succession of George III was, in Ireland, fought (where there was any contest at all) over the proposals for a limited Parliament for seven years. It was in this election that the radical CHARLES LUCAS was returned as MP for DUBLIN, campaigning for general reforms including a triennial Parliament. Under the terms of POYNINGS' LAW, the Irish Parliament sent to England proposals for a septennial act, although it was widely believed in the administration that the matter would not be pressed vigorously. In consequence, the proposal or 'head of a bill' was not turned into a bill for consideration in the Irish Commons. In the session of 1765/6 the proposal was raised again, and the head of a bill for a septennial Parliament was passed by the Irish Commons on 14 March 1766, and viewed as 'necessary to the preservation of their fundamental rights'. The future PATRIOT leader, HENRY FLOOD, actually pressed for annual Parliaments but got little support. The British choice of an Octennial Act, which encountered little opposition in the Irish Commons, was a not unexpected assertion of the primacy of the British Parliament over that of Ireland.

O'Doherty, Sir Cahir (1587–1608)

The terms by which the Earl of TYRONE submitted to the English crown at MELLIFONT in 1603 were, by design of MOUNTJOY the LORD DEPUTY, generous. O'Doherty had been a Gaelic chieftain developed by the administration in DUBLIN as a force against the Earl of Tyrone, his knighthood a reflection of the faith reposed in him. The Mellifont terms gave to the earl and to his former Gaelic enemies ostensible security in their estates. O'Doherty was confirmed in his lands in Innishowen. Mountjoy's successor as Lord Deputy, ARTHUR CHICHESTER, did not favour the status quo, not least because of his own territorial interest within ULSTER, and a proclamation of 1605 made the settlement of 1603 a matter of question. O'Doherty had relied upon the goodwill of the Governor of DERRY, Sir Henry Docwra, in his loyalist position and in the control he exercised over his territory. Two years after the 1605 proclamation, Docwra was replaced with Sir George Paulet, who shared the views of Chichester and Sir JOHN DAVIES, and went out of his way to alienate and unsettle O'Doherty, informing the authorities in Dublin that O'Doherty was in a state of rebellion by November 1607. In fact, he rose in April 1608, stormed and took Derry, killed Paulet and burned the city. On 20 June he defeated a government force commanded by Sir Henry O'Neill, another Gaelic instrument of the English government, and was then shot dead in action at Kilmacrenan, County Donegal on 5 July. His head was despatched to Dublin. O'Doherty's treatment by the government indicated to former followers of Tyrone that little could be expected of the settlement of 1603, if the authorities could destroy one of their own nominees in such a way.

O'Donnell, Rory (1575–1608)

Rory O'Donnell was the younger brother of 'Red' Hugh O'Donnell (1571–1602) who had been a prominent rebel during the TYRONE rebellion, and had been murdered in exile in Spain in 1602. Rory, heir to 'Red' Hugh's title of 'The O'Donnell' was also in arms with Tyrone, but, by the submission at MELLIFONT in 1603, had been confirmed in his estates and granted the title of Earl of Tyrconnell. Like Tyrone he took full advantage of the Mellifont terms to extend and to consolidate his power in Donegal, but under increasing pressure from the English authorities in DUBLIN, he seems to have resorted to conspiracy to raise further rebellion. With Tyrone, he fled to Ireland in 1607 (see FLIGHT OF THE EARLS) after direct accusation by the Dublin authorities. He died in Rome of a fever a year later. His fall and that of Tyrone opened up ULSTER to the full implementation of the policy of PLANTATION, and marked the collapse of the ancient Gaelic hierarchy in the province.

O'Donovan Rossa, Jeremiah (1831–1915)

O'Donovan Rossa was a grocer in County Cork of nationalist sympathies, who in 1856 founded at Skibbereen the PHOENIX (National and Literary) SOCIETY which very shortly became part and parcel of the organization of the IRISH REPUBLICAN BROTHERHOOD, the revolutionary movement. He became involved in the production of the *Irish People* newspaper, and was arrested in September 1865 on a charge of treason and felony, along with THOMAS LUBY. The paper's suppression was welcomed by Cardinal CULLEN because of what he saw as its overtly revolutionary, PHYSICAL FORCE sentiments. During his imprisonment, O'Donovan Rossa was nominated and returned as MP for the Tipperary constituency, defeating his opponent by 1,131 votes to 1,028. As a convicted felon, he was unable to take his seat in the Parliament at WESTMINSTER, but the result of the election was nonetheless a shock to the authorities, coming as it did within two years of the suppression of the FENIAN rising of 1867. In January 1871 the British government released 33 Fenian prisoners, amongst whom was O'Donovan Rossa, and he went into exile in America. He took up writing, and was active in the formation of the SKIRMISHING FUND and in financing the DYNAMITE WAR in England. In 1877 he was chief of the Fenian movement in America. Attitudes to O'Donovan Rossa in the nationalist and republican movements were mixed, but PADRAIC PEARSE accorded him considerable posthumous fame when he spoke at O'Donovan Rossa's funeral at Glasnevin cemetery in 1915. Pearse in his speech made O'Donovan Rossa into a symbol of the generations of Irishmen who had struggled for independence, and made him an example for the new generation to follow.

Official Punishments

The term 'official punishments' was British government jargon for the 'authorized reprisals' carried out against the Irish by the BLACK AND TANS, AUXILIARIES and ROYAL IRISH CONSTABULARY during the WAR FOR INDEPENDENCE of 1919–21. It conveyed official support for the campaign of terror which, counterproductively, increased sympathy and support for the IRISH REPUBLICAN ARMY.

O'Halloran, Sylvester (1728–1807)

O'Halloran was a Limerick surgeon and physician, specializing in head injuries, and a member of the Royal College of Surgeons who played an important part in the revival of interest in Gaelic and Irish history. O'Halloran was a Catholic. His concern for the survival of the records of Ireland's past was expressed in his *Insula Sacra* of 1770, and he laid emphasis upon the proper study of ancient Ireland (*Ierne Defended* of 1774). His major work, published in that same year, was *General History of Ireland* which looked at what was known of Irish history prior to the Anglo-Norman invasions of the twelfth century.

O'Hanlon, Redmond *see* TORIES

Old English, The

According to King James I, the Old English in Ireland were only 'half his subjects'. The opinion reflected the attitude of the NEW ENGLISH settlers, who regarded the Old English as either lost in Catholicism or partly or wholly swallowed up in the native culture of the GAELIC IRISH. Certainly, the Old English had had centuries in which to assimilate with the native people of Ireland, although it was never as thorough an assimilation – and sometimes was most markedly not so – as the newcomers of PLANTATION and Tudor and Stuart settlement pretended. The Old English in Ireland, 'English of Irish birth' as they tended to be styled up until 1600, traced their association with the country to the Anglo-Norman conquests of the mid-twelfth century and later. Indeed, the term is ordinarily applied to any 'English' families established in Ireland prior to the reign of King Henry VIII (1509–47). Their chief area of control was DUBLIN and its PALE, and by 1600 they were most conspicuous in urban centres predominantly in the provinces of Leinster, Munster and in Connacht, where they had a strong presence in County Galway. Although there were some powerful aristocratic families – the Butlers and the Burkes, for example – the majority of the Old English were of gentry status, intermixing closely with their Gaelic neighbours (except in the Pale where an exclusive Englishness long survived, until it was crushed by New English administrators and enforcers of doctrinaire Protestantism). The antiquity of English landholding in Ireland made them as potentially vulnerable as the Gaelic Irish to concerted government questioning of titles to land, which became more comprehensive in the seventeenth century as the plantation schemes were promulgated. This, and the onslaught on Catholic religious observance which was far from a unifying factor between the Gaelic Irish and Old English, forced the Old English to politicize themselves. Indeed, it can be argued that the Old English view of themselves, was in fact forced upon them by external factors: that their community of interest and 'Anglo-Irish' self-identity was a response to the threat of religious change and land expropriation. They endeavoured to be seen as distinct from the restive Gaelic people (the great ULSTER uprising of the Earl of TYRONE having ended only in 1603), and to have their own Catholicism seen as no threat to their continuing loyalty to the English crown and the Protestant government. The effort was wasted, because it was inherent in the imposition of New English settlement that Catholicism should eventually be crushed. In the first two decades of the seventeenth century, as the Irish House of Commons was crammed with Protestant New English MPs from specially created boroughs, the Old English found themselves treated, and came to regard themselves, as a beleaguered group. Thus their attempt to bargain with the crown (see MATTERS OF GRACE AND BOUNTY) can be seen as an attempt to reassert their old power. Failure to find accommodation led them to involvement with the Gaelic rebels of the IRISH REBELLION of 1641, and the creation of the Gaelic and Old English CATHOLIC CONFEDERACY. Of course, their rebellion was by no means solid: many Old English remained loyal to King Charles I who was engaged in a bitter struggle with the English Parliament. A victory for the king might, after all, alleviate the problems of the Old English, and anyway, loyalty to the crown (such as that personified by the Earl of ORMOND) was a crucial element in the Old English psyche. The defeat of royalists and rebels alike, and the massive land expropriations of the 1650s, completed the downfall of the Old English, and put them on a par with the Gaelic Irish, united both by a common religious faith and, henceforth, by a common history of dispossession and disenfranchisement. By 1700 power in Ireland had passed conclusively to the Protestant ASCENDANCY which was, by and large, the New English comfortably established as the 'new Irish'.

Old Irish

This term would appear to have two applications. It was used of themselves by the GAELIC IRISH of the CATHOLIC CONFEDERACY of 1641, and consequently must be taken in its sense of 'native' Irish, Irish not of English origin. However, it can also be used of the native Irish and of the Old English together, to distinguish

them from the NEW ENGLISH and the Protestant ASCENDANCY.

Old Ross, battle of

The battle of Old Ross, County Wexford, was fought on 18 March 1643 between government forces under the Earl of ORMOND, and troops of the CATHOLIC CONFEDERACY commanded by PRESTON. Ormond was making for New Ross near by when he turned to meet the Leinster rebels and defeated them.

O'Leary, Art (Airt Uí Laoghaire/Art Ó Laoghaire)

Art O'Leary's death in 1773 at the hands of soldiers, was commemorated in a 'lament' written by his wife Eibhlin Dubh Ní Chonaill. O'Leary was a Catholic exile in Europe, who had served in the forces in Hungary, and had returned to his native lands in County Cork. On 4 May 1773 he refused to sell his horse to the Protestant Abraham Morris, and was shot dead by soldiers in Morris's company. Morris was acquitted of murder on 9 September. The lament, 'Caoineadh Airt I Laoghaire', was an expression of a literary form that was peculiarly female, and was used to record for all time the injustice of the killing. It was also a Gaelic revival of considerable importance.

O'Mahony, John (1816–77)

John O'Mahony was one of the founders of the YOUNG IRELAND group, which emerged from the REPEAL ASSOCIATION of DANIEL O'CONNELL as a PHYSICAL FORCE movement that rejected O'Connell's constitutionalism. O'Mahony was in arms during the abortive Young Ireland rebellion of 1848, and escaped into France with JAMES STEPHENS. By 1853 O'Mahony was in New York, where, in 1855, he was involved in the formation of the revolutionary EMMET MONUMENT ASSOCIATION. By 1858 he was involved in the FENIAN movement, and trying to organize Irish-American soldiers to journey to Ireland to train the Fenians there in the use of arms. His project to seize the island of Campo Bello on behalf of America, using Irish-American Fenian soldiers in April 1866, had failed and discredited O'Mahony amongst the Fenians, who looked instead to James Stephens to bring on the general rising in Ireland for which the movement had been formed. Stephens' procrastination on this led to his own eventual replacement by Colonel Thomas Kelly (see SIXTY-SEVEN, The). O'Mahony commanded Fenian troops which fought for the Union during the American Civil War, developing the military expertise he needed, but it was never put to the test apart from the Campo Bello incident.

O'Malley, Ernie (1898–1957)

O'Malley came into the revolutionary republican movement in 1917, in the wake of the EASTER RISING, when he joined the IRISH VOLUNTEERS. During the rising of 1916 he had been involved in spontaneous and undirected harassment of the British troops in DUBLIN, one of those inspired immediately by the events. He became an officer in the IRISH REPUBLICAN ARMY under MICHAEL COLLINS in 1919 and fought in the WAR FOR INDEPENDENCE of 1919–21. O'Malley was the first important IRA commander to reject the terms of the ANGLO-IRISH TREATY of 1921 which effectively PARTITIONED Ireland, excluding SIX COUNTIES of ULSTER from Irish self-government. Captured wounded by the pro-government IRA in 1922 during the civil war, he went on HUNGER STRIKE and was released in 1923. O'Malley wrote a major account of the IRA's struggle, *On Another Man's Wound*, which was published in 1936.

O'More, Rory (d. 1652/3)

Rory O'More was the descendant of a previously extensively-landed Gaelic family in County Armagh and the Irish midlands, although by 1641 he was in reduced circumstances, directly attributable to the PLANTATION policy pursued by the English administration in DUBLIN. He may have been the prime mover in fomenting the IRISH REBELLION which broke out in October 1641, for his familial connections with Gaelic families were extensive, and he certainly involved prominent ULSTER Gaelic figures in the rising. It was through his influence that OWEN ROE O'NEILL came over from Europe to command the Ulster insurgents. O'More was also influential in bringing the OLD ENGLISH to the talks that led to the creation of the CATHOLIC CONFEDERACY, but he was tied closely to O'Neill and followed his political stance, which in 1648 was to ally them alongside RINUCCINI, the papal envoy, against the Confederacy itself, which wished to form an alliance with the Irish royalists (see CESSATION). In the decline of the rebel and royalist parties from 1649 onwards, O'More disappeared into the struggle under the command of CLANRICARDE and died somewhere in Ireland, in 1652 or 1653.

O'Neill, The

'The O'Neill' was the type of Gaelic title that the English government sought to suppress during the sixteenth century (and in earlier centuries), the assumption of which by the Earl of TYRONE in 1595 was seen as a direct challenge to English dominance in Ireland. It was a denial of the policy of ANGLICIZATION to which leading Gaelic nobility such as Tyrone subscribed, theoretically, in adopting and using English titles such as 'earl'. The use of 'The O'Neill' implied the readoption of Gaelic forms of control and influence over the 'clan', and heralded the approach of Tyrone's rebellion against the English crown which ended in 1603 at MELLIFONT.

O'Neill, Daniel (1612–64)

Daniel O'Neill was the Protestant, but Gaelic, nephew of OWEN ROE O'NEILL whose military career lay primarily in England, where he was a commander in the royalist armies during the ENGLISH CIVIL WAR. In 1649 he was in Ireland as a royalist agent seeking to bring together the royalist ORMOND and the rebel leader Owen Roe O'Neill, and commanded Owen Roe's forces for a time in ULSTER during the latter's illness that led to his death. Daniel O'Neill was serving in Scotland in 1650 when his command of the Ulster forces was transferred to the bishop of CLOGHER. He ended his career as Postmaster General in England, an indication of what a Gaelic Irishman might achieve in England by the profession of the Protestant religion.

O'Neill, Hugh *see* TYRONE, Earl of

O'Neill, Owen Roe (1590–1649)

Owen Roe O'Neill, the nephew of the Earl of TYRONE who fled from Ireland in 1607 (see FLIGHT OF THE EARLS) had pursued a military career in the armies of Spain, until drawn back to Ireland to head the rebel Gaelic forces during the IRISH REBELLION which began in 1641. He arrived in Ireland, in County Donegal, on 9 July 1642, by which time the rebellion had grown to a nation-wide insurrection comprehending the OLD ENGLISH as well in the CATHOLIC CONFEDERACY. O'Neill's attitude to Irish affairs was blunt: he 'held him no better than a devil' who saw any distinction actual or to be made, between the OLD ENGLISH and the GAELIC IRISH. He would 'call and term all, Irish'. He was somewhat in the mould of the committed Catholic crusader of earlier rebellions, James FitzMaurice FitzGerald, who had inspired the Desmond wars at the close of the sixteenth century. O'Neill was an accomplished soldier. After his defeat at Clones in County Monaghan by the Scottish PRESBYTERIAN army of the LAGGAN, inflicted upon him in June 1643 when his forces were in desperate need of training, he never suffered another defeat in the field. He won the crushing victory of BENBURB in 1646. His unbending Catholicism, Spanish in temper, led him to support the papal envoy RINUCCINI when the latter obstructed all attempts to arrive at an alliance with the royalists under ORMOND (see CESSATION), in consequence of which, when the alliance did come, in 1649, it was far too late. O'Neill fell ill in that year and the command of his army was briefly exercised by a Gaelic Irish royalist, DANIEL O'NEILL, Owen Roe's uncle. He died at Cloughoughter, County Cavan on 6 November 1649, his final year marred by a brief but (for the royalists) damaging alliance with the government troops in ULSTER against the now royalist Scots.

O'Neill, Phelim (1604–53)

Sir Phelim O'Neill was, with RORY O'MORE, a prime mover of the IRISH REBELLION of 1641. He was an ULSTER Gaelic Catholic, with estates in County Armagh and County Tyrone, and in 1641 was the foremost of his name in the province which, in terms of raising native Irish in arms, was crucial. It was Phelim O'Neill who issued the rebels' proclamation denying they were in arms against the king, Charles I, and urging they had risen for the defence of their liberties (grossly infringed upon by 40 years of PLANTATION by the government and its mercantile allies in England and in DUBLIN). In November it was Phelim O'Neill who declared that the rebels acted under the authority of the king himself, something that historians have, by and large, tended to disbelieve but which may have had an element of truth in it. Upon the arrival of OWEN ROE O'NEILL in Ulster, Phelim handed command over to him, and served as one of Ulster's spokesmen on the Supreme Council of the CATHOLIC CONFEDERACY at Kilkenny. He served as Lord President of Ulster from 1642, the assumption of which office was in keeping with the attempt to show the legality of the rebellion. Phelim favoured, where Owen Roe O'Neill did not, the conclusion of an alliance with the royalists in Ireland in 1646/7, but sided with the papal envoy RINUCCINI when the latter denounced the compromises of principle inherent in any such alliance. He surrendered to the government in 1650, and was tried and executed on 10 March 1653. He might have saved his life had he stated that the rebellion of 1641 had been fomented by King Charles I (who had preceded O'Neill to the block in 1649), and as had been claimed by the rebels in 1641. But O'Neill denied that this was so, and was beheaded.

O'Neillism

An historiographical term which contends that the rebellion of the Earl of TYRONE which ended at MELLIFONT in 1603, was nothing to do with a national, Gaelic uprising, but everything to do with the Earl of Tyrone's perception of his own self-interest, which meant, political independence from interference from England and the English administration in DUBLIN. This arose, it is contended, from the pronounced localism of Gaelic aristocratic awareness, and expressed itself in concern for the way things used to be, rather than in any genuine attempt to create a unified Irish national movement. Thus, Gaelic assertiveness was O'Neillism, tending to the greater freedom of action of 'THE O'NEILL', the Earl of Tyrone. The contention has limited applicability, in that it explains away a rebellion of short duration but draining on the English exchequer, without showing that there was any continuum in subsequent risings, such as that, for example, of O'DOHERTY in 1608, which was presumably 'O'Dohertyism', whilst the IRISH REBELLION of 1641–53 was a compound of residual and even more parochial 'O'Neillism', 'O'Moreism' and 'Maguireism'. O'Neillism is an historiographical tendency that seeks to deny to Gaelic uprisings any ideological commitment beyond that of extreme conservatism, and as such, fails to perceive that that is in itself an ideological commitment. For it is an assertion of the Gaelic order against ANGLICIZATION, and as such is, in its implications, beyond the parochial, or merely local.

O'Rahilly, The (Michael Joseph O'Rahilly) (1875–1916)

The O'Rahilly was a Catholic country gentleman with estates in Kilkenny, who became involved in revolutionary republicanism through his membership of the GAELIC LEAGUE. He wrote articles for SINN FÉIN. He was deeply involved in the HOWTH GUN RUNNING in 1914, but when the EASTER RISING was imminent in April 1916, he accepted orders countermanding the involvement of the IRISH VOLUNTEERS that emanated from EOIN MACNEIL. Nevertheless, as a 'volunteer', he took part in the defence of the GPO in DUBLIN and was killed during the fighting.

Orange Order and Orangeism

The Orange Order is the oldest of all the Irish political or sectarian movements, originating in 1795 in ULSTER after the

Battle of the DIAMOND between Catholics and Protestants. Following the battle, Protestant militants went onto the offensive in County Armagh, burning out Catholics and driving refugees before them. They were condemned as 'lawless banditti' by the authorities, 'a rebellious and insurrectionary' attitude amongst them 'running contradictorily to the channel of Allegiance'. In its early stages the Orange Order subsumed the violently sectarian Protestant PEEP O'DAY BOYS, and took on from its inception the colour of loyalty to the British connection that was seen as threatened by resurgent Catholic political activism and the struggle for EMANCIPATION. By 1835 there were some 200,000 Orange men in Ulster (and in other parts of Ireland). The Orange Order presented, and presents, itself as organized LOYALISM, a loyalty directed towards the British crown, the guarantee of Protestant religious freedom, and the maintenance of the British connection. It was, and is, in its basic philosophy, antagonistic towards the creation of a Republic of Ireland covering all 32 counties, with its concomitant ascendancy (as it was, and is, perceived) of Catholicism, the majority religion in Ireland. But 'loyalty' in the Orange Order was always a qualified loyalty – loyalty to the crown so long as the crown 'supports the Protestant ASCENDANCY' was an early declaration of principle. It linked itself by name and ceremonial to the memory of King WILLIAM III, William of Orange, who deposed the Catholic king, JAMES II, in 1688, and destroyed the JACOBITE cause in Ireland between 1689 and 1691. The Order therefore, in its very nature, identified with the overthrow of legitimate authority for the sake of a perceived political (and religious) purpose. Its conditional loyalty is, therefore, inherent. In its early years, the Orange Order was both secretive and ritualized, borrowing heavily from Masonic practice in its regalia (although there were, as early as 1802, clashes between Masonic and Orange Lodges in the Belfast area). Its first ritualized observance of 12 July (as the anniversary of the battle of the BOYNE where the Jacobites were roundly defeated) was in 1796, and was accompanied by violence against, and from, Catholic crowds. In 1797 Masters of the Orange Lodges met to formulate a declaration of their principles, which included support for the CHURCH OF IRELAND as the established church (and the guarantee of the Ascendancy). A great period in Orange Order revival was to come with the move towards DIS-ESTABLISHMENT of that church in the 1860s, but the association of Orangeism with PRESYBTERIANISM has tended to blur that earlier commitment. When Presbyterians, particularly in Ulster, split in 1798 for and against the UNITED IRISHMEN rebellion – the United Irishmen movement itself rooted in radical Presbyterianism – the Orange Order was solidly behind the government. General LAKE, in his repressive measures against the United Irishmen in Ulster in 1797, used the Orange Lodges as an additional weapon, and personally countenanced their 12 July parades of that year. When UNION of Britain and Ireland was inevitable in 1800 (it came into practice in 1801) the Orange Order was split between opposition to Union, and support for it. Lodges at Maze, County Down, denounced the Union as the 'inevitable ruin' of Ireland, and they had support from Lodges elsewhere, although the Grand Orange Lodge in County Antrim regretted the divisions the Union had occasioned the movement. Although the government could use the Orange Order when it chose, as an intimidatory force, it was also clear that the potential of the Order was not necessarily compatible with the interests of stable government. On 9 March 1825 the Unlawful Societies (Ireland) Act sought to limit the activities of all bodies, Protestant or Catholic, which claimed to be representative of opinion and designed to promote changes in the law. The ban on Orange Lodge meetings was implicit, and the Grand Orange Lodge warned its component members against continuing to meet. But by reforming itself as a benevolent society, 'The Loyal and Benevolent Orange Institution of Ireland' it got around the legislation and remained intact. It was headed by a Grand Master. In fact, Orangeism as an alternative to the effective campaigning of the CATHOLIC BOARD and CATHOLIC ASSOCIATION had achieved very little. As it

became apparent that major concessions to the Catholics on emancipation were imminent, militant Protestantism underwent a revival through the BRUNSWICK CLUBS, but these were essentially aristocratic. There was almost a pitched battle between militant Protestants and supporters of DANIEL O'CONNELL in County Monaghan in 1828: sectarian conflict seemed imminent, and the government had deployed more than 20,000 troops throughout Ireland to meet it. The Catholic Emancipation Act of 1829 led to a wave of Orange disturbances all over Ulster, both reacting to measures already enacted, and in opposition to the Repeal campaign which O'Connell intended to mount, to break the Union of 1801 which, by now, the Protestants had taken as something to be protected. The Order, which laid emphasis upon its benevolent side, had successfully infiltrated itself into the peace-keeping forces, with committed magistrates and JPs on its side. The government in Britain was alarmed, a select committee reported unfavourably, and the Order felt obliged to dissolve itself in 1836, at the height of its influence and strength. In 1845 meetings at Enniskillen proposed to revive the Order, in keeping with the laws against secret societies and oath-taking, and in May of 1849 the Grand Orange Lodge adopted new rules to govern the Loyal Orange Institution. Between then and 1850, the Loyal Orange Institution became a predominantly urban movement, with particular strength in Belfast, and it owed much to the flamboyant WILLIAM JOHNSTON who challenged outright legislation against processions. The HOME RULE issue gave to the Orange Order an identifiable object for its enmity: and the association between Unionism and Orangeism was almost total by 1880, although the one was, theoretically at least, constitutional, the other, by definition, extra-parliamentary. Sectarian violence, which exploded in the summer and autumn of 1857, became a necessary adjunct of assertive Orange Order parades and ceremonials, which were a direct challenge to Catholics. The sectarian issue in Irish politics was maintained by Orange violence. Although it never reached the strength it had enjoyed in 1835, by 1912 there were about 125,000 Orange men throughout Ireland (predominantly in Ulster) and they contributed massively to the ULSTER VOLUNTEER FORCE raised to defend the Union against Home Rule. Colonel R.H. Wallace, the secretary of the Grand Orange Lodge of Ulster, was drilling men with magisterial approval in 1912. Many of them died in the British Army on the Somme in the FIRST WORLD WAR of 1914–18. Orangeism, because of its association with Unionism and its commitment to the Union which its founding lodges had felt so ambivalent about, has proved to be a most effective barrier to the spread of class consciousness that men like LARKIN and CONNOLLY, socialists and Irish nationalists, saw as necessary for the creation of a true free republic in Ireland.

Contemporary republicans and nationalists, for whom the sectarian division is inherently prejudicial to the recognition of an 'Irish' interest that embraces all 32 counties, come up against the cross-class alliance of Protestants and Unionists that the Orange Order still maintains more or less solidly. The Orange Order is the oldest surviving organization in Ireland, because the struggle to which it became committed, remains the same, and it is, therefore, comparable with the IRISH REPUBLICAN ARMY, for which the cause of a united Ireland remains the same. They represent entrenched opposites: historians who profess to see the TYRONE rebellion which ended in 1603 as O'NEILL-ISM, conservative and concerned with the status quo, must also interpret Orangeism in the same way. It was, and remains, primarily defensive, beset by an Irish nationalism perceived as Catholic in colour, which grew steadily from emancipation, Repeal and Home Rule into revolutionary Irish Republicanism.

Orange Peel

'Orange' Peel was DANIEL O'CONNELL's opprobrious nickname for the politician ROBERT PEEL, and was applied when Peel, as CHIEF SECRETARY in DUBLIN, evinced little or no enthusiasm for the cause of Catholic EMANCIPATION.

Ó Rathailie, Aodhagán (1670–1726)

The name is anglicized as Égan O'Rahilly. He was a poet of the Gaelic tradition, noted for his commitment to the cause of the Stuarts, and to JACOBITE Ireland, a commitment which was linked to sending up the NEW ENGLISH and their 'planter' culture. He developed the image of Ireland as a woman wronged, waiting upon her Stuart deliverer, the deliverer who, though Ó Rathailie never knew it, did not come. He lived through the Jacobite wars that in 1691 broke the back of Catholic Ireland, and his poetry was an expression of the sadness of the defeated. Poets such as he preserved a tradition that made possible the later, nineteenth-century Gaelic cultural revival.

Order of Liberators

The Order of Liberators represented another political ploy by DANIEL O'CONNELL following upon the virtual suppression of the CATHOLIC ASSOCIATION In February 1825, which was legislated for by the Unlawful Societies Act of March. The ban applied to Protestant ORANGE Lodges as well as to the Catholic Association. This measure was followed by the defeat in the House of Commons of a bill for EMANCIPATION of Catholics. In the General Election campaign of June to July 1826, O'Connell mobilized the FORTY-SHILLING FREEHOLD vote on an unprecedented scale to oust the government man, Beresford, in County Waterford, in favour of the successful candidate Henry Villiers Stuart, and on 30 August in Waterford initiated the 'Order of Liberators'. It was intended to honour any man who had performed some act of service to the well-being of Ireland and its people, and, at the same time, to promote effective use of the Catholic vote. It was also intended as a force to prevent the prevalent FEUD AND FACTION fighting which damaged the image of the Catholic peasantry.

Organization, The

A term by which members of the IRISH REPUBLICAN BROTHERHOOD, the revolutionary republican movement, referred to it.

Ormond(e), James Butler, 12th Earl of (1610–88)

From 1642 until his departure for France in 1650, the Earl of Ormond was the epitome of Irish loyalty to the English crown. Of OLD ENGLISH family, but a Protestant, the earl sustained the royalist party in Ireland as long as it was militarily possible to do so, and until his authority was cut from under him by the DUNFERM-LINE DECLARATION of King Charles II. He spoke on behalf of the fallen LORD DEPUTY, THOMAS WENTWORTH, in 1641. Ormond took command of government troops against the IRISH REBELLION which broke out in October of that year, although his efforts were hampered by the LORDS JUSTICES, Borlase and Tichborne, who were close to the English Parliament which was steadily encroaching upon royal authority. The ENGLISH CIVIL WAR complicated Ormond's task of reducing the rebels to obedience. Not until 1643 was he appointed LORD LIEUTENANT by the king, and required to reach a CESSATION with the Catholic rebels in order to free troops for service in England on the king's behalf. Ormond's efforts were plagued by resistance within the CATHOLIC CONFEDERACY of the papal envoy RINUCCINI. When peace was at last concluded, in 1646, it was too late to assist the defeated king militarily, and was, anyway, rapidly denounced by Rinuccini who was backed by the military strength of the rebel commander OWEN ROE O'NEILL. In 1647 Ormond entered into an agreement with the English Parliament against the Confederacy, handed over DUBLIN to their forces, and went into France temporarily. In 1649, having returned to Ireland, and Rinuccini no longer a problem, Ormond concluded alliances with the Confederacy (or what was by then left of it) and with Owen Roe O'Neill, but again, too late to be of any real effect. CROMWELL's Irish campaigns, begun in 1649, destroyed piecemeal rebel and royalist resistance in Ireland, and Ormond quit the country in 1650, handing over what was left of his command to CLANRICARDE. At the restoration of King Charles II in 1660, Ormond was instrumental in the restoration of the CHURCH OF IRELAND, and in the enforce-ment of the Acts of SETTLEMENT and EXPLANATION which were intended to tackle the land problem created by the mass expropriations of the 1650s. He was appointed Lord Lieutenant until 1669, and again from 1677 to 1682. His resolute sense of loyalty led him to support King JAMES II, though he viewed with dislike and attempted to resist, the Catholic policies of the king. His successor and nephew James Butler sided with WILLIAM III. Ormond had been created a marquess in 1642 and elevated to the dukedom of Ormond in 1661, an acknowledgement of his long record of service to the crown under unenviable conditions.

Ormond Treaties *see* CESSATION

Orr, William *see* INSURRECTION ACTS

O'Sullivan-Beare, Philip (c. 1590–1660)

Philip O'Sullivan-Beare was the nephew of the O'Sullivan chief of County Cork, who had fought under TYRONE during the rebellion which ended at MELLIFONT in 1603, and who had then entered Spanish service. Philip himself commanded in the Spanish navy, but was primarily a writer and champion of the Earl of Tyrone's cause. His work, *Zoilomastix* of 1625 was a survey of the leading Irish Catholic clergy of his and his uncle's generation, as well as those working in academic posts in Europe. O'Sullivan-Beare's importance as a writer, at a time of some prolific Irish-Gaelic output, lies in the fact that he was not himself a cleric, but a layman educated in Spain, and writing of recent events in Ireland. As well, therefore, as producing works on St Patrick, and vigorous criticism of the CHURCH OF IRELAND Primate USSHER, he wrote *Historiae Catholicae Iberniae Compendium* (1621), which work was part of a genre of writings aimed at the English represen-tation of events in Ireland over the previous half century. It was both a survey of Irish history, and a first-hand account of the Tyrone rebellion against Queen Elizabeth, a catalogue of the perfidies of the English and of the virtues of Tyrone himself.

Oulart Hill, battle of

The battle of Oulart Hill was fought on 27 May 1798 during the WEXFORD RISING of that year, between rebels under the leadership of Father JOHN MURPHY and MILITIA and YEOMANRY forces which over-confidently attempted to storm an entrenched rebel position on Oulart Hill. The rebels, equipped with captured muskets, inflicted a comprehensive defeat on the government troops.

P

Páirlimint Cloinne Tomáis

The 'Páirlimint' was an anonymous poem of the late seventeenth century, which whilst lamenting the downfall of the Catholic gentry who had patronized Gaelic learning and poetry, was chiefly a satire at the cost of the changing social makeup of the Irish countryside. The poet depicted mockingly the Irish peasantry who had replaced the gentry on their lands, as tenants of the English landlords: peasants who made a pretence of being gentry, but were only too keen to fit into the new order of things by acquiring the use of the English language. The poet used throughout his work, the vernacular expressions of the peasantry in the province of Munster, and thereby recorded them at a time when they were undergoing change; and his depiction of English as used by the Irish peasantry, intended to lampoon the users, vividly illustrated the problems of the native Gaelic speaker coming to terms with the intrusive and dominant tongue of the settlers.

Pale, The (English)

The term 'Pale' has two meanings. In the one case it was used to define that area of Ireland solidly settled by and under the administrative control of the English. In the second usage, which is linked to the first, the Pale is conceived of as a limit to the spread of ANGLICIZATION and CIVILITY, and is therefore something that is constantly moving, until, at the logical end of the Anglicization process, the whole of Ireland would be 'the Pale'. The Pale was that area in which the OLD ENGLISH settled extensively during the medieval period, in the counties grouped around DUBLIN, with the eastern seaboard at their backs. It marked the place where English law and custom ran, and beyond it lay native Irish folk, BREHON LAW, and the customs of the Gaels. Dublin, Kildare,

Louth and Meath retained, within the Pale, their separateness, the 'county' structure, imposed from England, being crucial to the settlement of the land. There had been a time, during the fourteenth century, when the Pale had extended to cover the counties of Waterford, Wexford, and Tipperary, but the shrinkage to an area centred upon Dublin was so complete by 1495 that a 'pale' or wooden fence had been conceived of (though never installed) to mark it off, a symbolic Hadrian's Wall beyond which dwelt the savage Irish. Beyond its confines there were Old English settlers, some of them, of considerable power and landholding, but they were closely interwoven with the existing fabric of Gaelic society, and there was, on the part of the 'Palesmen' a sense of social and racial exclusivity peculiar to the Pale. On the eve of the FLIGHT OF THE EARLS of 1607, and the PLANTATION policy, the Pale around Dublin, or the Dublin Pale, had smaller scale imitations, with Pales centred upon Cork, Galway, Limerick and Waterford: they represented spheres of English influence. Early in the seventeenth century, however, the Pale came to be largely something that belonged to antiquity: NEW ENGLISH settlement, made possible on a major scale by plantation, regarded the whole of Ireland as to be subjected to English control and law. There was no defensive, Pale-oriented thinking but rather, the Pale of Dublin was a leaping-off point for the scramble into the rest of the country. When the OLD ENGLISH presence in the Pale turned, almost to a man, to support of the rebels when the IRISH REBELLION of 1641 broke out, the significance was that they created a military threat to the government on its very doorstep. But the struggle of the civil wars that followed was not waged around control of the Pale. The taking of the war into the rebel heartlands indicated strongly that the concept of an area of English influence was dead, that the whole of Ireland was to be thus controlled.

Parliament, The Irish

The Parliament in Ireland was a direct intrusion of an English institution during the Middle Ages. Like the English Parliament, which from the 1690s claimed and for a time exercised supremacy over it, the Irish version was bicameral, with a House of Lords and an elective House of Commons. Its subordination to the English crown via the LORD LIEUTENANT or Chief Governor and the English Privy Council, was made explicit in 1495 by POYNINGS' LAW which, amongst other things, stipulated that the Irish Parliament must be summoned by the sovereign, and legislative matter must receive prior crown approval. The Irish Parliament was, therefore, intended to be an extension of English authority in Ireland, itself a colony of the English crown. Not until the last 20 years or so of the eighteenth century, did it achieve anything like legislative independence, and that brief and not altogether promising period came to an end with the UNION of Britain and Ireland which took effect in 1801. Thenceforth, Ireland would be represented by 100 MPs at WESTMINSTER (later increased, moderately, in number), and the Irish Parliament as it was, never met again. There was a precedent for that, although an unhappy one, in the brief Union of the 1650s when Irish MPs sat in the Long Parliament in England.

Because of the ebb and flow of the area of Ireland under direct English control or indirect influence during the Middle Ages, the Irish Parliament was a fluid assembly. Its expansion, however, was concurrent with the PLANTATION policy vigorously imposed, particularly in ULSTER, following the failure of the TYRONE rebellion in 1603. New boroughs were created with speed, their charters of incorporation giving them the right to representation in the Parliament at DUBLIN. By 1613 there were 36 new seats in Ulster, 18 in Munster, 16 in Leinster and 12 in Connacht. This policy gave to the Irish House of Commons a preponderance of NEW ENGLISH, Protestant, representation, at the expense of the OLD

ENGLISH and the dwindling handful of GAELIC IRISH MPs, who never again (until 1689, and then briefly) achieved a dominance in the house. The Old English did manage to have a few of the new charters called in question, but by doing so they accepted the legitimacy of the rest. As it was, the questioning of borough representation was used against the Old English before the Parliament of 1640 and, coupled with the decline in Old English seats inherent in the merger of counties Tipperary and CROSS TIPPERARY, gave the New English a majority of 89 seats in that Parliament.

The IRISH REBELLION of 1641–53 ended with the complete subjugation of Ireland by the forces of the English Parliament. In March 1653 the Rump of the Long Parliament at Westminster voted that there should be Irish representation at their meetings, which heralded a form of Union of the two kingdoms. Some 30 representatives of Irish seats sat in the Long Parliament's sessions of 1654, 1656 and 1659. Direct government in Ireland remained, as it always had done, in the hands of English appointees. LORD DEPUTY FLEETWOOD, succeeded by HENRY CROMWELL, ruled with the aid of a Council of State, itself a copy of that instituted in England after the abolition of monarchy in 1649.

In 1661 the Irish Parliament was restored in Dublin with much the same preponderance of Protestant members as in 1641, but this time with a number of MPs representative of settlement during the 1650s. There was no barrier as such to Catholic members, but the effectiveness of the land expropriations and the guilt of involvement in the 1641 rebellion, precluded their election. The unrepresentative nature of the Irish Parliament, true even of the Parliament summoned in 1689, was already its most prominent feature, and it proved far from pliable. It ceased to meet at all in 1666. (Theoretically, a Parliament, summoned by a monarch at his or her accession, could last as long as the life of the sovereign, meeting in occasional sessions. Not until the 1768 OCTENNIAL ACT was the life of a Parliament circumscribed and limited to an eight-year duration).

The Parliament of 1689, summoned by

JAMES II to support his military effort to regain his throne from which he had been ousted by his rival WILLIAM III in 1688, was predominantly Catholic and Old English, thanks to the manipulation of boroughs by the Earl of TYRCONNELL, and thanks also to the fact that Protestant areas like Ulster and others under WILLIAMITE control, returned no members. Nevertheless, allowing for its unrepresentative nature, the 1689 Parliament challenged the assumptions of Poynings' Law, and the right of the English Parliament to legislate for Ireland. King James disliked the assertiveness, but gave his assent to it. He also was faced with a concerted effort by the Parliament to overturn the land settlements of the 1660s and the 1650s and to restore things to what they had been on the eve of the rebellion of 1641. Had the JACOBITE cause triumphed, King James would have been hard put to it to restrain the Parliament that he had summoned. But by 1691 James II was in exile and his followers dispersed. The first Williamite Parliament of 1692, however, showed itself as obstinate on the issue of English legislative supremacy as had that of 1689. The Commons rejected a money bill because it had not originated within that House (which, under Poynings' Law, it did not need to) and then passed a resolution that it 'was and is the sole ... right of the (Irish) commons to prepare heads of bills for raising money'. The government got around this by compromise: it merely provided a money bill proposal for the commons to initiate themselves.

The Irish Parliament's direct answerability to the English Parliament (the British Parliament after the Union of Scotland and England) became steadily a matter of importance within Ireland itself. It had been protested at by PATRICK DARCY and, more recently, by WILLIAM MOLYNEUX, and the DECLARATORY ACT of 1720 which put the proposition in no uncertain terms, remained a matter of contention until it was repealed in the first stages of the emergence of Irish legislative independence known as GRATTAN'S PARLIAMENT of the 1780s and 1790s. During the eighteenth century, the Irish Parliament became a symbol of minority rule, wholly dominated by the ASCENDANCY, Protestant in the CHURCH OF IRELAND sense, and, in the eyes of many, a place where 'men of interest' were more in evidence than 'men of conscience'. The 32 counties of Ireland, the 117 boroughs and TRINITY COLLEGE, each returned two members to sit in the house of 300 MPs. The vast majority of them were influential landowners, and they never fell below 50 per cent of the whole, the bulk of the other seats being held by representatives of the 'professions'. There was widespread corruption, not least in the way in which the British administration secured compliance in its policies by bribery. The assertion of 'nationalist' ideology, such as it was, through the oratory of men like GRATTAN and FLOOD, which found sympathy amongst whigs in the British Commons, led to the reassertion of Irish parliamentary freedom, and the period of Grattan's Parliament which immediately preceded the Union of 1801. Although Grattan derided the corruption of the Irish house, the 'borough parliament' as he called it, he and his fellow reformers achieved little beyond gaining for that Parliament more control over the legislation that passed through it. There was certainly no fundamental reform, and it was less receptive of Catholic EMANCIPATION than was the Parliament at London.

Opponents of the Union of 1801 drew attention to the venality of the Irish Parliament by illustrating (see BLACK LIST) the bribery that enabled the British administration to force through legislation whereby the Irish Commons dissolved itself. Campaigners for the repeal of that Union were never entirely clear what they wished to replace it with, although the nature of the Irish Commons, at least, must have changed with the enfranchisement of Catholic FORTY-SHILLING FREEHOLDERS in legislation of 1793 (see EMANCIPATION). The Irish Parliament never met again, in any form. It was for a long time remembered, in Ireland, and on the strength of that brief period of its existence associated with the name of Grattan, as an expression of Irish freedom. The fact was, Parliament was always, from 1613 until 1801, representative of sectional, not of national, aspirations. It enshrined, for the whole of the eighteenth century, the power and dominance of a minority of the Irish POPULATION.

Parliament Act, The

The legislation of 18 August 1911, which limited the ability of the House of Lords to delay the enactment of bills for more than two years, was a decisive move in the long-drawn-out campaign for HOME RULE for Ireland. In 1893 the House had thrown out a Home Rule Bill, and thereafter the legislation had been dropped, until it became known that the government intended to introduce new legislation in 1912. To clear the way for its passage, the Parliament Act of 1911 was passed. For the Unionists, who opposed the principle of Home Rule, it was a decisive blow: it obliged them to think, not in terms of resistance to legislation, but of damage limitation, to have ULSTER, or part of it, excluded from Home Rule legislation. In January 1913 the new Home Rule bill passed its third reading in the Commons and was immediately jettisoned by the Lords, but their power was now only to delay, and in June 1914 they were giving their attention to an amendment providing for PARTITION in the event of self-government for Ireland. The outbreak of the FIRST WORLD WAR in August 1914 shelved the legislation, and the EASTER RISING of 1916 and the WAR FOR INDEPENDENCE of 1919–21 changed the nature of the debate.

Parnell, Charles Stewart (1846–91)

More, perhaps, than DANIEL O'CONNELL Parnell has symbolized the assertion of Irish national identity in the nineteenth century. He was born in Avondale, County Wicklow – the 'blackbird of Avondale' of Irish ballad – of Anglo-Irish parentage, though his animosity towards England was pronounced. He was associated with ISAAC BUTT, and in 1875 became MP for Meath, before sitting for Cork in 1880. He quickly rose to prominence in the IRISH PARLIAMENTARY PARTY by his militancy and involvement in the OBSTRUCTIONIST tactic, and for a time at least, in the late 1870s and as a result of a

visit to America, appeared to countenance FENIAN revolutionary activities, although the Fenians of the post SIXTY-SEVEN rising period were a degree less radical than their original movement. He brought the land question squarely into the HOME RULE struggle by involvement with and Presidency of the LAND LEAGUE of 1879, which campaigned for peasant proprietorship and fair rents amongst other things. With the backing of the Parliamentary Party, and sympathy from the Catholic hierarchy, Parnell played a prominent part in the agitation of the LAND WAR of 1879–82, advocating the policy known as BOYCOTTING. He was arrested and gaoled in 1881 for sedition, which in itself won him widespread sympathy, but the 1881 LAND LEGISLATION of GLADSTONE's government went so far towards meeting Land League demands that the agitation declined, despite Parnell's attempt to resurrect it through the NO RENT MANIFESTO issued from his prison. His own release was secured by the 'deal' made with the government known as the KILMAINHAM TREATY, by which Parnell undertook to curb agrarian unrest in return for amendments to the 1881 legislation. By 1886 Parnell was deeply involved in parliamentary politics, pursuing Home Rule through the Liberal alliance, and losing touch with the land issue, which the 1881 Act had by no means resolved. The Irish NATIONAL LEAGUE, a revived form of the Land League but bringing together Home Rule issues, land reform and industrial development, was Parnell's constituency organization, but, in the atmosphere of revived rural unrest in 1888, was suppressed by the LORD LIEUTENANT. Parnell was never far from being accused of involvement in violence. The Land League and the National League were both suppressed because, it was argued, of their tendency towards creating unrest, and Parnell himself had been (falsely) accused in the PHOENIX PARK incident, where revolutionary INVINCIBLES had murdered the CHIEF SECRETARY in 1882. In a sense, Parnell needed that association to make himself palatable to the revolutionary elements in Irish political life, if he was to attempt to contain them, and win them to the constitutional methods he was himself pursuing. For, above all, Parnell was a constitutional nationalist, a creature of the political world of the House of Commons who, when he found himself caught up in the tradition of the Irish felon as in 1881, compromised his way out, as with the Kilmainham Treaty. Parnell was ruined when he was cited as co-respondent in the O'Shea divorce case in November 1890. Gladstone professed to be shocked by it and unable to work alongside Parnell any longer, and the Irish Parliamentary Party split with the majority disavowing Parnell's leadership. In the ensuing struggle to repair his reputation and to rebuild his power, Parnell died in Brighton in Sussex. He had married O'Shea's divorced wife, Katherine, a few months before. If Parnell did lose touch with Irish popular feeling through his involvement with the political dealings of the House of Commons, it did not lose touch with him. The scandal that was allowed to wreck him in 1890 blew away in the context of his death, and the affection he had inspired contrived to preserve his memory in Irish tradition.

Parnellism and Parnellites

Parnellism is a term that is ordinarily applied to the type of political activity which CHARLES PARNELL pursued in the struggle for HOME RULE and land reform. In the LAND LEAGUE and the NATIONAL LEAGUE, he developed constituency organizations working on behalf of the MPs in Parliament, the first real political parties that Ireland had known. Parnellism was constitutional nationalism, seeking to control and to divert PHYSICAL FORCE nationalism, and aiming at nationwide organization. The Parnellites were those who, after the scandal of 1890 which split the IRISH PARLIAMENTARY PARTY, remained loyal to Parnell himself. They were always a minority within Parliament, and came to move to a more radical posture in consequence, adopting FENIAN rhetoric of a quasi-revolutionary kind. Nevertheless, it was the Parnellite leader, REDMOND, who reunited the Irish Parliamentary Party in 1900 and who brought it closer to Home Rule than Parnell himself ever did.

Parsons, Sir William (1570–1650)

Parsons, knighted in 1620, was a career member of the English administration in Ireland, to which he had been introduced by his uncle and whom he succeeded as Surveyor-General in 1602. He acquired extensive estates during the process of PLANTATION, and Parsonstown in King's County takes its name from him. A Privy Councillor in 1623 and MP for County Wicklow in 1640, he was appointed LORD JUSTICE. With his partner, Borlase, he ruled Ireland after the disgrace, trial and execution of THOMAS WENTWORTH. Parsons was undoubtedly responsible for concocting the plot to seize Dublin CASTLE which was attributed to conspirators within the PALE, on the eve of the IRISH REBELLION of October 1641. He seems to have sought to push the Catholic OLD ENGLISH into alliance with the GAELIC IRISH rebels. As Lord Justice, Parsons countenanced the visit to DUBLIN of delegates from the English Parliament in 1642, when that Parliament was engaged in the ENGLISH CIVIL WAR against King Charles I. The king commanded Parsons to expel them from Dublin, but thereafter bypassed the Lord Justice and dealt more and more with the loyal and reliable Earl of ORMOND. Parsons was deprived of his office, and arrested by Ormond. In 1648 he returned to England where he died.

Partition

On 7 March 1917 Lloyd George, speaking in the House of Commons, referred to ULSTER as possessed of 'a population as hostile to Irish rule as the rest of Ireland is to British rule'. He drew attention to its religious difference, its racial difference, its distinctive, pro-UNION, Imperial outlook. The Irish nationalist MPs in the House walked out in protest. Lloyd George had been charged by the Prime Minister, Asquith, with finding a solution to the Irish problem following the EASTER RISING of 1916, and he had already demonstrated that he favoured immediate implementation of HOME RULE legislation that had lain dormant since July 1914, with exclusion of SIX COUNTIES of Ulster. In May 1917 he was to make much the same recommendation, but with the exclusion of those counties for a five-year term. The principle of Partition was not invented by Lloyd George. When the Home Rule Bill had been introduced into the Commons in 1912 (the power of the House of Lords to reject it severely cut by the PARLIAMENT ACT of 1911), Ulster's Unionists and their political allies, the Conservative party of Great Britain, had made it plain that they would resist, by force of arms if necessary, any attempt to force them to live under government from DUBLIN. In 1913 they had formed, and by 1914 fully equipped, the ULSTER VOLUNTEER FORCE. CARSON, the Unionist leader, had repeatedly spoken of exclusion for the full nine counties of historic Ulster, and in September 1913 had said that a provisional government for the north would be formed in the event of Home Rule if the legislation did not take account of Ulster's opposition. Such a government would be formed from the ruling council of the Unionist movement. In May 1914, therefore, Prime Minister Asquith had introduced an amendment to the HOME RULE LEGISLATION of 1912, to permit Ulster counties to opt out of Home Rule on a temporary basis. It was replaced by a second amendment which allowed for permanent exclusion of the province, and at that point the FIRST WORLD WAR had intervened to cause postponement of final legislation. Lloyd George's proposals, therefore, of 1916 and 1917 remained firm to the commitment for Ulster exclusion, and the six county option had emerged clearly. (There had been earlier proposals for exclusion of four counties, Antrim, Armagh, DERRY and Down, but these proposals had never found favour. The Unionists themselves chose the six instead of the nine county solution, because the Protestant majority was clearly defined in the six – Antrim, Armagh, Derry, Down, Fermanagh and Tyrone). Lloyd George's second recommendation of May 1917 carried with it an alternative in the shape of an IRISH CONVENTION to thrash out some other solution, but this achieved little more than the abortive BUCKINGHAM PALACE CONFERENCE of 1914 which had sought to find a middle way between the demands

of the Unionists and the Nationalists. Nothing was done by the time of the General Election of 1918, in which the constitutional nationalist MPs in the Parliament at WESTMINSTER were virtually swept away by a vast surge of popular electoral support for SINN FÉIN, a party which would have nothing to do with partition and nothing to do with involvement in the British legislative process. It established its own DÁIL ÉIREANN, whilst the IRISH REPUBLICAN ARMY conducted the effective guerrilla WAR FOR INDEPENDENCE that induced the British to negotiate with the republican movement. On 23 December 1920 the GOVERNMENT OF IRELAND ACT became law, virtually a revised version of the Home Rule Bill of 1912: it accepted partition as a reality, and provided a Parliament for the six counties and a Parliament for the rest of Ireland, with a Council of Ireland to decide on matters of mutual importance. At this point the expression 'Northern Ireland', representative of the truncated Ulster, came into use. The 'Northern Irish' leadership accepted the Act, the southern republicans and nationalists did not, and that refusal, coupled with the independence struggle, forced the British to talk to Sinn Féin. Delegates from the Dáil were despatched to London to talk to Lloyd George and his cabinet and advisors, who had tantalizingly held out the prospect of 'dominion status' within the Empire. Doctrinaire republicanism rejected any such commitment within the Empire, but the mere fact of negotiation implied some give from them. They were not going to discuss partition, but rather to discuss what could be arrived at given the reality of partition. As historians have pointed out, the resulting Treaty was not the cause of partition, but rather, partition being accepted, made the Treaty into a realizable goal for both sides. It is considered likely that Lloyd George and the British government had given cast-iron guarantees to the Unionists that partition would not be negotiable. But in the conference between the Dáil delegates and the British, Lloyd George conveyed the impression that a subsequent boundary commission might well make the Ulster position so impracticable as to oblige the province, or that part of it excluded, to join with the rest of Ireland. Thus the ANGLO-IRISH TREATY gave to Ireland dominion status within the Empire, from which they might one day secede and declare themselves as a Republic. The Ulster issue, the issue of partition, was left to be resolved. During the Irish Civil War that ensued, between pro and anti-Treaty forces of the IRA, both sides nevertheless continued to co-operate in operations in 'Northern Ireland'. It was the dominion status that split the IRA, and Sinn Féin, the abandonment of the pure Republic as the Treaty was seen by its opponents. But concurrent with that was the resistance to the abandonment of a part of Ireland, without which an Irish Republic would anyway have been incomplete. The problem of partition is as yet, unresolved, three-quarters of a century on.

Party Processions Acts

The Party Processions Acts were legislation aimed at preventing sectarian conflict in Ireland, by imposing bans upon the open display of religious and political commitment, with the paraphernalia of banners, music and symbols. The first such act was passed in August 1832, directed primarily at the violent excesses of the ORANGE ORDER in the BELFAST area. The Act of March 1850 banned the display of emblems and weapons as well as marches and processions intended to incite disturbance. A further act of 1860 imposed more rigorous controls, and it was this act that led to the challenge against its provisions from the Orangeman WILLIAM JOHNSTON of Ballykilbeg, County Down, who, in time-honoured style on 12 July 1867, paraded 10,000 Orangemen at Bangor, County Down. The legislation of 1850 and of 1860 was repealed by an Act of 27 June 1872. The Acts had, anyway, proved of little worth. Prevention of sectarian violence, where it was prevented, owed more to the activity of the reformed CONSTABULARY than to Acts of Parliament. Significantly, a nationalist challenge to the Acts had been the funeral of TERENCE BELLEW MACMANUS, the YOUNG IRELAND revolutionary, in DUBLIN in 1861, a massive display of nationalist fervour which, presented as a funeral procession, escaped the terms of the Act – just as the organizers had intended that it should.

Patriot Parliament

Patriot Parliament is the term given to the Parliament of 1689 summoned by King JAMES II, and was first applied by writers in the early nineteenth century. Ireland was, in 1689, on the edge of major hostilities between supporters of King James, the JACOBITES, and the armies of his rival for the throne of England, King WILLIAM III. The Parliament summoned to DUBLIN was, for the first time since the sixteenth century, a Catholic and OLD ENGLISH assembly – there were, perhaps, half a dozen Protestant MPs in attendance. It met from 7 May to 18 July, with 228 members in the Commons and some 46 peers in the House of Lords, as well as seven bishops of the CHURCH OF IRELAND. The Parliament was important primarily for its passage of an act, assented to somewhat reluctantly by James II, which rejected the principle of English legislative supremacy enunciated in POYNINGS' LAW. The assertiveness of the Catholic MPs in that respect was emulated by their Protestant successors in the first Parliament summoned after James II's defeat, and became a crucial issue during the course of the eighteenth century. The Patriot Parliament also repealed the 1662 Act of SETTLEMENT, as a means toward undoing the land expropriations and re-settlement of the 1650s, and by an act of attainder against some 2,000 known supporters of King William, sought to extend the land reorganization through confiscation of estates. Since the Parliament was intended to vote funds to support King James's war effort, he was obliged to go along with its extreme Catholic measures, although once known, they served to further alienate the Protestants of Ireland and arouse alarm amongst some that might otherwise have been sympathetic to the Jacobite cause on grounds of the king's legitimate right to hold the throne. The land measures came to nothing: the Parliament did not reassemble, and the basis of its authority, the kingship of

James II and his military power, was swept away in war by 1691.

Patriots, The

The Patriot group of MPs in the Irish PARLIAMENT emerged during the mid-eighteenth century around the persons of HENRY FLOOD, and then HENRY GRATTAN. The sense in which the word 'patriot' is applied to them is narrow. They were, without exception, members of an exclusive ruling elite in Ireland, the Protestant ASCENDANCY, whose power was based upon the suppression and disenfranchisement of the Catholic majority in the country. Their nationalism was colonial, and their identification of themselves as 'Irish' was an identification of their group interest with that of the national interest, of which they saw themselves as the rightful expression. As early as the 1720s, 'patriot' MPs had been critical of the DECLARATORY ACT of 1720 which had unequivocally subordinated the Irish Parliament to that of Britain. Indeed, their great achievement was the repeal of that Act in 1782, and the passage of a Renunciation Act by which the British Parliament disclaimed the right to legislate further in the fashion of the 1720 Act. As a group within the House of Commons, the 'patriots' are identifiable from around 1760, with Flood as their primary spokesman, although when he accepted office from the British administration, the mantle of 'patriot' oratory passed to Grattan, whose name is attached to the last 20 years of the Irish Parliament (GRATTAN'S PARLIAMENT) subsequent to the repeal of the Declaratory Act. If the Patriots possessed a 'policy' – and they were not in any sense a party – it revolved around the economic and constitutional interests of Ireland. As well as legislative independence, they sought to introduce a limit of seven years for the duration of a Parliament (the British offer of the OCTENNIAL ACT in 1768 satisfied them) and to reduce the drain on the revenues of Ireland from ABSENTEE LANDLORDS and the extensive pension list charged upon those revenues. But their Protestantism, the basis anyway of their authority, made them largely unsympathetic to Catholic EMANCIPATION. Thus

their 'patriotism' was exclusive, it was never a popular extra-parliamentary movement as well, unless the title can be applied to the VOLUNTEERS upon whose organization men like Grattan depended to add weight to their constitutional struggle. The AMERICAN WAR FOR INDEPENDENCE stimulated Patriot tendencies within the Irish Parliament, but effective lessening of trade restrictions by the British soon undermined sympathy for the American colonists. The Patriots were really Protestant gentry nationalists with a limited view of who it was that the Irish nation comprised, and their failure was the passage of the UNION of 1801 which combined the British and Irish Parliaments and abolished that separate assembly in DUBLIN.

Peace Preservation Force, The

The Irish Peace Preservation Force may be said to represent an intermediate measure between the relative lack of policing of the eighteenth century, and the reorganized CONSTABULARY of 1836 onwards. The creation of the Peace Preservation Force in 1814 was in response to widespread AGRARIAN OUTRAGES and sectarian violence.

Thus the powers of the Act establishing it applied to disturbed areas of the country, where there was a need for stronger policing. The onus was on the LORD LIEUTENANT to identify such areas, and to appoint within them a chief magistrate, a chief constable and a force of sub-constables, to be paid from the localities, but answerable to the executive in DUBLIN, at the CASTLE. Local Justices of the Peace (see MAGISTRATES, JUSTICES OF THE PEACE) could request a force for their area as well. The first force to operate was in action in County Tipperary by September 1814, although some historians have ascribed its first appearance to Roscommon in November 1819. The police took their name of 'Peelers' from the man who was the architect of the 1814 Act, ROBERT PEEL, then CHIEF SECRETARY in Ireland. Subsequent legislation, such as the Suppression of Disturbances Act of April 1833, empowered the Lord Lieutenant to establish court martials in proclaimed districts. The Peace Preservation

Force was expected to work alongside the military in cases of major unrest. Constabulary reform in 1836, restructuring of the peace-keeping force and creation of a new police body, led to the submerging of the Peace Preservation Force in that general reorganization.

Pearse, Padraic (1879–1916)

'I do not know' said Pearse in America on a fund-raising trip in 1914, 'how nationhood is achieved except by armed men'. He was the strenuous advocate of PHYSICAL FORCE nationalism rooted deep in the history of Irish republicanism, that saw the FIRST WORLD WAR between Britain and Germany of 1914–18 as the opportunity for Ireland to seize her freedom. Pearse was a scholar and poet, deeply versed in Gaelic history and literature, who drew inspiration from the memory of ROBERT EMMET above all others, and who believed that some kind of blood sacrifice was necessary for the birth of an Irish nation. He joined the IRISH REPUBLICAN BROTHERHOOD in 1913, and was a commander in the IRISH VOLUNTEERS when, in 1914, they split over the support given to Britain's war effort by the constitutional nationalists of REDMOND's parliamentary party. How far Pearse imprinted his personality and vision upon the EASTER RISING of 1916, and how far he reflected the ideology of the visionary SÉAN MAC DIARMADA, may be debated: but he was closely involved in planning a rising as a member of the Military Council of the IRB, and was Director of Military Operations. He was head of the Provisional Government of the Irish Republic when he read the PROCLAMATION of that Republic on the steps of the GPO on 24 April 1916. Captured when the rising was suppressed, Pearse was tried and was shot on 3 May 1916. His name, along with that of the socialist JAMES CONNOLLY, is that most associated with the Easter Rising. In his assessment of the impact of the blood sacrifice he and his fellows made, he was absolutely right. Irish independence arose from the brief Republic he established.

Peel, Robert (1788–1850)

Peel's first connection with Ireland was as MP for Cashel in the British Parliament in 1809. A seat purchased for him by his father, Sir Robert Peel (d. 1830). Between 1812 and 1818 he held the influential post of CHIEF SECRETARY in Ireland, during which time he carried through legislation to establish the 'Peelers' – the PEACE PRESERVATION FORCE – in 1814. His view of the Irish was jaundiced: 'the Irishman's natural predilection for outrage and a lawless life' he believed, 'nothing can control'. Thus his policing measure of 1814 was clearly intended to contain violence rather than bring an end to it. He was an opponent of EMANCIPATION for Catholics, and resigned government office in 1827 because he suspected measures would be introduced to grant it, as they were, in 1829. DANIEL O'DONNELL nicknamed him 'Orange' Peel because of his unbending Protestantism. But the emancipation measure of 1829 was partly the result of Peel's efforts, when it became plain that it was necessary, as the British government saw it, to fend off insurrection. He became Prime Minister in 1834, resigned in 1835, and, in opposition, formed the revived Tory party which became known as the Conservatives. He was constantly involved in Irish issues, and was responsible for the establishment of ST PATRICK'S COLLEGE at Maynooth, a Catholic seminary, for which he introduced legislation into the Commons in April 1845. The prevalence of POTATO BLIGHT in Ireland, reported widely in September 1845, led him, on his own initiative, to purchase £100,000 worth of grain from America as an emergency measure, and he appointed a relief commission in Ireland. His enforced resignation in June 1846 turned around further relief measures for Ireland, although his general attitude was to favour the workings of free trade. He died as a result of a riding accident, ironically, on Constitution Hill, London, in 1850.

Peep O'Day Boys

The Peep O'Day Boys, so named for their first-light raids, were a violently Protestant sectarian movement which developed during the 1780s, with some kind of formal foundation at Markethill in County Armagh in July 1784. They were, to all intents and purposes, self-appointed enforcers of the PENAL LAWS against Catholics which, they considered, had suffered from neglect by the Protestant gentry and MPs in the Irish PARLIAMENT. They represented an artisan and working-class Protestantism in ULSTER, alarmed by softening attitudes to Catholics and dismayed by industrial problems in the province. In a sense, Catholics were a scapegoat for other problems. The Peep O'Day Boys developed as an alternative to the VOLUNTEERS in some ways, particularly after movements within the Volunteer movement to include Catholics and to call for EMANCIPATION, and were in time subsumed within the more organized ORANGE ORDER. They provoked, by their violent attacks on Catholic homes and attempts to drive Catholics out of lands in the Ulster counties, a Catholic counter-movement, the DEFENDERS, and it was a clash between the Defenders and Peep O'Day Boys that directly led to the formation of the Orange Order.

Penal Laws

The Penal Laws were a series of Acts of Parliament devised to disenfranchise and otherwise disadvantage the Catholic population of Ireland, whether of GAELIC IRISH or OLD ENGLISH origin. Some historians have chosen to lay emphasis, however, upon the laws as directed specifically against the Irish as a people, who incidentally happened also to be Catholics, and it was certainly the case that the Protestant ASCENDANCY of the eighteenth century rested upon the enforcement of such laws. The Protestants of the Ascendancy were, for the most part, of NEW ENGLISH origin, that is, descended from settlers of the seventeenth-century PLANTATIONS. The first significant penal law was the 26 June 1657 act 'for convicting, discovering and repressing of popish recusants' (recusants were non-attenders of the services of the Protestant churches in the 1657 context. The CHURCH OF IRELAND had been abolished but had been, prior to the IRISH

REBELLION of 1641–53, and was to be again after 1660, the 'test' for conformity). The 1657 legislation required suspected Catholics to take the Oath of ABJURATION denying papal supremacy, or suffer the sequestration of two-thirds of their property. This law reflected those already in force in England, where anti-Catholicism had reached a pitch during the ENGLISH CIVIL WARS of 1642–51. On 24 December 1691, following the defeat of the JACOBITE forces of King JAMES II in Ireland, a law of the English Parliament barred Catholics from holding public office in Ireland and from entering the Irish Parliament. The period after 1691 saw a spate of anti-Catholic laws, originating in the fear of Jacobitism (given that there was a Catholic pretender to the English throne), and in reaction to the sweeping pro-Catholic legislation of James II's PATRIOT PARLIAMENT of 1689. Historians have pointed out, however, that the laws were irregularly enforced, but the point is, that the laws existed and could be enforced, for much of the ensuing century or more. Acts of September 1695 prohibited Catholics from sending their children abroad to receive a Catholic education, prohibited Catholics from teaching in Ireland, denied them the right to have weapons or to possess any horse worth in excess of £5 purchase. In January 1699 Catholics were forbidden to work as solicitors. The most far-reaching of the penal laws was that of 1704 which denied to Catholics the right to buy land, to act as guardians to the heirs of estates, and imposed a stringent sacramental test for office holders that worked against DISSENTERS as well as Catholics. The tendency of the penal laws was to prevent the Catholic Irish from owning land, to force them to become a dispossessed peasantry. In May 1728 an act deprived the Catholics of the right to vote, making law something that was already inevitably bound up in denying them entitlement to possess land, the qualification for the franchise. Those Catholics who, for the sake of their property, underwent real or pretended conversion to the Church of Ireland, were legislated against in 1734, when, if they had Catholic wives, they were prohibited from permitting their children to be educated in the mother's faith. They were also barred from serving as Justices of the Peace, if their marriage was to a Catholic. Despite these laws, Catholics were able to engage in trade, and during the eighteenth century a comfortably-off Catholic middle class began to emerge in the towns and cities of Ireland. By 1783, when the Bank of Ireland was set up, it has been shown that such Catholics held 10 per cent of the capital fund of the new bank. They were, anyway, some 75 per cent of the total population of Ireland, and where they held land, were predominantly leaseholders limited by law in the duration of their leases. As freeholders, they may have enjoyed only 5 per cent of the land of Ireland. Moves towards the repeal of the penal laws began in the 1770s, attributable to the falling risk of Jacobite resurgence, and to a general atmosphere of toleration that was common to much of Protestant Europe. But, in the Irish Parliament, there was never a coherent body of MPs working towards EMANCIPATION in the light of new attitudes. Much depended upon outside agitation, both by Catholics themselves, and by liberal Protestants (see EMANCIPATION).

Petty, William (1623–87)

William Petty came into Ireland as Physician-General to the Cromwellian invasion armies of 1649–53. In 1654 he was appointed to undertake the important DOWN SURVEY of the country, as part and parcel of the expropriation of the rebel and royalist Irish, to make way for new settlers from England and Scotland. He produced the first accurate maps of Ireland (and in 1685 published his map *Hiberniae Delineato*), having surveyed 22 counties in the course of a little over a year. Petty was an important figure in the development of Irish intellectual life after the restoration of Charles II, who knighted him in 1662. He was also one who held the view that Ireland was unreasonably at the mercy of the English Parliament, and his (posthumously) published work *The Political Anatomy of Ireland* of 1691 argued that case, which was reflected in the debates in the Irish PARLIAMENT of that period.

Phoenix Park

On 6 May 1882 CHIEF SECRETARY Lord Frederick Cavendish and Under Secretary T.H. Burke were assassinated during a knife attack in Phoenix Park, DUBLIN. The target of the assassins was probably meant to be Burke, but the INVICIBLES who carried it out were uncertain as to the identity of the two men. The incident, a particular outrage to Protestant and British opinion, provided an opportunity for enemies of CHARLES PARNELL to link him with PHYSICAL FORCE nationalism. In April 1887 the *Times* newspaper in London published what was purported to be a letter linking Parnell with the Invincibles and with the assassinations. A Special Investigative Commission was set up in August 1888, which found the letter to be a deliberate forgery, and thus exonerated Parnell from all involvement. Parnell's traducer, Pigott, shot himself in Madrid in 1889.

Phoenix Society and Phoenix Conspiracy

The 'Phoenix National and Literary Society' (the symbolism of the name of which will be self-evident) was founded in 1856 at Skibbereen, County Cork by O'DONOVAN ROSSA as a front for revolutionary republicanism. The Phoenix Conspiracy was a rather shadowy 'plot' to promote an invasion of Ireland by FENIANS from America in 1858/9. The leader of the plot was JAMES STEPHENS. In December 1858 the police raided the Society's Skibbereen offices, arrested 15 members, and suppressed it. From this society was to emerge the IRISH REPUBLICAN BROTHERHOOD, in that the personnel of the latter conformed to that of the Society, in County Cork.

Physical Force

The doctrine of 'physical force' is best expressed by PADRAIC PEARSE's remark of 1914 that nationhood can only be won by armed men. But the issue of 'physical' as against 'moral' force became prominent in the 1840s, during the rift in the REPEAL ASSOCIATION between constitutionalists led by DANIEL O'CONNELL, and the radical nationalists who became known as the YOUNG IRELAND movement. Physical force was an inherent aspect of the struggle for an independent Irish nation or an independent Irish legislature. It was used as a threat (as by the VOLUNTEERS of the 1780s, implicit rather than explicit) and was resorted to by the UNITED IRISHMEN in 1798 and ROBERT EMMET in 1803. O'Connell's Repeal movement, like his campaign for EMANCIPATION, rested upon the persuasive power of moral force, the self-evident rightness of the cause eventually being held to prevail. The tradition of moral force was inherited by the parliamentary-based HOME RULERS and land reformers of the 1870s. The case of the Young Ireland movement, and of the radical theorist FINTAN LALOR, in the 1840s, was that the struggle for repeal of the UNION of 1801 was getting nowhere, that some resort to armed force was essential if Ireland were ever to approach separate identity. The Young Ireland movement resorted to arms in 1848, and failed, but the physical force doctrine itself did not therefore cease to find exponents. The FENIANS of the 1860s, the IRISH REPUBLICAN BROTHERHOOD, and the men who rose in arms in 1916 in the EASTER RISING, could trace their method back for a century or more. In the end, after the WAR FOR INDEPENDENCE of 1919–21, it was justified, it did win a nation.

Place Act

The 'Place' Act of 16 August 1793, marked a further but belated success for the PATRIOT party of the House of Commons. CHIEF SECRETARY Hobart, who had already conceded substantial Catholic EMANCIPATION in the same year, acceded to the Place Act with other legislation, to bring the constitutional position in Ireland into line with that in Britain. Effectively, the Place Act 'for securing the freedom and independency of the House of Commons', excluded from the Commons all those who enjoyed pensions or otherwise held places of profit under the crown, although it was not retrospective. It required any member who accepted such a position to resign his seat. One of the Patriot grievances had been the numbers

of government-associated MPs in the Commons, who could be expected to act in accordance with the wishes of the British administration (although FLOOD, a vehement critic of the system, himself accepted government office and withdrew from Patriot politics for a time). Legislation such as the Place Act and the Emancipation Act of 1793 were prompted as much by fear of impending revolution within Ireland (perhaps inspired from France) as by any concern that matters should be amended.

Plan of Campaign (*see also* SIEGE OF SAUNDERS' FORT)

The Plan of Campaign represented an attempt by the NATIONAL LEAGUE (the successor body to the LAND LEAGUE of 1879–82) to revive the LAND WAR in the continuing interest of peasant proprietorship and expropriation of the landlords. It was announced on 23 October 1886, and was drafted by WILLIAM O'BRIEN and JOHN DILLON with the approval of PARNELL, although he later, in May 1888, distanced himself from the agitation. The objective of the Plan was to obtain blanket withholding of rents on certain estates, the rents to be paid into the hands of trustees. On 16 December 1886 O'Brien, Dillon and other National League figures arrived in Galway to receive the rents of tenants on the estates of the Lord Clanricarde. Two days later the LORD LIEUTENANT proclaimed the Plan, 'a criminal conspiracy'. The arrest of O'Brien and others, and their subsequent trial, indicated the government's determination, but the jury failed to agree on their verdict. There may have been more than coincidence in the fact that at this time, the *Times* newspaper published damaging material linking Parnell to the INVICIBLES and the PHOENIX PARK assassinations of 1882. Ensuing law suits and the Special Commission set up to look into Parnell's complaint against the *Times*, in 1888, led Parnell to disassociate himself from the 'criminal conspiracy' of the Plan of Campaign, which had also been condemned by the Catholic Church. Nevertheless, the Plan was still active in 1889, when the CHIEF SECRETARY established a secret group, known as the

'Syndicate' to protect the estates of the Ponsonby family in County Cork. In September 1890 O'Brien and Dillon were arrested, but released on bail. They fled to France. In their absence they were sentenced to six months' gaol for conspiracy, and were seized upon their return to Ireland in 1891. Their prosecution and Parnell's disgrace in 1890 led to the virtual cessation of the Plan of Campaign.

Plantation (*see also* CONNACHT, LEINSTER, MUNSTER, ULSTER, Plantation in)

Plantation – the expropriation of landholders, and the conversion of some or all of their land to provide settlement for colonists – was the most direct assault made by the English government upon the native GAELIC IRISH, and, eventually, the OLD ENGLISH, during the seventeenth century. Less moderate in impact than ANGLICIZATION, and concerned with the creation of a semi-urban network of settlements throughout Ireland, it was a policy that looked to a transformation of the propertied section of Irish society in the interests of English governmental stability as well as in the name of religious reformation. Plantation on a small scale had been tried during the sixteenth century, but it was resorted to as a major act of policy after the collapse of the TYRONE rebellion in ULSTER in 1603. The procedure was fairly uniform: title to land would be called into question, and submitted to the consideration of a jury drawn from the area in which the lands were located, which jury ordinarily found in favour of the king's right to the land. This right was often based upon ancient claims, such as those in County Wexford which were dated back to the reign of King Richard II in the fourteenth century. Forfeiture, whereby a rebel against the government lost his lands, was an easier method of getting control. When PARSONS, as LORD JUSTICE, in 1641 connived at a spurious plot to implicate the Old English of the PALE in the IRISH REBELLION of that year, he, an avid 'planter', was looking to a time when the rebellious Old English, like the Gaelic Irish, would forfeit their property. In the usual case of a jury decision in favour of the royal claim, some portion of the surrendered land would be reserved for the previous proprietor(s), the rest would be available for sale or grant to new settlers. In the case of Ulster, direct forfeiture by the Earls of Tyrone and TYRCONNELL resulted from their FLIGHT (OF THE EARLS) in 1607, and previously loyal Gaelic landholders were goaded into situations that made them subject to forfeiture as well. The Irish Rebellion of 1641 gave the English government a chance to open up Ireland for full-scale resettlement. To finance the war effort against the rebels, ADVENTURERS were induced to advance money against blocks of land to be made available to them once the rebellion was crushed. The outbreak of the ENGLISH CIVIL WAR in 1642 extended the potential reservoir of forfeited Irish lands, by making rebels out of those who, in arms against the Gaelic rebels of 1641, were, because of their loyalty to King Charles I, treated as rebels also by the English Parliament. The alliance of the royalists and the rebels, which came belatedly, was partly forced upon the royalists by the land settlement policy of the English Parliament. By the Settling of Ireland Act of 1652, the lands of rebels were subject to confiscation on a sliding scale of one-fifth, one-third or two-thirds according to the degree of guilt that could be established against them. This procedure opened the way for corrupt information to be laid against many, and the Cromwellian land settlement of the 1650s led to the mass expulsion of the Catholic landowners, whether Gaelic or Old English, from their estates, and their enforced transportation into less fertile and profitable Connacht. The measures for plantation taken between 1607 and 1660 were never effectively undone, although there was some restitution. The sweeping repeal planned by the JACOBITE 'PATRIOT' PARLIAMENT of 1689 never came about.

Plantation put the native and Old English landowners of Ireland, unless they were openly and committedly Protestant and acceptable, into the role of expendable undesirables. The Old English, who had come to dominate Irish affairs over the native Gaelic Irish, were themselves displaced by the NEW ENGLISH and the Scots who came in with plantation, and whose religious orthodoxy of the Protestant kind made them preferable to the English government. Plantation, and especially the Cromwellian land settlement (when land was set aside for soldiers in lieu of arrears of pay) introduced the speculator and the quick-profit motive into Ireland, as it also introduced the absentee landowner living off rents. There was, in fact, more land available than there were fit men to take it, with the result that a landless Irish peasantry was often kept on in a tenant position. The origins of the dreadful poverty and the 'monstrous evil' of the Irish land question of the nineteenth century lay in the policy of plantation in the seventeenth.

Plantation was a method by which the English government asserted its authority over Ireland; more, it was the method by which English values and social usage were imposed upon another culture; it was the means by which England brought to a finality the piecemeal encroachment on Ireland begun in the twelfth century, and was thus the affirmation of a right to possess Ireland which the English had assumed, padded out as it was with useful if less than trustworthy medieval grants and submissions to the English crown. It is clear that the vigour with which plantation was pursued after 1607 owed a lot to Protestant assertiveness against a Catholic and, potentially, hostile neighbour. But the approach of the seventeenth-century policy was less savage than that which had been contemplated during the reign of King Henry VIII (1509–47), when wholesale genocide had been mooted, but jettisoned not because of the enormity of the idea, but because it was felt that England had not the surplus population to fill satisfactorily an empty land. The plantation policy implemented in the area of Leix and Offaly in Leinster in the 1530s was that which was followed in subsequent schemes. The Irish PARLIAMENT of 1537 legislated to turn the native-held land into the counties of King's and Queen's (see ADMINISTRATIVE STRUCTURE), where local juries could declare the land of former rebels to be the property of the crown. Two-thirds of the forfeited land was thus reassigned, the remaining third left to the former possessors of the whole.

Plunkett, Joseph Mary (1887–1916)

Joseph Plunkett, the son of George Noble Plunkett (1851–1948) hereditary papal count, was a signatory of the PROCLAMATION OF THE IRISH REPUBLIC read from the steps of the GPO at the onset of the EASTER RISING of 1916. Joseph had been Director of Operations in the IRISH VOLUNTEERS in 1913 and a member of the IRISH REPUBLICAN BROTHERHOOD, and he sat in the latter's Military Council when the plans for an uprising were made. He had also been involved in acquiring guns from Germany, in collaboration with ROGER CASEMENT. Joseph Plunkett was shot on 4 May 1916 for his part in the rising. His father was returned as an independent MP on an ABSTENTIONIST platform (like the SINN FÉIN MPs) in 1917, and opposed the ANGLO-IRISH TREATY.

Plunket(t), St Oliver (1629–81)

Oliver Plunkett was born in County Meath of OLD ENGLISH family, and was educated at the Irish College in Rome where he was ordained in 1654. He became Professor of Theology in the College de Propaganda Fide, a post he held until 1669. He was appointed archbishop of Armagh in that year, and arrived in Ireland in 1670. Of strong ultramontane views (that is, an advocate of the doctrine of papal supremacy), he set himself to overhaul the church in Ireland. He became a victim of anti-Catholic hysteria, of the ever-present ghost of the 1641 IRISH REBELLION. In 1678 he was accused of implication in the spurious POPISH PLOT, and when a court in Ireland failed to convict him, he was taken to London and re-tried, with a similar result. A third trial led to his conviction for 'propagating the Catholic religion', and he suffered the penalty for treason. Like all the victims of the Popish Plot, his trial was a travesty of justice, his execution a judicial murder. He was the last Catholic to suffer martyrdom at Tyburn, and he was canonized in 1975.

Police *see* CONSTABULARY

Poor Law, The Irish

Irish poor relief legislation aimed, in theory, at the alleviation of distress and want, failed to face the crisis of the FAMINE of 1845–49. Within 10 years of the passage of the important 1838 Act, the system had shown itself unsuited to Irish conditions. One hundred years earlier, in 1741 the YEAR OF THE SLAUGHTER, another major famine had struck Ireland, attempts to alleviate which were wholly down to private initiative. The personal initiative of the LORD LIEUTENANT, the Duke of Bedford, in his official capacity, led to expenditure to alleviate distress in the face of severe harvest failures prior to the crisis years of 1756/7. There was no system of poor relief in Ireland commensurate with that which had prevailed in England since the early seventeenth century. Private alms-giving, the creation of localized, often parochial, charitable trusts, were wholly inadequate in the face of the distressed state of the Irish peasantry. The first legislative measure to remedy this came in 1772, with Woodward's Act named after a CHURCH OF IRELAND dean who had published his arguments in favour of a tax-financed relief scheme in 1768. Known as the 'mendicity act', that of 1772 was a long way from the system envisaged by Woodward: it required that beggars be badged, and that workhouses be set up. In each county a body of commissioners was created to expend monies raised by subscription and church collections, on the provision of indoor (workhouse) relief. The measure was so half-hearted as to be meaningless. Unless there was a diversion of funds from the GRAND JURIES, little was achieved because the funding was wholly unsuited to the task, and there was a certain air of indifference amongst those who could afford to help. Only in BELFAST, where a substantial workhouse was opened in 1774, and in DUBLIN where the 'house of industry' – run on spartan lines – was able to cope with several thousand indigent and sickly poor in times of crisis, was there any real outcome of the Act. Not until 1817 was there any further legislation, and that came in face of the agricultural depression ensuant upon the ending of the wars with France in 1815. In July 1817 asylums for the lunatic poor were legislated for, but the important Act was that of 16 June, the Poor Employment Act, pushed through in face of famine and disease and widespread agrarian unrest. PEEL, the CHIEF SECRETARY, took steps in his official capacity, with permission from the British government, to appoint a co-ordinating committee to make grants for relief to local committees in afflicted areas. He also provided a similar system to deal with the prevalent typhus epidemic that accompanied famine conditions. The 1817 Act gave powers to the Lord Lieutenant to organize public works financed out of the rates. In April 1819, the House of Commons appointed a select committee to enquire into the condition of the poor in Ireland, but legislation did not come anywhere near meeting the Irish problem. By 1822 there was widespread crop failure and famine conditions in Munster and Connacht, and the House of Commons passed an act to provide funds for the construction of roads to provide paid employment for the destitute. The Irish administration responded with, as Peel had in 1817, a central committee organized to disburse funds made available by the government, to those areas most in need, where local commissioners assessed requirements and disbursed the funds given them. The important factor of the responses of 1817 and 1822 was that it had established that intervention by the government was necessary if there was to be any large-scale alleviation of want. The British Parliament was, therefore, steadily conditioned to pass legislation that the Irish Parliament, up until its abolition in 1801, had never seriously entertained or concerned itself with. The principle of intervention lay behind the 1838 Poor Relief (Ireland) Act, which, in brief, introduced the English Poor Law of 1834 into Ireland, with its Boards of Guardians, its Poor Law commissioners and its workhouse system of indoor relief. According to the Chancellor of the Exchequer, the 1838 legislation was less concerned with alleviation of distress than in 'loosening [the poor man's] grip upon the land'. The utter unsuitability of the English system for Ireland had been pointed out to the government by its own commission of enquiry chaired by the archbishop of Dublin, which had reported by 1836, laying emphasis upon the need for public works. Its recommendations were ignored, and the 1838 law, which would be implemented on a selective basis – that is, the proposed workhouse system within which all relief would be administered, could only cope with 80,000 poor people at one time. In Irish terms, that was nothing. The Act created 130 Poor Law Unions run by elective Boards of Guardians, who were answerable to the Poor Law commissioners. The creation of the Boards of Guardians introduced another tier into the system of local administration quite apart from their first purpose in implementing the Poor Law. All manner of additional concerns came to be imposed upon them in subsequent government reform of local administrations, heralded by the MUNICIPAL REFORM Act of August 1840. The new system of 1838 came into being in April 1839, having been organized under the direction of Commissioner George Nicholls, who had been instrumental in the decision of government to abide by the methods of the 1834 English system. The famine of 1845–49 revealed the helplessness of the system, with its emphasis upon indoor relief, and famine relief measures came to depend upon extraordinary efforts of private initiative and hurried government legislation. In February 1847 the Destitute Poor Act provided for temporary 'soup kitchens' and for a measure of outdoor relief, and the Act of 8 June 1847 instructed the Poor Law Guardians to provide outdoor relief to the aged and the sick and to widows with dependent children, and allowed for temporary, short-term relief to the able-bodied unemployed. It contained an exclusion clause, however, whereby anyone possessed of a quarter acre of land or more was exempt from its provisions. That merely encouraged the poverty-stricken tenant to abandon his holding. By 4 July 1847 there were 680,000 persons in receipt of outdoor relief, and as many again were dead and dying in the countryside. The workhouse system survived the famine intact, and in 1861 another select committee of the Commons investigated the workings of the Poor Law in Ireland.

Legislation in August 1862 abolished the quarter-acre clause of the 1847 Act, and extended provision for outdoor relief. In 1872 the functions of the Poor Law Commission for Ireland (established in 1847) were transferred to the new Local Government Board, to whom the Guardians reported. Mounting distress in Ireland in 1879/80 was met by further legislation empowering the Local Government Board to extend outdoor relief provisions, but the basis of the Poor Law remained workhouse oriented (the workhouse system was ultimately abolished in Ireland by the FREE STATE government in 1922). How far the imposition of a thoroughly unsuitable Poor Law on Ireland in 1838 critically affected the impact of the famine may be debatable: but a system of indoor relief, appalling enough in its English context, was horrendous in the poverty-stricken countryside of Ireland with the destitute of which, the workhouse system was unable to cope. Dean Woodward had made his recommendations for tax-based relief in 1768. The practicality of his idea was never put to the test, but what came after his suggestion, proved in no way more efficacious.

Pope's Brass Band

A pejorative term for the IRISH BRIGADE.

Popish Plot, The

In January 1681 the English House of Commons found that there was a Catholic plot aiming at the massacre of the English and the subversion of Protestantism. The plot was a concoction of Titus Oates (1649–1705) whose profession, according to the *Dictionary of National Biography* entry, was that of 'perjurer'. How his fantastic revelations came to be credited so widely, reflects the incipient fear of Catholicism deeply embedded in the English Protestant subconscious since the sixteenth century, and the (hardly fortuitous) fact that the magistrate to whom Oates first revealed his plot, was murdered shortly after. The terror that the 'plot' unleashed lasted from 1678 until 1685, when Oates was exposed for the liar he was, but it served the interests of prominent Protestant politicians who wished to create an atmosphere conducive to the exclusion of the Catholic heir, James Duke of York, from the throne of England. In Ireland, the LORD LIEUTENANT gaoled the archbishop of DUBLIN in 1680, and closed down all Catholic religious houses (see CATHOLIC CLERGY, Legislation Against). The great victim of the plot was ST OLIVER PLUNKET(T), dragged through three trials to his eventual execution in London in July 1681, hounded by the virulent polemicist Henry Jones, bishop of Meath in the CHURCH OF IRELAND. Otherwise, the 'plot' in Ireland took the form of a suspected French invasion connived at by Plunkett, Richard Power Earl of Tyrone (briefly gaoled) and some others. The hysteria evident in England did not manifest itself in Ireland.

Population

Precise figures for the population of Ireland, assessed by census at 10-yearly intervals, become available for Ireland, as for England, in the nineteenth century. Prior to that, demographers' estimates convey a picture of numbers from 1600 onwards. In that year, the population stood at 1.4 million, and had risen to 2 million by 1641. The impact of the IRISH REBELLION of 1641–53 and consequent economic upheaval may account for the figure of 1.7 million arrived at for 1672, the 2 million of 1641 being arrived at again by 1687. Using tax returns and other incidental sources, estimates of between 2.5 and 3 million have been offered for the early part of the eighteenth century. The major period of population growth in Ireland occurred between 1780 and 1830: growth seems to have peaked before the FAMINE of 1845–49 made such an inroad into the population. A figure of 4.4 million has been given for c.1790, and the census returns of 1821 show 6.8 million. Thereafter the decline of the Irish population can be demonstrated at precisely 10-yearly periods:

1831	7.7 million
1841	8.2 million
1851	6.5 million
1861	5.7 million
1871	5.4 million
1881	5.1 million
1891	4.7 million
1901	4.4 million (as in 1790)
1911	4.3 million

The devastating effect of the famine and of subsequent mass EMIGRATION reduced the population to its late eighteenth-century levels within 50 years. Between 1841 and 1851 alone there was a 19.8 per cent decline in the overall figures. Between 1841 and 1911 the number of inhabited dwellings in Ireland fell from 1,328,839 to 861,057, and the number of families over the same period declined from 1.4 million to 912,000. The first census after the creation of the FREE STATE showed a population of 2.9 million (and, in Northern Ireland, 1.2 million) in 1926. As recently as 1971 the population of the former Free State, now Republic of Ireland, remained around the 2.9 million level.

Potato Blight (*see also* FAMINE of 1845–49)

Historians continue to debate the process by which the potato became a staple in the Irish diet. It certainly increased in importance as a crop as the seventeenth century wore on, and the association of the Irish with potatoes was apparent in English anti-Irish demonstrations in the 1680s, when potatoes were stuck upon poles or sticks to symbolize the Irish. Reliance upon the potato in diet first became apparent in Munster, where it was a major element in winter food by the 1750s. Within 30 years it was consumed as a staple all year round, and there was sufficient surplus production for export to America. The spread of the potato led to the widespread practice of keeping pigs, which lived off the peelings. The renewed emphasis upon arable agriculture, and the reclamation of 'waste' lands, during the wars at the end of the eighteenth century, saw a natural increase in potato as well as in grain crops. By 1840, it has been argued, the potato was a common dietary staple, and still there was sufficient to permit the export of some 20 per cent of the total produced. The blight that struck at the crop in 1845 was first noted in England in August (where dependence upon the potato was less marked). By the autumn it was identified in Ireland. It appears to have been a new fungus disease – *Phytophthora infestans* – which literally rotted the crop in the soil. Since the potato is extremely nutritious, it can support life; but some balance in the consumption of milk and fish is necessary. Agricultural decline from 1815, the developing unemployment as land shifted away from arable to pasture, forced the poor onto reliance on the potato exclusively. Thus the blight of 1845 destroyed not only the foodstuff for the next year, but likewise the seed potatoes for the next cropping.

Poynings' Law

Sir Edward Poynings (1459–1521) was LORD DEPUTY in Ireland to King Henry VII charged, amongst other things, with rooting out the latent support for the House of York there. Its last king, Richard III, had been overthrown by Henry in 1485, but subsequent attempts on the throne had a strong Irish connection. Poynings summoned a Parliament in 1494 and under his direction it passed acts the burden of which is known as Poynings' Law. The measures must be understood in the context of Poynings' political task, to deprive pretenders to the English throne of Irish support. Thus, all laws that had been passed by the English Parliament prior to 1494 were held to have validity in Ireland as well – which meant, the enactment of Henry VII's right to the throne and the parallel attainder of his dead rival, Richard III. Of more long-term consequence was the requirement that all proposed legislation in the Irish PARLIAMENT, be submitted to the English Privy Council for its approval, and that this submission be made through the office of the Lord Deputy who could put a check on legislative proposals if he chose. If the bills were to be proposed, they were returned to the Irish Parliament to be passed or voted out as occasion might fit. Amendments to bills subsequent to the approval of the bills, had to go through the approval process as well. Once the English crown had obtained this measure of control over Ireland's legislature, it did not let go, although there were occasions when it could be irksome. For example, the English Parliament in 1642 – on the verge of (ENGLISH) CIVIL WAR with King Charles I – attempted to bypass the procedure to hurriedly enforce anti-Catholic laws. Challenges to Poynings' Law were articulated by, among others, PATRICK DARCY in the 1640s and WILLIAM MOLYNEUX in the 1690s. The PATRIOT PARLIAMENT summoned by King JAMES II in 1689 actually voted for its repeal, with the assent of a reluctant monarch, but that Parliament was swept away with the rest of JACOBITE Ireland in 1691. Following the revolt which toppled James II in 1688 and replaced him with King WILLIAM III, the Privy Council's authority over Irish legislation passed to the English Parliament, which in 1720 – aware of continued mutterings in the Irish Parliament against the ancient law – passed a DECLARATORY ACT which emphatically emphasized the supremacy of the British Parliament over the Irish. The repeal of that Act was one of the objectives of the PATRIOTS in Ireland, who in 1782 secured its repeal and a renunciation by the British Parliament of the right to vote similar legislation again. The 1782 repeal effectively overturned Poynings' Law.

Precincts

In January 1651 commissioners from the Parliament in England arrived in Ireland to take over the government there. Edmund Ludlow and John Jones (with responsibility for civil affairs) and Miles Corbet and John Weaver, replaced the abolished LORD LIEUTENANCY. The territory which had been brought under English military control was divided up into 'precincts' each with its own military governor and collectors of taxes. The precincts were a temporary measure: by 1656 the county-structure was as before, presided over by sheriffs and Justices of the Peace (see MAGISTRATES AND JUSTICES OF THE PEACE).

Precursors, The

The Precursors were established in 1838 by DANIEL O'CONNELL to commence work on the formation of a movement to agitate for repeal of the Union of 1801. They were, therefore, the forerunners or precursors of the Loyal National REPEAL ASSOCIATION.

Presbyterianism

Presbyterianism came into Ireland with Scottish settlement, predominantly in ULSTER, during the late sixteenth century. As a religious doctrine, it was based upon the teachings of John Calvin as these were transmuted by the Scottish reformer John Knox. Pure Presbyterianism believed in one ministry, dispensed with 'priesthood' and with bishops or episcopacy, and adhered to a church structure in which congregations were grouped together in Presbyteries which were likewise organized into Synods. Organized Presbyterianism may be traced, in Ireland, to the IRISH REBELLION of 1641 which broke out in Ulster. A Scottish Presbyterian army under ROBERT MONRO was sent into the province to counter the rebels there, and established its base at Carrickfergus where the first Irish Presbytery was established as well. This, and the continued influx of Scottish settlers into Ulster, turned its north and eastern areas into a Presbyterian stronghold, which it has remained. In 1672 WILLIAM PETTY estimated that, of the 300,000 Protestants that he reckoned were in Ireland, one-third at least were Scottish Presbyterians grouped in Ulster. The link between Ulster and Scotland was maintained by the settlers, particularly as they continued to arrive in large numbers at the end of the seventeenth century. In consequence, divisions within the Scottish Presbyterian Church found reflection in Ulster (see NEW LIGHT), but, interestingly, the Irish Presbyterians were more willing to work alongside the state. The grant of government money to finance the ministry – the REGIUM DONUM – was accepted gladly in Ulster, but somewhat brusquely rejected by the higher-principled Scottish ministers when it was first offered to them in 1669. Presbyterians, as DISSENTERS, non-communicants of the CHURCH OF IRELAND which was the test of respectability in eighteenth-century Ireland, suffered some of the

disadvantages suffered by the Catholics of Ireland. Anti-Catholicism was not expressly a religious issue. It was much bound up with matters of land and legality, and the Presbyterians were by no means as committed to anti-Catholicism for their own defence as was the Church of Ireland and the Protestant ASCENDANCY. Indeed, among Presbyterians radical political doctrines had wide currency. The UNITED IRISHMEN movement of the 1790s, which brought on a full-scale rebellion for Irish independence in 1798, was initially a Presbyterian radical movement with Ulster origins, that spread to include Catholic republicans elsewhere. There would have been no Ulster uprising in the NINETY-EIGHT had it not been for Presbyterian leadership. The structure of the Presbyterian Church was more or less democratic, the most important element being the congregation and the lay elders of it – 'moral policemen' as they have been called – the most significant members. The congregations, through their elders, chose their ministers and financed their salaries. Congregations met in Kirk Sessions, which grouped together would form a Presbytery (there were nine Presbyteries in Ulster in 1702). The Presbyteries in their turn formed a General Synod, but when that Synod met to deliberate, lay representatives of every individual congregation were in attendance. Given the fact that the Presbyterians were, like the Catholics, barred from office-holding, school-teaching and so forth by the same PENAL LAWS which required a sacramental test, and given also that Presbyterians like Catholics, paid TITHES to support the established church, there was plenty of scope for militancy. In actuality, by the 1740s most of the disabling laws affecting Presbyterians were either repealed or in abeyance.

Historians have remarked upon the relative lack of vituperative theological and doctrinal debate in Ireland amongst the Protestants in the early seventeenth century. This has been ascribed to the presence of the numerous common enemy, the Catholics. Again, when the Catholic struggle for EMANCIPATION began to take effect at the end of the eighteenth century, and certainly by 1829, Presbyterians moved away from their radicalism (with some exceptions) to collaborate with the Church of Ireland. The growth of the avowedly ORANGE ORDER, which was sectarian before it was commemorative of William of Orange (see WILLIAM III), relied heavily upon Presbyterian membership. LOYALISM became an Ulster-based phenomenon because it was Presbyterian in colour, and the ultimate 'Northern Ireland' state that emerged in 1921 was based upon the commitment of the majority Presbyterian population (with some exceptions) to the UNION of 1801 of Britain and Ireland.

Presidents and the Presidency System

The Presidency system affected the provinces of Connacht and Munster. There was no need for it in Leinster, because of the domination of the DUBLIN administration, and proposals for its institution in ULSTER came to nothing. The idea of a President in each of the provinces had been discussed in the 1540s, but nothing had come of it. The role of the President was to enforce ANGLICIZATION, English law and usages, on the inhabitants. His task was both civil and military, and depended upon the active support of the LORD DEPUTY and the Dublin administration. The first President to be appointed was Sir Edward Fitton in Connacht in 1569, an appointment that gave warning to the lords of Munster that they would be next. Resistance to the Presidency system accounts in some measure for the Munster rebellion of that year, but a President was nevertheless imposed in 1570 in the person of Sir John Perrot, who held office until 1576. The precise powers of the provincial Presidents were never clearly defined: because they were dependent upon the Lord Deputies they were vulnerable to conspiracy against them amongst the leaders of society within the province. Their military role was, at least until 1600, the most crucial. Indeed, in July 1576 Captain Malby was appointed as 'military governor' in Connacht in succession to President Fitton, but was not appointed President himself until 1579. His successor, Bingham, was charged with misgovernment, and when

he was exonerated, was ordered to campaign against the O'Rourkes in County Leitrim. The Presidency system's usefulness depended upon the lack of tighter centralized control from Dublin. It was swept away by the English Parliament, but restored in 1660 as part of a parcel of measures by King Charles II to undo the consequences of the IRISH REBELLION of 1641–53 and the ENGLISH CIVIL WARS. The Presidencies of Munster and Connacht survived until 1672, when they were formally abolished for good. Cromwellian government in Ireland, through efficient commissioners and Lord Deputies, had shown that the Presidencies were not necessary: their revival had been a piece of politicking by King Charles, and their disappearance yielded all authority to Dublin.

Preston, Thomas (1585–1655)

'A gentleman of English race' THOMAS WENTWORTH observed of Preston, 'well affected to the King'. He was educated in the Spanish Low Countries, and served in the Spanish armies with OWEN ROE O'NEILL, whom he came cordially to detest. When the IRISH REBELLION broke out in 1641, Preston offered his services to the rebels, and arrived at Waterford in September 1642. His rival O'Neill was commanding the CATHOLIC CONFEDERACY army of ULSTER, and Preston was given that of Leinster. He won an immediate victory over government troops at Timahoe on 5 October, but was beaten by the Earl of ORMOND at Old Ross in March 1643. After the battle of BENBURB, he accommodated himself to O'Neill and the papal envoy RINUCCINI, but in 1649 was decisively beaten at DANGAN HILL by the forces of MICHAEL JONES commanding for the English Parliament. He formed an alliance thereafter with the royalists of the Earl of Ormond, became Governor of Galway, and in 1650 defended Waterford against IRETON. King Charles II created him Viscount Tara in that year in acknowledgement of his services. Preston escaped to France in 1652, having been excluded from pardon by the government in England, and died in exile.

Prevent the (Further) Growth of Popery, 1704 Act for *see* Penal Laws

Prince of Ireland

A title accorded to Hugh O'Neill, Earl of TYRONE by European leaders with whom he negotiated for the purpose of military support for his rebellion against the English crown. Spanish aid was forthcoming, but was destroyed in a single battle at KINSALE in 1601. Tyrone submitted to the crown in 1603.

Proclamation of the Irish Republic

The Proclamation was read on the steps of the GPO in DUBLIN on 24 April 1916 at the start of the EASTER RISING. It was signed by THOMAS J. CLARKE, SÉAN MAC DIARMADA, THOMAS MACDONAGH, P.H. PEARSE, EAMONN CEANNT, JAMES CONNOLLY and JOSEPH PLUNKETT. The text read: 'The Provisional Government of the Irish Republic to the People of Ireland. Irishmen and Irishwomen: In the name of God and of the dead generations from which she receives her old tradition of nationhood, Ireland, through us, summons her children to her flag and strikes for her freedom.

Having organized and trained her manhood through her secret revolutionary organization, the IRISH REPUBLICAN BROTHERHOOD, and through her open military organizations, the IRISH VOLUNTEERS, and the Irish CITIZEN ARMY, having patiently perfected her discipline, having resolutely waited for the right moment to reveal itself, she now seizes that moment, and, supported by her exiled children in America and by gallant allies in Europe, but relying in the first on her own strength, she strikes in full confidence of victory.

We declare the right of the people of Ireland to the ownership of Ireland, and to the unfettered control of Irish destinies, to be sovereign and indefeasible. The long usurpation of that right by a foreign people and government has not extinguished the right, nor can it ever be extinguished except by the destruction of the Irish people. In every generation the Irish people have asserted their right to national freedom and sovereignty; six times during the past three hundred years they have asserted it in arms. Standing on that fundamental right and again asserting it in arms in the face of the world, we hereby proclaim the Irish republic as a sovereign independent state, and we pledge our lives and the lives of our comrades-in-arms to the cause of its freedom, of its welfare, and of its exaltation among the nations.

The Irish republic is entitled to and hereby claims, the allegiance of every Irishman and Irishwoman. The republic guarantees religious and civil liberty, equal rights and equal opportunities to all its citizens, and declares its resolve to pursue the happiness and prosperity of the whole nation and of all its parts, cherishing all the children of the nation equally, and oblivious of the differences carefully fostered by an alien government, which have divided a minority from the majority in the past.

Until our arms have brought the opportune moment for the establishment of a permanent national government, representative of the whole people of Ireland, and elected by the suffrages of all her men and women, the Provisional Government, hereby constituted, will administer the civil and military affairs of the republic in trust for the people. We place the cause of the Irish republic under the protection of the Most High God, whose blessing we invoke upon our arms, and we pray that no one who serves that cause will dishonour it by cowardice, inhumanity, or rapine. In this supreme hour the Irish nation must, by its valour and discipline, and by the readiness of its children to sacrifice themselves for the common good, prove itself worthy of the august destiny to which it is called.'

Property Defence Association

The Association was established in DUBLIN in December 1880 by landlords, to organize self-help and resistance to the LAND WAR tactics of the LAND LEAGUE. Amongst their objectives was to bring in labourers to work the lands of those subjected to BOYCOTTING, and they came to work closely with the ORANGE ORDER which did the same.

Propositions, The

Following the repeal of the DECLARATORY ACT of 1720 in 1782, and the further renunciation act, the British government was constrained to try to establish a new working relationship with the assertive Irish PARLIAMENT. To that end, a series of Propositions were laid before it, although the purpose of the British House of Commons seems to have been to cut back on the degree of legislative independence won by their counterparts in DUBLIN. Amongst measures to allow for equity in import duties, abandonment of import restrictions and a mutual trading preference, was the requirement that surpluses from the revenues of Ireland should go towards expenditure on the fleet. The Propositions were debated in Dublin in February 1785 after presentation by the CHIEF SECRETARY, Orde, and were generally approved of. Back in WESTMINSTER, however, they were modified and approved provided that the Irish Parliament pass all the legislation at once. The Irish Commons voted to consider the revised bill in August, but the extent of opposition to them obliged the administration to abandon them.

Q

Quarterage

Quarterage was an anti-Catholic 'tax' levied within Irish boroughs by the Protestant-controlled Gilds. Because of the severity of the PENAL LAWS, Catholics were more or less obliged, if they had any ambition, to move into trade. The Protestant trade Gilds were prepared to admit Catholics as 'quarter' brothers upon payment of an entry fine and quarterly fees – hence, 'quarterage'. Thus the Catholics were entitled to enjoy the benefits accruing from Gild membership without actually being members, although they were not barred by law from becoming such. For much of the eighteenth century up to 1778 the Gilds endeavoured to have statutory endorsement of the quarterage system, but the Catholics resisted it strenuously and the Gilds gave way.

Quebec Act

The Quebec Act of 22 June 1774 extended to Catholics in Quebec, Canada, the right to exercise their religion freely, and no longer required them to take an oath of supremacy denying papal authority. The granting of political rights to the Quebec Catholics created a strong impression in Ireland, where their co-religionists were still labouring under the extensive range of the PENAL LAWS. EMANCIPATION in Ireland was still 20 years or so away, but the Quebec Act signalled a change in the British attitude towards the Catholics. The apprehension of lingering JACOBITISM and the fear of the consequence of setting at liberty the majority of the Irish population was beginning to fade.

Queen's Colleges

The educational institutions known as the Queen's Colleges (from Queen Victoria) were introduced by ROBERT PEEL in May 1844 as a direct attempt to undermine the control exercised by Catholic education upon the recently enfranchised and burgeoning Catholic bourgeoisie in Ireland. The proposal for these non-denominational colleges came at the same time as Peel was organizing increased funding for the Catholic ST PATRICK'S COLLEGE at Maynooth. Catholic leaders split over the issue, DANIEL O'CONNELL siding with the church hierarchy which denounced the principle of non-denominational education, WILLIAM SMITH O'BRIEN coming out in favour. Foundation legislation passed the House of Commons on 31 July 1845, with colleges prescribed for BELFAST, Galway and Cork, but not for DERRY or for Limerick as had originally been envisaged. The Catholic bishops were advised by Rome to establish a Catholic university in Ireland in opposition to the new colleges. But within weeks of a Catholic Synod at Thurles which re-emphasized church hostility, though somewhat qualified, the new colleges were drawn together by act as the Queen's University of Ireland. That resistance by the church did not diminish. Reform attempts by GLADSTONE failed in the Commons in 1873, but in August 1879 the Queen's University was abolished, and a new Royal University established by charter came into effect on 27 April 1880. In 1884 PARNELL, moving towards rapprochement with the CATHOLIC CHURCH to increase support for his NATIONAL LEAGUE, condemned the system as 'godless' and campaigned for denominational education in consort with the church hierarchy. The ultimate resolution of the issue came in a typically British way. In 1908 the Irish Universities Act abolished the Royal University of 1880, and provided for the National University of Ireland at DUBLIN, embracing Dublin, Cork and Galway, whilst a Queen's University was provided in Belfast based on the original Queen's College there. Although non-denominational education was implicit in the new legislation, in practice the division between north and south, Ulster and the rest of Ireland, meant virtually a Protestant/Catholic division as well.

R

Races of Castlebar

A derisory term for the battle at Castlebar fought on 27 August 1798, where the French expeditionary force under HUMBERT, which had landed to support the republican UNITED IRISHMEN in their rebellion, routed government troops and drove them in flight from the field. This battle inaugurated the short-lived Republic of Connacht, proclaimed on 31 August by Humbert. Government troops were back in control in Castlebar by 4 September.

Rakehelly Horseboys

The poet Edmund Spenser (1552–99) employed the term to describe the KERNS, Irish soldiery and household retainers of the Gaelic chiefs. Spenser was established on an estate in County Cork by 1588 and lived in Ireland until his house was destroyed in a Gaelic uprising and he was forced back to England, where he died.

Ranelagh Undertaking

Farming of the revenues was a common financial practice in seventeenth-century England. In 1669 Alderman John Forth of London on behalf of a consortium of financiers and merchants, undertook to 'farm' the entire Irish revenues, paying to the government £204,500 per annum. The consortium then collected the revenues from taxation in Ireland at their own expense, but reckoned to make a profit well over the annual prescribed payment. In August 1671 Charles II was persuaded by Richard Jones Earl of Ranelagh heading a new consortium, to impose Ranelagh's group upon Alderman Forth's, so that Forth paid the money due to the government, to Ranelagh. It was a quite extraordinary arrangement, Ranelagh undertaking to cover government expenditure direct from the monies he received, and to ensure the king £80,000 as a 'fee' to be paid upon conclusion of the undertaking. The scheme simply failed, and ended in 1675 with Forth's own original 'farm'. The Irish government then took over the farm, remitting to England £300,000 in 1678.

Rapparees

The word 'rapparee' comes from the Irish word for the short pike, 'rapaire'. The Rapparees were a kind of late seventeenth-century equivalent of the FLYING COLUMNS of the IRISH REPUBLICAN ARMY. They were JACOBITE guerrillas working behind the WILLIAMITE lines during the period 1689–91. An act for their suppression was passed in September 1697, when they and the TORIES were still active. Rapparees were still operating in Connacht early in the eighteenth century.

Rebels

It needs to be understood that, in Irish nationalist and republican terms, the word 'rebel' is honourable, as was, for much of the nineteenth century, the word 'felon' applied to YOUNG IRELAND and FENIAN revolutionaries who were executed or TRANSPORTED for rebellion. 'Rebel' conveys resistance to authority, a denial of established government, a movement to set up an alternative. Since all authority in Ireland, in the view of the 'rebels', was imposed and alien in origin, then resistance to it might be justified not in terms of rebellion alone, but in terms also of legitimate reassertion of suppressed nationhood. In that context, action would not be rebellion, but would only be defined as rebellion by the authority seeking to repress it. Thus the word 'rebel' was applied by government, and assumed by the nationalist cause in much the same way as the Tory political party took over and made honourable the opprobrious term 'TORIES' applied to them by their political enemies.

Redmond, John (1856–1918)

Although Redmond has been derided by Irish republican opinion, which looked upon him as a nationalist willing to concede crucial issues to the British, his role as leader of constitutional nationalism between 1900 and 1918 was extraordinarily difficult. Redmond was one of the minority of MPs of the IRISH PARLIAMENTARY PARTY who stood firmly by its old leader PARNELL when, in 1890, scandal led to a bitter division within its ranks. He maintained the leadership of the PARNELLITE minority through the difficult 1890s, and restored unity in 1900, heading a party committed to HOME RULE and laying more emphasis than perhaps Parnell had done, upon its achievement through the constitutional processes of the British House of Commons where he sat as MP for Waterford from 1891 to 1918. Commitment to parliamentary processes led Redmond to ignore the fact that, during the early 1900s, republicanism and the old PHYSICAL FORCE nationalism was emerging as a major political factor in Ireland, encouraged by and encouraging the spread in Gaelic revivalism which emphasized Irish distinctiveness. For Redmond, victory seemed to be within Ireland's grasp when the 1912 Home Rule Bill was introduced into the Commons, the resistance of the House of Lords having been rendered negligible by adroit legislation in 1911 (see PARLIAMENT ACT). Redmond, however, was willing to concede PARTITION (the exclusion of all or part of ULSTER from a self-governing Ireland) which was in theory anathema to doctrinaire republicanism and the emerging SINN FÉIN movement. The FIRST WORLD WAR of 1914–18 broke Redmond's influence. He had tried to take over or at least to limit the militancy of the IRISH VOLUNTEERS. In 1914 he urged those Volunteers to enlist in the British army to fight against Germany, on the grounds that a grateful Britain would hasten Home Rule through once Germany was beaten. In fact, at his WOODENBRIDGE meeting in September 1914 he appeared to present himself as the leader of the Volunteers. All he succeeded in doing was in fact splitting them, and from the anti-enlistment Volunteers emerged, after the EASTER RISING of 1916, the IRISH REPUBLICAN ARMY which did not countenance the British constitutional process. Redmond failed in his objective, saw his support in Parliament drastically cut by the successes of Sinn Féin's radical programme in 1917 and 1918, and felt himself betrayed by the British proposals for conscription in Ireland which surfaced alongside further Home Rule proposals in 1918. He was not, any more than Parnell had been, 'leader of the Irish race': but in the rarefied atmosphere of WESTMINSTER he might pass as such. His career was in many ways as tragic as that of his mentor, Parnell.

Reform Association, The Irish

The Irish Reform Association was founded in August 1904 by Windham Wyndham-Quien, Earl of Dunraven (1841–1926), former Colonial Under Secretary and a landowner in County Limerick. The Association's objective was to press for devolution for Ireland, although Dunraven thought it should be qualified, since he did not feel the Irish were yet ready for self-government. He had written on the Irish problem in 1880, and in 1897 published *The Outlook in Ireland: The Case for Devolution and Conciliation*. The Reform Association's foundation came with the dissolution of the Land Conference. Dunraven adopted a high profile in the moderate, constitutionalist cause, and was present at the IRISH CONVENTION proposed by Lloyd George in 1917 to try to arrive at a settlement of the HOME RULE issue. He sat in the Senate of the FREE STATE from 1922.

Regency Crisis, The

The Irish dimension of the Regency Crisis which erupted over the illness and insanity of King George III in the autumn of 1788, became another aspect of the assertion of legislative independence achieved in 1782 by the repeal of the DECLARATORY ACT. Given the need for a regency, the British Parliament had the choice either of the passage of a bill appointing the Prince of Wales as regent, or simply of requesting him to do so. It was a constitutional crisis with no immediate precedent to draw upon. The Prince of Wales' known predilection for the Whigs would mean that appointment by request might lead to the exercise of royal powers in favour of his political allies. The Tory government would prefer a bill by which regency powers could be limited. On 16 February 1789 GRATTAN in the Irish Commons proposed support for the idea of an 'address' requesting the prince to assume the regency, thus throwing his weight behind the Whig position. The Lords and Commons in Ireland together, on 18 February, voted to extend the invitation to the Prince. Their motive was to further emphasize their independence established in the repeal legislation of 1782 which rid them of the Declaratory Act. The LORD LIEUTENANT, however, refused to pass on the result of the vote to England. The Irish Commons censured his behaviour and appointed a delegation to convey their wishes to London. It arrived after the king had recovered his wits, and their journey was pointless.

Regium Donum

The Regium Donum was a state subsidy paid to the PRESBYTERIAN Church in Ireland. The architect was Sir Arthur Forbes (1623–96), who acted as an intermediary between the crown and the ULSTER Presbyterians during a period of unrest amongst their fellows in Scotland. The Regium Donum was also a limiting measure on the spread of Presbyterian congregations, because it was spread among the serving ministers to augment their incomes, but was a fixed sum, which meant that additional appointments would thin down the individual share of the money. In 1672, the year of institution, the sum was pegged at £600. After the JACOBITE wars of 1689–91, King WILLIAM III doubled the sum concerned, to be paid out of the customs collected in BELFAST, although later payment was transferred to the Irish Exchequer. The Regium Donum was suspended in 1714 but was revived by King George I. CASTLEREAGH used the promise of further

money to win Presbyterian support for the UNION of 1801 between Britain and Ireland. In 1792 the figure had stood at £7,700 per annum. Castlereagh doubled it, virtually, to £15,000 a year. By 1869 the sum involved was £41,000 but with the DISESTABLISHMENT of the CHURCH OF IRELAND, the Regium Donum was abolished, and instead the Presbyterian Church received compensation of £769,600 which was invested by the General Assembly Trustees, and the interest used for the ministers.

Remonstrance, The (Catholics')

In December 1661 a group of Irish OLD ENGLISH Catholics drew up an address, or Remonstrance, to King Charles II in which they declared their full obedience to him, and denied that the Pope could absolve them from that obedience. In 1661 there was still high anticipation that the king, restored to his throne in 1660, would act in such a way as to meet the grievances of the dispossessed Catholics that had suffered during the Cromwellian land settlement in the 1650s. Whatever the king's private intentions, there was no major reversal of what had been done whilst he was an exile in France (see Act of SETTLEMENT). The Catholic bishops and clergy met in DUBLIN in June 1666 to consider the wording of the Remonstrance, and modified it so as to exclude references to papal authority. The Earl of ORMOND, the LORD LEIUTENANT, rejected the address and dissolved the assembly, banishing the archbishop of Armagh. St Oliver Plunket(t)'s Synod in 1670 asserted its loyalty to the crown as well.

Remonstrant Synod

The Remonstrant Synod of the PRESBYTERIAN Church in ULSTER was formed in August 1829 as the result of a resurgence of fundamental orthodoxy within that church. During the eighteenth century a general air of tolerance towards the 'NEW LIGHT' movement had informed the attitudes of the church's leaders in the province. The early nineteenth century, however, saw a reaction to the pro-EMANCIPATION doctrines of men such as Henry Montgomery (1788–1865) who became Moderator of the General Synod of Ulster in 1818. Within weeks of his appointment, a secessionist synod had emerged, accusing him of Unitarianism and his opponents, the Trinitarians, took control of the Synod of Ulster in 1827. Montgomery and his supporters devised a Remonstrance against the activities and beliefs of their more numerous rivals, and in 1829 were obliged to develop their own Remonstrant Synod. Their departure enabled the General Synod and the anti-Montgomery seccession synod to reunite, which they did by 1840, imposing full orthodox emphasis upon the Westminster Confession of Faith, which the New Light movement of 100 years before had challenged. The creation of the Remonstrant Synod, therefore, marked a decisive split within the Presbyterian Church. The newly orthodox synod became politically conservative, committed to the UNION (which Montgomery and his supporters were not) and confrontational with the Catholic Church.

Renunciation Act *see* DECLARATORY ACT

Repeal Association, The Loyal National

The Repeal Association (the words 'Loyal National' were intended to convey its constitutional approach to repeal and its universal appeal within Ireland) was formed in April 1840 from the NATIONAL ASSOCIATION OF IRELAND formed only four months previously. The Association was DANIEL O'CONNELL's next political campaign, the objective of which was the repeal of the UNION of 1801 of Britain and Ireland, which led to the abolition of the Irish PARLIAMENT. O'Connell argued for the illegitimacy of that arrangement, and for the need to relegislate, but it was never altogether clear what he would have accepted or wanted if repeal had gone through. He may well have settled for some kind of temporary Irish Parliament effectively subordinate to WESTMINSTER, but reflective of the majority in Ireland and, therefore, predominantly Catholic. From that position it might then

be possible to move towards what BUTT and PARNELL would define as HOME RULE in later years. On the other hand, O'Connell may have settled for a concession from the British government that went only so far as to accept the need for new legislation. Catholic Church support was fully behind the movement from 1841, although it possessed its radical wing as well, the future YOUNG IRELAND revolutionaries, for whose PHYSICAL FORCE doctrines O'Connell had no sympathy, nor they for his constitutionalism. The year 1843 was launched as the Year of Repeal, with massive open-air meetings all over Ireland (except in ULSTER), but it came to a mixed end with the cancellation of the CLONTARF meeting in October at the insistence of the government. Although most of the Repeal Association's supporters accepted O'Connell's decision to pull back from the brink, the Young Irelanders later adduced the decision as part of their disenchantment with the Association's lack of progress.

Repeal Rent *see* CATHOLIC RENT

Republic of Connacht *see* RACES OF CASTLEBAR; HUMBERT

Revolt of the Towns (of 1603), The

The 'revolt of the towns' is an historiographical term to describe what was an OLD ENGLISH protest and assertion of strength after the collapse of TYRONE's rebellion in 1603. In April of that year, Catholic worship was restored in a number of towns, and LORD DEPUTY MOUNTJOY moved against them. Waterford held out for two days, Cork a little longer. DUBLIN was chosen as the chief target, where the oath of Supremacy requiring Catholics to reject papal authority, was imposed upon leading citizens. The government, particularly after Mountjoy's departure, pressed hard upon the Old English-dominated urban centres, rescinding trading rights, and seizing their customs' farm in 1613. The Old English in general took warning from the administration's reaction to the tepid 'revolt': Catholics, whether GAELIC IRISH or otherwise, were aware that they were now under siege.

Ribandmen/Ribandism *see*
RIBBONMEN

Ribbonmen (also Ribandmen)

When first formed, the Ribbonmen were so named from the red ribbon or riband which they favoured, though this later became a green ribbon. (A green ribbon had been the badge of association of the radical Levellers during the ENGLISH CIVIL WARS.) They represented a complex ideological development in the history of agrarian secret societies. Historians have identified an 'old' and a 'new' Ribbonism, the former associated with the Ulster movement and the latter with its appearance in Leinster. Catholic, and emerging from the DEFENDER tradition that had arisen to combat Protestant violence, they were anti-Protestant and nationalist. They seem to have been linked with, or to have endeavoured to organize, nascent trade unionism. Their activities show them to have been revolutionary and apocalyptic. There were distinct links with WHITEBOYISM and with the ROCKITE movements, and there is a connection between Ribbonism and the development of the revolutionary and powerful FENIAN movement of the 1860s. But much of what is known of them is inferred, though it is certain that, like the Defenders before them, they were a response to provocation. In August 1815 some 1,500 Ribbonmen were reported gathered in DERRY to attack a public house where ORANGE men and Freemasons held lodge meetings. There were disturbances in DUBLIN, Galway and Limerick in 1819/20 attributed to the movement, and in 1820 it was reported that Ribbonmen were trying to restrain the activities of the Rockites in the interest of future, organized agrarian revolt. Some Ribbonmen, like the Rockites, attached importance to the 'prophecies' of Pastorini, from whom they deduced that a great anti-Protestant uprising would take place in 1825 which would bring deliverance to the Catholics of Ireland. O'CONNELL went out of his way

to denounce them. A resurgence of Ribbonism was reported in April 1868 (the year after the Fenian rising of SIXTY-SEVEN) and associated with the assassination of a landlord at Killucan, County Westmeath, but by that time it may be that the term 'Ribbonmen' was applied indiscriminately to various groups with localized grievances expressed in violence. The June 1871 Protection of Life and Property in Certain Parts of Ireland Act (called the Westmeath Act) was directly aimed at what was reportedly Ribbon resurgence, and allowed for the indefinite suspension of habeas corpus in cases of AGRARIAN OUTRAGE. The Ribbonmen found a place in popular Irish legend in which their confrontational attitude towards Protestants was central.

Richmond Commission, The

The Royal Commission on Agriculture, called the Richmond Commission after its chairman the Duke of Richmond, was set up in August 1879 (on the eve of the LAND WAR in Ireland) to enquire into the depressed state of agriculture in the United Kingdom. It delivered its preliminary report in January 1881, at the time that the more narrowly defined BESS-BOROUGH COMMISSION presented its own recommendations. The final report of the Richmond Commission was delivered in July 1882, at the end of the first phase of the Land War. The Commission was not concerned solely with Ireland, although some of its members did go along with the Bessborough proposals (see LAND LEGISLATION). The burden of its conclusions was that there should be government funding for EMIGRATION out of Ireland for the surplus poor, organized re-settlement within Ireland, programmes for land drainage and reclamation, and the improvement of the road system. The Commission had visited Ireland in the middle of 1880 and taken evidence from accredited witnesses.

Rightboys, The

Historians regard the Rightboys as the most powerful of all the secret agrarian movements which developed in Ireland in the eighteenth century, perhaps not least because they aroused the sympathy and support of some of the gentry. They were a Munster movement, appearing first in 1785 in any strength but, according to research, had some links with an unsuccessful parliamentary candidate Sir John Colthurst. Colthurst resisted the TITHES exacted by the CHURCH OF IRELAND, and one of the primary targets of the Rightboys were tithe collectors and their agents. The anti-Tithe agitation spread across into Leinster by 1786, when the movement was at its height. There is no evidence that the Rightboys were sectarian: the Tithe issue was not a sectarian but rather an economic issue, and distinctive sectarianism (such as evidenced, for example, by the RIBBONMEN) was dependent upon identifiable Protestant groups for its origin and focus. The Rightboys gathered together the old rural grievances against high rents as well as tithes, and were indiscriminate as to religious faith in their challenge to church levies, whether for the Church of Ireland or to support Catholic priests. They were, it was said, 'poor honest Tradesmen, Farmers and Labourers' who occasioned very little physical violence and few deaths. The Tumultuous Risings Act of March 1787 was aimed at their interference with tithe collection, and rigorous policing was enforced by the Police Act of May that year. They faded away as a distinct movement after this legislation, but there were subsequent, episodic and random outbreaks of unrest attributed to them.

Rinuccini, Giovanni Battista (d. 1653)

Rinuccini, archbishop of Fermo, papal nuncio and high in the command structure of the CATHOLIC CONFEDERACY from his arrival in Ireland in October 1645, was committed above all else to the interests of the CATHOLIC CHURCH in Ireland. He allied himself with the GAELIC or OLD IRISH interest in the Supreme Council of the Confederacy and won the support of the powerful OWEN ROE O'NEILL. He effectively disrupted attempts at peace with the royalist Earl of ORMOND in 1646 and 1648 and thereby reduced the

prospects of the alliance when it did become effective after his return to Rome in February 1649. Rinuccini's task, as he understood it, was to maintain the integrity of the church in Ireland, and not to compromise its liberties through alliances with former enemies. Such alliances had to be clearly based upon recognition of the Catholic Church and guarantees for its future. Hence his bitter animosity towards MURROUGH O'BRIEN, who sought to come to terms with the Confederacy in 1648 and whose career until then was savagely anti-rebel if not primarily anti-Catholic.

Rockites

The Rockite movement carried with it a bitter memory of the excesses involved in the suppression of the UNITED IRISHMEN revolt of 1798. They were noted for their hatred of the YEOMANRY, and they combined this with a violent opposition to ORANGEISM, although, since they were largely a movement of Munster and southern Leinster, they came into little direct contact with large bodies of the Protestant enemy. But they burned Protestant churches and disrupted the activities of those evangelical Protestant missions that flourished in the euphoria of the SECOND REFORMATION of the early nineteenth century. They may be shown to fit into a millenarian tradition of peasant protest, and appear to have believed in the imminent doom of the Protestant nation. The year 1825 was held as the year for retribution and the necessary slaughter of the heretics, and there were contacts between the Rockites and the RIBBONMEN of ULSTER and Leinster. Alternatively, they were known as 'Lady Rocks' and their leaders subscribed to the name 'Captain Rock'. 'Lady Rocks' is an allusion to their adoption of female dress during their activities, less to conceal their identities, than to register their protest against the upside-down world in which they lived. The adoption of female garb by male protesters, found also in Britain as well as in Ireland, was symbolic of unease at perceived distortions in the balance of society. In October 1821 they were responsible for the killing of a chief constable of the PEACE PRESER-VATION FORCE in Munster. The failure of the millennium to come in 1825 seems to have taken the energy from the movement, which, like most such phenomena, faded.

Rowan, Archibald Hamilton (1751– 1834)

Rowan was born in London, adopted Whig political principles, and removed to County Kildare in 1784. In 1791 he joined the UNITED IRISHMEN movement, where he adopted fiercely republican ideas. In 1794 he visited revolutionary France where he talked with Robespierre and others, and impressed upon them the view that Ireland would rise in arms if a French invasion should be launched. Rowan's significance as a leader of the United Irishmen at this time was largely due to the government singling him out for prosecution with one or two others. Before arriving in France, he had escaped from Newgate Gaol in London where he had been lodged since January 1794 on a charge of sedition. From France, he went to America, where he digested his experience of revolution in France, and found himself unable to further condone revolution in Ireland. He secured a pardon from the British government and returned home in 1803. Thereafter, he was associated with reform movements on behalf of Catholics.

Royal Dublin Society, The

The 'Dublin Society for Improving Husbandry, Manufacturing, and other Useful Arts' became the 'Royal Dublin Society' in 1820 when it received the patronage of King George IV. Originally, at its foundation in June 1731 by Samuel Madden (d. 1765) and others, it was an expression of that developing association of the Protestant ASCENDANCY with 'Irishness' that produced the PATRIOTS of the Irish PARLIAMENT in the 1760s, and nurtured a form of colonial nationalism during the eighteenth century. The Society's purpose was to encourage improvements within agriculture and industrial enterprise in Ireland, and encouraged also the membership of resident landowners committed to liberal principles. By the same token, it was a strenuous critic of LANDLORD ABSENTEEISM. The Society looked to Irish initiative and to self-help to promote the economic interests of Ireland, but it had a wider field of interest as well, as its survey of 23 counties to provide a statistical estimate of the survival of the Irish language demonstrates. Royal interest had been evidenced in 1746 when the Society had received £500 from the privy purse. In 1834 it launched an Industrial Exhibition in DUBLIN, and in 1863 received the huge Joly Collection of books and manuscripts relating to the history of Ireland. It continues to function, and may be compared with the British 'Royal Society'.

Royal Irish Academy

The Irish Academy was founded in 1785 as, simply, the Irish Academy, to promote research into and the collection of materials relating to, the history and antiquities of Ireland. In a sense, it was a further expression of the colonial nationalism of eighteenth-century Ireland, but its preoccupation with the GAELIC IRISH and OLD ENGLISH Catholic past inevitably led it away from the ASCENDANCY view of that past. Our knowledge of the POPULATION of Ireland in 1790 is due to the work of the academician Gervase Bushe, who computed figures from study of the extant Hearth Tax returns, and whose findings were published by the Academy in its *Transactions*. Between 1913 and 1976 it undertook the preparation and publication of a *Dictionary of the Irish Language*.

Royal Irish Constabulary (*see also* CONSTABULARY)

The Constabulary organized and reformed by THOMAS DRUMMOND in the 1830s, acquired the prefix 'Royal' in 1867 for its efforts in the suppression of the FENIAN revolutionary uprising of that year. It was a centralized, paramilitary force which, in 1870, numbered 13,000 men in Ireland with the separate Dublin Metropolitan

Police accounting for a further 1,000. It was paid from government funds, and controlled by an Inspector General assisted by three Assistant Inspector Generals. The style of the force was to influence British colonial police forces in Africa and elsewhere. In theory the RIC should have been purged of ORANGE and other sectarian influences – that had been Drummond's intention – and the resignations of some officers in the WAR FOR INDEPENDENCE period of 1919–21 reflects a lack of uniform political attitude in the force. That said, it was seen as an instrument of British repression in Ireland quite as much as the regular army, and the BLACK AND TANS and the AUXILIARIES sent into Ireland in 1920 to fight the IRISH REPUBLICAN ARMY were sent in as support for the RIC, a move which led to a 'mutiny' amongst RIC officers at Listowell, County Kerry in June 1920 and resignations in protest against the tactics of the government.

The cost of policing in Ireland was high: in 1912, before any widespread republican military activity, it was estimated at a cost of six shillings and eight pence per head of the population of 4.3 million, whereas in the whole of England and Wales the cost was three shillings and four pence per head, in a population of 36 million.

In November 1921 the RIC in ULSTER were taken over by the new government of Northern Ireland, as part of the PARTITION leading to the creation of the FREE STATE in the south, and it became the Royal Ulster Constabulary in May 1922.

Republican animus against the RIC arose from the incidents of the SIXTY-SEVEN rising, and subsequent encounters such as the Mitchelstown Massacre of September 1887 in Cork, where RIC opened fire on an unarmed crowd. Armed RIC officers assassinated the republican Lord Mayor of Cork in March 1920. The RIC was disbanded in the Free State in August 1922.

The 'Royal Irish Republicans', an agrarian group active in County Cork in 1881, assumed their name in derision of the RIC.

Russell, Thomas (1767–1803)

Russell was an associate of the revolutionary leader ROBERT EMMET, and, for his part in the rising of 1803, was tried and hanged at Downpatrick in October of that year. Russell was a Cork man, who had been an active member of the UNITED IRISHMEN movement in the 1790s, but had been gaoled between 1796 and 1802 and so not involved in the NINETY-EIGHT rising. Russell was the link-man between Emmet's movement and potential French support, but when he quit France to join Emmet in DUBLIN on the eve of the rising, the communication with France ceased. Russell did not put much faith in French help, and seems to have spurred Emmet on to strike on their own, to secure support by initial success. He went into ULSTER to try to revive United Irishmen sympathies there, but with limited success, although he, like Emmet, expected that some direct action would lead to spontaneous risings throughout Ireland. Named a member of the provisional government of the Irish Republic in July 1803, he appealed to the 'Men of Erin' to rise in its support. Russell was captured after an attempt to get back into Dublin to rescue Emmet. Emmet's subsequent insistence that he, and he alone, was the sole instigator of the rising of 1803, intended to deflect government wrath from his associates, has subsequently tended to obscure the importance of Thomas Russell.

S

St Patrick, (Royal) College of

The devastating impact of the French revolution on Catholic seminaries in France enabled the British government to make a gesture to the Catholics of Ireland. The Act of 5 June 1795 which established St Patrick's College at Maynooth followed upon the brief and hopeful LORD LIEUTENANCY of the Earl FITWILLIAM, whose recall had made the progress towards further EMANCIPATION seem at an end. An annual grant of £8,000 was instituted, and the college opened with a complement of 10 professorships. The college thereafter served the interests of Catholic emancipation in a broad sense, for it produced an Irish-trained clergy who were able to relate closely with their subsequent parishioners, and to prove influential in such campaigns as DANIEL O'CONNELL's emancipation struggle before 1829, and the movement for repeal of the UNION of 1801. In 1845, coincidentally with the government's move for non-denominational university education, the Maynooth College Act increased the annual endowment from government to £26,000, and made a capital grant of £30,000 – which excited Protestant animosity through Britain. By 1853 it was estimated that of 2,291 parish priests working in Ireland, 1,222 had passed through the Maynooth seminary, and 23 of the 28 Catholic bishops had been educated there also. In July 1976 the college became an independent university.

Saint-Ruth, Charles Chalmont Marquis de (d. 1691)

Saint-Ruth was a Catholic nobleman who, in May 1691, arrived from France to support the JACOBITE cause in Ireland. He arrived with a reputation as a bitter enemy of the French Huguenots, and imbued his Irish campaign with something of the atmosphere of a Catholic crusade. He was killed in action at the fierce battle of AUGHRIM on 12 July 1691 below Kilcommodon Hill, and his death deprived the Irish army of victory over GINKEL's WILLIAMITE army.

Sarsfield, Patrick (d. 1693)

Sarsfield was the grandson of the rebel leader RORY O'MORE, who was instrumental in the IRISH REBELLION of 1641. After a career in the English army of King Charles II, he was associated with TYRCONNELL in the reorganization of Irish forces under King JAMES II. As commander of Irish troops in England in 1688, he went into exile with the king after the coup which put WILLIAM III on the English throne, and accompanied James II when he landed in Ireland to organize against the usurper. He swept the WILLIAMITES out of Connacht, but at the vital battle of the BOYNE he performed poorly through the disposition of the JACOBITE army. His fame in Ireland attaches to his spirited defence of Limerick. James II created him Earl of Lucan in 1691, and he fought at AUGHRIM where the French general SAINT-RUTH was killed in action on 12 July 1691. Sarsfield pushed hard for the far-ranging terms by which Limerick was surrendered to the Williamite General, GINKEL. The Treaty of LIMERICK, which attempted to protect Catholics at large, was broken by the Irish PARLIAMENT. Sarsfield, by the terms of the Treaty, took his army into France – the flight of the WILD GEESE as his departure was termed – and into French service. He died in action at the battle of Landen in 1693, fighting the Anglo-Dutch army of William III.

Satisfaction, Act of (see also BLACK BOOKS of Athlone)

The Act of Satisfaction was passed on 26 September 1653, following upon the final suppression of the GAELIC IRISH and OLD ENGLISH rebels who had waged a sustained rebellion since 1641. As the Act's title conveys, its purpose was to satisfy the expectations and entitlements of the ADVENTURERS (who had advanced money to finance the war against the rebels) and the soldiers who were to receive grants of forfeit land in lieu of pay. It enshrined the policy of transplanting native Irish from areas to be re-settled, into Connacht, as well. The counties of Waterford, Limerick, Tipperary, Queen's, King's, Meath, Westmeath, Armagh and Down were set aside to meet all the claims for land. The native Irish were commanded to leave for Connacht by 1 May 1654. Commissioners were appointed to allocate land to those thus transplanted, and in January 1654 allocations of the forfeited land were decided by lot. The removal to Connacht was unenthusiastic: the government applied constraints, such as making those reluctant to move subject to martial law (19 March 1655). In 1657 pardon was extended to all former rebels and papists who had made the prescribed removal, but they were required to be in Connacht by September of that year.

The act of Satisfaction, therefore, was concerned solely with the English government's obligations to the Adventurers and the soldiery with which it had conquered Ireland. Some 12,000 soldiers were settled on forfeited land, and of those, 7,000 or more had their titles to that land confirmed during the reign of Charles II, who, it had been hoped, would restore the expelled landowners.

Scarrifhollis, battle of

The battle of Scarrifhollis, fought near Letterkenny County Donegal on 21 June 1650, saw the defeat of the CATHOLIC CONFEDERACY army commanded by Heber MacMahon bishop of CLOGHER, by government troops under the veteran Sir CHARLES COOTE. Clogher was despatched to DERRY where he was hanged, and there were numerous killings after the surrender of the Irish forces.

Schomberg, Frederick Herman, 2nd Duke of (1615–90)

Schomberg was born in northern Germany, but his mother was English. His career was wholly military, serving during the Thirty Years War in Europe, and acting as Gentleman of the Chamber to the Protestant William II of Orange in 1645. He was given an English lordship by Charles II, and served for a time as a commander under Prince Rupert in 1673. In 1687 he was Commander-in-Chief of the armies of the Protestant Elector of Brandenburg, and amongst those who accompanied WILLIAM III to England in 1688 to seize the throne from King JAMES II. He commanded the army which set off for Ireland from England and landed near Bangor, on 13 August 1689. He took Carrickfergus Castle on 28 August, where he showed remarkable leniency towards the enemy. He was killed in action at the battle of the BOYNE in 1690.

Second Reformation

The term is applied to an explosion of Protestant religious fervour, particularly in the missionary field, in the early and mid-nineteenth century. In Irish terms it is recognized in the proliferation of societies (such as the HIBERNIAN BIBLE SOCIETY and the Irish Evangelical society) which, through educational programmes and the distribution of tracts, attempted to wean away Catholics from their ancient faith. There was also a concomitant development of missionary work from within the CHURCH OF IRELAND. Half-hearted attempts at converting Catholics had been made in the eighteenth century, but it did not become a pressing matter until, through EMANCIPATION, they became politically active. Thus the missionary movements, despite an origin in profound religious revival, were a cynical attempt to defuse the perceived threat posed by Catholic resurgence. They met the unequivocal opposition of a progressively Irish-trained priesthood and hierarchy (see ST PATRICK'S COLLEGE) and made little headway.

Seneschals

The Seneschal was an official of 'manorial courts' which, like much else in Irish local administration, was introduced into Ireland during the sixteenth and seventeenth centuries, although Ireland was never manorialized to the extent that England was. Irish manors were, for the most part, created by royal patents directed to specific named individuals which created organs of local administration presided over by manorial courts. The Seneschals selected the juries of the courts, which in their turn appointed parish officers such as the constable. The English equivalent of the seneschal would have been the bailiff of the court.

Servitors

The servitors were ordinarily army veterans who had a share in the distribution of lands in ULSTER following the PLANTATION plans of the early seventeenth century. Their allocations were primarily in counties Donegal, Tyrone and Fermanagh. They were permitted some discretion in the number of native Irish tenants which they retained upon their new lands.

Settlement, Act of

The Act of Settlement of 31 July 1662 gave the force of law to Charles II's DECLARATION of 1660, touching the matter of the lands seized and redistributed by the government in the 1650s. By the terms of the new Act, all lands confiscated in Ireland since 23 October 1641 were deemed to be vested in the crown as trustee pending resolution of rival claims. The date reflected the outbreak of the IRISH REBELLION. The crown had an interest in the land problem, because of the way in which the English Parliament of 1642 – on the eve of civil war (see ENGLISH CIVIL WAR) against King Charles I – had taken it upon itself to dispose of forfeited lands without reference to the king, whose perquisite it was to control rebel lands and oversee their disposal. The Act of Settlement made provision to confirm the claims of ADVENTURERS (those who had advanced money to finance the war effort against the rebels) and soldiers whose grants pre-dated 7 May 1659; to look at the problem of arrears due to royalist soldiers of the Earl of ORMOND incurred before June 1649; and to consider the claims of the expropriated Catholics and Protestant royalists,

whether GAELIC IRISH, OLD ENGLISH or, more rarely, NEW ENGLISH. A Court of Claims was set up with seven commissioners to hear cases involving the last group, and to arrange for the compensation of present holders of lands that were to be restored to their original owners.

The Act in fact incorporated within it a degree of anti-Catholic policy. A classification of 'innocents' was applied to those who had had no part in the Irish Rebellion, but had suffered by association. Theoretically they were to be admitted to their forfeited lands without delay – the new holders would be simply expelled in their turn. But if, as happened, the 'innocents' possessed land in boroughs, they were not to be reinstated at all, but to be found equivalent acreage beyond the boundaries of the town.

The Act was not efficacious. Its court of claims sat for barely eight of the 12 months it was intended to sit, and preoccupied itself with sifting appeals from 'innocents'. Only 700 or so claims were allowed, and one-fifth of those were Protestant. There was some corruption – some known rebels were reinstated, often with the backing of powerful advocates in England and Ireland. After three years of inadequate revision, the Act of EXPLANATION was required which sought to simplify matters by confiscating a straight third part of the forfeited lands for restitution.

The PATRIOT PARLIAMENT of 1689, summoned by King JAMES II to support him in his struggle against WILLIAM III, repealed the Act of Settlement amongst other legislation intended to assert Irish legislative independence. They intended a thorough redistribution of the land, such as the 1662 Act had not contemplated, in favour of the Catholics and, specifically, of the Old English. But that Parliament did not survive long enough to achieve its objectives. In consequence, the Cromwellian land settlement remained, largely unaltered.

Settling of Ireland, Act for (*see also* SATISFACTION, Act of)

The Act for the Settling of Ireland passed in the English Parliament on 12 August 1652, should be seen as a preliminary measure preparing the way for the Act of SATISFACTION of 1653 which redistributed forfeited and seized land. The 1652 Act categorized the Irish in terms of their involvement with the CATHOLIC CON-FEDERACY during the IRISH REBELLION of 1641–53, and was intended to make ready for the allocation of lands to satisfy the ADVENTURERS who had financed the war effort against the rebels. Pardon was denied to those who had been in arms before the creation of the Confederacy at Kilkenny; those who were Catholic priests and had been involved in the rebellion; those who had slaughtered civilians or, being themselves civilians, had killed soldiers; and all those still in arms against the government who did not render themselves before 28 days had expired from publication of the Act. There were some specific exceptions from pardon, including the rebel leader RORY O'MORE, and the royalists ORMOND and CLANRICARDE.

Seven Ill Years, The

The Seven Ill Years began with the summer of 1695 in Scotland, and the term refers to a sequence of bad harvests and bitterly cold winters which gave a great incentive to renewed Scottish emigration into ULSTER. For the most part this meant an expansion in the numbers of the PRESBYTERIAN community in Ulster.

Shakers *see* CARDERS

Shan Van Vocht/Sean Bhean Bhocht

In Irish tradition, the Shan Van Vocht was a euphemism for 'Mother Ireland', who in popular imagery and song has long been represented as a 'Fine Old Woman'. It became the title of a radical feminist journal founded in 1896 by the biographer of WOLFE TONE, Alice Milligan (d. 1953). It was linked to the revolutionary movement INGHINIDHE NA HÉIREANN.

Shanavests *see* CARAVATS and SHANAVESTS

Sheehy, Father Nicholas (1728–66)

Father Sheehy was the victim of government repression of the WHITEBOY movement which the authorities chose to see as evidence of French designs upon Ireland. In February 1766 Father Sheehy, accused of complicity in Whiteboy activism, was tried in DUBLIN where the jury acquitted him. He was removed to Clonmel in County Tipperary, where a rigged jury found him guilty of treason and he was hanged on 15 March 1766. His executioner was identified and stoned to death in Philipstown, King's County, in September 1770 by an angry peasant crowd.

Shinners

Shinners was British army slang for the SINN FÉIN movement during the period 1917–21, but it could also be applied indiscriminately to any Irish supporting self-government.

Shoneen/Séoinín

The Gaelic phrase literally translates as 'little Johnny', and was a pejorative term applied to the members of the British administration in Ireland centred upon the CASTLE, and to their supporters amongst the Protestant ASCENDANCY.

Shrule, County Mayo

Shrule was the scene of a massacre, on 16 February 1642, of Protestant settlers by forces of the CATHOLIC CONFEDERACY which had emerged from the IRISH REBELL-ION begun in October 1641. The Protestants were theoretically under the protection of Viscount Mayo. The Catholic commander present was Edward or Edmund Burke of Connacht.

Sidney, Henry 1st Viscount (1641–1704)

Henry Sidney, created Viscount in 1689 by a grateful WILLIAM III and, five years later, Earl of Romney, was a prime mover in the intrigues which overthrew King JAMES II in 1688. He was a younger brother of the English republican Algernon

Sidney (d. 1683). He served in the Dutch armies and established good relations with William of Orange, and it was through Sidney that the offer of the throne was made to the Dutch prince. Sidney fought at the BOYNE in July 1690, in which year he was appointed LORD JUSTICE to govern Ireland alongside Thomas Coningsby. In March 1692 he secured office as LORD LIEUTENANT, but his experience in Ireland was not happy. He was amazed by the attitudes of the dominant Protestant majority, complaining at the dominance of England in Irish affairs, and was forced to dissolve the Irish PARLIAMENT in face of its reaction to the Treaty of LIMERICK which had ended the JACOBITE wars with considerable leniency towards Catholics. Sidney left Ireland in 1693.

Siege of Saunders' Fort

The 'Siege of Saunders' Fort' was an incident of the LAND WAR of the 1880s, and highlighted the grievance of EVICTION. Between 20 and 27 August 1886, some 20 men and women resisted all attempts by 700 police and companies of British troops to enforce eviction orders on Thomas Saunders at Woodford, County Galway. The evicting landlord, Clanricard, became the target of the national compaigners including WILLIAM O'BRIEN, who rallied the tenancy to withhold their rents, and then offered them at a discount) to Clanricard on the understanding that he would reinstate the evicted. O'Brien's experience in the Galway evictions helped formulate the PLAN OF CAMPAIGN, a massive programme for rent strikes as a weapon against the landlord interest.

Sinn Féin

The English translation of the name Sinn Féin is ordinarily given as 'Ourselves' or 'Ourselves Alone'. It was a political party founded to pursue the achievement of an Irish Republic, and, despite varying electoral performance, remains the only Irish political party dedicated to the reunification of Ireland and the ending of the PARTITION imposed in 1921. ARTHUR GRIFFITHS enunciated the policy that was

to be that of Sinn Féin, in November 1905, and it was an associate, Maire Butler, who summed up that policy in the words 'Sinn Féin'. 'The people of Ireland are a free people and no law made without their authority or consent is, or can ever be, binding on their conscience'. On 21 April 1907 the Sinn Féin League emerged from the DUNGANNON CLUBS and CUMANN NA NGAEDHEAL and from 1908 the word 'League' was dropped. It was essentially a PARNELLITE movement as Griffiths conceived it, committed to change through electoral success. It fought its first by-election in February 1908, when former nationalist MP Charles Dolan was defeated by another nationalist, when he stood on the Sinn Féin ticket. There is no doubt that some of the IRISH PARLIAMENTARY PARTY or HOME RULE PARTY looked with interest upon the new party, but it could only become a threat to them if the movement towards Home Rule should fail. It failed in 1914, when REDMOND and the nationalists agreed to the shelving of legislation for the duration of the FIRST WORLD WAR, and campaigned for Irish support for the British war effort. The EASTER RISING of 1916 and, more particularly, the brutal British response, gave to Sinn Féin political capital; as Redmond warned in the House of Commons, the executions would also alienate those who had no sympathy with the ideals of the rebels. What actually happened was more than that: the ideals of the rebels, came to be seen in contrast with the realities of British rule, and appeared preferable. On 5 February 1917 the father of a dead rebel of Easter Week, was returned as Sinn Féin MP for North Roscommon in a by-election, breaking the constitutional nationalist grip on the constituency. The same thing happened in May in South Longford, and in Kilkenny city in August. At the tenth Sinn Féin conference in DUBLIN in October 1917, EAMON DE VALERA was elected President. The attempt by the British government to introduce conscription into Ireland in 1918 gave Sinn Féin a ready-made campaign, in which opposition to British rule merged with pro-Germanism. In May 1918 the LORD LIEUTENANT made a further political mistake in arresting Sinn

Féin's leadership on the grounds of a spurious GERMAN PLOT in which they were supposed to be involved. In the General Election in December 1918 the new party swept away the old constitutional nationalists of Redmond, who kept six seats against Sinn Féin's 73. The destruction of the constitutional movement was thus accomplished. All Sinn Féin candidates stood and were elected on the understanding that they would not sit at WESTMINSTER, and in January 1919 they organized the first DÁIL ÉIREANN. Due to electoral reform in February 1918 (Representation of the People Act) the franchise had been extended to all Irish males aged 21 or over, and to most women of the age of 30 or more. This, and the fact that membership of Sinn Féin stood at more than a quarter of a million in 1918, meant that its support was massive and widespread. They took 48 per cent of the total vote in Ireland in the General Election, and some 65 per cent in the counties that were to form the FREE STATE in 1921. In the local government elections in January 1920, the party took 172 of the available 206 boroughs and urban councils. Sinn Féin supported the IRISH REPUBLICAN ARMY during the WAR FOR INDEPENDENCE of 1919–21, and it was with representatives of the party in the Dáil that the British negotiated in 1920 leading to the ANGLO-IRISH TREATY and the creation of the Free State. Sinn Féin, like the IRA, split over the failure to achieve full republican status for Ireland, and the Partition which left a separate state of Northern Ireland in the SIX COUNTIES. In the Free State General Election of June 1922, the anti-Treaty Sinn Féin candidates won 36 seats, the pro-Treaty 58. Other parties took 34. By the time of the 1927 General Election, Sinn Féin's fortunes were in decline. As a doctrinaire republican party, it secured only 5 seats.

Sinn Féin's triumph in the period from 1916 to 1921 was due to the fact that it exactly caught the mood of the Irish people, and appealed to the Irish conscience. Because it was a political party, the propensity to split over the crucial issue of the Treaty of 1921 and its implications, was unavoidable. Although subsequent Irish parties have continued to claim commitment to reunification, Sinn Féin alone has remained consistent in its lack of equivocation on the matter.

Six Counties, The

The Six Counties which form 'Northern Ireland', the separate state established as part of the agreement between the British government and representatives of DÁIL ÉIREANN in 1920/1, are Antrim, Armagh, DERRY, Down, Fermanagh and Tyrone. They form a part of the ancient province of ULSTER, which had nine counties. The three contained within the FREE STATE (the present Irish Republic) are Cavan, Monaghan and Donegal. The use of the term 'six counties' conveys political belief. Those who regard Ulster as partitioned, and regard Ireland as partitioned, would allude to the state of Northern Ireland as 'the six counties': similarly, they would not equate Northern Ireland with Ulster because one-third of the ancient province is divided from it.

Sixth of George I *see* DECLARATORY ACT (of 1720)

Sixty-Seven, The (Rising of)

The FENIAN insurrection in Ireland, aimed at overthrowing British rule and establishing an Irish Republic, was long in the preparation. The planning was carried on in America, where the Fenian movement was divided over the wisdom of an Irish rising: some favouring attacks on British power through Canada. The outbreak of the American Civil War entailed postponement, and many Fenians learnt the trade of arms fighting, predominantly for the North, during that war. The end of the war in 1865 made an Irish rising a pressing issue, with hundreds of ex-soldiers available for service. JAMES STEPHENS, the leader of the movement, procrastinated as to the date to be chosen, and was replaced by Colonel Thomas Kelly who left for Ireland to prepare for insurrection. By 1867 there were some 80,000 Fenians in the United Kingdom, offering the chance of a war on two fronts, in Ireland and in England. The nominal commander of the Fenian forces was to be Gustave Cluseret, a French veteran of the American Civil War.

The scheduled date for the rising was to be the night of 11/12 February 1867, but it was postponed to 5 March. On the eve of the original date, an attack on the arsenal at Chester was betrayed by spies and thwarted. The Fenian commander, John McCafferty, was arrested in DUBLIN. Colonel John O'Connor kept to the February date and led a rising in County Kerry. But the bulk of the action centred around the 5 March. The main area of action was to be Dublin, Cork, Tipperary and Limerick. There were battles at Glencullen and at Tallaght near Dublin, and at Limerick and Kilmallock, 'the hottest fight of all'. Peter Crowley was shot dead by a British soldier in Kilcloney Wood on 31 March 1867. In May a shipload of arms was landed in Sligo Bay, sent from America aboard the *Erin's Hope*. The rising disintegrated rapidly into localized, sometimes heroic, attempts by handfuls of men. Colonel Kelly was apprehended in Manchester in September 1867. A virtual one-man war was waged by Captain William Mackey Lomasney, who seized weapons in Cork in November, and went on the run until he was taken in a shoot-out in Market Street, Cork, in February 1868.

If the Fenian rising achieved anything, it may have forced a shift in British public opinion towards resolution of the Irish problem. But it did more than that, for the Sixty-Seven passed into nationalist and republican lore, a further inspiration to add to those of 1848, 1803 and 1798.

Skirmishing Fund

The Skirmishing Fund was founded in America in March 1876 by former FENIAN activist O'DONOVAN ROSSA, to provide fund-raising organization. Money raised by the fund financed the DYNAMITE WAR in Britain.

Smashing of the Van, The

'The Smashing of the Van' was how an incident of the FENIAN uprising of 1867 was to be remembered in Irish nationalist lore. In September 1867 Colonel Thomas Kelly and Captain Deasy had been apprehended in Manchester, and their rescue was planned by Colonel Richard O'Sullivan Burke. On 18 September O'Sullivan Burke's men attacked the police van transporting the prisoners, and blew the doors, in the process of which a police sergeant was killed. In October William Allen, Michael Larkin and Michael O'Brien were arraigned for the man's murder, convicted on 1 November, and hanged on 23 November. They became the 'Manchester Martyrs', celebrated in republican circles and the subject of numerous ballads, reflecting their demeanour upon the scaffold. The song 'God Save Ireland', which rapidly assumed the role of an anthem, was in honour of them. Some 60,000 mourners followed their funeral in DUBLIN in December, and 10 years later PARNELL would publicly defend their memory in the House of Commons.

Solemn League and Covenant

The Solemn League and Covenant, signed throughout ULSTER on 28 September 1912, was modelled upon a similar document of defiance, the Scottish National Covenant of 1638, drafted to illustrate Scottish PRESBYTERIAN hostility to reforms in the Scottish church proposed by King Charles I. That of 1912 was also intended to demonstrate to the British government, if they were not already aware of it, the hostility felt in Ulster towards the HOME RULE proposals that the government intended to push through by 1914. On the day in question, some 237,300 men appended their signatures to the Covenant, and some 234,000 women signed a separate document. The CHURCH OF IRELAND gave the act its blessing by officiating alongside Presbyterians at the ceremony in BELFAST. The burden of the Covenant was that the signatories pledged themselves to do whatever should be deemed necessary to defeat the imposition of Home Rule upon them. Historians have seen it as the last defiant gesture of the Protestant ASCENDANCY, and have remarked, too, upon the cross-class profile of the signatories. The Covenant has to be seen in the context of a long sustained campaign by the Unionists against Home Rule, but it ushered in an intensification of activity symbolized by the formation of the ULSTER VOLUNTEER FORCE.

Soloheadbeg Incident, The

The fight at Soloheadbeg, County Tipperary, was the first engagement of the WAR FOR INDEPENDENCE waged by the IRISH REPUBLICAN ARMY against British authority in Ireland. An IRA unit led by Séamus Robinson, Dan Breen and Séan Treacy, attacked an explosives convoy guard by the ROYAL IRISH CONSTABULARY. The police were defeated, two of their number killed.

Sons of Freedom

The Sons of Freedom was a name adopted by RIBBONMEN in Leinster in and around 1838. They were an intensely anti-Protestant movement, somewhat more sectarian than their Ribbonmen counterparts in ULSTER.

Sons of the Shamrock

The name was used of and by RIBBONMEN in the 1820s, particularly in ULSTER. Other names adopted by this radical anti-Protestant movement were 'Society of St Patrick', and 'Patriotic Association of the Shamrock' and 'Brotherhood of St Patrick'.

Soup Kitchen Act *see* FAMINE RELIEF

Spailpín

Anglicized as 'spalpeen', the term meant a migrant agricultural labourer, a crucially important element in the Irish rural economy. In 1841, for example, some 3 per cent of the entire population of Mayo would leave to find work in harvest time in Britain. They were usually marginal farmers or labourers needing the income from abroad to support their families over the winter months. There was much spalpeen involvement in the CARAVAT movement, a class-based agrarian group which came to prominence in the early nineteenth century in FEUD with the SHANAVESTS.

Stanley Letter, The

The 'letter' took its name from Edward Smith-Stanley, CHIEF SECRETARY in Ireland from 1830 to 1833 and later the 14th Earl of Derby, and Prime Minister in 1852, 1858/9 and 1866–68. In September 1831 in the House of Commons Stanley moved successfully that a grant of £30,000 be made available to the LORD LIEUTENANT to be expended on a 'national system' of education for Ireland. The principles behind that system were laid down by Stanley in a letter to the Duke of Leinster, upon which he was working in October and November of 1831. Stanley's innovation was dramatic. A full 40 years before any such system was attempted in Britain, he created a system of education funded by central government, with salaried teaching staff appointed by local 'boards of governors' and uniform issue of text books. He aimed to meet the avidity of the Irish for learning, and to avoid even the taint of Protestant missionary zeal that had marred the KILDARE PLACE SOCIETY and other educational programmes. In consequence, he aroused the suspicion both of the CHURCH OF IRELAND and of the PRESBYTERIANS. In the end, his non-denominational schools were effectively denominational by choice. Stanley wanted to provide denominational religious education, but in all other respects have Protestant and Catholic mix together and be taught together. The very principle of localized control worked against this, for the leading figures in most communities were either clergy or of distinct religious persuasion. Thus their appointments reflected their views. Presbyterian reaction in places degenerated into arson attacks on school buildings and the physical intimidation of teachers not of their persuasion. Nonetheless, the Stanley letter was an insight into the workings of a reformer's mind who was ahead of his time in his own country, and attempting to apply to Ireland a function for education for which Ireland was not suited.

Star Chamber

The Prevention of Crimes Act of 16 July 1882 gave to the ROYAL IRISH CONSTABULARY and the Dublin Metropolitan Police power to summon and to question under oath, and to take depositions from any person as often and whenever they chose to do so. The system was employed to break the INVINCIBLES movement implicated in the PHOENIX PARK assassinations of the CHIEF SECRETARY and the Under Secretary. The powers of the police were referred to as the 'Star Chamber', because, as in the seventeenth-century court of Star Chamber, they were used to harass suspects, and there was no remedy for their abuse.

Starvation, The Great *see* FAMINE of 1845–49

Steelboys/Hearts of Steel

The Steelboys were an ULSTER agrarian movement of strongly PRESBYTERIAN character which developed in southern Antrim around 1769. Their targets were initially the heavy fines demanded for renewal of leases on the estates of Lord Donegal, and the evictions that were enforced when the fines were not met. On Christmas Eve of 1770 some 1,200 farmers styling themselves the 'hearts of steel' marched on BELFAST to protest against evictions, and were met by the military, who opened fire on them, killing several. In January 1771 a proclamation against the spreading unrest was issued by Viscount Townshend, the LORD LIEUTENANT. Legislation followed in March 1772 when the government passed an act to cover five of the Ulster counties to repress Steelboy outbreaks. By 1774 it was considered safe to repeal it. As it spread, the Steelboy movement encompassed protests against TITHES and high rents, so that it adopted a broad programme for reform which rested upon avowals of loyalty and a radical Presbyterianism that later manifested itself in the VOLUNTEERS and UNITED IRISHMEN.

Stephens, James (1825–1901)

Stephens was a civil engineer by profession, and came from County Kilkenny. He was involved with REPEAL ASSOCIATION politics when he joined the YOUNG IRELAND movement of revolutionary nationalists, and by 1848 was amongst its leadership. Following the failure of their rising in 1848, he fled to France. Convinced of the potential for a successful rising against the British, Stephens was instrumental in the foundation of the IRISH REPUBLICAN BROTHERHOOD in 1858, and established contacts with the FENIAN movement in America, where he raised funds for the cause of insurrection. The American Civil War deferred revolutionary action, although the date of September 1865 was fixed upon. In 1862 he wrote *On the Future of Ireland*. Stephens' authority over the proposed revolt was conditional, and when he postponed action in 1866, he was deposed by MEAGHER and Thomas Kelly, who engineered the SIXTY-SEVEN rising without him. Stephens went into France and remained there in exile until 1891, when he returned to Ireland and lapsed into retirement.

Survey and Distribution, Books of

The Books of Survey and Distribution were compiled to record the holders of forfeited and expropriated lands allocated during the Cromwellian land settlement of the 1650s, which followed the suppression of the IRISH REBELLION of 1641–53 and the suppression of the Irish royalists. They showed the holders as they were prior to the 1650s, and the holders at the restoration of King Charles II in 1660. The restoration was expected to usher in a general redistribution of land (see Act of SETTLEMENT), although it was neither so widespread nor so thorough as the dispossessed had hoped for. The books show how few of those who received grants of lands actually made any use of them, preferring to sell on to speculators.

Swift, Jonathan (1667–1745)

Swift was educated in Ireland, and passed through TRINITY COLLEGE. He was ordained in 1694, by which time he had been involved in efforts to secure a fixed term Parliament – a triennial Parliament – from King WILLIAM III. In 1704 he published the *Battle of the Books* and *Tale of a Tub*, which was an attack on religious hypocrisy and theological pedantry. By then he was Prebendary of St Patrick's, DUBLIN, and a Doctor of Divinity. In 1708 he launched an attack on the Irish PRESBYTERIANS in his *Letter on the Sacramental Test* which also signalled his disenchantment with Whig politics, against which he wrote vigorously in London papers. He became Dean of St Patrick's in 1713 – he is thus ordinarily referred to as 'Dean Swift' – and from 1715 was ordinarily resident in Ireland, although his contempt for the Catholic Irish was barely concealed. Nevertheless, he saw in their treatment a weapon for his Tory political armoury. In 1724 he launched the famous DRAPIER'S LETTERS attack on the patent for WOOD'S HALF-PENCE. He signally failed to interest Prime Minister Walpole in Irish conditions, and, after the publication of *Gulliver's Travels* in 1726, brought into print his *A Short View of the State of Ireland*. This work links with his much earlier (1701) piece, *A Discourse of the Contests and Dissensions between the Nobles and the Commons in Athens and Rome* which was an attack upon the way in which Irish land was granted to the favourites of William III, especially his Dutch associates. His *Short View* dealt with the desperate poverty of Ireland. Swift was a polemicist rather than a political theorist, and he did not long associate with any political grouping, partly, it seems, from personal pique. His importance is largely posthumous: much of his published work was anonymous.

Swordsmen

The Swordsmen appear to have occupied a place in Gaelic society that distinguished them from the GALLOGLASS and from the KERNS, although it may also be that English observers implied a distinction that was not actual. They were armed followers of GAELIC IRISH chiefs who continued to flourish after the suppression of the TYRONE revolt in 1603 at MELLIFONT. In 1609 there were reckoned to be 12,000 of them in the country at large, and CHICHESTER planned to ship them out of Ireland to serve in European armies. Three ships loaded with Swordsmen were sent into Sweden that year. There was still a strong presence in Ireland as late as 1631, when similar proposals were made but not followed up. Thus the Swordsmen, or what was left of them, finally disappeared in the IRISH REBELLION of 1641–53.

T

Tandy, James Napper (1740–1803)

Tandy was Protestant by religion, a tradesman by occupation, and, from the early 1770s embarked upon a radical political career that was further inspired by the AMERICAN WAR FOR INDEPENDENCE. He joined the VOLUNTEER movement, organized an ostentatious parade of its artillery in DUBLIN in November 1783, and was active in 1784 in promoting reform measures through the Irish PARLIAMENT, although these came to nothing because of their extra-parliamentary origin. A national congress was organized for October 1784 in Dublin to draft a reform programme, in which Tandy was prominent, but this, too, ended in failure. The French Revolution fired Tandy's enthusiasm again: in 1792 he was a member of the UNITED IRISHMEN republican movement, and behind the call of the United society of December for the formation of a new Volunteer or National Guard movement. He was accused of involvement with the Catholic militants of the DEFENDER movement, and of taking proscribed oaths of association, and so fled to France, by way of America. In France he gave the impression of being the leading figure in the United Irishmen plans for a seaborne invasion to back rebellion, and this brought him into conflict with WOLFE TONE, to whom the French accorded most credit. He became a close associate of ARTHUR O'CONNOR, and the rift within the Irish group in France deepened, not least because of Tone's contempt for his opponents. Tandy led an invasion of Ireland in 1798 by 200 Irishmen and some 80 or so French artillery officers, which was intended to link up with the force under the command of HUMBERT, and support the native rebellion of that year. The Irish leaders were intended to assume control of forces in ULSTER. The ship, the *Anacreon*, landed at Rutland Island, County Donegal in September, where they learned of the defeat suffered by Humbert's expedition. The enthusiasm of the peasantry was insufficient to persuade Tandy to remain, and the invaders put off rapidly. He was later seized in Hamburg in circumstances of extremely doubtful legality, and returned to Ireland where he was tried in 1800 for treason.

Tanistry

In the early part of 1608 the Court of King's Bench pronounced 'tanistry' to be illegal in Ireland. Ten years before, the administration had charged rebel leaders in ULSTER with an attempt to bring the whole country back to obedience to 'the tanist law'. Tanistry was the doctrine of elective succession, by which, during the lifetime of a king or chief, his successor would be determined upon from amongst his kin. The system is integral to the Tuath, which was a tribal unit of land, of anything up to 400 square miles in extent. Within the territory, leadership was devoid of customary rights of inheritance in the possession of the land. It was the basis of native Gaelic society, promoting extended kinship links over land held in common, a tiny portion of which only was held by the chief by hereditary right. It is unlikely that TYRONE, in his rebellion which ended in 1603 and hastened suppression of Gaelic survivals such as Tanistry, aimed at anything like its resurgence. The point about the earl was, that he accepted the process of ANGLICIZATION (as in the case of his title of earl as against 'THE O'NEILL') where it strengthened his position, and he accepted English law where it underwrote his authority. Tanistry was a challenge to him rather than an asset.

Tate Expedition, The

William Tate was an aged American sea captain who became involved in the French plans to support the UNITED

IRISHMEN rising in Ireland to throw off British rule. He has been described as 'a sophisticated pirate' by one historian of the period. Tate was to sail for the west coast of England with a force of 1,000 or so ruffians from French gaols, descend upon Bristol, and then make for DUBLIN. On 22 February 1797 the expedition landed in Pembrokeshire thanks to contrary winds, Tate and his men went ashore, and the French commander, Castagnier, put back to sea immediately. Tate surrendered on 23 February, having found his situation quite impossible. The British government shipped the captured French back home, much to the alarm of the French authorities. Most of them ended up in the prisons they had come from.

Teachta Dála (TD)

The Irish equivalent of MP and meaning a member of DÁIL ÉIREANN, the Irish PARLIAMENT, founded by SINN FÉIN following its spectacular election results in the General Election of 1918.

Teague-Land

The term 'teague-land' was English slang for Ireland that became prevalent during the late seventeenth century, at a time of increasing anti-Irish feeling. The expression is found, for example, in the racist pamphlet *Bog Witticisms* of 1687 (which ran into several further editions). Teague is the anglicized form of 'Tadhg', used by the Irish of themselves, and meaning, loosely, 'Irishman'.

Tenant League, The

The national Tenant League organization was founded as a consequence of the proliferation of localized tenant societies in the late 1840s, such as that established in September 1847 by FINTAN LALOR in County Tipperary. A similar group emerged in Callan, County Kilkenny in October 1849, and by 1850 there were 20 or so such groups throughout Ireland, all sharing the same objective of securing realistic rents from landlords by arbitration, and representative of respectable farmers. In August 1850 an umbrella

organization, the Tenant League, was formed by CHARLES DUFFY and FREDERICK LUCAS (amongst others) to co-ordinate efforts towards legislative involvement in the rent issue. Their organization also came to be referred to as the 'League of North and South' because of their emphasis upon the extension of ULSTER CUSTOM to the rest of Ireland, perhaps through legislative enactment of its 'tenant-right' principles. The Tenant League was the first extra-parliamentary party in Ireland which sought to influence MPs to espouse its objectives at WESTMINSTER, and by so doing was instrumental in bringing down an unsympathetic ministry. Following the General Election of July 1852, the League convened a conference in DUBLIN in September, at which Liberal MPs undertook not to co-operate with the government unless there were guarantees of action to meet the tenants' case. Those MPs were instrumental in the overthrow of Lord Derby's government in December, which was replaced by a ministry headed by Lord Aberdeen. Thereupon the united front in the Commons broke, and two Tenant League MPs defected to Aberdeen's ministry, and the League's grouping in the Commons broke down. By this time, however, the unity of the League itself was in doubt, as Protestant Ulster supporters began to back away from developing Catholic politicization manifested by the influence of Duffy and others.

The idea of the 'tenant league' remained within Irish politics, because the issues which it had addressed remained potent. In 1869 ISAAC BUTT founded an Irish Tenant League in Tipperary, and between 1875 and 1878 at least 30 Tenants' Defence Associations sprang up especially in Munster and the counties of Dublin, Kilkenny, and Louth in Leinster. Tenant issues became subsumed within the LAND WAR of 1879–82 (see also, IRISH BRIGADE; IRISH PARLIAMENTARY PARTY).

Tenant Protection Societies *see* TENANT LEAGUE

Terry Alts

The Terry Alts were a rural secret society which arose over the issue of TITHES, and is evidenced in Counties Clare, Limerick, Galway and Westmeath between 1829 and 1832. They interfered with tithe collection, and attempted to organize resistance to assessment. There was little violence associated with them, no specific legislation aimed at them, and they disappeared during the Tithe Wars of the 1830s.

Test Act

The Test Act, a matter of grievance for PRESBYTERIANS and other non-conformists in Ireland, is associated inseparably with the Act to Prevent the Further Growth of Popery of 1704 (see PENAL LAWS), which imposed the sacramental test upon candidates for public office. That is, they were required to take the sacraments of the CHURCH OF IRELAND and to show themselves to be communicants of that church. The first such 'test' had been applied in an act of March 1673 in England. The 1704 Act did not prevent Presbyterians and DISSENTERS from voting or sitting as MPs, but it did deny them, as it denied Catholics, civil and military office. This aspect of the 1704 Act was repealed, in favour of Dissenters only, in May 1780 (the English Act was repealed in 1828). The 'test act' represented the hostility of the Church of Ireland towards Protestant dissent, and is therefore an indication of the church's power in Ireland in 1704.

Thorough or Rule of Thorough

The term 'thorough' encapsulates the policy of THOMAS WENTWORTH in his capacity as LORD DEPUTY in Ireland from 1633 to 1641: 'Thorough government' he said, was needed, 'to make every Irishman a loyal and prosperous English citizen'. Upon his arrival in Ireland the most pressing need was to finance administration and balance the Irish budget. He perceived that Ireland had the means to fund itself, and thereby to make his rule there independent of reliance upon the goodwill of interest groups such as the NEW ENGLISH and the OLD ENGLISH, divided as they were by religious faith, and pursuing divergent objectives. He developed a particular dislike for the self-evident self-interest of the New English – 'a company of men the most intent upon their own interests that ever I met with'. The purpose of 'thorough' was, therefore, to make the office of Chief Governor independent of such narrow interests, and moreover, to eliminate the influence of those interests in the government of Ireland. If he could do it, he meant to use the divergent interest groups against each other, and Wentworth was fortunate in enjoying the explicit confidence of King Charles I. This meant that, given also the lack of a Parliament in England, he could work without interference from home, and confident in the knowledge that his critics in Ireland could not get at him through sympathetic ears in England. The threat to 'thorough' would come from pursuing it in such a way as to unite disparate tendencies against him and his administration, and there was also the risk that the policy, if not pursued effectively in England or in Scotland, would of itself fail. 'Thorough' was the policy of a crown appointee determined to increase the power and independence of the crown. Any decisive challenge to it anywhere – as in Scotland in 1638 – was the major risk it ran. Once Charles I was forced by events to deal with an English Parliament, as happened in 1640, the power upon which 'thorough' rested was weakened.

Three Fs, The

The Three Fs were a fair rent, a fair sale and fixity of tenure. On 21 January 1881, 20,000 ULSTER farmers signed a memorial to demand legislation. The demands were the requirements of the more substantial farmers in Ireland. They became a major issue during the crisis of the LAND WAR of 1879–82. The LAND LEGISLATION of 1881, GLADSTONE's major political move of the Land War period, sought to meet the demand for the Three Fs by enacting security of tenure subject to conditions (such as the payment of rent), and in this he was following the recommendations of the BESSBOROUGH COMMISSION of enquiry which had accepted the justice of the Three Fs case in totality. Thus arbitration courts to fix rents were also established (although PARNELL and the fragmented LAND LEAGUE did not uniformly welcome the measure). The problem of the 1881 Act was that it did not go far enough, but, insofar as the larger farmers were concerned, it met their demand for the Three Fs. It left out of consideration smallholders with arrears of rent, and also leaseholders, who found themselves abandoned by the better-off once the latter had secured what they required from government.

Threshers *see* CARDERS

Tithe and Tithe Wars

The tithe or 'tenth' was an annual tax levied by the established church (in Ireland, the CHURCH OF IRELAND) upon the produce of the land, either in kind or in cash. In practice, tithes were bought and sold like other goods, so that the tithe owner need not be the church, but a speculative layman, the tithe farmer. It was not only the exaction of the tithe that created grievance: in Ireland, particularly (but it was also so in England to a lesser degree) there was resistance amongst the majority non-communicants of the established church towards paying in any way for its support. Tithe was an issue in most of the outbreaks of agrarian unrest in the eighteenth and early nineteenth century, with attacks on tithe farmers, proctors who collected tithes for their employer, and general interference with the process of assessment. The Tithe Wars were merely an extension of that resistance on a grand scale.

Tithe legislation was complex and often 'tinkered' with the system. In 1736 the House of Commons had come out against 'tithe of agistment' which meant that it was no longer to be collected on pasture land. This decision favoured the development of large-scale grass farms, with concomitant fall in rural employment. It was an isolated measure – hardly a reform – that served to aggravate the tithe issue whilst benefiting a few. The intermittent outbreaks of anti-tithe violence and agitation led, in 1787, to the Tumultuous Risings Act, which attempted to suppress interference with tithe collection. It was made perpetual in 1800. On 19 July 1823 the Irish Tithe Commutation Act made it possible for the clergy of the Church of Ireland, through arbitration, to agree to commute tithe in kind to cash payments. This same Act made grassland eligible for tax, and thus it failed in two respects. Firstly, it did not meet the anti-tithe grievance, that tithe was insupportable, so that it meant very little difference whether it were collected in cash or in kind. Secondly, it alienated the larger farmers who, since 1815 and the French wars, had gone further in the direction of replacement of arable with pasture land. The first confrontation of the resultant Tithe War came in March 1831 at Graiguenamanagh, County Kilkenny, when a force of 120 police (see PEACE PRESERVATION FORCE) was moved in to seize cattle from farmers refusing to pay tithes. In May there were deaths in anti-tithe riots at Castlepollard in Westmeath, and on 18 June at Newtownbarry, County Wexford, the YEOMANRY opened fire on a crowd of protesters and killed several. There was a particularly savage incident at Carrickshock in County Kilkenny in December, when a chief constable and 12 police officers were killed in a pitched fight with an anti-tithe crowd. In May 1832 a select committee of the House of Commons was appointed to report on the disturbances over tithes, and in August a preliminary act aimed at commutation came into effect, but this was preceded by an act to facilitate recovery of arrears of tithe and to assist the clergy of the Church of Ireland who, in the general strike against tithe payments, were suffering badly from depleted incomes. The unrest was still widespread: in April 1833 the LORD LIEUTENANT was empowered to suppress public rallies and to establish court martials in areas of severe disturbance. The Church Million Act, as it was called, of 29 August 1833 advanced £1 million of government money to the relief of tithe owners, whoever they were, deprived of their income. The government hoped to recover this money in time. In legislation in June 1832, which had preceded the proposal for commutation in August, the government had already undertaken to pay some arrears, but had also set itself to collect outstanding arrears for 1831 by force if necessary. The government's fierce reactions have to be seen in the light of the view of tithes as private property, sacrosanct and to be protected by government. In February 1834 the CHIEF SECRETARY in Ireland, Littleton, proposed in the Commons that the tithe be commuted into a form of Land Tax, the first indication that tithes, as they had always been known, might be abolished. The Tithe War, however, was far from over. In December 1834 there was another major engagement at Rathcormac, County Cork, in which at least nine people were killed in a clash between rioters and the authorities. The agitation was so effective that over the period 1833–35, less than one-third of the estimated tithe due was collected. DANIEL O'CONNELL, who by some was accused of inspiring anti-tithe agitation by his rhetoric, in August 1835 gave his support to the government's Insurrection Act 'for speedy punishment of offences', the last attempt by the government to legislate the agitation away. It was never applied and lapsed in 1840. By then the necessary concessions had been made.

The reform measure of 1838 came during the Under Secretaryship of the liberal reformer, THOMAS DRUMMOND, who reminded landlords and others that 'property has its duties as well as its rights' in May of 1838. The Tithe Rent-charge Act of 15 August 1838 converted the tithe into a rent-charge estimated at 75 per cent of normal tithe value, and the legislation made landlords responsible for paying the rent-charge. At one fell blow the government swept away, therefore, the tithe farmers and proctors, abolished tithe in its old form, and passed it on to the proprietors of land, who could, of course, allow for it in the rents and fines imposed upon their tenants, but at a reduced rate. The Irish legislation followed that in England of 1836. Since tithe resistance in England had never been so bitter as it had been in Ireland, it may be argued that the reform

of 1838 merely extended provisions already applied to England. But the tithe rebels of Ireland had forced the government's hand: their campaign had been so successful, that they had forced the government to expend money to make good the losses due to the 'war', and the thousands of small and large farmers all over Ireland, whatever their religious persuasion, had forced the removal of a system they had long challenged.

Toleration Act

The Toleration Act of November 1719 was aimed at the DISSENTERS of Protestant persuasion by excusing them from the requirement to attend services of the CHURCH OF IRELAND, and by easing the laws applying to dissenting clergy. The 'sacramental' TEST ACT of 1704, however, was left unaltered and was not repealed until 1780.

Tommy Downshires

The Tommy Downshires were an anti-TITHE movement that appeared in Counties Armagh and Down during the Tithe War of the 1830s. They were within a tradition of rural unrest, but, because of the general anti-tithe agitation, their efforts were not isolated. In consequence their activities merged with the general campaign.

Tone, Theobald Wolfe (1763–98)

Tone came of Protestant family in DUBLIN, was educated at TRINITY COLLEGE, and was called to the Irish Bar in 1789. He was already committed to nationalist politics, and in 1790 published *Hibernicus*, which asserted the Irish right to independence. His *Argument on Behalf of the Catholics of Ireland* which advocated emancipation, appeared in 1791. He was not particularly pro-Catholic, but rather, had come to the conclusion that the Catholic religion was certain to fade before the rationalism of the European enlightenment. He wished to see a united DISSENTER and Catholic cause for Irish freedom. He became a member of the VOLUNTEERS, and in 1792 helped found the UNITED IRISHMEN movement in

Dublin. In that same year he was secretary of the CATHOLIC ASSOCIATION, pressing for reform of the PENAL LAWS. For him, in his move towards revolution, Ireland was 'a conquered, oppressed and insulted country' for which the French revolution provided hope and for which French aid might be forthcoming. His attempts to induce the French to invade Ireland proved fruitless in 1797, but in 1798 he came with French help to County Donegal, after the United Irishmen's rising of that year was already mostly over. He was captured at Buncrana, County Donegal, in October, was tried in November by court martial and was sentenced to be hanged. When he was unable to have this sentence changed to death by firing squad, he committed suicide in his prison, and died on 19 November 1798. His son, William, was brought up by the French and educated, and came to exercise a command in their armies.

Tories

The English word 'Tory' is an anglicization of the Gaelic word 'Toraidhe', which, literally, meant 'raider' but came also to mean 'outlaw' when it might be applied to political undesirables, such as the English 'Tory Party' that emerged during the late seventeenth century. The Tories were renegades, the dispossessed Catholic Irish gentry of the 1650s who had supported the IRISH REBELLION of 1641–53 or had fought for King Charles I, and found themselves landless as a consequence. Their activities were not confined to guerrilla action against new settlers and the English forces in Ireland during the 1650s. They became an important lawless element in the Irish countryside for much of the rest of the seventeenth century, 'lawless bandits' as they were termed in the 1670s, 'under the pretence of defending the national rights [they] infest the country'. They produced not a few Irish folk heroes, including the Brennan Brothers in Kilkenny, 'Count' Redmond O'Hanlon (who was eventually murdered by a kinsman in 1681) and Dudley Costello (who in 1666 had a price of £20 on his head and who was killed in a fight in County Mayo in March 1667).

As late as 1695 the government issued an act for the suppression of Tories and RAPPAREES, but as a phenomenon they faded away soon after. They were, after all, first-generation dispossessed Catholic Irish or OLD ENGLISH minor gentry. Their cause was immediate and died with them. They were representative of themselves, but also, in that their existence perpetuated the memory of the expropriations of the 1650s, they served a 'national' Irish interest as well.

Towns and Urban Centres

'Living dispersedly' was equated with GAELIC IRISH society in the eyes of the English. Urban centres, unless grouped around ecclesiastical buildings of importance, were not characteristic of Gaelic society. As late as 1600, despite centuries of English encroachment, the chief towns were confined to the coastal areas, serving as ports, the most important of which were Limerick, Cork, Waterford and Dublin, each with its PALE of English influence around it. Lesser ports were those at Wexford, Dundalk, DROGHEDA, New Ross and Youghal.

Towns were an instrument of PLANTATION. By 1690 there were some 117 incorporated boroughs in Ireland returning MPs to the Parliament, and of that figure, no fewer than 80 had been established after the surrender of the rebel Earl of TYRONE in 1603, whose eventual flight to France (see FLIGHT OF THE EARLS) opened ULSTER up to full-scale plantation and town foundation. The town was an instrument of NEW ENGLISH political control in Ireland, the tool by which, with its charter, they challenged and came to dominate the Catholic OLD IRISH who enjoyed control of the older, and fewer in number, towns of Ireland. Towns were also islands of ANGLICIZATION and CIVILITY in a savage-inhabited wilderness that plantation would gradually bring under order. Very often, towns owed their origin to the decision to settle in a certain place, of an individual planter, who drew to him others for mutual protection and, as often, they imposed strict limits upon the admission of native Irish to the towns. Hence the development, as in Limerick, and at DERRY, of distinctive 'English' and 'Irish' towns side by side. Often, Irish 'suburbs' developed around the periphery of English-controlled commercial centres, and that type of demarcation was marked as late as 1770 in Armagh, where there was also a distinction between Catholic labourers and Protestant professional and trading classes within the town area. The growth in numbers, and the expansion, of the towns more than anything else implanted upon the Irish landscape the symbol of English control. By virtue of the anti-Catholic PENAL LAWS and deliberate Protestant exclusivity, the New English and their political heirs maintained urban control well into the nineteenth century.

Townshend, George 4th Viscount (1724–1807)

Viscount Townshend, after a long military career begun before the battle of Culloden in 1746 (at which he fought) became LORD LIEUTENANT of Ireland in 1767, a post which he held until 1772 when he was recalled. He was the first of the permanently resident Chief Governors of Ireland, charged with restoring power to the British administration at the CASTLE, and having to deal with the assertiveness of the developing PATRIOT element in the Irish PARLIAMENT. It was during his Viceroyalty that the 1768 OCTENNIAL ACT came into force, which met Patriot demands for limited-term Parliaments. He was also charged with securing an increase in the Irish military establishment from 12,000 to 15,000 men, the unpopularity of which he constantly tried to impress upon the government. When the proposal reached the Irish Commons, it produced an address to the effect that the state of the finances was such that the measure could not be contemplated. Townshend believed that to avoid this sort of resistance in future, he needed to be able to dispose of much more government patronage, that is, he needed to be able to buy votes. The General Election which followed the Octennial Act returned members to Parliament who Townshend and his CHIEF SECRETARY Macartney thought they could manipulate, and he succeeded in having the increase in the armed force passed. Very soon after he had to prorogue Parliament because of Patriot resistance to a money bill introduced from England. During 1770 Townshend worked hard to develop a government party by the exercise of patronage, and came under severe personal attack in the published 'Baratarania' letters which were circulated widely in printed form. When Parliament met again in 1771, the personal attacks on Townshend continued, although they did not carry the support of a majority in the House. Townshend's impatience and somewhat tactless approach to the problem of reasserting administration control over the Commons, was largely responsible for his recall: he had, effectively, prepared the ground for a confrontation between the British administration and the Patriots of the Commons, who produced a motion in 1771 congratulating the Lord Lieutenant on the way he had disposed of various sinecures and Viceregal patronage by which 'he had excited gratitude sufficient to secure an expression of confidence in your administration'. Townshend's majority in the House did not countenance the motion, thus, for the Patriots, underlining its purpose.

Tralee Bay

In April 1916 JOSEPH PLUNKETT, one of the leading planners of the EASTER RISING of that year, notified ROGER CASEMENT in Germany of the intending rising, to the end that Casement should organize a shipment of arms for the rebels. On 20/21 April – three days before the PROCLAMATION OF THE IRISH REPUBLIC in DUBLIN – the ship *Aud* arrived in Tralee Bay, but was scuttled when British naval patrols approached it. It had carried on board 20,000 rifles and ammunition necessary for the IRISH VOLUNTEERS.

Transport and General Workers' Union

The Irish Transport Workers' Union was founded at the end of December 1908 by JAMES LARKIN, with JAMES CONNOLLY as the BELFAST organizer in 1910, by which time it had become the TGWU of Ireland. Larkin, indifferent to the political struggle with Britain, and more interested in the industrial strength of the working class, maintained a determination that the union should be non-sectarian. Connolly, whilst he accepted that, was more concerned with its political value and the struggle against British influence in Ireland. The TGWU published its own paper, *Irish Worker* from May 1911 (suppressed in December 1914). Its recruitment campaign ran into trouble in Wexford in August 1911, where the foundrymen were locked out by their employers over the issue of union membership. Two years later in 1913 the TGWU took on the DUBLIN employers in the LOCK-OUT over the issue of union membership in the city. In October 1914, upon Larkin's departure, Connolly took over as secretary of the Union, and he was executed in 1916 for his part in the EASTER RISING of that year.

Transportation

In May 1848 the YOUNG IRELAND revolutionary leader JOHN MITCHEL was transported for 14 years under the terms of the Treason-Felony Act of April of that year. The government used a rigged jury to secure a conviction, and that, and the rigour of the sentence, drew increased attention to the system of transportation, as well as making Mitchel famous as a 'Felon' of Ireland. Transportation to Australia had begun in 1788 in general, and from Ireland alone in 1791. Between then and 1835, some 40,000 'felons' underwent transportation, although it has been shown that of those only about 600 were nationalist rebels transported for political offences, although there were many that had been involved in rural agitation and protest over land, TITHE and related issues. Mitchel was the first of several Young Irelanders to be transported. In the trials following upon the failure of the rising of 1848, four Young Irelanders including SMITH O'BRIEN and MEAGHER, were sentenced to death. When they failed to oblige the government by petitioning for the pardons that would permit commutation of their sentences to transportation, the government passed legislation in June 1849 which allowed for the imposition of transportation in cases

of treason and justified the decision to commute their sentences.

Trevelyan, Charles Edward (1807–86)

Trevelyan became assistant secretary to the Treasury, in London, in 1840, after a career in the Indian civil service, to which he returned, with a knighthood, as Governor of Madras in 1859. During the period of the FAMINE in Ireland – 1845–49 – it fell to Trevelyan to administer relief. Trevelyan, through published writings in the midst of the crisis, indicated pretty clearly that he saw the famine as a mechanism to reduce surplus population. His views reflected prevailing Whig opinion, and he was in step with the Prime Minister Lord John Russell who held office from 1846 until 1852. Russell had direct experience of Ireland and, indeed, had favoured the commutation of TITHE into a rent-charge which was a major reform measure 10 years before the famine struck. But Trevelyan implemented a government policy that was interventionist to a very limited degree: not until 1847 was there direct, outdoor relief (see POOR LAW; FAMINE) rather than attempts to increase public works to provide money for the poor to purchase food.

Trinity College

Trinity College, DUBLIN received its charter of foundation as the College of the Holy and Undivided Trinity, in March 1592, to rise on land granted to the citizens of Dublin in 1539 for their loyalty during a recent rebellion. The new college became the intellectual heart of the Protestant ASCENDANCY: W.B. Yeats observed that if there was any religious veneration in the Protestant mind, it was directed towards that venerable institution. The College acquired extensive landed interest during PLANTATION in the early seventeenth century, particularly in the counties of Fermanagh, Armagh and Donegal, and all subsequent legislation relating to confiscations during the 1650s dealt with Trinity College property (and that of the CHURCH OF IRELAND for which it was a training ground) in separate categories. During the period of the IRISH REBELLION of 1641–53, and indeed until 1660, the College (purged of its LAUDIAN statutes of 1637) was at a low ebb, but its future was assured by King Charles II who, amongst other things, diverted into its keeping the extensive library of the archbishop of ARMAGH, and saw the establishment of further chairs, including Mathematics and Law. By this time the College was wholly Protestant in its student body. Under JAMES II a Catholic provost was appointed, Michael Moore, but the chief service he rendered it was to protect its library during occupation by JACOBITE troops in September of 1689. During the eighteenth century the College expanded. By 1711 it had a medical school, a new library designed by Thomas Burgh a year after that, and in 1762 it acquired its first chair of history. King George III in 1776 provided annual grants towards professorships in French, German, Spanish and Italian. John Hely-Hutchinson (1724–94) as provost of the College from 1774, was instrumental in the introduction of foreign languages, and, in 1782, promoted the idea of Catholic admission to the College. He also favoured EMANCIPATION in general. Catholic admission to the College came in 1794, and in 1798 the favourers of the UNITED IRISHMEN movement amongst the fellows, were purged. Trinity did, to a degree, reflect PATRIOT nationalist politics of the period after 1760, but it remained a bastion of the Protestant domination in Ireland despite the intrusion of Catholic undergraduates. In 1838, however, the governing body of the College instituted a chair in Irish, and made its first professorial appointment two years later. The 'Heron Case' of 1845 drew attention to the exclusivity of the College. Denis Heron was denied the right of election to a scholarship because of his Catholicism, and the governing body's decision was upheld on appeal by Heron to the College 'Visitors'. In 1854 a concession to those like Heron, came with the creation of 16 non-denominational scholarships, but by this time a Catholic UNIVERSITY COLLEGE had opened its doors to meet the non-Protestant need for advanced educational opportunities. Not until 1867 were the religious tests partially abolished, and in 1873 by 'Fawcett's act'

they were swept away entirely. Nonetheless, the Catholic hierarchy, hostile to all government university legislation because of its avowedly non-denominational character, maintained its disapproval of Trinity as well, re-emphasizing it in the Synod at Thurles in 1875. During the EASTER RISING of 1916, guns were mounted by the British at the College which shelled the GPO and other republican garrisons in the city. Some radical development in the student body had been noted in 1913, when a group organized itself to assist the Dublin workers during the LOCK-OUT dispute over the membership of the TRANSPORT AND GENERAL WORKERS' UNION, but in November 1919 there was fighting in Dublin between Trinity Students commemorating the dead of the FIRST WORLD WAR of 1914–18, and University College students opposed to them.

If the test of belonging to the Ascendancy in the eighteenth century was communion with the CHURCH OF IRELAND, then Trinity College was the intellectual training ground of Ascendancy figures, as countless biographies of those times demonstrate. GRATTAN, FLOOD and other Patriot leaders were there, as well as solid government men such as FITZGIBBON and BERESFORD. The College perpetuated and sustained a distinctive 'Irishness' born of the NEW ENGLISH settlement of the seventeenth century, which it nurtured from its inception.

Troubles, The *see* WAR FOR INDEPENDENCE

Tuath *see* TANISTRY

Tubberneering, battle of

The battle of Tubberneering, County Wexford, was fought on 4 June 1798 during the WEXFORD RISING, part of the UNITED IRISHMEN rebellion of that year. A British column under a Colonel Walpole was destroyed and Walpole killed by the rebels.

Tullaghoe Stone, The

The Tullaghoe (County Tyrone) stone was in all probability a prehistoric or early Christian standing stone, upon which THE O'NEILL had customarily been inaugurated as chief of the clan. Early in September 1602, during the final campaigns by MOUNTJOY against the rebellious Ulster Irish led by the Earl of TYRONE, Mountjoy ordered the destruction of the stone. It was a symbolic move, demonstrating that for Mountjoy and thus for English administration, IRISH GAELIC usage was at an end.

Tyrconnell, Richard Talbot Earl of (1630–91)

Around the person of the Earl of Tyrconnell evolved the pro-Catholic policy for Ireland of the last Stuart king, JAMES II. Tyrconnell's earldom dated to 1685. During the IRISH REBELLION of 1641–53, he had fought alongside the royalist forces under THOMAS PRESTON, and was in the defence of DROGHEDA, but escaped the slaughter CROMWELL inflicted on the garrison in 1649. He was later arrested in London and charged with conspiracy to murder the Lord Protector. From 1660 he was attached to the household of the future James II, then Duke of York, and in Ireland was reckoned the spokesman for the Catholic interest, and an enemy of the Earl of ORMOND. During the POPISH PLOT scare, Talbot was briefly gaoled. Created earl at the accession of James II, Talbot's fierce Catholicism had ample scope to reveal itself, and it has been remarked of him that he was more loyal to that than he was to the king he served. In February 1687 he replaced the recently appointed Earl of Clarendon as LORD DEPUTY, which he combined with control of the armed forces. These he purged of their Protestant officer corps. When WILLIAM III usurped the throne in 1688, Tyrconnell accompanied James II into exile in France, but was back in Ireland in 1690 to take command of the JACOBITE armies operating there. Now styled Duke of Tyrconnell, he fought at the BOYNE in July, and commanded at AUGHRIM in 1691, where he died from a heart attack after the battle was over, and lost. The song 'Lillibullero' was a contemporary political satire aimed at him.

Tyrone, Hugh O'Neill Earl of (1540–1616)

O'Neill was a GAELIC IRISH Catholic, carefully nurtured in England to act as an instrument of ANGLICIZATION in his native ULSTER, but, as his whole career shows, his subservience to England was more apparent than real. He used English authority to support him where necessary, and he flouted it and ignored it to further his own interest. He overcame rivalries within Ulster that undermined his authority, particularly when, in 1593, he and his enemy Turlough O'Neill came to terms and the earl was recognized as THE O'NEILL by the clan. Suspicious of English policy towards Ulster, and because of that jealous of his own power, Tyrone rose in arms in 1594, 1597 and lastly in 1598, in a massive rebellion that was Irish in context rather than merely an Ulster insurrection. He courted Spanish aid, and won the victory of the Yellow Ford in 1598 against Henry of the Battleaxes, the English commander Henry Bagenal. Tyrone's Spanish help was forthcoming, and was rapidly destroyed at KINSALE in 1601. Thereafter, the earl fell back upon the defensive, and in 1603 came to terms with LORD DEPUTY MOUNTJOY at MELLIFONT. At the end of the year he was pardoned yet again by the king, James I, following the policy of his predecessor, Elizabeth. It is clear that the English, with plans for PLANTATION in Ulster, would allow Tyrone little leeway in his control of his own territory. The Dublin administration encouraged disputes with Ulster, playing upon rivalries, and in 1607 Tyrone had little choice but to flee the country (see FLIGHT OF THE EARLS). He died in Rome in 1616.

U

Ulster, and Plantation in

Of the four provinces of Ireland (see ADMINISTRATIVE STRUCTURE), Ulster was that which held out against English conquest and CIVILITY the longest. Not until the defeat of the Earl of TYRONE in 1603, indeed, not until his flight to Europe in 1607 (see FLIGHT OF THE EARLS) was Ulster opened to English encroachment on a major scale. In 1600 there were only five major urban centres (see TOWNS), Newry, Carrickfergus, DERRY, Armagh and Downpatrick, and of those, Carrickfergus was primarily a military garrison, and Downpatrick's importance was ecclesiastical. By 1613 there were 36 incorporated boroughs returning MPs to the Irish PARLIAMENT, such was the speed of PLANTATION once Tyrone and his allies had fled their lands. There was already some Scottish settlement in Down and Antrim by the time of the survey of the province which began in July 1608. The commissioners declared Armagh, Cavan, COLERAINE (Derry), Donegal, Fermanagh and Tyrone to be crown property and disposable. All existing land titles were held to be invalid, and native Irish occupiers, now become tenants, were permitted to remain only on lands granted to the CHURCH OF IRELAND, TRINITY COLLEGE or to the SERVITORS. Land grants were in precise bundles – the 'great' of 2,000 acres, the 'middling' of 1,500 acres and the 'small' of 1,000 acres, with fixed rents to the crown of £5.6s.8d. per 1,000 acres. All of Coleraine (Derry) was given to the city of London. Some 500,000 acres were thus thrown open to new settlement, and 'UNDERTAKERS' were expected to be resident, to create urban centres, and to maintain English presence. In 1622 there were some 12,000 adult settlers in the counties confiscated, and in the counties of Down and Antrim a mix of Scots and English to the total of some 7,500. A handful of GAELIC IRISH proprietors remained, on marginal soils, and there were numerous Gaelic Irish tenants retained for practical purposes. LORD DEPUTY WENTWORTH, after 1635, as part of his policy to reduce the power of the NEW ENGLISH, extended the powers of the COURT OF WARDS to some two-thirds of the newly settled lands, and imposed altered land tenure thereby. But Wentworth's attack on the New English was limited in its application: he fell from power in 1641, and in that same year a far more serious threat came into reality, a native Gaelic uprising, the IRISH REBELLION which, aided by Catholic support from the OLD ENGLISH, plunged Ireland at large into war for 12 years. The dispossessed Irish fell upon the planters in Ulster with ferocity, scattering them in droves of refugees into England, where their coming heightened anti-Catholic panic which was a constant feature of the English character at that time. Scottish settlers, aided rapidly by troops from Scotland, clung on to territory in Ulster, but the province was for the most part quickly overrun and repossessed. But this was a temporary restoration. The rebellion failed in 1653, and the Cromwellian land settlement that followed had additional forfeited lands to dispose of. By the eighteenth century, the most Gaelic province of Ireland had become the most ANGLICIZED of them all, developing an increasingly dominant Protestant majority, and pursuing an industrialized future that separated it more and more, in economic terms, from the rest of Ireland.

Ulster Convention

The Ulster Convention met on 17 June 1892 in BELFAST, presided over by the Duke of Abercorn. It represented in its 12,000 delegates 'the wealthy, the orderly, the industrious, the enterprising portion of Ireland' – according to Arthur Balfour. It was a demonstration of intransigent opposition to HOME RULE. In the 1885 General Election, the Home Rule MPs returned from Ireland numbered 85, and held an effective balance of power between the Liberals and the Conservatives. Within days of the election, GLADSTONE's decision to promote Home Rule had become known – the price of Irish support – and in January 1886 Salisbury's Conservative government fell. The plans for Home Rule developing in the Liberal party, led to countermeasures in ULSTER, supported both by the English Conservatives and by elements of Gladstone's own Liberal party. In January 1886 the Ulster Loyalist Anti-Repeal Committee, a Conservative front, appeared in Belfast, with subsequent rallies. The Convention, therefore, of 1892 was a part of the reaffirmation of opposition to Gladstone's determination to introduce Home Rule despite setbacks in the House of Lords. A second Home Rule Bill was introduced in February 1893 and failed again in the Lords: thereafter legislative activity lapsed until 1912. The Convention had, for the time being, no further purpose.

Ulster Covenant *see* SOLEMN LEAGUE AND COVENANT

Ulster Custom

Ulster Custom was, to tenants seeking security of tenure in nineteenth-century Ireland, the desirable norm which prevailed in ULSTER. Historians are still unclear as to how far the custom prevailed in the province by the end of the eighteenth century, but that is largely a reflection of the lack of legislative standing. Ulster Custom did not give tenants fixity of tenure by any means, it applied only to what may be called their saleable interest in their holdings, and for it to be effective, it had to be recognized by landlords and tenants alike. It meant an option on renewal of lease for the sitting tenant, and the right to receive from an incoming tenant the value of any improvements carried out on the holding, and monetary payment for the outgoing tenants' 'interest'. An attempt to legislate for it in 1847 failed and was not renewed. Commissions looking into

the state of agriculture and the poor in Ireland recognized that the Custom lacked precise definition, and the Landlord and Tenant Act of August 1870 (see LAND LEGISLATION) left it to the land courts to determine where it prevailed, putting the onus of proof upon the tenant. This meant that the Custom did not spread throughout Ireland but was, in practice, limited to those areas where it quite clearly could be shown to prevail. Nevertheless, the importance of Ulster Custom lies in its fact of existence: it was something to which the Irish peasant smallholders compared their insecure position *vis-à-vis* their landlords, and aspirations to share in it became part of the campaigns of Tenant movements and land reform movements for much of the middle part of the nineteenth century.

Ulster Day *see* SOLEMN LEAGUE AND COVENANT

Ulster Defence Union

The Ulster Defence Union was a support group outside Parliament, for the UNIONISTS in the Conservative party, and emerged during the 1890s run-up to the second attempt to pass HOME RULE legislation through Parliament in 1893. Its purpose was to raise funds to promote the anti-Home Rule cause, and to plan for emergency action in the event of Home Rule becoming law. The guiding spirit was Edward Saunderson (1837–1906) a former Liberal who had voted against GLADSTONE on the issue of DISESTABLISHMENT of the CHURCH OF IRELAND, and become a Conservative. As Deputy Grand Master of the ORANGE ORDER he was very influential, and largely responsible for rallying the Unionists within the Conservative party.

Ulster Rebellion (of 1641)

The Ulster Rebellion of October to November 1641 was short-lived only because it merged into the general conflagration of the IRISH REBELLION of 1641–53. Nevertheless, it was the prime begetter of that larger alliance of Catholic interests, the CATHOLIC CONFEDERACY, which subsumed a basically GAELIC IRISH revolt engineered by, among others, RORY O'MORE and PHELIM O'NEILL. It was very much a revolt of the dispossessed and expropriated Irish, chafing under the policy of PLANTATION which had ensued upon suppression of the ULSTER revolt of TYRONE in 1603. There had been some unrest between then and 1641. CAHIR O'DOHERTY's revolt of 1608 had been crushed, and there were many arrests in 1615 when report of a conspiracy to massacre Protestants surfaced – how much truth there was in that is debatable. Unlike the other provinces of Ireland – Connacht, Leinster and Munster – where the process of ANGLICIZATION had been piecemeal and prolonged, Ulster took the full impact of a vigorous re-settlement policy begun in 1608 and virtually completed by 1613, when the vast expansion in urban centres gave the Protestant NEW ENGLISH control of Parliament in DUBLIN. The speed of the process, and the existence of exiles in Europe trained in the art of war in European armies, created a reservoir of discontents. The opportunity to act came with the downfall of LORD DEPUTY WENTWORTH in 1641, and the preoccupation of the king, Charles I, and his Parliament with their own struggle, and the problem of Scottish resistance to the crown's religious policies.

The original leaders of the Ulster Rebellion were not themselves the 'dispossessed' though they were, by virtue of the terms of PLANTATION, holding lesser lands than they might have held, and their families had held, prior to 1608. They nevertheless represented the dispossessed, and their objectives were, primarily, to reassert their power against the NEW ENGLISH domination of the province and, secondly, to press for religious liberties for Catholics. They certainly hoped that the king would look favourably upon them, although it was never entirely politically expedient for him to do so, even had he wished. They may even have seen themselves as the potential military arbiters of the contest between the king and Parliament. They unleashed a major nation-wide rebellion, however, in which original aims were lost sight of, and an 'Irish' crusade against English domination developed, coupled with intransigent Catholic assertiveness, particularly under the influence of RINUCCINI and his right-hand man, OWEN ROE O'NEILL, a true 'dispossessed' Irishman.

Ulster Special Constabulary

The 'Special Constabulary Force' was set up in the midst of the WAR FOR INDEPENDENCE, as a back-up to the ROYAL IRISH CONSTABULARY in their fight against the IRISH REPUBLICAN ARMY. They were classified into three groups, the A Specials (full-time but temporary constables); the B Specials (part-time and intended to operate within their localities); and the C Specials, a large emergency reserve force intended to meet specific crises as and when they arose. Their purpose was two-fold. It was intended that they should encompass the ULSTER VOLUNTEER FORCE, raised in 1913 to defend ULSTER against HOME RULE, and thus give absolute legality to their activities. Secondly, in the event of an independent southern Ireland, and the consequent drastic cut in the extant police force, to provide a reservoir of reinforcement for what would be left of it in the north. Needless to say, the Specials were for the most part Protestant. In later years the B Specials were to earn an unsavoury reputation as practitioners of decidedly sectarian forms of peace-keeping. In November 1921 control of the Royal Irish Constabulary in the SIX COUNTIES that would make up the separate 'state' of Northern Ireland, passed to the Northern Ireland government. In December Prime Minister Craig increased the strength of the Specials, to 4,200 in the A group, 8,500 in the B group, and 22,000 in the C category, the emergency reserve. In 1925 the A Specials were disbanded after a mutiny to secure favourable terms for their discharge. The B Specials were disbanded in April 1970, and many of them enlisted in the Ulster Defence Regiment.

Ulster Tenant Right Association

The Tenant Right Association was formed in ULSTER, at DERRY, in May 1847 by William Sharman Crawford (1781–1861) a radical Protestant MP for Rochdale, Lancashire, who had favoured Catholic EMANCIPATION but had disassociated himself from DANIEL O'CONNELL's struggle for repeal of the UNION of 1801. Crawford was deeply involved in tenant agitation for security of tenure and recognition of a tenant's 'interest' in his holding. He believed that ULSTER CUSTOM, which guaranteed certain rights to the tenants, should be given legislative status, but his attempt to move a bill in the House of Commons failed to get a second reading in 1847. The Tenant Right Association was a defensive measure, intended to maintain campaigns for preservation and extension of Ulster Custom, and it was part and parcel of a much greater movement which became the TENANT LEAGUE, merging smaller groups all over Ireland. The Tenant Right Association had heavy PRESBYTERIAN backing, a reflection of the numbers of tenant farmers of that persuasion in Ulster.

Ulster Unionist Council

A major conference of ULSTER Unionist MPs took place in BELFAST in December 1904, which resolved to form what became known in the following year as the Ulster Unionist Council, to resist HOME RULE for Ireland. Its executive committee spread the number of Unionist Clubs in Ulster, to provide local bases on which to organize resistance to devolution if it should come, and an Irish Unionist Council was similarly set up in DUBLIN to co-ordinate Unionist activism nation-wide. In 1912 Bonar Law made a pledge of unconditional British Conservative and Unionist support for whatever steps the Council might take in face of the renewal of Home Rule legislation by the government. The Council since its inception had organized a large body of opinion in Ulster, and drawn together the ORANGE ORDER, various Unionist Associations, and a sympathetic majority in the House of Lords, to present itself as powerful enough to challenge the British government if an attempt were to be made to impose rule from Dublin. In September 1913 a standing committee of the Council organized itself as a provisional government in waiting for Northern Ireland, with every likelihood that Home Rule would go through. Its leader was EDWARD CARSON, who under such circumstances, looked to be the first Prime Minister of the Northern Ireland state. The ULSTER VOLUNTEER FORCE was already on foot and recruiting, to provide the 'army' of the proposed secessionist state. The FIRST WORLD WAR beginning in 1914 obliged the government to shelve its Home Rule measures, but in June 1916 – following the significant EASTER RISING in Dublin by the IRISH REPUBLICAN BROTHERHOOD to wrest independence from Britain – Lloyd George proposed immediate Home Rule with the temporary exclusion of the SIX COUNTIES of Ulster from its provisions. The Council accepted the proposal, thereby indicating its final abandonment of the Unionists in the rest of Ireland. Their acceptance of Lloyd George's proposal was a defeat, but the temporary exclusion clause did not last. Permanent exclusion of the six counties of the future Northern Ireland was written into the legislation of December 1920 which established a Parliament at Belfast. The first Unionist Prime Minister of the new 'state' was Carson's successor as leader of the Ulster Unionist Council, Sir James Craig.

Ulster Volunteer Force

The purpose of the Ulster Volunteer Force, set up by the ULSTER UNIONIST COUNCIL in 1913 under the command of General Sir George Richardson, was to defend ULSTER against HOME RULE government from DUBLIN. Sir EDWARD CARSON advanced £10,000 of his own money towards equipping it, and there were no problems in bringing in weapons from Britain and elsewhere. By the spring of 1914 it was 23,000 strong and quite capable, in the first instance, of enforcing a declaration of Ulster's independence if the leadership resolved upon it. The foundation of the UVF led to republican imitation in the rest of Ireland, and the formation of the less numerous and less well-equipped IRISH VOLUNTEERS from which was to emerge the IRISH REPUBLICAN ARMY. When the FIRST WORLD WAR broke out in 1914, and the threat of immediate Home Rule was lifted, the UVF formed the bulk of the 36th (Ulster) Division which bled to death in courageous fighting on the Somme in one day's fighting on 1 July 1916. The Force was refounded in 1920 by Carson, who threatened to use it against the IRA if the British government proved unable to deal with the guerrilla WAR FOR INDEPENDENCE.

With the creation of the Northern Ireland Parliament in 1921 and the 'state' of Northern Ireland, the bulk of the UVF merged into the vastly increased ULSTER SPECIAL CONSTABULARY. An Ulster terrorist group emerged in 1966 under the name of the UVF, and embarked upon a series of murders of Catholics in Ulster.

Undertakers

In the context of Irish history, the term 'Undertakers' has two distinct meanings. The PLANTATION of ULSTER after 1608 rested upon the commitment of the Undertakers, persons of means who undertook upon acquisition of land (which was made available in grants of between 1,000 and 2,000 acres) to fulfil the government's requirements that they be resident by 1610, and that by 1613 they demonstrate the imposition of agricultural and tenurial practices on the English pattern (and as already prevailed in the PALE), and dispense with Irish tenants in favour of settlers. The term 'Undertaker' is also applied to those ASCENDANCY figures who controlled and managed business in the Irish PARLIAMENT during the eighteenth century. Their power was identified closely with the British administration at the CASTLE, and depended upon the infrequent presence in Ireland of the Chief Governor, whether LORD LIEUTENANT or LORD DEPUTY. They were the target of opposition criticism, particularly from the PATRIOTS who emerged during the 1760s in the Commons and who in 1782 won virtual legislative independence from Britain, but their power was also effectively if quite as corruptly challenged by Lord Lieutenant the VISCOUNT TOWNSHEND (1767–72). The Undertakers, by their control of patronage, sinecures and pensions, were able to 'buy' votes in the Parliament and thus could ensure the smooth passage of government legislation.

Union, of Britain and Ireland, 1801

England and Scotland were United by act in 1707. Two years later, the Irish House of Lords expressed a desire for a similar Union between Britain and Ireland. The issue occasionally arose during the eighteenth century – there were, for example, anti-Union riots in DUBLIN in 1759 – but, from the British viewpoint, Union was neither desirable nor necessary until the aftermath of the UNITED IRISHMEN rebellion of 1798. The rebellion itself may have been the factor which brought William Pitt to favour Union, but the mood in Britain towards Ireland had undergone change for more than 20 years. The PATRIOT element in the Irish PARLIAMENT won an impressive degree of legislative independence in 1782 by the repeal of the 1720 DECLARATORY ACT, which had stipulated the supremacy of the WESTMINSTER Parliament over that in Dublin. Although the Irish Parliament did not reform itself from the BOROUGH PARLIAMENT that GRATTAN had termed it, during the dominance of the Patriot group, it remained an unpredictable and formidable body for the British administration at the CASTLE to manipulate. The 1798 rebellion thus provided an immediate excuse to do something which the British government had long contemplated. In January 1799, a week after the British House of Commons had thrown out a measure for full legislative independence for Ireland, Pitt expressed himself of the opinion that Union of the two Parliaments was necessary. In May 1800 CASTLEREAGH introduced the bill into the House of Commons to create the United Kingdom of Great Britain and Ireland. The case was presented to the Irish Parliament as a guarantee of the survival of the Protestant ASCENDANCY in face of Catholic EMANCIPATION, since it was the intention to limit Irish representation at Westminster to 100 MPs, 28 Peers to enter the House of Lords, and four Bishops. Those who were opposed to Union declared, with truth, that it was pushed through the Irish Parliament by corruption and jobbery (see BLACK LIST). The

Irish Commons voted in favour of their own abolition on 7 June 1800, the royal assent was given in August, and the Act came into force on 1 January 1801. It was greeted generally by the Catholics with approval; the Ascendancy was split over it, and the ORANGE ORDER likewise. The office of LORD LIEUTENANT and the British administration at the Castle survived Union, with a concomitant rise in the power of the CHIEF SECRETARY. The campaign for repeal of the Union became, under the direction of DANIEL O'CONNELL, identified closely with Catholic political aspirations, which in turn made Union palatable to the majority of Protestants. The REPEAL ASSOCIATION during the 1840s mounted a massive campaign, with no effect, nor was it ever precisely clear what they would have in place of the Union of 1801. For Irish nationalism and republicanism, Union was a particular blessing, for it became possible to identify British rule and the government of Ireland as wholly one and the same, particularly given the surviving administration at the Castle headed by the Lord Lieutenant. It was possible, if they did not look too closely, to see the last 20 years of the Irish Parliament – GRATTAN'S PARLIAMENT – as an expression of Irish self-identity, whereas it was nothing more than the cumulative result of Ascendancy aggrandizement. For a long time the return of an independent Irish legislature limited the objectives of the constitutional nationalists, but their campaign for HOME RULE came to a bitter end in 1918. The British government only let go of Ireland when it became too troublesome to continue to try to control it, and it was not Repealers or Home Rulers who made that so, but the armed forces of the IRISH REPUBLICAN ARMY and popular support for SINN FÉIN.

United Britons *see* UNITED ENGLISHMEN

United Englishmen

Revolutionary republicanism, epitomized in France, spread not only into Ireland, where it formed the doctrine, ultimately, of the UNITED IRISHMEN movement. There was a corresponding response in Britain, too, and the violent republican United Englishmen movement which emerged in 1797 owed its inspiration both to Ireland and to France. There were other developments, the United Scotsmen and the United Britons, and all of them were linked to the movement in Ireland. The obvious point of contact was through the Scottish link with ULSTER, where the United Irishmen had their first origin, and the missionary zeal of Ulster republicans created a major network of United men in Manchester. The United Englishmen movement spread throughout the northwest, and into Leicestershire and Staffordshire as well. It was induced by the Irish movement to look towards French help, and it took its oaths and rules from the Irish source as well: most importantly, it was committed to insurrection in support of an insurrection in Ireland. Documents of the United Englishmen were seized in London in early 1798 by the police, as its London organization was in the process of creation. Historians have shown that the United Englishmen were a loose amalgamation of radical reform groups, in despair of constitutional government, with whom the United Irishmen made contact as a means of carrying their influence beyond the confines of Ireland. Thus there emerged a cross-border identity of purpose which reflects the universality of republican principles, echoed in the firm belief that the French would liberate England. The United Englishmen were effectively broken up by government action in 1798, but they re-emerged in 1799, and DESPARD's conspiracy of 1803 was a manifestation of English-based republicanism working again in consort with the remnants of the United Irishmen under ROBERT EMMET in DUBLIN.

United Irish League

The success of the United Irish League can be seen as a major factor in the reunification of the IRISH PARLIAMENTARY PARTY which had split in 1890 between pro- and anti-PARNELL factions. The League was founded in Connacht, in County Mayo, in 1898 under the slogan 'The Land for the People', to represent the western smallholders who had gained little from the LAND LEGISLATION of recent decades. Its primary target was the grazier, whose grassland farms developed at the expense of arable. From 1899 the League's newspaper, the *Irish People*, began to appear, and in that year membership was reckoned at around 33,000. By 1900 it was almost 100,000 strong. Co-founders WILLIAM O'BRIEN and MICHAEL DAVITT had created a movement that threatened to have more political importance than the body of MPs from Ireland in the Parliament at WESTMINSTER, and REDMOND's reunification of the parliamentary party led to its co-opting of the League as a constituency force.

United Irish Society *see* UNITED IRISHMEN

United Irishman, The

The *United Irishman* was founded as a journal for the promotion of his ideas, by the YOUNG IRELANDER JOHN MITCHEL, in February 1648 after he had split from the IRISH CONFEDERATION. It sold 5,000 copies on the first day of publication. The paper's policy was to advocate the violent overthrow of British rule in Ireland and, in the context of the FAMINE then raging in Ireland, that was a policy that excited widespread support.

The title *United Irishman* was applied to a journal founded in 1899 by ARTHUR GRIFFITH, who also edited it. It provided a platform for the ideas that later came to be espoused by SINN FÉIN, the republican movement established by Griffith, most particularly withdrawal from WESTMINSTER and the creation of an Irish DÁIL ÉIREANN in DUBLIN. From 1906 the paper became known simply as *Sinn Féin*.

United Irishmen

The Society of United Irishmen was founded in BELFAST in October 1791 as a radical and largely Protestant movement aiming at reform of the Irish PARLIAMENT, and frustrated by the inability or unwillingness of the PATRIOT element in that Parliament, to reform itself. The constitutional origins of the Society should not be obscured by its later, revolutionary republicanism which erupted in the 1798 rebellion. The Belfast founders were Samuel McTier and Robert Simms, and in November a DUBLIN branch was established with NAPPER TANDY as secretary. In January 1792 the first issue of SAMUEL NEILSON's paper the *NORTHERN STAR*, organ of the Belfast Society, appeared. The United Irishmen were, in their early years, far from being a Catholic nationalist movement: their strength lay amongst the Whig Protestants of ULSTER, where there had been sympathy for the American colonists in the AMERICAN WAR FOR INDEPENDENCE, and where there was friendliness towards the revolution in France. They regarded the wars against France as inimical to Ireland's true interests. The very existence of the Society owed a lot to the precedent of the VOLUNTEER movement, which leading parliamentary figures like GRATTAN had been happy to exploit to secure control of Parliament, but which they had long since (with the notable exception of FLOOD) found to be an embarrassment. It was no coincidence, therefore, that in December 1792 the Dublin Society called upon the Volunteers to re-arm themselves and to assemble again, to counterbalance the influence of the government-backed Irish MILITIA. In February 1794 proposals for parliamentary reform were made public, originating amongst the Dublin Society, and calling for universal male suffrage. By this time the government was moving against the Dublin Society. Archibald Hamilton Rowan was gaoled for two years for his part in the calling of the Volunteers to arms in 1792, and in May of 1794 the Dublin Society was suppressed by the police. At this point the constitutional nature of the United Irishmen began to undergo change. In the spring of 1795 the Belfast Society opted to go underground in a new, secret organization, bound by oath, led by a central Directory, committed to republicanism and separation from Britain. This was a response to the fall of the short-lived LORD LIEUTENANT, the Earl FITZWILLIAM, who had tried to push ahead with reforms, including Catholic EMANCIPATION, too fast for the Protestant ASCENDANCY to take. With FitzWilliam, many, not only the members of the United Irishmen, believed constitutional hopes to be at an end. At this time, contacts began to be made, not only in England with proto-republican groups such as would later emerge as the UNITED ENGLISHMEN, but in America and in France as well, marking the beginnings of a plan aiming at armed insurrection. It is at this point also that the Catholic nationalism notable in United Irishmen groups throughout Ireland, began to surface, and the links established with the militant Catholic defence movement known as the DEFENDERS. In September 1796 the government arrested the Belfast leadership on charges of treason. The *Northern Star* paper was raided the following year, and the first victim of repression, William Orr, was hanged for allegedly administering the oath of the movement. In 1797 the government gave General LAKE a free hand to repress the revolutionary movement in Ulster, which he did with the utmost rigour and considerable brutality (see NINETY-EIGHT), and in March of that year the Leinster Directory of the United Irishmen was raided in Dublin and its leaders arrested, which seriously impeded plans for revolt. Nevertheless, it broke out in Leinster on the night of 23/24 May 1798. In the ensuing widespread fighting, some 30,000 were killed, and the government forces, actively involving Militia and YEOMANRY, committed a series of appalling atrocities. The United Irishmen virtually disappeared in the havoc of the Ninety-Eight, although there was a brief resurgence of their principles in EMMET's revolt of 1803. The example of the United Irishmen would later inspire other nationalist and republican movements, not least because of the non-sectarian nature that it had possessed, and its example of commitment to the overthrow of British dominance.

University College

University College, DUBLIN, opened in 1854 as the Catholic University. The name changed in October 1882, and shortly thereafter it was transferred to the Jesuits. Its foundation in 1854 reflected Catholic hierarchy disgust with government proposals and progress in the field of non-denominational university education (see QUEEN'S COLLEGES), what

Cardinal Newman (first Rector of the Catholic University) described as the 'stupid forcing on [Irish] Catholicism of … godless education'. Rome had urged upon the Irish bishops the idea of a Catholic university, and in 1850 a committee headed by archbishop CULLEN was established. Cardinal Newman (1801–90) lectured in Dublin in 1851 on the 'Idea of a University', and saw the proposal for Ireland as a means to create 'the Catholic University of the English tongue for the whole world'. It was to be modelled on the University of Louvain, with an Oxford collegiate structure, and it was intended to provide an alternative to the entry of Catholics into Oxford and Cambridge. There was a marked lack of enthusiasm amongst the laity towards the project, they seeming to believe it was an entirely negative response to the government's system. It opened without endowments and without recognition of its degrees, and not until 1879 did it receive £6,000 from the government to establish scholarships.

University Legislation *see* QUEEN'S COLLEGES

Unlawful Societies Act, The

The bill to suppress 'unlawful societies' was introduced into the House of Commons by CHIEF SECRETARY Henry Goulburn and became law on 9 March 1825. It was aimed at the CATHOLIC ASSOCIATION and at the ORANGE ORDER in their various capacities as representative assemblies, petitioning pressure groups or campaigners for law reform. On 18 March the Catholic Association dissolved itself, to be relaunched in July in a manner to avoid the terms of the Act. The Orange Order circulated its lodges to the effect that lodge meetings would henceforth be construed as in breach of the Act.

Up, To be

In the eighteenth and nineteenth centuries, the expression 'to be up' meant membership of a secret society, such as the DEFENDERS or the RIBBONMEN, two militant Catholic movements hostile to Protestants.

V

Veto Controversy, The

In January 1799 a meeting of Catholic bishops in DUBLIN resolved to accept the right of the government to vet appointments to bishoprics in Ireland, as part and parcel of a general compromise on the position of the church. Following the presentation of Catholic petitions to the House of Commons in 1805, a debate was opened in May 1808 in which the government presented draft plans for the operation of just such a veto which, they claimed, already had the consent of the Irish hierarchy. The Catholic bishops, in synod in Dublin in September, flatly repudiated any such agreement. The 'veto controversy' erupted in 1814, when a letter from the secretary of the Sacred Congregation for the Propagation of the Faith, in Rome, was published in full in Dublin. The letter expressed the view that the bishops should go along with the veto, and permit the government to examine correspondence between them and Rome. Pope Pius VII (1800–23) favoured concordats between the papacy and the governments of countries, such as Britain, where there was a substantial Catholic minority. In Ireland, DANIEL O'CONNELL issued a warning to the papacy and to the Catholic hierarchy that any acceptance of the government's power of veto would lead to revolt amongst the Catholic faithful and the parochial clergy. In April 1815 the authorities in Rome withdrew their offer of making correspondence open to government inspection, but reiterated in the 'Genoese' letter its acceptance of veto. The Catholic bishops rejected the rescript in August and prepared resolutions to put their case in Rome. The Pope instructed them that his view remained adamant, that the veto should be established, and in 1817 the bishops' spokesman in Rome was forcibly ejected from the Vatican. The veto issue arose again in an attempt to introduce a bill for Catholic EMANCIPATION into the Commons in 1821, when the proposers endeavoured to link emancipation to a government right of veto, but the measure was rejected. The issue thereafter lapsed, but the hostility of the Irish bishops had alarmed the papacy.

Vinegar Hill, battle of

The battle of Vinegar Hill, fought on 21 June 1798, was the last major action of the WEXFORD RISING of that year, part of the nation-wide UNITED IRISHMEN revolt to establish an Irish republic. The rebel forces under Father JOHN MURPHY were defeated by government troops, including YEOMANRY and MILITIA units.

Volunteers, The

In 1784 HENRY GRATTAN, regarding the extra-parliamentary reform agitation of the Volunteer movement as intimidatory of the Irish PARLIAMENT, referred to them as 'the armed beggary of the nation'. They had, insofar as he was concerned (his colleague FLOOD did not share his view), fulfilled their purpose. They had provided militant backing for the PATRIOT group of MPs which, in 1782, had achieved legislative independence from Britain, and for Grattan, their task was accomplished. But the Volunteers, as an expression of developing Protestant Irishness, were not to be so easily dismissed. They had emerged during 1778 in ULSTER (although a similar movement appeared for a time in County Wexford in 1776), inspired by the actions of the American colonists in the AMERICAN WAR FOR INDEPENDENCE, and committed to vigorous assertion of Irish national interest. They were largely Protestant in membership and outlook, although there were early and isolated calls for Catholic membership. Therefore, the Volunteer movement was respectable: so much so that in 1779 the LORD LIEUTENANT, the Earl of Buckinghamshire, authorized the issue of arms to it, and it was not infrequently employed in policing duties. In 1780 – when it was about 40,000 strong – its Commander-in-Chief was the anti-Catholic James Caulfield Viscount Charlemont, who was to be a bitter enemy of the UNION of Britain and Ireland of 1801. Thus, until the Irish PARLIAMENT secured the repeal of the 1720 DECLARATORY ACT in 1782, the Volunteers were the voice of Ireland, or at least, of Protestant Ireland: Grattan could claim to speak for the 'beggary' as he later called them, and use their assertiveness to press home the legislative reform he wanted. Once that was won, however, the Volunteers could only be a problem, as they evidenced directly in the DUNGANNON CONVENTION of 1783. There, with delegates from 300 Ulster groups representing 150,000 men, they moved on from legislative reform to the reform of Parliament itself, demanding secret ballot votes and an annual Parliament, amongst other things. Their proposals were thrown out by the House of Commons in November of that year. Moves toward Catholic EMANCIPATION were also evident. The nature of the Volunteer organization encouraged the development of radical tendencies; the Conventions held at Dungannon and elsewhere, brought together representatives of the various Volunteer corps scattered predominantly in Ulster, but throughout Ireland wherever there was a sufficiency of Protestants to form. They had not been formed by Grattan and other MPs, but had developed, as an extra-parliamentary force, independently of moves within Parliament. They had found a common cause in the assertion of Parliament's integrity, but the Volunteers expected further reform of the system itself in

keeping with democratic principles. It was not forthcoming, and by 1784 they were a spent force, still in being, but of no account. When resurgence for the movement did come in the 1790s, it created a split within it, some moving along the reform lines established in 1783, some – alarmed by Catholic assertiveness – becoming recruiting material for the YEOMANRY. In 1793 a Reform Convention met in Dungannon representing a Volunteer movement that had been dramatically radicalized and become not only pro-Catholic reform, but heavily reliant upon Catholic membership. In 1792 the Belfast Volunteers had taken up the cause of emancipation, although there was reluctance to embrace the notion of armed force to secure their objectives. The influence of the French Revolution on the resurgence of the movement was enormous, and the UNITED IRISHMEN, the republican movement that looked to France both for example and potential help, regarded the Volunteers as the basis of an insurrectionary movement. The links with the aristocratic Ascendancy were thus broken, although there were Volunteer elements in Ulster which, alarmed by the DEFENDER activities of militant Catholics, moved closer to support of the administration. It was a confused picture, but the government believed it perceived the way the movement was going and in March 1793 proclaimed the Ulster Volunteers illegal and suppressed them, following a clash between armed Volunteers and regular soldiers. Thus the Volunteer movement virtually disappeared, some by involvement in the preparations for rebellion that came in 1798 – heavily infiltrated by the United Irishmen and the Defenders – and some merging with government-sponsored forces such as the Militia and Yeomanry.

W

Wadding, Luke (1588–1657)

Wadding was a member of the Franciscan order, born in Waterford, who in 1617 became President of the Irish College at Salamanca. Although not the instigator of the IRISH REBELLION of 1641, he was certainly its principal external, European organizer, and the man responsible for recruiting OWEN ROE O'NEILL as a commander for the CATHOLIC CONFEDERACY. In 1642 he was accredited as papal agent to the Supreme Council of the Confederacy at Kilkenny, and it was he who arranged for the appointment of the papal envoy RINUCCINI in 1645.

Walwyn, William

As far as is known, William Walwyn did not visit Ireland. Of his birth and death there is no extant record. He came to prominence during the later stages of the ENGLISH CIVIL WAR of 1642–51, as a prolific pamphleteer in the cause of the radical Leveller movement. In 1649 he was arrested for inciting the NEW MODEL ARMY to mutiny on the eve of its departure for Ireland to suppress the IRISH REBELLION that had raged since 1641, and to deal with the last royalist elements in the country. Walwyn's significance lies in his espousal of the rights of Irishmen as fellow human beings: in the context of the times in which he lived, his humanitarian attitude and abhorrence of generations of English policy in Ireland were exceptional and provocative.

War for Independence, 1919–21

The War for Irish Independence opened in January 1919 with the SOLOHEADBEG ambush by the IRISH VOLUNTEERS of a ROYAL IRISH CONSTABULARY convoy in County Tipperary. It came to an end with the formal truce of 11 July 1921, which preceded the creation of the FREE STATE through the ANGLO-IRISH TREATY. In the General Election of December 1918, SINN FÉIN, the republican party, had won 73 Irish seats on an ABSTENTIONIST policy, disavowing involvement with WESTMINSTER. On the day of the Soloheadbeg action, Ireland's own Parliament, DÁIL ÉIREANN, met in DUBLIN. It is unlikely that the military action, which rested upon the political success, was organized by Sinn Féin, but was the decision of the IRISH REPUBLICAN BROTHERHOOD and the Irish Volunteers to strike against Britain. In July 1919 the British suppressed Sinn Féin, the Volunteers and CUMANN NA MBAN throughout County Tipperary; in January the journal An t'Oglach had stated the moral justification for the Volunteers to kill police and soldiers, as instruments of continued British oppression in Ireland. In May there had been a fight at Knocklong in County Limerick. By August the centre of revolutionary activity had shifted into County Clare, where the IRISH REPUBLICAN ARMY (as the Volunteers were now styled) were operating, and in County Cork, at Fermoy, on 7 September Liam Lynch and the 2nd Cork Brigade of the IRA attacked regular troops. In retaliation the Shropshire Light Infantry destroyed and looted shops in the town. Regular troops struck again in November in Cork where they plundered Patrick Street. By this time there were some 43,000 British regular soldiers stationed in Ireland, costing the government £860,000 a month. By the time that a truce was declared, their reprisal burnings and lootings and those of the BLACK AND TANS and of the AUXILIARIES (who came into Ireland in 1920) had given rise to compensation claims totalling £4.3 million, whilst the cost of the war against the IRA alone was £20 million a year. The IRA, lacking the manpower and technology to meet the government forces in pitched battles, conducted widespread guerrilla warfare, developing the speedy and effective FLYING COLUMNS. The Royal Irish Constabulary and the regular army supporting them, were unable to sustain the war. In consequence, early in 1920, two additional back-up forces, the Black and Tans and the Auxiliaries, were introduced, licensed by the British government to use whatever force or terror was necessary to destroy the basis of support for the IRA, a fighting force rooted amongst the civilian population and sustained by them. During 1920 the war intensified, with serious sectarian anti-Catholic riots in BELFAST orchestrated by the ORANGE ORDER, and a distinctive spread of retaliatory actions. In Lisburn, for example, the killing of a police inspector (himself involved in a murder in Cork in March) led to concerted attacks on the homes of Sinn Féin supporters, and their flight from the town. The government, in August, hurried through a Restoration of Order Act which gave the military and police arbitrary powers to arrest Sinn Féin members and to use courts martial in lieu of civilian courts and coroners' courts. Secret courts began to sit in September, and the ULSTER SPECIAL CONSTABULARY was formed to provide further back-up for the hard-pressed RIC, some of whose officers were themselves disgusted by the activities of the Black and Tans and the Auxiliaries. The morale of the government forces was low, that of the IRA commensurately high. By October 1920 the rebels had destroyed 490 police barracks, killed 117 police officers, and 23 regular soldiers. MICHAEL COLLINS had penetrated and discovered the identity of the British intelligence operation in DUBLIN, in consequence of which 14 agents were assassinated in November, and in that same month 18 Auxiliaries were wiped out in a Flying Column ambush at Kilmichael, County Cork. The measure of the government's desperation is the official sanctioning of reprisals, a step taken in January 1921 and symbolized by the execution of six IRA prisoners in Cork: the IRA struck back with the shooting of six British soldiers. In Dublin, a strike that paralysed the city greeted the execution of IRA men in March.

During the course of the war, moves of a political nature towards meeting the Irish demand for independence proceeded. The future GOVERNMENT OF IRELAND Act was introduced into the Commons in February 1920, and became law in December. It provided for a PARTITIONED Ireland, with separate Parliaments in Belfast and in Dublin, for which elections took place in May 1921. The 124 Sinn Féin candidates and 4 independents standing in the 26 counties of southern Ireland were returned unopposed (six Sinn Fein MPs were returned in Ulster, where the old constitutional nationalists still had six seats as well). The Sinn Féin MPs abstained from the proposed Parliament and assembled in the Dáil after the conclusion of the truce which became effective on 11 July 1921, and the Anglo-Irish Treaty which resulted from negotiations with the British government was signed on 6 December, bringing the War for Independence to a formal conclusion.

Despite the British government's military commitment in Ireland, and the resort to terror to intimidate the Irish people, the eventual success of Sinn Féin and of the IRA was inherent in British political attitudes. It had resolved Ulster obstructionism by agreeing to partition, and the tide that had carried Home Rule virtually into reality in 1914 remained unstoppable. The question for the British really was, the precise nature of Irish relations with Britain following upon independence: it was not a question of seeking to maintain control of Ireland. The War for Independence, therefore, can be seen in some ways as a perpetuation of Ireland's subjugation, and an explosion of frustration amongst the politically active of republican principles within the country. It is unquestionable that the IRA wore down British resolution, such as it was. Whether the IRA won, however, would have been debatable, in view of the ensuant civil war over the precise terms of the Treaty of 1921.

Wards and Liveries, Court of

The Court of Wards and Liveries was

developed in England in the sixteenth century to enforce the rights of the crown over the heirs of estates held of the crown. In 1615 a commission was set up to examine the management of wardships in Ireland, primarily to secure revenues for the crown, and from 1616 some monies began to come in. The Lord High Treasurer, the Earl of Middlesex, in 1622 established the Court permanently in Ireland, a matter of grievance for the OLD ENGLISH. The new estates of PLAN-TATION and the NEW ENGLISH settlers were exempt from the Court's provisions. Only the long-established property of the Old English came under its brief. Moreover, under-age heirs to the estates of Catholic Old English landlords, tended to be brought up as Protestants by guardians appointed by the Court for their minority. When an heir came of age to 'sue out his livery', he was expected to take an oath of supremacy renouncing papal authority. In 1662 King Charles II abandoned the Court in return for alternative revenues, including a grant in perpetuity of internal customs dues. His decision to be rid of the Court (that in England had been abolished in 1646) reflected the change in the pattern of landownership following upon the IRISH REBELLION of 1641–53 and the Cromwellian land settlement of the 1650s. He needed to satisfy the new holders of former Old English estates.

Waterford

In 1600 Waterford was the second city of Ireland, a major coastal port trading with Europe, and dominated by the OLD ENGLISH urban culture. It was one of the towns which challenged, briefly, in 1603 (see REVOLT OF THE TOWNS) the intentions of the LORD DEPUTY. In 1618 its charter was rescinded because of the influence in the town of the Catholic population. In 1646 RINUCCINI summoned a Legatine Synod to Waterford to excommunicate the adherents of the alliance between the CATHOLIC CONFEDERACY and the royalists of the Earl of ORMOND. CROMWELL came against Waterford in November 1649, but was obliged to abandon the siege in December, and the port held out until August 1650 when it finally yielded to IRETON without the slaughter that had occurred at DROGHEDA and Wexford.

Wentworth, Thomas (1593–1641)

Wentworth's task, as he saw it, as LORD DEPUTY in Ireland from 1632 until his recall in 1641, was to make Ireland remunerative for the crown, loyal, and yet dependent upon England. This meant confrontation with NEW ENGLISH and OLD ENGLISH interests: he did not consider native GAELIC IRISH to be of any moment, and when he referred to 'native Irishmen' he expressly meant the Old English in contrast to the first- or second-generation settlers of the PLANTATION period. When he eventually fell, and was arraigned by the Parliament in England for treason, no fewer than 20 of the articles of impeachment levelled against him concerned the nature of his administration and his policy of THOROUGH in Ireland. As the king's Chief Governor, he built up an estate of almost 60,000 acres based in Kildare and Wicklow, and began construction of a never completed viceregal palace at Jigginstown. His acquisitiveness was that of a typical Englishman in Ireland, but he entertained only contempt for the venality of the New English, whose opposition towards him was epitomized by Richard Boyle, the Earl of CORK. Yet Wentworth's personal dislike of the planters did not make him any particular friend of the Old English, for both parts of Ireland's power were to be controlled in the interests of strong monarchy. Thus, although in the MATTERS OF GRACE AND BOUNTY (which Wentworth inherited), he, and the king, appeared to try to meet the grievances of the Catholics, in effect they were interested only in the subsidies promised in return, and when these were forthcoming, the 'graces' were not proceeded with as far as the legislative standing promised. Wentworth unsettled Ireland: he attacked New English interests by questioning land titles and the use of the Court of CASTLE CHAMBER, and he offended the Old English by, for example, his challenge to the Earl of CLANRICARDE over resettlement of the Earl's property in Galway (see CONNACHT, PLANTATION IN). He controlled the Parliament in DUBLIN, however, and moreover, made inroads upon Old English representation by the time it met in 1640. By then,

Wentworth's primary value to the king was in developing an Irish army capable of supporting royal authority, initially against the Scots, perhaps in time – as the English Parliament certainly professed to fear – against his English subjects. Wentworth, created Earl of Strafford in 1640, had temporarily found himself at a disadvantage with the king over the latter's courting of the Catholic Earl of ANTRIM in ULSTER, whose Scottish connections the king thought to use to enforce authority in Scotland. Wentworth considered Antrim to be of no account, and that the king must come to rely upon Wentworth's own Irish army of some 8,000 men. But in the end he hastened his own downfall, by recommending that the king summon a Parliament in England in 1640. The second Parliament, necessarily summoned in 1641 in face of the mounting Scottish threat, impeached Wentworth with charges that relied heavily upon his administrative record in Ireland. He was executed the same year.

Westmeath Act *see* RIBBONMEN

Westminster, Irish Representation at

Westminster was the seat of the English Parliament. In the 1650s, the Irish PARLIAMENT had ceased to exist for a short period and a handful of members were sent to sit in the assembly at London. The Irish Parliament was restored in 1660 and continued to meet until the UNION of Britain and Ireland in 1801, which brought the distinct Irish Parliament to an end. Under the terms of the Act of Union, 100 seats were allowed at Westminster for Irish MPs, with commensurate representation of lay and spiritual peers in the House of Lords; in 1832 the number of seats was increased to 105. In 1793 the EMANCIPATION of Catholics, so far as it then went, enfranchised the FORTY-SHILLING FREEHOLDERS, which enabled them to exercise their vote for members of Parliament, but did not offer them the chance to have Catholic MPs, who were still barred from Parliament. The first major emancipation legislation after Union came in 1829, by which

Catholics were at last entitled to sit, but the reform of 1793 was nullified, the property qualification rising from 40 shillings to £10. This reduced the Irish electorate from 216,000 to no more than 37,000 voters. The Representation of the People Act of August 1832 which, as has been said, increased Irish seats at Westminster to 105, also extended the franchise based on the £10 qualification to boroughs, with a marked increase in the voting population from the 37,000 of 1829 to some 92,000, which, historians have pointed out, represented a little over 1 per cent of the Irish population, or, voters represented 1 in 115 people in Ireland as against the 1 in 24 which prevailed in England. Under the 1832 legislation, the first General Election was held in January 1835, and Ireland's 105 seats were divided 37 to the Conservatives, 34 to the Liberals and 34 to O'CONNELL'S REPEAL ASSOCIATION candidates, committed to the ending of the Union of 1801 and its ensuant under-representation of the Irish in Westminster. A further Representation of the People Act, applying to Ireland, was passed in 1850, which effectively increased the county electorate but cut that in the boroughs by one-quarter, through the £8 rated occupation qualification. The Act extensively overhauled the system of registering voters by opting for an occupation qualification giving the vote to ratepayers on a £12 Poor Law valuation in the counties. The electorate thus increased to 163,000. The electorate had suffered a dramatic fall in numbers after the FAMINE of 1845–49: it has been estimated that, in the counties, there was a collapse in numbers of 40,000 voters. The 1850 Act, therefore, moved the electorate towards a more respectable figure. The Representation of the People Act of 1868 applied only to the parliamentary boroughs, and dealt with the inequity of the £8 qualification of 1850, which it cut to £4, and extended the franchise to lodgers. Subsequent legislation for the whole of the United Kingdom in 1884 increased the Irish electorate to 738,000 in a population of close to 5 million. In that same year, GLADSTONE made known his intention of introducing a bill to redistribute parliamentary seats, and the ensuing Act, of June 1885, removed the franchise from 22 Irish boroughs and altered the boundaries of BELFAST, Antrim and Down, cutting the number of Irish seats at Westminster from 105 to 103. The last legislative measures adopted by the British or Imperial Parliament that directly affected Ireland's (potential) representation at Westminster came in 1918. In February of that year an act extended the franchise to all males aged 21 or over, and to most women aged 30 or more, at the same time redrawing constituency boundaries to provide roughly equal populations in each. The number of seats at Westminster to be filled by MPs from Ireland rose again to 105, but they were not to be filled. SINN FÉIN won 73 of them in the 1918 General Election and, having been elected on an ABSTENTIONIST platform, formed their own DÁIL ÉIREANN in DUBLIN. Thus the 1918 election, in so far as the majority of the Irish electorate were concerned, marked the end of association with the British Parliament.

Wexford Rising, The

The Wexford Rising was a part of the general rebellion of 1798 led by the UNITED IRISHMEN republican movement, to throw off British rule. Religious issues were not those over which the struggle was fought: PRESBYTERIAN rebels fought against Catholic MILITIA units throughout the country, alongside Catholic rebels fighting the same enemy. The Wexford Rising, however, has been seen by historians as primarily a religious issue, and a republican one more or less by association. Wexford was an area where there was particular hostility towards the new Militia forces at their creation, and the rising in 1798 seems to have been provoked by the authorities. Under the command of Father JOHN MURPHY, Father Philip Roche and others, the rebels adopted a markedly anti-Protestant position, vengeful and, in consequence, brutally suppressed. There were striking rebel victories – at OULART HILL, and at TUBBERNEERING – and equally as striking failures. At VINEGAR HILL Father Roche was taken and hanged, at Kilcomney Hill Father Murphy was apprehended and brutally put to death. There were bitter engagements when Enniscorthy was taken by the rebels, and at New Ross, Newtownbarry and Gorey where they were worsted. The vehemence of the rebels in Wexford impressed itself upon their enemies: arms were few and far between, pitchforks and scythes and hurriedly made pikes were used against the musketry of the Militia and the regulars. At the battle of New Ross on 5 June 1798 wave after wave of rebels stormed the defences, some 2,000 or more of them were left dead in the place, and the victorious government troops were stunned by their commitment. The defiance shown at New Ross may have been the single event of the 1798 rising that caused the British government to suppose that the revolt was a serious threat to its dominance. Moreover, if there was then a tendency to see the rising of the United Irishmen as a 'Catholic' insurgency, and if historians have described it as such, it must largely be due to the Wexford Rising, which was seen by both sides as a conflict of religions and the settling of old scores (see NINETY-EIGHT).

Whateley Commission *see* IRISH COMMISSION

Whig Clubs

The Whig Clubs were founded in DUBLIN in 1789 by the Earl of Charlemont, and HENRY GRATTAN, and in BELFAST in 1790, with the express purpose of organizing opposition to any attempt at legislative UNION of Britain and Ireland (which came in 1801). They may be said to represent the residual and limited radicalism of the VOLUNTEER movement, and they were intended to be socially exclusive, a typical development of the PATRIOT party in the Irish PARLIAMENT seeking to develop and to control limited extra-parliamentary activity. They were interested in a limited degree of parliamentary reform, but were neither pro-Catholic nor particularly concerned about EMANCIPATION. The UNITED IRISHMEN movement, republican and non-sectarian, has been seen as a counter to the Whig Clubs.

Whiteboys and Whiteboyism

The Whiteboy movement, which began to appear in the 1760s in Counties Tipperary, Cork, Limerick and Waterford, was a widespread example of rural agitation aimed at specific grievances, and was, despite what hostile contemporaries said, Catholic but non-sectarian. The targets of the Whiteboys were TITHE, particularly that on potatoes, the fees levied by the Catholic priests in their parishes, enclosures, rents and the shift to pasture at the expense of arable and, thus, of rural employment. They encompassed therefore, in their several manifestations, the perennial grievances of the Irish peasantry. Whiteboy activity was of long duration – they seem still to have been active in the early nineteenth century, so that the term 'Whiteboyism' came to be applied with a certain lack of discrimination to the outbreaks of other groups such as the TERRY ALTS and the WHITEFEET. Historians found the name 'Whiteboy' a useful generic label to apply to a type of rural unrest. There may well have been a correlation between Whiteboy activity in Munster and the OAKBOYS outbreak in ULSTER that came in 1763. The government reacted against the Whiteboy menace with some vigour. In 1762 forces were despatched from Ulster into Munster to deal with the outbreak, and in 1762 magistrates and and others charged with their suppression were indemnified against prosecution for their actions. A Catholic priest, Father Nicholas Sheehy, was executed in March 1766 for allegedly encouraging Whiteboys to commit a murder and in June of that year a Tumultuous Risings Act was drafted to deal with them. The Whiteboys appeared in Kildare, Kilkenny and Queen's County in 1775, and two of their leaders, Owen Carroll and John Duggan were executed at Newtownbarry, County Wexford, in September. Further legislation came in April 1776 and was made perpetual in 1800. The CATHOLIC CHURCH denounced the Whiteboys from its pulpits, and again the movement died away, only to flare up in 1787 targeting tithe collectors and the landlords and their agents identified with rent increases. The English Riot Act was introduced into Ireland to cope with this fresh outbreak, to prevent the taking or administering of oaths of association, and empowering the LORD LIEUTENANT to appoint reliable constables in BARONIES where there was unrest. In view of the fact that the Whiteboy movement was reportedly active again early in the nineteenth century, it is worth noting that they were not, as a group, identifiable in the 1798 uprising of the UNITED IRISHMEN. This serves to underline the point that organizations such as the Whiteboys were not political: they served to harness the energies of rural resentment against traditional causes of grievance. Whilst individual Whiteboys may well have been DEFENDERS or United Irishmen, any stronger link imputing sectarian or republican principles to the movement as a whole would be wrong.

Whitefeet, The

The Whitefeet movement, identifiable in LEINSTER, particularly Queen's County, King's County and Kilkenny, in the early 1830s, was a combination of rural protest movement (sometimes referred to as WHITEBOYISM) and FEUD, in a revival of the old combat of the CARAVATS AND SHANAVESTS. Their rivals took the name of the Blackfeet. By this date, the localized or regionalized feuds within Irish peasant society were on the wane, and the Leinster phenomenon of the Whitefeet probably owed much to the tensions of the TITHE WAR. Their appearance, like that of the TOMMY DOWNSHIRES, for example, was brief and it is likely that the feud element rode on the back of genuine anti-tithe unrest.

Widow McCormack's Cabbage Patch

This is the derisory term for the action at Ballingarry, County Tipperary, fought between YOUNG IRELAND rebels and the police on 29 July 1848. It is used to point out the folly of the attempted insurrection, and to contrast it with the rising of EMMET in 1803, and subsequent nationalist rebellions such as that of the FENIANS in 1867.

Wild Geese, The

The Wild Geese were the Irish JACOBITES who left Ireland to serve in the armies of the French king after the Treaty of LIMERICK in 1691, which brought to an end the struggle in Ireland between the rival kings JAMES II and WILLIAM III. Several thousand Irishmen took ship for France and they, and those who followed after them, and their descendants, formed the IRISH BRIGADES which served the French crown for much of the eighteenth century. The original Wild Geese fought, for example, at Steenkirk in 1692 where the forces of William III were defeated by the French.

William III, King (d. 1702)

William of Orange was married to Mary the daughter of the then James Duke of York, in 1677. In 1685, upon the death of his brother King Charles II, Duke James ascended the throne of England as JAMES II, the first Catholic monarch since Mary Tudor in the mid-sixteenth century. Anxiety about the future, entertained by many Protestant nobles and men of influence in England, was increased when James' wife Mary of Modena gave birth to a son and heir in June 1688. A group of Tories and Whigs invited William of Orange to invade England and to assume the crown in consort with his wife. William, engaged in war with the French, accepted the invitation as a means of enhancing his strength, landed in England on 5 November 1688 and in February he and his wife became joint monarchs of England and Ireland. A declaration was at once issued calling upon the supporters of the deposed King James to surrender by 10 April 1689. In March 1690 a Danish mercenary army, hired by William, arrived in Belfast Lough to begin operations against the JACOBITES, and on 14 June William III landed at Carrickfergus to take command. On 1 July he won the major victory of the BOYNE, and drove James II in flight from Ireland to France. The Boyne did not, however, mark the end of the struggle. The new king occupied DUBLIN at once, and issued another demand for Jacobites to surrender themselves, but he came up against fierce opposition at ATHLONE and at Limerick (see LIMERICK, SIEGE OF). On 5 September he returned to England, leaving the war to be conducted by his generals. The war was ended by the Treaty of LIMERICK agreed between PATRICK SARSFIELD the Jacobite leader following the death of TYRCONNELL and GINKEL the commander of William III's siege army.

William III's achievement in Ireland was less than the honour done him in subsequent centuries. He became the symbol of Protestant Ireland, the guarantee of the repression of the Catholic majority, and the talisman of the ORANGE ORDER of the nineteenth and twentieth centuries. His name, in Protestant lore, is inextricably linked with the massive action at the Boyne where the Jacobite and Catholic Ireland of Tyrconnell and Sarsfield was first dealt a major blow. Following his triumphant retention of the throne he had usurped, William's administration and Parliaments in Ireland, and their successors, implemented draconic PENAL LAWS against the Catholics that held them in subjugation for a century and more. Thus, his importance as a saviour in Protestant popular belief, is equalled by his symbolizing repression and expropriation for Catholic Irishmen.

Williamites

The supporters of King WILLIAM III are termed Williamites, to distinguish them from the JACOBITES who supported his rival for the throne, JAMES II. The application of the term 'Williamite', however, is of shorter duration. Jacobites and Jacobite sympathies were as much in evidence in the mid-eighteenth century as in the period of the Jacobite-Williamite struggle of 1689–91.

Woodenbridge

Woodenbridge in County Wicklow was the location chosen by JOHN REDMOND on 20 September 1914 to deliver a speech committing, or presuming to commit, the IRISH VOLUNTEERS to active involvement in the British war effort against Germany. The Volunteers had been founded in 1913 as a nationalist force on a par with the ULSTER VOLUNTEER FORCE raised to resist

HOME RULE. Redmond, as leader of the IRISH PARLIAMENTARY PARTY at WESTMINSTER, had managed to secure representation of his constitutional nationalist grouping on the directorate of the Irish volunteers. When war with Germany broke out in August 1914, and Home Rule had to be (temporarily) postponed for the duration, Redmond had committed his party to support of Britain. The Woodenbridge speech, therefore, was in keeping with his established position, but it served to split the Volunteers. Some 10,000 or so declined to be led by him into enlistment for the British army, and they, within two years, were involved in the EASTER RISING of 1916 against British rule. The pro-Redmond element formed the National Volunteers. In Irish political terms, Redmond had made a grave mistake, although that was not apparent until after the 1916 rising, when popular opinion moved towards radical republicanism in the shape of SINN FÉIN. Redmond's opposition to CONSCRIPTION in 1918 did not repair the damage, for he was seen as the lackey of British imperialism.

Wyndham's Act *see* LAND
LEGISLATION

Y

Year of the Slaughter (Bliadhain an áir)

The Year of the Slaughter was 1741, when a FAMINE of unparalleled ferocity swept over Ireland killing 300,000 people at the least. It was induced by chronic harvests and bad weather in 1739 and 1740, and the summer of 1741 was marked by epidemics of typhus and dysentery. A century later, a greater and even more destructive famine struck Ireland.

Yelverton's Act

The Act took its name from its first mover as a bill in the Irish Commons, Barry Yelverton (1736–1805), a leading figure in the VOLUNTEER movement, and later ennobled as Lord Avonmore, when he lent his weight to the government proposal for UNION in 1801. Yelverton's Act was that legislation which repealed the DECLARATORY ACT of 1720, and ended Irish parliamentary subordination to the British Parliament at WESTMINSTER (see also PATRIOTS, Irish PARLIAMENT). The Act amended POYNINGS' LAW of 1495, and deprived the LORD LIEUTENANT and his administration of any power to originate or to alter bills, which must be transmitted direct to the crown, and then returned under the Great Seal via the Lord Lieutenant to the Irish Commons. The king's power to suppress remained intact, but his power to alter, and consequently the power of the British Parliament to alter, legislation was effectively ended. The Renunciation Act of 17 April 1783 acknowledged the Irish Parliament's right to legislate exclusively for Ireland.

Yeomanry, The

The LORD LIEUTENANT the Earl Camden, in 1796, resolved to set up a Yeomanry Corps to make good the drain of regular troops out of Ireland for the French wars. Camden himself admitted that in the Yeomanry (or Yeos as they came to be called) he was 'arming Protestants against Catholics'. The timing of the Corps' recruitment explains that remark. The danger of revolution within Ireland from the UNITED IRISHMEN movement of republicans, backed by French arms, was very real. The old VOLUNTEER movement, which had displayed remarkable PATRIOT fervour in the 1770s and 1780s, had been either radicalized or simply folded. The radicalized elements that had come under United Irishmen influence had been suppressed. The MILITIA, raised to do much the same job of back-up military force as the new Yeomanry, was reckoned to be heavily infiltrated by revolutionaries and by the Catholic DEFENDER movement, and, because of its heavy Catholic recruitment, politically unreliable. Thus the Yeomanry, which aimed at exclusive Protestant enrolment, and which was 40,000 strong when the 1798 rebellion broke out, was the British administration's attempt to organize a reliable force. It was notoriously badly disciplined, despite its semi-gentry officer cadre, but it was loyal, which was all that mattered to the administration. ORANGE ORDER activists were welcomed into its ranks, and it was first used during General LAKE's repressive campaign in ULSTER during the build-up to the United Irishmen revolt. During the NINETY-EIGHT, it was involved in countless atrocities against the rebels, whoever they were (whether Protestant or Catholic), but in WEXFORD they fulfilled their sectarian purpose fully, evidenced by their murder of Father JOHN MURPHY and many of his followers.

Young, Arthur (1741–1820)

Arthur Young was the most prominent agricultural reformer and modernist of his age, though not himself a particularly accomplished farmer. He was in Ireland in 1776, where he became agent to Lord Kingsborough on his estates in County Cork, a post he held until 1779. As with his visit to France, Young compiled an account of the agricultural economy of Ireland, published in two volumes in 1780, in which, amongst other things, he drew attention to LANDLORD ABSENTEEISM and its deleterious effect upon agriculture.

Young Ireland

The Young Ireland movement, revolutionary in a gentlemanly fashion, arose from the Repeal campaign of DANIEL O'CONNELL, or, more accurately, from what they perceived to be the failure of that campaign. They represented the intellectual, urbanized, liberally Protestant elements of the REPEAL ASSOCIATION, increasingly disenchanted by O'Connell's emphasis upon Catholicism and nationalism as if the two were synonymous. As a movement, the Young Irelanders did not form a coherent organization. They first began to emerge around 1842 with the appearance of the journal NATION, and they might more properly be termed the 'Nation Group' at that time. O'Connell viewed with dismay their increasing attraction to PHYSICAL FORCE nationalism, Anglophobic, romantic in the way that PADRAIC PEARSE would one day be romantic. They fed upon the history of resistance to British rule, and disseminated accounts of it in their *Library of Ireland* publications which began to appear in 1845, the first volume being a history of the VOLUNTEERS of 1782 (see DUNGANNON CONVENTION), the armed force which, to the Young Irelan-

ders, was the implicit threat that the PATRIOT group in the Irish PARLIAMENT had used to win legislative independence from Britain in 1782. In 1846 the Young Irelanders split with O'Connell, or they repudiated constitutional methods for reform. JOHN MITCHEL and FRANCIS MEAGHER and others established the IRISH CONFEDERATION with its Confederate Clubs to promote their views and to maintain coherence outside of the Repeal Association. With more than a nod towards the NINETY-EIGHT rebellion, Mitchel produced the *UNITED IRISHMAN* journal to promote the group's increasing move towards revolt: FAMINE was destroying the Irish peasantry in their thousands, and relief efforts were ineffective. To the Young Irelanders, if ever there was a justifiable time to rise, it came in 1848. The rising was disastrous. The single engagement, called by some 'the battle of Ballingary', by the group's enemies 'the battle of WIDOW McCORMACK'S CABBAGE PATCH', in July 1848, was a victory for the authorities. Mitchel and Meagher had been apprehended before the rising, which was led by SMITH O'BRIEN a former MP in the Repeal Association interest. Whatever coherence Young Ireland had possessed as a revolutionary group, disappeared with the cabbage-patch encounter, and the leaders were condemned to TRANSPORTATION. But they were a reminder of something which O'Connell's constitutionalism and its noisy campaigns may have for a time obscured. The physical force aspect of Irish nationalism, of which the Young Ireland group was a part, and a link between 1798 and the FENIAN risings of 1867.

APPENDICES

Appendix 1a: Viceroys of Ireland 1603–1921

(LL = Lord Lieutenant.   LD = Lord Deputy.   LJ = Lord Justice.)
Appointments are given in *strict* chronological order

1603 Sir Arthur Chichester LD

1615 Thomas Jones archbishop of
Dublin LJ
Sir John Denham LJ

1615 Sir Oliver St John LD

1622 Sir Adam Loftus LJ
Richard Viscount Powerscourt LJ

1622 Henry Carey Viscount Falkland
LD

1629 Adam Viscount Loftus LJ
Richard Earl of Cork LJ

1633 Thomas Wentworth Viscount
Wentworth LD

1640 Thomas Wentworth Earl of
Strafford LL

1641 Robert Sidney Earl of Leicester
LL

1643 Sir John Borlase LJ
Sir Henry Tichborne LJ

1643 James Butler Earl of Ormond LL

1646 Philip Sidney Lord Lisle LL

1647 Arthur Annesley, Parliamentary
Commissioner
Sir Robert King, Parliamentary
Commissioner
Sir Robert Meredyth,
Parliamentary Commissioner
Colonel John Moore,
Parliamentary Commissioner
Colonel Michael Jones,
Parliamentary Commissioner

1648 James Butler Marquess of
Ormond LL

1649 Oliver Cromwell, Commander-in-
Chief and Governor-General

1650 Henry Ireton LD

1650 Edmund Ludlow, Commissioner
for Civil Affairs
Colonel John Jones,
Commissioner for Civil Affairs
Miles Corbet, Commissioner for
Civil Affairs
John Weaver, Commissioner for
Civil Affairs

1652 Charles Fleetwood, Commander-
in-Chief and Commissioner for
Civil Affairs

1652 Fleetwood, Corbet, Ludlow and
Jones, Commissioners for Civil
Affairs

1652 Cromwell, Fleetwood, Ludlow,
Jones, Corbet and Weaver,
Commissioners for Civil Affairs

1654 Charles Fleetwood LD

1655 Henry Cromwell, acting
Commander-in-Chief

1657 Henry Cromwell, LD and
Commander-in-Chief

1658 Henry Cromwell LL

1659 Colonel John Jones,
Commissioner for Civil Affairs
William Steele, Commissioner for
Civil Affairs

Robert Goodwin,
Commissioner for Civil Affairs
Matthew Tomlinson,
Commissioner for Civil Affairs
Miles Corbet, Commissioner for
Civil Affairs

1659 Edmund Ludlow, Commander-in-
Chief

1660 John Weaver, Commissioner for
Civil Affairs
Robert Goodwin, Commissioner
for Civil Affairs
Sir Charles Coote, Commissioner
for Civil Affairs
Sir Hardress Waller,
Commissioner for Civil Affairs
Colonel Henry Markham,
Commissioner for Civil Affairs

1660 George Monck, Duke of
Albermarle LL

1660 Sir Maurice Eustace LJ
Roger Earl of Orrery LJ

1662 James Duke of Ormond LL

1668 Thomas Earl of Ossory LD

1669 John Baron Robartes LL

1670 John Lord Berkeley LL

1672 Arthur Earl of Essex LL

1677 James Duke of Ormond LL

1685 Michael Boyle archbishop of
Dublin LJ
Arthur Earl of Granard LJ

1685 Henry Earl of Clarendon LL

1687 Richard Earl of Tyrconnell LD

1689 KING JAMES II PRESENT IN
IRELAND – VICEROYALTY
LAPSES

1690 KING WILLIAM III PRESENT IN
IRELAND – VICEROYALTY
LAPSES

1690 Henry Lord Sidney LJ
Thomas Coningsby LJ

1690 Henry Viscount Sidney LJ
Sir Charles Porter LJ
Thomas Coningsby LJ

1692 Henry Viscount Sidney LL

1693 Sir Charles Porter LJ
Sir Cyril Wyche LJ

1693 Henry Lord Capel LJ
Sir Cyril Wyche LJ
William Dunscombe LJ

1695 Henry Lord Capel LD

1696 Morrogh Viscount Blessington LJ
William Wolseley LJ

1696 Sir Charles Porter LJ

1696 Sir Charles Porter LJ
Charles Earl of Mountrath LJ
Henry Earl of Drogheda LJ

1697 Henry Earl of Galway LJ

1697 Charles Marquess of Winchester
LJ
Henry Earl of Galway LJ
Edward Viscount Villiers LJ

1699 Charles Duke of Bolton LJ
Henry Earl of Galway LJ
Edward Earl of Jersey LJ
Narcissus archbishop of Dublin
LJ

1699 Charles Duke of Bolton LJ
Charles Earl of Berkeley LJ
Henry Earl of Galway LJ

1700 Laurence Earl of Rochester LL

1703 James Duke of Ormond LL

1707 Thomas Earl of Pembroke LL

1708 Thomas Earl of Wharton LL

1710 James Duke of Ormond LL

1713 Charles Duke of Shrewsbury LL

1714 Charles Earl of Sunderland LL

1717 Charles Viscount Townshend LL

1717	Charles Duke of Bolton LL
1720	Charles Duke of Grafton LL
1724	John Lord Carteret LL
1727	John Lord Carteret LL
1730	Lionel Earl of Dorset LL
1737	William Duke of Devonshire LL
1745	Philip Earl of Chesterfield LL
1746	William Earl of Harrington LL
1750	Lionel Duke of Dorset LL
1755	William Marquess of Hartington LL
1757	John Duke of Bedford LL
1761	George Earl of Halifax LL
1763	Hugh Earl of Northumberland LL
1765	Thomas Viscount Weymouth LL
1765	Francis Earl of Hertford LL
1766	George Earl of Bristol LL
1767	George Viscount Townshend LL
1772	Simon Earl of Harcourt LL
1776	John Earl of Buckinghamshire LL
1780	Frederick Earl of Carlisle LL
1782	William Duke of Portland LL
1782	George Earl Temple LL
1783	Robert Earl of Northington LL
1784	Charles Duke of Rutland LL
1787	Richard archbishop of Armagh LJ James Viscount Lifford LJ John Foster LJ
1787	George Marquess of Buckingham LL
1789	John Earl of Westmorland LL
1794	William Earl FitzWilliam LL
1795	John Earl Camden LL
1798	Charles Marquess Cornwallis LL
1801	Philip Earl of Hardwick LL
1805	Edward Earl of Powis (did not take up the post)
1806	John Duke of Bedford LL
1807	Charles Duke of Richmond LL
1813	Charles Viscount Whitworth LL
1817	Charles Earl Talbot LL
1821	Richard Marquess Wellesley LL
1828	Henry Marquess of Anglesey LL
1829	Hugh Duke of Northumberland LL
1830	Henry Marquess of Anglesey LL
1833	Richard Marquess Wellesley LL
1835	Thomas Earl of Haddington LL
1835	Henry Earl of Mulgrave LL
1837	Henry Earl of Mulgrave LL
1839	Hugh Viscount Ebrington LL
1841	Thomas Earl de Grey LL
1844	William Lord Heytesbury LL
1846	John Earl of Bessborough LL
1847	George Earl of Clarendon LL
1852	Archibald Earl of Eglinton LL
1853	Edward Earl of St Germans LL
1855	George Earl of Carlisle LL
1858	Archibald Earl of Eglinton LL
1859	George Earl of Carlisle LL

1864	John Lord Wodehouse LL	**1889**	Laurence Earl of Zetland LL
1866	James Marquess of Abercorn LL	**1892**	Robert Lord Houghton LL
1868	John Earl Spencer LL	**1895**	George Earl Cadogan LL
1874	James Duke of Abercorn LL	**1902**	William Earl Dudley LL
1876	John Duke of Marlborough LL	**1905**	John Earl of Aberdeen LL
1880	Francis Earl Cowper LL	**1915**	Ivor Lord Wimborne LL (resigned 1916, reappointed)
1882	John Earl Spencer LL	**1918**	John Viscount French LL
1885	Henry Earl of Carnarvon LL	**1921**	Edmund Viscount FitzAlan LL
1886	John Earl of Aberdeen LL		
1886	Charles Marquess of Londonderry		

Appendix 1b: Deputies in Ireland 1603–1800

1614	Thomas archbishop of Dublin LJ Sir Richard Wingfield LJ	**1701**	Narcissus archbishop of Dublin LJ Henry Earl of Drogheda LJ Hugh Earl of Mount Alexander LJ
1636	Adam Viscount Loftus LJ Christopher Wandesford LJ	**1701**	Narcissus archbishop of Dublin LJ Henry Earl of Drogheda LJ
1639	Sir Robert Dillon LJ Christopher Wandesford LJ	**1702**	Hugh Earl of Mount Alexander LJ Major-General Thomas Erle LJ Thomas Keightley LJ
1640	Christopher Wandesford LD		
1640	Robert Lord Dillon LJ Sir William Parsons LJ	**1704**	Sir Richard Cox Hugh Earl of Mount Alexander Major-General Thomas Erle
1640	Sir William Parsons LJ Sir John Borlase LJ	**1705**	Sir Richard Cox LJ John Lord Cutts LJ
1660	John Lord Robartes LD	**1707**	Narcissus archbishop of Armagh LJ Sir Richard Cox LJ
1664	Thomas Earl of Ossory LD		
1668	Thomas Earl of Ossory LD	**1707**	Narcissus archbishop of Armagh LJ Richard Freeman LJ
1671	Michael archbishop of Dublin LJ Sir Arthur Forbes LJ		
1682	Robert Earl of Arran LD		
1687	Sir Alexander Fitton LJ William Earl of Clanricard LJ	**1709**	Richard Freeman LJ Richard Ingoldsby LJ

1710	Richard Freeman LJ Richard Ingoldsby LJ		**1728**	Thomas Wyndham LJ Hugh archbishop of Armagh LJ William Connolly LJ
1710	Narcissus archbishop of Armagh LJ Richard Ingoldsby LJ		**1730**	Hugh archbishop of Armagh LJ Thomas Lord Wyndham LJ Sir Ralph Gore LJ
1710	Sir Constantine Phipps Richard Ingoldsby		**1732**	Hugh archbishop of Armagh LJ Thomas Lord Wyndham LJ Sir Ralph Gore LJ
1711	Sir Constantine Phipps Richard Ingoldsby		**1733**	Hugh archbishop of Armagh LJ Thomas Lord Wyndham LJ
1712	Sir Constantine Phipps LJ John archbishop of Tuam LJ		**1734**	Hugh archbishop of Armagh LJ Thomas Lord Wyndham LJ Henry Boyle LJ
1714	Thomas archbishop of Armagh LJ Sir Constantine Phipps LJ John archbishop of Tuam LJ		**1740**	Hugh archbishop of Armagh LJ Robert Jocelyn LJ Henry Boyle LJ
1714	William archbishop of Dublin LJ John archbishop of Tuam LJ Robert Earl of Kildare LJ		**1742**	Hugh archbishop of Armagh LJ Robert Jocelyn LJ Henry Boyle LJ
1715	Charles Duke of Grafton LJ Henry Earl of Galway		**1742**	John archbishop of Armagh LJ Robert Jocelyn (Lord Newport) LJ Henry Boyle LJ
1717	Alan Lord Brodrick LJ William Connolly LJ William archbishop of Dublin LJ		**1744**	John archbishop of Armagh LJ Robert Lord Newport LJ Henry Boyle LJ
1717	Alan Viscount Middleton LJ William archbishop of Dublin LJ William Connolly LJ		**1747**	George archbishop of Armagh LJ Robert Lord Newport LJ Henry Boyle LJ
1719	Alan Viscount Middleton LJ William Connolly LJ		**1749**	Robert Lord Newport LJ Henry Boyle LJ
1722	William archbishop of Dublin LJ Richard Viscount Shannon LJ William Connolly LJ		**1749**	George archbishop of Armagh LJ Robert Lord Newport LJ Henry Boyle LJ
1722	William archbishop of Dublin LJ Richard Viscount Shannon LJ William Connolly LJ Alan Viscount Middleton LJ		**1754**	George archbishop of Armagh LJ Robert Lord Newport LJ Brabazon Earl of Bessborough LJ
1724	Alan Viscount Middleton LJ Richard Viscount Shannon LJ William Connolly LJ		**1756**	Robert Viscount Jocelyn LJ James Earl of Kildare LJ Brabazon Earl of Bessborough LJ
1726	Hugh archbishop of Armagh LJ Richard West LJ William Connolly LJ		**1758**	George archbishop of Armagh LJ Henry Earl of Shannon LJ John Ponsonby LJ
1726	Thomas Wyndham LJ Hugh archbishop of Armagh LJ William Connolly LJ			

1765	John Lord Bowes LJ John Ponsonby LJ	1789	Richard archbishop of Armagh LJ Lord FitzGibbon LJ John Foster LJ
1766	John Lord Bowes LJ Charles Earl of Drogheda LJ John Ponsonby LJ	1795	William archbishop of Armagh LJ John Viscount FitzGibbon LJ

No further Deputy Viceroys were appointed after the Union of 1801

Appendix 2: Chief Secretaries in Ireland 1603–1921

1605	Sir Henry Piers	1703	Edward Southwell
1616	Sir Henry Holcroft	1707	George Dodington
1622	Sir John Veele	1708	Joseph Addison
1644	Sir George Lane	1710	Edward Southwell
1660	Matthew Lock	1713	Sir John Stanley
1662	Sir Thomas Page	1714	Joseph Addison
1669	Sir Henry Ford	1715	Martin Bladen Charles Delafaye
1670	Sir Ellis Leighton	1717	Edward Webster
1672	Sir Henry Ford	1720	Horatio Walpole
1673	Sir William Harbord	1721	Edward Hopkins
1676	Sir Cyril Wyche	1724	Thomas Clutterbuck
1682	Sir William Ellis	1730	Walter Cary
1686	Sir Paul Rycaut	1737	Sir Edward Walpole
1687	Thomas Sheridan	1739	Thomas Townshend
1688	Patrick Tyrrell	1739	Henry Legge
1690	John Davis	1741	William Viscount Duncannon
1692	Sir Cyril Wyche	1745	Richard Liddell
1695	Sir Richard Aldworth	1746	Sewallis Shirley
1696	William Palmer	1746	Edward Weston
1697	Matthew Prior	1750	Lord George Sackville
1699	Humphrey May	1755	Henry Seymour Conway
1700	Francis Gwyn		

1757	Richard Rigby	1806	William Elliot
1761	William Gerard Hamilton	1807	Sir Arthur Wellesley
1764	Charles Earl of Drogheda	1809	Robert Dundas
1765	Sir Charles Bunbury	1809	William Wellesley Pole
1765	Francis Seymour Conway, Viscount Beauchamp	1812	Robert Peel
1766	Augustus Hervey	1818	Charles Grant
1767	Theophilus Jones	1821	Henry Goulburn
1767	Lord Frederick Campbell	1827	William Lamb
1769	Sir George Macartney	1828	Lord Francis Leveson Gower
1772	Sir John Blaquiere	1830	Sir Henry Hardinge
1776	Richard Heron	1830	Edward Lord Stanley
1780	William Eden	1833	Sir John Cam Hobhouse
1782	Richard FitzPatrick	1833	Edward John Littleton
1782	William Wyndham Grenville	1834	Sir Henry Hardinge
1783	William Windham	1835	George Viscount Morpeth
1783	Thomas Pelham	1841	Edward Lord Eliot
1784	Thomas Orde	1845	Sir Thomas Francis Fremantle
1787	Alleyne FitzHerbert	1846	Henry Earl of Lincoln
1789	Robert Hobart	1846	Henry Labouchere
1793	Sylvester Douglas	1847	Sir William Meredyth Somerville
1794	George Viscount Milton	1852	Richard Lord Naas
1795	Thomas Pelham	1853	Sir John Young
1798	Robert Viscount Castlereagh	1855	Edward Horsman
1801	Charles Abbot	1857	Henry Herbert
1802	William Wickham	1858	Richard Lord Naas
1804	Sir Evan Nepean	1859	Edward Cardwell
1805	Nicholas Vansittart	1861	Sir Robert Peel
1805	Charles Long	1865	Chichester Parkinson-Fortescue

1866	Richard Lord Naas	**1886**	Sir Michael Hicks-Beach
1868	John Wilson-Patten	**1887**	Arthur James Balfour
1868	Chichester Parkinson-Fortescue	**1891**	William Lawies Jackson
1871	Spencer Marquess of Hartington	**1892**	John Morley
1874	Sir Michael Hicks-Beach	**1895**	Gerald William Balfour
1878	James Lowther	**1900**	George Wyndham
1880	William Forster	**1905**	Walter Hume Long
1882	Lord Frederick Cavendish	**1905**	James Bryce
1882	George Otto Trevelyan	**1907**	Augustine Birrell
1884	Henry Campbell-Bannerman	**1916**	Henry Edward Duke
1885	Sir William Hart Dyke	**1918**	Edward Shortt
1886	William Henry Smith	**1919**	James Macpherson
1886	John Morley	**1920**	Sir Hamar Greenwood

CHRONOLOGY

1601	*24 December* Battle of Kinsale
1603	*30 March* Treaty of Mellifont
1607	*4 September* The Flight of the Earls
1608	*18 April* Cahir O'Doherty's Revolt
1625	*27 March* Accession of King Charles I
1626	*22 September* King offers the 'Graces'
1628	*24 May* Offer of 51 'Matters of Grace and Bounty'
1633	*25 July* Thomas Wentworth becomes Lord Deputy
1639	*21 May* The 'Black Oath' imposed in Ulster
1641	*12 May* Execution of Thomas Wentworth *23 October* Outbreak of Irish Rebellion
1642	*19 March* Adventurers' Act in English Parliament *9 July* Owen Roe O'Neill arrives in Ireland *22 August* Outbreak of the English Civil Wars
1643	*13 November* Earl of Ormond appointed Lord Lieutenant
1645	*25 August* Earl of Glamorgan's treaty with the Irish rebels
1646	*5 June* Battle of Benburb
1647	*7 June* Arrival of Michael Jones at Dublin
1649	*17 January* Royalists and rebels make alliance *30 January* Execution of King Charles I *2 August* Battle of Rathmines or Baggot-Rath *11 September* Massacre at Drogheda *11 October* Massacre at Wexford *6 November* Death of Owen Roe O'Neill
1652	*12 August* Act for the Settling of Ireland
1660	*14 May* Charles II proclaimed king
1662	*31 July* Act of Settlement
1672	*October* First grant of Regium Donum
1678	*28 September* Popish Plot 'revealed'
1685	*6 February* Accession of King James II
1687	*12 February* Tyrconnell becomes Lord Deputy

1688	*5 November* William of Orange lands in England		**1795**	*4 January* Earl FitzWilliam becomes Lord Lieutenant *23 February* Earl FitzWilliam dismissed *21 September* Battle of the Diamond *September* Foundation of the Orange Order
1689	*18 April* Siege of Derry begins			
1690	*1 July* Battle of the Boyne			
1691	*12 July* Battle of Aughrim *3 October* Treaty of Limerick		**1796**	*October* Establishment of the Yeomanry Corps
1695	*7 September* First of the Penal Laws		**1798**	*23 May* Outbreak of the United Irishmen rebellion *21 June* Battle of Vinegar Hill *27 August* The 'Races of Castlebar' *19 November* Suicide of Wolfe Tone
1704	*4 March* Further Penal Laws			
1720	*7 April* Declaratory Act passes British Parliament			
1728	*6 May* Disenfranchisement of Catholics		**1799**	*31 January* Union of Britain and Ireland is advocated by William Pitt
1768	*16 February* Octennial Act		**1800**	*1 August* Irish Act of Union
1774	*22 June* Quebec Act		**1801**	*1 January* Implementation of the Act of Union
1778	Spread of the Volunteer movement			
1782	*15 February* Volunteers' Dungannon Convention *21 June* Repeal of the Declaratory Act		**1803**	*23 July* Emmet's Rebellion
			1814	*25 July* Peace Preservation Act
1791	*14 October* United Irishmen founded in Belfast *9 November* United Irishmen of Dublin meet		**1822**	*1 August* Irish Constabulary Act
			1823	*12 May* Foundation of the Catholic Association
1793	*9 April* Franchise extended to Catholics		**1828**	*14 August* Foundation of the Brunswick Clubs
1794	*23 May* Administration suppresses Dublin United Irishmen		**1829**	*13 April* Catholic Emancipation Act

1832 *16 August*
Tithe commutation legislation

1834 *22 April*
Daniel O'Connell opens the
    Repeal campaign

1835 *25 July*
Thomas Drummond becomes
    Under Secretary in Ireland

1836 *20 May*
Irish Constabulary Act

1838 *31 July*
Irish Poor Law

1840 *15 April*
Repeal Association founded

1842 *15 October*
Journal *Nation* first published

1843 Year of repeal

1845 *9 September*
Potato blight notified in Ireland
Famine begins

1847 *13 January*
Irish Confederation of Young
    Irelanders founded
15 May
Death of Daniel O'Connell in Italy

1848 *29 July*
Young Ireland rebellion

1850 *9 August*
Formation of the Tenant League

1854 *3 November*
Catholic University opens in
    Dublin

1858 *17 March*
Foundation of the Irish
    Republican Brotherhood

1859 *April*
Fenian Brotherhood founded in
    America

1866 *22 June*
Paul Cullen archbishop of Dublin
    created a cardinal

1867 *February*
Fenian uprising begins

1868 *3 August*
Amnesty Association for Fenian
    prisoners starts campaign

1869 *26 July*
Disestablishment of the Church of
    Ireland

1870 *19 May*
Isaac Butt founds Home Rule
    movement
1 August
Gladstone's land legislation

1873 *21 November*
Home Rule League founded

1877 *28 August*
Parnell becomes President of the
    Home Rule Confederation

1879 *21 October*
Irish National Land League
    founded
Land War begins

1881 *22 August*
Gladstone's second land
    legislation

1882 *6 May*
Phoenix Park assassinations

1885 *December*
Gladstone's conversion to Home
    Rule known

1886 *8 June*
Home Rule Bill defeated
23 October
Plan of Campaign announced

1887 *23 August*
Land legislation

1889 *24 December*
O'Shea divorce scandal,
    involving Parnell, breaks

1890 *6 December*
Irish Parliamentary Party splits for
    and against Parnell

1891	*6 October* Parnell dies in England		*24 September* Irish Volunteers split over the war
1893	*2 September* Second Home Rule Bill defeated	**1915**	*May* Irish Republican Brotherhood sets up its Military Council

1891   *6 October*
Parnell dies in England

1893   *2 September*
Second Home Rule Bill defeated

1898   *23 January*
United Irish League established

1900   *30 January*
Irish Parliamentary Party reunites

1903   *14 August*
Wyndham's Land Act

1905   *March*
Dungannon Clubs founded in
    Ulster

1907   *21 April*
Sinn Féin League founded
5 September
Sinn Féin established as political
    party

1912   *11 April*
Third Home Rule Bill in Commons
28 September
Solemn League and Covenant in
    Ulster

1913   *31 January*
Ulster Volunteer Force founded
19 November
Formation of the Citizen Army in
    Dublin
25 November
Irish Volunteers founded

1914   *25 May*
Home Rule Bill passes the
    Commons
23 June
Partition of Ireland proposed
4 August
Britain declares war on Germany
15 September
Home Rule suspended

24 September
Irish Volunteers split over the war

1915   *May*
Irish Republican Brotherhood
    sets up its Military Council

1916   *24 April*
The Easter Rising in Ireland
29 April
Surrender of the rebel leaders
May
Executions of rebel leaders in
    Dublin

1917   *5 February*
Sinn Féin wins first by-election

1918   *18 April*
Legislation for conscription in
    Ireland
December
Major Sinn Féin victory in General
    Election

1919   *21 January*
Outbreak of War for
    Independence
Dáil Éireann meets for first time
12 September
Dáil Éireann proscribed

1920   *2 January*
Black and Tan recruitment begins
27 July
Auxiliary recruitment begins
21 November
Bloody Sunday in Dublin
23 December
Government of Ireland Act

1921   *11 July*
Truce between IRA and British
    forces
6 December
Anglo-Irish Treaty signed

BIBLIOGRAPHY

Barnard, T.C., *Cromwellian Ireland: English Government and Reform in Ireland 1649–1660*, Oxford 1975.

Beames, M., *Peasants and Power: The Whiteboy Movements and their Control in Pre-Famine Ireland*, Brighton 1983.

Beckett, J.C., *Protestant Dissent in Ireland 1687–1780*, London 1948.

Beckett, J.C., *Confrontations. Studies in Irish History*, London 1962.

Beckett, J.C., *The Making of Modern Ireland 1603–1923*, edn., London 1981.

Berleth, R., *The Twilight Lords*, London 1979.

Bew, P., *Land and the National Question in Ireland 1858–1882*, Dublin 1979.

Bolton, G.C., *The Passing of the Irish Act of Union*, Oxford 1966.

Bottigheimer, K., *English Money and Irish Land. The Adventurers in the Cromwellian Settlement of Ireland*, Oxford 1971.

Boyce, D.G., ed., *The Revolution in Ireland 1879–1923*, London 1988.

Brady, C., & Gillespie, R., eds., *Natives and Newcomers: The Making of Irish Colonial Society 1534–1641*, Dublin 1986.

Broeker, G., *Rural Disorder and Police Reform in Ireland 1812–1836*, London 1970.

Childs, J., *The Army, James II and the Glorious Revolution*, Manchester 1980.

Clark, S., *Social Origins of the Irish Land War*, Princeton 1970.

Clark, S., & Donnelly, J., *Irish Peasants: Violence and Political Unrest 1780–1914*, Manchester 1983.

Clarke, A., *The Old English in Ireland 1625–1642*, London 1966.

Connell, K.H., *The Population of Ireland 1750–1845*, Oxford 1950.

Connell, K.H., *Irish Peasant Society*, Oxford 1968.

Connolly, S., *Priests and People in Pre-Famine Ireland 1780–1845*, Dublin 1982.

Corish, P.J., *The Catholic Community in the Seventeenth and Eighteenth Centuries*, Dublin 1981.

Cullen, L.M., *Anglo-Irish Trade 1660–1800*, Manchester 1968.

Cullen, L.M., *An Economic History of Ireland since 1660*, London 1972.

Cullen, L.M., *The Emergence of Modern Ireland 1600–1900*, London 1981.

Curtis, L.P., *Anglo-Saxons and Celts: A Study of Anti-Irish Prejudice in Victorian England*, Bridgeport, Conn., 1968.

Davis, R., *The Young Ireland Movement*, Dublin 1987.

De Rosa, P., *Rebels. The Irish Rising of 1916*, London 1990.

Dickson, D., *New Foundations: Ireland 1660–1800*, Dublin 1987.

Dickson, R.H., *Ulster Emigration to Colonial America 1718–1785*, Belfast 1966.

Edwards, R.D., *Patrick Pearse: The Triumph of Failure*, London 1977.

Edwards, R.D., & Williamson, T.D., *The Great Famine*, London 1956.

Elliott, M., *Partners in Revolution: The United Irishmen and France*, London 1982.

Falkener, C.L., *Illustrations of Irish History and Topography, Mainly of the Seventeenth Century*, London 1904.

Fanning, R., *Independent Ireland*, Dublin 1986.

FitzPatrick, B., *Seventeenth Century Ireland. The War of Religions*, Dublin 1988.

Foster, R.F., *Modern Ireland 1600–1972*, London 1988.

Freeman, T.W., *Pre-Famine Ireland: A Study in Historical Geography*, Manchester 1957.

Garvin, T., *The Evolution of Irish Nationalist Politics*, Dublin 1981.

Gibbon, P., *The Origins of Ulster Unionism*, Manchester 1975.

Gilbert, J.T., *History of the Irish Confederation and the War in Ireland 1641–1649*, Dublin 1882–1890.

Hoppen, K.T., *Ireland Since 1800. Conflict and Conformity*, London 1989.

Kee, R., *The Green Flag. A History of Irish Nationalism*, London 1972.

Laffan. M., *The Partition of Ireland 1911–1925*, Dundalk 1983.

Lee, J., *The Modernization of Irish Society 1848–1918*, Dublin 1973.

Loughlin, J., *Gladstone, Home Rule and the Ulster Question 1882–1893*, Dublin 1986.

Lyons, F.S.L., *Ireland since the Famine*, London 1971.

MacCarthy-Morrogh, M., *The Munster Plantation: English Migration to Southern Ireland 1583–1641*, Oxford 1986.

McConville, M., *Ascendancy to Oblivion: The Story of the Anglo-Irish*, London 1986.

MacDonagh, O., *States of Mind. A Study of Anglo-Irish Conflict 1780–1980*, London 1983.

McDowell, R.B., *Irish Public Opinion 1750–1800*, London 1944.

McDowell, R.B., *The Irish Administration 1800–1914*, London 1964.

Miller, D., *Queen's Rebels. Ulster Loyalism in Historical Perspective*, Dublin 1978.

Miller, K., *Emigrants and Exiles: Ireland and the Irish Exodus to North America*, Oxford 1985.

Mitchell, A., *Labour in Irish Politics 1890–1930*, Dublin 1974.

Moody, T.W., *The Londonderry Plantation 1609–1641*, London 1939.

Moody, T.W., Martin, F.X., Byrne, F.J., eds., *A New History of Ireland Volume III, Early Modern Ireland 1534–1691*, Oxford 1976.

Moody, T.W., Vaughan, W.E., eds., *A New History of Ireland Volume IV, Eighteenth Century Ireland 1691–1800*, Oxford 1986.

Murphy, J.A., *Ireland in the Twentieth Century*, Dublin 1975.

O'Brien, R.B., ed., *Life of Theobald Wolfe Tone … Written by Himself and Continued by His Son*, 2 Vols., London 1893.

Ó Broin, L., *Revolutionary Underground: The Story of the Irish Republican Brotherhood, 1858–1924*, Dublin 1976.

O'Farrell, P., *England's Irish Question: Anglo-Irish Relations 1534–1970*, London 1971.

O'Ferrall, F., *Catholic Emancipation: Daniel O'Connell and the Birth of Irish Democracy*, Dublin 1985.

Ó Tuathaigh, G., *Ireland before the Famine 1798–1848*, Dublin 1972.

Pakenham, T., *The Year of Liberty*, London 1969.

Perceval-Maxwell, M., *The Scottish Migration to Ulster in the Reign of James I*, London 1973.

Philpin, C.H.E., ed., *Nationalism and Popular Protest in Ireland*, Cambridge, 1987.

Quinn, D.B., *The Elizabethans and the Irish*, Ithaca N.Y., 1966.

Renwick, W.L., ed., *Edmund Spenser's 'A View of the Present State of Ireland'*, Oxford 1970.

Richter, M., *Medieval Ireland, The Enduring Tradition*, London 1988.

Ryan, D., *The Rising*, Dublin 1949.

Senior, H., *Orangeism in Ireland and Britain 1795–1836*, London 1960.

Sheehy, J., *The Rediscovery of Ireland's Past: The Celtic Revival 1830–1930*, London 1980.

Short, K.R.M., *The Dynamite War. Irish-American Bombers in Victorian Britain*, Dublin 1971.

Simms, J.G., *The Williamite Confiscation in Ireland 1690–1703*, London 1956.

Simms, J.G., *Jacobite Ireland 1685-1691*, London 1969.

Solow, B., *The Land Question and the Irish Economy 1870–1903*, Cambridge, Mass., 1971.

Stewart, A.T.Q., *The Narrow Ground. Aspects of Ulster 1689–1969*, London 1977.

Thornley, D., *Isaac Butt and Home Rule*, London 1964.

Townshend, D., *Political Violence in Ireland: Government and Resistance since 1848*, Oxford 1983.

Vaughan, W.E., ed., *A New History of Ireland, Volume V, Ireland Under the Union, I, 1801–1870*, Oxford 1989.

Wall, M., *The Penal Laws 1691–1760. Church and State from the Treaty of Limerick to the Accession of George III*, Dundalk 1961.

Ward, M., *Unmanageable Revolutionaries: Women and Irish Nationalism*, London 1983.

Wells, R., *Insurrection: The British Experience 1795–1803*. Gloucester 1983.

Williams, T.D., ed., *Secret Societies in Ireland*, Dublin 1973.

Winstanley, M.J., *Ireland and the Land Question 1800–1922*, London 1984.

MAPS

Ancient Provinces of Ireland

Counties of Ireland established from the Middle Ages to the seventeenth century

Plantation and resettlement

Miles
0 10 20 30 40

Donegal

Derry   Antrim

Tyrone

ULSTER

Fermanagh

Leitrim

Monaghan

Armagh

Down

Sligo

Cavan

Louth

Mayo

Roscommon

Longford

Meath

CONNACHT

Westmeath

Dublin

LEINSTER

Galway

Offaly

Kildare

Clare

Laios

Wicklow

Tipperary

Kilkenny

Carlow

Wexford

Limerick

MUNSTER

Waterford

Kerry

Cork

///// Plantations of James I

····· Land involved in Cromwellian
Clearances of the 1650s

Variations in land war activism 1879–1882

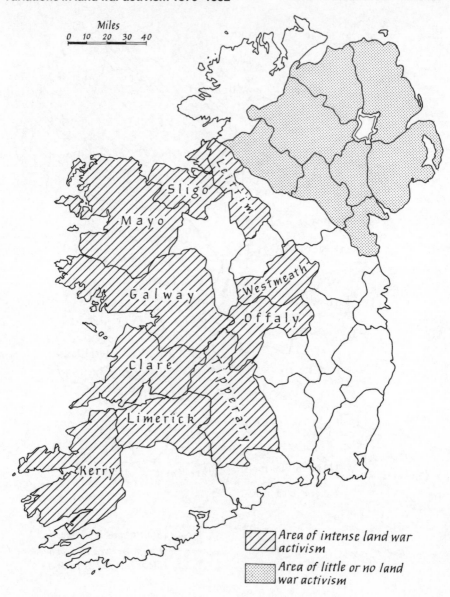

Miles
0 10 20 30 40

Sligo

Leitrim

Mayo

Galway

Westmeath

Offaly

Clare

Tipperary

Limerick

Kerry

░▓ Area of intense land war
      activism

░░ Area of little or no land
      war activism

Areas of substantial Sinn Féin membership 1919

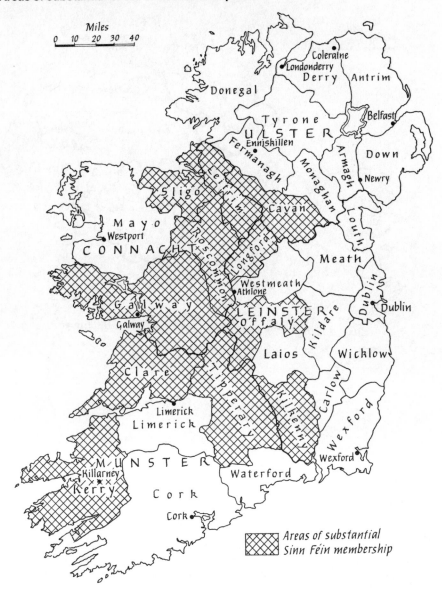

Ancient province of Ulster and the six counties of Northern Ireland from 1921

Miles
0 10 20 30 40

Donegal

Derry
Co. Derry
Antrim
Tyrone
Lough Neagh
Belfast
Fermanagh
Monaghan
Armagh
Down
Cavan

Galway

Dublin

Boundary of Ancient Province of Ulster
The Six Counties of Northern Ireland